PRAISE FOR *THE LONG HONDURAN NIGHT*

"Dana Frank has written a searing portrait of a nation in crisis, a book that is startling, enraging, and humane all at once. Her most important accomplishment is never losing sight of the hardships and treachery that ordinary Hondurans have had to endure these last several years, nor the dignity with which they have survived it all."
—Daniel Alarcón, executive producer of Radio Ambulante, author of *At Night We Walk in Circles*

"*The Long Honduran Night* breaks the deafening silence that has followed recent American intervention in Honduras. It graphically documents the awful legacy of this intervention. By showing how directly the United States crashed into a Honduran presidential election, it also exposes the hypocrisy of our outrage at foreign interference in our own politics."
—Stephen Kinzer, award-winning author and foreign correspondent

"If you've any interest at all in Honduras, US foreign policy, Central America, why so many Central Americans are migrating north . . . or in a powerful, informative, and extremely good read, do pick up Dana Frank's book, *The Long Honduran Night*. It's a surprisingly readable book that tells not only the tragic story of another failed state and the forces that continue to work against establishing real democracies in Central America, but also inspires in its stories of everyday people— in Honduras and the United States—who work against difficult odds to create change, often by placing their lives at risk."
—María Martin, independent journalist

"Free from academic jargon, conversant with modern Honduran history, and steeped in passion, this testimonial book is the best primer in English about the coup, and resistance to it, that destroyed Honduran democracy on June 28, 2009. . . . Almost ten years after the coup, Frank's book transits seamlessly between the social fabric and the intimate lives of hundreds of Hondurans she has met personally during her many years in the countr͟ ͟ ͟ ͟ ͟while referencing key historical processes and their current legacies, an important and necessary feat on its own, but also valuable because it informs the current plight of Hondurans who flee their country into the US seeking asylum in the aftermath of the 2009 coup."

—Dario A. Euraque, professor of history and international studies, Trinity College

"I have covered Honduras ever since the 2009 coup. Dana Frank's insightful and very human portrait of the country's resistance is required reading for anyone who wants to understand what's really going on in Honduras and why it matters."

—Adam Raney, journalist, Al Jazeera English and Univision

"I congratulate and thank Dr. Dana Frank, a North American concerned about Honduras, for giving us this book and for documenting the role of the United States in the long night of terror that we have lived in Honduras since the 2009 coup. Her contribution to historic memory stands as our witness."

—Bertha Oliva, general coordinator, Committee of the Families of the Detained and Disappeared in Honduras

THE LONG HONDURAN NIGHT

Resistance, Terror, and the United States in the Aftermath of the Coup

Dana Frank

Haymarket Books
Chicago, Illinois

Published in 2018 by
Haymarket Books
P.O. Box 180165
Chicago, IL 60618
773-583-7884
www.haymarketbooks.org
info@haymarketbooks.org

ISBN: 978-1-60846-960-4

Trade distribution:
In the US, Consortium Book Sales and Distribution, www.cbsd.com
In Canada, Publishers Group Canada, www.pgcbooks.ca
In the UK, Turnaround Publisher Services, www.turnaround-uk.com
All other countries, Ingram Publisher Services International,
IPS_Intlsales@ingramcontent.com

This book was published with the generous support
of Lannan Foundation and Wallace Action Fund.

Cover photo: Honduran military, police, and private security forces
occupying the town of Guadalupe Carney, Colón, December 15, 2010.
© Dana Frank.

Cover design by Jamie Kerry.

Printed in the United States.

Entered into digital printing December 2018.

Library of Congress Cataloging-in-Publication data is available.

To Stephen Coats and German Zepeda,

my two pole stars.

One in the North, one in the South.

One in heaven, at peace,

One on Earth, in struggle.

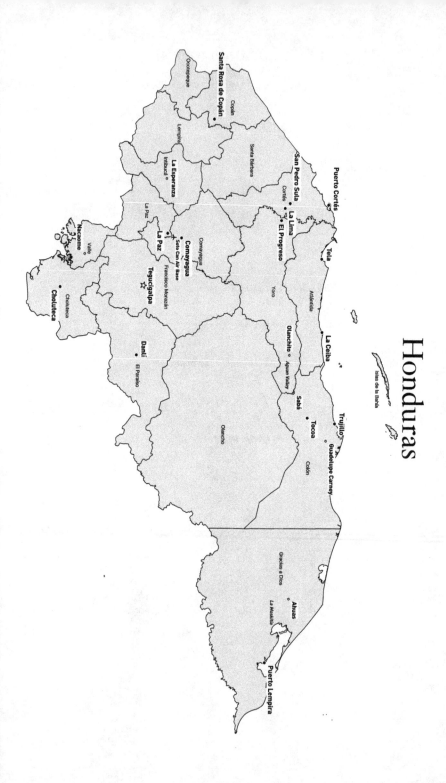

Honduras

Islas de la Bahía

Santa Rosa de Copán
Ocotepeque
Copán
Lempira
La Esperanza
Intibucá
Santa Bárbara
San Pedro Sula
Cortés
Puerto Cortés
La Lima
El Progreso
Tela
La Paz
Comayagua
Soto Cano Air Base
La Paz
Francisco Morazán
Tegucigalpa
Atlántida
Yoro
Olanchito
Olancho
Aguán Valley
La Ceiba
Sabá
Trujillo
Tocoa
Guadelupe Carney
Colón
Nacaome
Valle
Choluteca
Choluteca
Danlí
El Paraíso
Olancho
Gracias a Dios
Ahuas
La Moskitia
Puerto Lempira

Contents

Introduction

On June 28, 2009, at 5:30 in the morning, the Honduran military deposed democratically elected President José Manuel Zelaya Rosales, in the first successful Latin American coup in over two decades. The armed forces flew him to Costa Rica with the full collusion of the Honduran Supreme Court and the majority of the Honduran Congress. During the weeks that followed, the Obama Administration moved swiftly to recognize and then stabilize the post-coup regime. In the face of an international outcry against the coup, the United States helped the perpetrators play out the clock until a previously scheduled election arrived in November, then recognized the outcome of a completely illegitimate electoral process controlled by the coup leaders themselves—bringing to power a vicious and corrupt post-coup regime.

This book tells the story of eight years in the aftermath of that coup: how the Honduran elites wrought havoc under their illegitimate rule and were assiduously supported by the US government, and how the Honduran people and their allies abroad, in particular in the United States, fought back. Into that larger narrative I weave my personal experiences in Honduras and Washington, D.C., as I observed joyous demonstrations in the streets of San Pedro Sula, visited a *campesino* town that had just been burned down by the police, pleaded with aides in the United States Congress, and tried to do my best to help stop the horror.

What difference did the Honduran coup make? There was certainly no golden age in Honduras before 2009 against which to measure it. On the eve of the coup, Hondurans were overwhelmingly

1

poor, seeking incomes in a weak economy based on agriculture and *maquiladoras*—export processing zones. A dozen intermarried elite families, known as the "oligarchs," many of them of Palestinian-Christian descent, owned most of the Honduran economy and ruled through two conservative parties, the Liberal Party and National Party, which had shared power for decades through backroom deals brokered behind a veneer of electoral democracy. In contrast to its neighboring countries, Honduras never had much more than a tiny middle class. The oligarchs presided over a state rife with corruption. The judiciary, prosecutors, and police answered in some cases to drug traffickers and organized crime, as did some politicians.[1] But before the coup the forces of complete corruption remained at bay, the state functioned at a basic level, and the rule of law was largely intact, however bent. Most people got by, economically, albeit poor and facing marginal prospects.

Honduras had remained under tight control of the United States since the beginning of the twentieth century—a "captive nation" in the eyes of scholars.[2] Beginning in the 1910s, the United Fruit Company and its counterpart, the Standard Fruit Company, largely controlled Honduran politics, as their banana plantations spread across vast enclaves over which the companies had near-complete control, with tentacles extending throughout the Honduran state and economy.

In 1954, though, fifty thousand banana workers and their allies rose up in a sixty-nine-day general strike that marked the most important moment in twentieth-century Honduran history. The strike's outcome, machinated from above by the US government, was a Cold War compromise in which strong unions were permitted to wrest concrete gains from the banana corporations and raise living standards for a sector of the working class, but only if they stayed assiduously out of electoral politics, fought Communists, and stayed silent about US domination. During the late 1950s and early 1960s, as part of its anticommunist project, the US brokered the creation of a Honduran welfare state that included a respectable system of labor laws—if usually not enforced—and a national health service and pension system that, while only covering a portion of the population, nonetheless delivered a measure of quality services.[3]

From the 1970s onward, leftists eventually came to lead some of the unions. But during the 1970s and 80s, no large-scale uprising of the armed left erupted in Honduras on the scale of uprisings in neighboring Nicaragua, Guatemala, and El Salvador. Some scholars argue that Hondurans followed a different path in part because a measure of agrarian reform enacted in the 1970s diffused revolutionary impulses from below.[4]

During the 1990s and 2000s multilateral development banks and the Honduran elites, in lockstep with transnational corporations and the US government, began to promote neoliberal policies that chipped away at the Honduran state and its services, especially under the presidency of Ricardo Maduro (2002–2006), the predecessor of deposed President Zelaya. Maduro also launched vicious *"mano duro"* ("hard hand") policies against alleged gang members.[5]

Honduras had long held strategic importance to the US imperial project. In 1954, the United States used Honduras as the base from which to launch a CIA-organized coup that overthrew the democratically-elected socialist president of Guatemala, Jacobo Árbenz, ushering in decades of state-sponsored genocide against the Guatemalan people.[6] During the 1980s, the United States used Soto Cano Air Base at Palmerola, jointly operated with the Honduran government, as a base for the murderous Contra War against the left-wing Sandinista government of Nicaragua. Throughout the 1980s, under the watch of US Ambassador to Honduras John Negroponte (1981–85), the United States worked closely with repressive Honduran armed forces, including the famous Battallion 3-16 death squad responsible for the deaths of Honduran leftists.[7] On the eve of the 2009 coup, Soto Cano, staffed by six hundred US troops, remained strategically important to US military interests in Latin America and the Caribbean.[8]

For all that, Honduras in 2009 was nonetheless far from the cesspool of corruption and state-sponsored terror it would soon become. It was safer than Guatemala, for example, where teenaged soldiers with assault rifles patrolled the streets, drug traffickers amassed fortunes eerily visible in empty high-rises laundering their money, and the genocidal military remained at large and largely in control. In Honduras during the ten years before the coup, around a dozen people were assassinated for political reasons—including four environmental activists and two trade unionists—a far lower number than would be seen after the coup. The major newspapers were all owned and controlled by the elites, but some allowed diverse political conversations, especially on the editorial page of *El Tiempo* in San Pedro Sula. Independent publications were few but published openly and without being harassed. Community-owned radio stations flourished. Honduras also still boasted the strongest labor movement in Central America, the legacy of the 1954 General Strike. In this relatively free context, grassroots social movements from below flourished during the 1990s and 2000s, especially among women and Indigenous peoples, who forged strong horizontal ties within the country and across the continent, along with a nascent LGBTI movement.[9]

What difference did the coup make? Its success sent shock waves throughout the hemisphere. The coup precipitated a rapid downward spiral that cast the Honduran people into a maelstrom of repression, violence, and increasing poverty. The post-coup regime destroyed the rule of law and gutted the country's welfare state—indeed, the state itself. It paved the way for spectacular corruption and the free reign of gangs and organized crime. The murder rate shot to the world's highest. The democratic space for freedom of speech and association tightened like a noose. In response to their country's devastation, hundreds of thousands of Hondurans fled the country and traveled north in the worst of dangerous circumstances. The 2009 coup had an enormous and terrible long-term impact on the Honduran people.

But Hondurans also, in turn, made an enormous difference themselves in response. This book is about that story, too: how the coup brought forth a broad, powerful grassroots resistance movement in support of constitutional order and social justice, supported by new transnational networks of solidarity. To their great surprise, Hondurans built a beautiful new culture of resistance and with it, a new sense of national pride. Immediately after the coup the new National Front of Popular Resistance built on decades of previous struggles to mount enormous resistance. Small farmers known as campesinos rose up collectively to recuperate lands they had once held as cooperatives but that had been robbed from them by magnates planting African palms. Indigenous and Afro-Indigenous activists defended their land against elite and corporate predators. Through all the next years, the labor, women's, and LGBTI movements continued to organize and challenge entrenched powers. By 2013, the first mass political party of the center-left in Honduran history spread across the country, gained the second-largest number of seats in the Honduran Congress, and may have even won the presidential election that year. In 2015, political refugees from the two traditional ruling parties, some of whom had supported the coup, themselves took to the streets by the tens of thousands, shouting "No to the dictatorship!" of criminal President Juan Orlando Hernández.

Finally, this book is also about the difference the coup made in my own life, and how I, too, tried to make a difference in response to it. I first started working in Honduras in 2000, when I was invited by the US Labor Education in the Americas Project (USLEAP), a Chicago nongovernmental organization (NGO), to help the Coalition of Latin American Banana Unions (COLSIBA) develop a union label for the US market. At that point, Chiquita, the inheritor of United Fruit, was almost forty-five percent unionized on its Latin American plantations and receptive to social responsibility initiatives from its unions. After a couple of years, the union label project fizzled out, but I continued to travel regularly to Central America to research women's empowerment projects in the banana unions of Latin America, especially Honduras, during the 1980s, 1990s, and 2000s.[10] In 2006, I began a new research project about the history of the US labor movement's anticommunist intervention in the Honduran labor movement during the Cold War.

The year before the coup, I was wrapping up that historical research and beginning to separate myself emotionally and professionally from my nine-year involvement in Honduras. I thought, I can't handle the heat and humidity; I'm moving on in my projects— although my social and personal ties to Hondurans on the north coast were ever-deeper.

Then the coup hit, and my life changed altogether, from the very first day into the next eight years. My efforts to stop the coup regime and US support for it brought barely relenting anguish, but also the beautiful gift of becoming part of the struggle to bring justice to Honduras. Into this book's larger narrative I weave the halting arc of my own process of trying desperately to figure out how I, too, could make a difference in response to the coup, as a North American—by reporting on Honduras, serving as an academic expert in the media, writing for policy journals, and eventually traveling to Washington and trying to influence the US Congress, while still traveling to Honduras two or three times a year and always working within expanding circles of information-sharing and solidarity. That first morning of June 28, 2009, I jumped off a cliff and became someone else. This book, in part, is about what was on the other side of that cliff.

Because it is shaped by my own experiences, point of view, and positioning, what follows here is sharply limited. Most obviously, I am not Honduran. I pass through the world as a white, middle-class woman with a US passport, an academic title attached to my name, and all the privileges and limitations that go with that package. My pre-coup history within Honduras focused largely on the north coast, less on Tegucigalpa, the mountainous regions, or the country's south, and that regional emphasis is reflected in my post-coup experiences recounted here. I know the labor movement best, less about other social movements. In the United States, my experiences focused on the media and Congress; I didn't, for example, help organize speaking tours of Hondurans to the United States, lead delegations from the United States to Honduras, or train people to accompany at-risk Honduran human rights defenders and activists. I know there are thousands of other stories that can be told of individuals in the solidarity movement that arose in response to the coup. This is just mine, woven into scholarly analysis of Honduran politics and US policy that I have tracked on a daily basis. Above all, my account here should only be understood in service to the far more central stories of millions of Hondurans themselves.

The overall arc of the book reflects changes in my experiences over time, as well as the evolving context within Honduras. In the first chapter, I am in the streets of San Pedro Sula; in the second, I travel to the Aguán Valley. By the third, I am in Washington, D.C. Over the course of the book, I was increasingly engaged in tracking and trying to influence US policy, and so later chapters reflect that emphasis and analyze the US policy sphere in greater depth. In 2013 and 2014, as Juan Orlando Hernández took over the presidency and consolidated his dictatorship, he took up increasing attention: hence Chapter 4. I end the story with his criminal reelection, with a US blessing, in 2017.

Many essential themes unfortunately remain outside the scope of this book. This is not a comprehensive history of Honduran activism since the coup. It does not do justice, for example, to the LGBTI and women's movements or the struggles of the Indigenous Tolupan and the Afro-Indigenous Garifuna peoples. Nor is it comprehensive in its analysis of the solidarity movement within the United States. It focuses on the US-Honduras interface, moreover, and does not discuss the governments of Nicaragua, Canada, the European Union (especially Spain), Ecuador, Brazil, Taiwan, Venezuela, El Salvador, or Guatemala, all of which played important roles in the larger story. Similarly, it does not discuss the solidarity activism that developed in many of those countries as well as in Mexico, Australia, Switzerland, and elsewhere. Nor does it have space to address the long-term impact of the coup on other countries in Latin America and the Caribbean. Within its coverage of US policy, the book does not adequately address the enormous impact of, and strategies behind, the hundreds of millions of dollars of funding that flowed to Honduras during this period through the United States Agency for International Development (USAID).

Much is missing here, finally, because it is too confidential to discuss. My multiple meetings with US Ambassadors Lisa Kubiske and James Nealon and with other embassy personnel, however revealing, remain "off the record," for example, as do my forays to the State Department in Washington, D.C. Most of my meetings in Congress also remain confidential, along with much of the work my colleagues and I did there. A few congressional aides did generously give me permission to depict here some elements of our interactions. They are not responsible for any of the views expressed in this book. Most importantly, so much of what Hondurans told me or what they did remains unsafe to repeat. All Hondurans who speak out against their government, its backers, or its enforcers are at very real risk of being assassinated at any moment—as are their children and family members, who are often killed to send a message. Here I can share only what is safe to tell and what I have been granted permission to recount. I am grateful to the dozens of dedicated and brave Hondurans who allowed me to name them here, tell their stories, and quote them.

Although this book is about Honduras, it ultimately tells a much bigger story than that of one country. It speaks to the history of social movements and the left in Latin America, and to structures of transnational solidarity. It speaks to the neoliberal plots of regional and global elites, to the "drug war" and its damages, and to militarized security policy. Finally, it offers insights into the clever, creative, and often nefarious tactics and strategies of US imperialism in the twenty-first century. The fate of Honduras after the coup wasn't a special case. It was a spearhead, cast into the heart of emerging democracy throughout Latin America and the Caribbean.

Brace yourself: what follows here is littered with dead bodies, especially in the second chapter. But it is not just a tale of unrelenting horror. It is also about the joys of daily life, especially lives spent in struggle against injustice, inequality, and imperialism. In the end, it is about how ordinary people, in the face of state terror and imperial aggression, chose to hope they could achieve a different future, and to throw themselves—and their children—into the lifelong project of making those hopes maybe, someday, come true.

Labor activists with banner from the National Front of Popular Resistance, at a highway blockade in Choloma, Cortés, June 28, 2010, the first anniversary of the coup. Photo credit: Dana Frank.

CHAPTER ONE

In Struggle:
Resistance and Repression

Learning Curves

At 5:30 a.m., on Sunday, June 28, 2009, I got a phone call telling me that the Honduran military had surrounded the home of the country's president, Manuel Zelaya, and had flown him to Costa Rica in his pajamas at gunpoint.

I tried to call my loved ones in Honduras, but their phones didn't work. Alternative radio in Honduras, which normally streamed in through my computer, was silent. I spent the whole day in a higher and higher state of helpless, horrified panic, watching the coup unfold on Spanish-language television.

Finally, late that night, I reached Stephen Coats, the Director of the US Labor Education in the Americas Project (USLEAP) in Chicago. He was the one who had first pulled me into working in Honduras nine years before; he was my great mentor in solidarity work with the banana unions. He had decades of experience working in the human rights and policy world in Washington, D.C. "Tell me what to do!" I demanded. He asked me two or three quiet questions, then asked: "What's your strategic plan?"

"Stop the coup," I whimpered.

In fact, I had no idea what to do. I had no strategic plan. For the weeks, months, years that followed, I got up every morning, cried in

10

the shower, braced myself for emails or calls notifying me a friend had been killed, and asked myself: what powers do I have to stop this? So did the Honduran people, who in the next days, months, and years, in the face of unprecedented terror, would rise up in spectacularly creative and courageous resistance to the coup.

None of us had expected that there really would be a coup. President Zelaya, a member of the Honduran elite himself, came from one of the two traditional conservative parties that had ruled the country for decades on behalf of a dozen oligarchic families who controlled the vast majority of the Honduran economy, along with US and other transnational corporations. Elected in 2006, Zelaya had begun to take more progressive positions by 2009, influenced by democratically-elected governments of the left and center-left that had come to power throughout Latin America during the 1990s and early 2000s in Argentina, Bolivia, Brazil, Ecuador, El Salvador, Venezuela, Uruguay, and elsewhere. He brought Honduras into Petrocaribe and ALBA (*Alianza Bolivariana para los Pueblos de Nuestra América*, Bolivarian Alliance for the Peoples of Our America), regional economic blocs independent of US control. He supported a 50 percent increase in the minimum wage, opened the door to restoring the land rights of small farmers, and, most importantly, stopped multiple power grabs by the elites, who sought to privatize the publicly owned ports, education system, electrical system, and anything else they could get their hands on.[1]

Facing tremendous pushback, his control slipping, Zelaya, in April 2009, legally announced he was asking voters to decide a nonbinding survey question, known as the *Cuarta Urna*, or fourth ballot box, on June 28. Voters were to be asked whether they thought that the upcoming ballot in the November presidential election should also include the election of delegates to a constitutional convention, or *Constituyente*, to be held at some undetermined point in 2010 or 2011. Zelaya was trying to re-create recent constitutional conventions in Ecuador, Bolivia, and Venezuela that had approved new constitutions expanding democratic rights and the power of Indigenous people, women, small farmers, and others at the bottom. Grassroots social justice activists in Honduras, especially those united in *Bloque Popular*, a direct-action coalition that had originated the demand, picked up on the *Cuarta Urna* proposal and began to construct extensive networks to encourage voting in its favor, as a way of opening up a larger conversation about fundamental reforms.[2]

The Honduran elites seized on the *Cuarta Urna* ballot to claim, without any evidence, that Zelaya was using a constitutional convention to overthrow the extant constitution's ban on presidential reelection and get himself a second term. Yet Zelaya would have been long out of office by the time any change might have been made—and he himself never mentioned reelection as a reason for the proposed convention. On the eve of the June 28 election, as tensions mounted, the military refused to distribute the actual ballots—though under the Honduran Constitution they were legally required to do so when directed by the president. Zelaya commanded them to obey. Then the entire Honduran Supreme Court and most of the Congress fell into line to endorse the armed ouster of Zelaya. Roberto Micheletti, the President of Congress, from Zelaya's own party, announced that he was now president, and the full powers of the Honduran government were lined up against Zelaya—and against the great majority of the Honduran people.[3]

That first Sunday I was mostly paralyzed. On Monday I finally reached my two closest friends in Honduras, Iris Munguía, the Secretary for Women of the Coalition of Honduran Banana and Agroindustrial Unions (*Coordinadora de Sindicatos Bananeros y Agroindustriales de Honduras*, COSIBAH), and German Zepeda, the organization's president. Iris said that they'd been driving back together from Nicaragua to San Pedro Sula, on the Honduran north coast, as the coup broke out, and had gotten stranded in Tegucigalpa, the capital, five hours away from home. She said there were no military checkpoints on the highways, but only because the police and military were busy occupying government buildings throughout the country.

By Wednesday morning the full reality of the coup was becoming clear. Tanks roamed the streets. CNN was blocked. Military planes roared through the skies. Phone service was disrupted. The army surrounded, invaded, and shut down Radio Progreso, a Jesuit-owned opposition radio on the north coast, and took over the transmitters of Cholusat SUR, an independent television station in the capital, silencing it for the next eight days.[4]

But to everyone's surprise, an enormous resistance movement sprang up, too, seemingly out of nowhere. That first Sunday morning in the capital, people started streaming spontaneously into the streets in front of the Presidential Palace to back up Zelaya. One friend later told me that he'd gotten there early, as soon as the coup was announced, and there were only a few other people. We're doomed, he thought. But within a couple of hours tens of thousands of people had arrived—soon to be attacked by the military and police with tear gas and batons.

On Monday, Tuesday, and Wednesday, demonstrations against the coup and in support of constitutional order erupted all over the country. Micheletti's new de facto government, in response, declared a state of siege, imposed a 6:00 p.m. curfew, and cracked down with ferocious repression. When demonstrators on Tuesday morning blocked the big "Bridge of Democracy" over the River Ulúa into El Progreso to demand the restoration of constitutional order, police and military tore into them brutally, sending ten to the hospital and arresting forty. Military checkpoints sprang up all over. The government shut off electricity to neighborhoods where protests were particularly strong. In Olancho, where Zelaya came from, the military reportedly began breaking into houses and capturing young people, forcing others to flee into the hills.[5]

On Thursday, July 2, hundreds of thousands marched in Tegucigalpa and San Pedro Sula, the country's second-largest city. At 3:05 p.m., I called German to see how the march in San Pedro Sula was going. He told me that Iris had just been grabbed out of the march by the police and thrown into the back of a military truck on top of fifteen other people and was being detained. That next hour, panicked, I called everyone I could think of in the NGO and labor worlds. But I had no idea who else to call—do I contact Human Rights Watch? Amnesty International? I knew nothing about them. An hour later I got a call that she'd been released after a crowd of local human rights defenders had shown up at the detention center. Iris was fine, but I never ever want to go through an hour like that again, during which I could only imagine what the police and military were doing to her, or if she were even still alive. That afternoon and its potential horrors hung over me for years.

That first week, it wasn't at all obvious that the coup would last. We knew that a coup attempt had been stopped in Bolivia the year before and that in 2002 a coup in Venezuela had been reversed after two days. We could feel how surprisingly strong the Honduran resistance was. We knew that the Organization of American States and dozens of countries throughout Latin America and all over the world had condemned the coup ferociously and called for Zelaya's immediate restoration.[6]

But the Obama Administration waffled. The day of the coup, Obama merely expressed hopes that Hondurans would "respect democratic norms, the rule of law and the tenets of the Inter-American Democratic Charter" and resolve their differences "peacefully through dialogue free from any outside interference."[7] By Monday, Obama was willing to call it a coup, but by mid-week the State Department had backed off from demanding Zelaya's immediate return.[8]

A week into the coup, on Sunday, June 5, deposed President Zelaya attempted to return to Honduras in a chartered plane, accompanied by his top ministers and Miguel D'Escoto, the President of the United Nations General Assembly. The presidents of Argentina, Ecuador, and Paraguay and the Secretary-General of the Organizations of American States followed in a second plane. Zelaya's plane finally crossed into Honduran air space after two hours. Eventually, the plane circled twice above Toncontín airport in Tegucigalpa, then tried to land. But just as the plane was about to drop down a second time, two large troop transport trucks from the Honduran Army pulled out and blocked the runway sideways. Zelaya's plane finally pulled up and away in defeat.[9] On live Venezuelan television, I could see the military and police swoop in on two hundred protesters who had reached the last fence before the tarmac. Snipers on top of the airport shot at the protesters, while troops forced the demonstrators back, toward the hundreds of thousands of additional protesters who had poured into the streets around the airport to welcome Zelaya upon his return. Later, photographs appeared of protesters carrying the horizontal body of Isis Obed Murillo, age 19, who'd been shot and killed by one of the snipers, blood streaming out from his head onto the ground.[10]

By that point, the opposition had consolidated into the National Front of Popular Resistance (*Frente Nacional de Resistencia Popular*, FNRP), known popularly as the Resistance or the *Frente*, bringing together a spectacularly broad coalition of the Honduran labor, campesino, Indigenous, Afro-Indigenous, and women's movements; progressive Catholics; middle-class and even elite members of Zelaya's Liberal Party; others across the political spectrum who were committed to constitutional order; and, most astonishingly amid a fiercely homophobic public culture, the LGBTI movement. The backbone was *Bloque Popular*, a direct-action coalition that had come together long before the coup to oppose privatizations, stop the Central American Free Trade Agreement (CAFTA), and define broad collective demands from the the state. Suddenly, everyone I knew, as they threw themselves into the Resistance, sounded like they were in France during World War II, and old-line Marxist trade unionists in their sixties were talking about their comrades in "*el movimiento gay*."[11]

The Frente, in turn, built on a coalition that had emerged in the previous year in solidarity with a thirty-eight-day hunger strike by seven federal prosecutors protesting corruption in the judicial system. The Indigenous Lenca people, Jesuits, and other allies had gradually joined the prosecutors' encampment in the open plaza underneath the Honduran Congress' building in Tegucigalpa. The alliances built during that campaign, including the new National Coordinating Committee of Popular Resistance (*Coordinador Nacional de Resistencia Popular*, CNRP), underlay the much broader progressive alliance that led resistance to the coup.[12]

That summer and fall of 2009, as the coup tore through Honduras and I tried to figure out what to do about it, I went nuts trying to explain my new life to others. It was like a huge wall rose up between me and other people I knew at home in Santa Cruz. "Don't you get it? There's been a coup!" I wanted to scream. "People are getting killed!" I couldn't stand it that no one seemed to care. As the days stretched into weeks, I had to work through the fact that most people I talked to weren't ever going to care—they were busy with their own problems, their own causes. I had to respect that. After a few weeks, when people asked what I was up to, I'd just tell them "I have a new life as a Honduran Freedom Fighter"—jokingly playing off President Ronald Reagan's 1983 reference to the US-funded Contra forces as "Nicaraguan Freedom Fighters."[13]

While the coup regime held on through the fall, the FNRP organized mass protests and got brutally attacked. The police and military launched into demonstrators with batons sporting new metal tips; they'd suddenly thrust the batons up into women protesters' crotches. At close range they unleashed dense thickets of tear gas, the kinds the make you vomit or cry or feel like you can't breathe, or all three at once. German joked to me that he was learning to distinguish the tastes of all the different brands of gas. By the end of September, when Micheletti suspended four articles of the Honduran Constitution— restricting freedom of transit, banning public meetings not autho- rized by security forces, and barring the media from criticizing the government—thirty-five hundred to four thousand people had been illegally detained for peacefully demonstrating, according to the Inter-American Commission on Human Rights.[14]

On August 14, the police grabbed Irma Melissa Villanueva, 25, from a demonstration in Choloma, outside San Pedro Sula, where she'd been marching alongside friends of mine, and took her away to a remote location, where four policemen gang-raped her for hours. "Now, bitch, now you're gonna see what happens to you for being where you shouldn't be," they told her. Three days later, with incred- ible bravery, her mother and husband at her side, she testified over Radio Progreso about what had happened.[15]

The terror escalated: one by one, activists disappeared or were assassinated. On July 11, armed men broke into the home of Roger Bados, a local union president and leader of the Resistance in San Pedro Sula, and shot him to death. That same night in Santa Barbara, to the west, men boarded a bus, ordered off Ramón García, an opposition activist, and killed him.[16] Incredibly, the Resistance nonetheless remained nonviolent, with the exception of rocks thrown at security forces on some occasions, after the forces had attacked first. In sharp contrast to the 1970s and 80s in Central America, no security forces were ever killed, and no armed struggle ever emerged, even after months of repression.

Despite the obviously criminal and illegitimate nature of the regime, the Obama Administration swiftly began treating de facto President Micheletti as Zelaya's legitimate diplomatic equal. On July 7, ten days after the coup, Secretary of State Hillary Clinton announced that the United States had persuaded both sides to agree to negotiations in San José, Costa Rica, by so doing successfully transferring power over the situation onto US-controlled terrain and away from the Organization of American States (OAS). The OAS, by contrast, did not recognize the post-coup regime, and the great majority of its member governments were adamant that Zelaya had to be returned to full powers immediately.[17]

The Obama Administration thus turned its back on supporting Zelaya as the only legitimate president of Honduras. A senior US official wrote Republicans in Congress on August 4: "Our policy and strategy for engagement is not based on supporting any particular politician or individual," he made clear. But then he criticized Zelaya for actions that "contributed to polarization of Honduran society and led to a confrontation that unleashed the events that led to his removal," a rather grammatically convoluted way of blaming the victim.[18]

The State Department did eventually suspend some visas of top *golpista* officials and business leaders associated with the coup and cut off a portion of police and military aid.[19] But the United States never condemned the vicious and ongoing human rights abuses by the de facto government. Obama and Clinton pointedly refused to ever use the phrase "military coup," which would have legally obligated the United States to stop almost all foreign aid to Honduras immediately. US law clearly states that funding to a foreign government must be immediately suspended in the case of a coup with significant military involvement.[20] Obama and Clinton chose to split hairs, and use "coup" but not "military coup."[21] Yet Hugo Llorens, the US Ambassador to Honduras, was unequivocal in a July 24 cable to Clinton, entitled "Open and Shut: The Case of the Honduran Coup": "There is no doubt that the military, Supreme Court and National Congress conspired on June 28 in what constituted an illegal and unconstitutional coup against the Executive Branch."[22]

Why did Obama and Clinton support the success of a military coup in Honduras—throwing US policy back to the twentieth century, when the United States armed and celebrated vicious Latin American dictatorships into the Reagan years? During the George W. Bush Administration (2001–2009), US foreign policy attention had been largely focused on the Middle East and Asia. The nations of Latin America enjoyed a brief hiatus in which to exercise a relatively greater degree of sovereignty—although the United States did bless the brief, unsuccessful coup attempt in Venezuela in 2002—and used that to open up democratic processes, institute more progressive policies, and establish greater independence from the United States. Regional alliances like ALBA flourished; Cuba's pariah status began to evaporate within the region; the United States lost its dominance over the Organization of American States. But when Obama came into office in January 2009, the eyes of the empire up north turned south and took notice of the slippage in US power; they saw the brakes the new governments were putting on neoliberal policies designed to serve the interests of transnational corporations and local elites.[23]

We don't yet have concrete evidence that the United States promoted the coup or approved it in advance. We do know that the plane in which the Honduran military flew Zelaya out of the country stopped to refuel at Soto Cano Air Force Base, a joint US-Honduran base, and we can presume that it would not have done so without US permission. We know that four of the six top generals who oversaw the coup were trained by the United States at the School of the Americas/Western Hemisphere Institute for Security Cooperation in Fort Benning, Georgia, and that it is unlikely that they would have perpetrated a coup without US approval.[24] A 2017 article by

Jake Johnston in *The Intercept* documented that the night before the coup, top Honduran military officials attended a party thrown by the US Embassy's defense attaché. At nine o'clock that night, Kenneth Rodriguez, the commander of US forces in Honduras, left the party to meet with Gen. Romeo Vásquez Velásquez, then returned to the festivities.[25] The next morning, Vásquez led the coup.

Whatever happened before the coup, we do know clearly what the Obama Administration did afterward to ensure the coup regime's permanence. To borrow a metaphor from the Vietnam War, Honduras was a first domino that the United States pushed over to counteract the new governments in Latin America. Zelaya was the weakest of the new center-left and left leaders; he lacked an independent party and a popular base. He made a good first victim, as US support for the coup warned all the other governments that they could be next.

US support for the coup stemmed from geopolitical interests in reasserting US power in the hemisphere. Soto Cano Air Base is one of the very few places in Latin America where the United States can land its big planes, especially after Ecuador evicted the United States from its base there in 2007. (President Rafael Correa famously quipped: "We'll renew the base on one condition: that they let us put a base in Miami—an Ecuadorean base."[26]) Those geopolitical concerns, in turn, serve transnational corporate interests in extracting wealth from Honduras and ensuring regional control more broadly. By the time of the coup, the Honduran economy boasted large export processing zones, or maquiladoras, in which transnational corporations produced garments and electronic parts, while mining corporations, especially from Canada, were moving in on mineral resources.[27] Corporate interests flourished as neoliberal economic policies, enforced by the International Monetary Fund and World Bank, promoted the elimination of basic governmental services and privatizations of state-owned entities.

For all my own ferocious commitment to stopping the coup, I still felt largely confused about what I should actually do. Most of what I did was only moving information around, recommending contacts to others, and trying to decode what was going on inside Honduras, while mobilizing what networks I knew of, made up largely of academics and labor activists. After I helped circulate and publicize a letter from a hundred fifty professors and Latin American experts calling on the United Nations Security Council to intervene in Honduras, it dawned on me that there should be some kind of academic delegation to Honduras—wasn't that what people did in these circumstances?—but I was clueless about how to organize one.[28] Deep inside, I was privately mourning that my beloved Honduras had become one of those places that needed delegations at all.

I dealt with a constant undertow of unrelenting brutality and real fear for my loved ones, and beyond that the knowledge that things in Honduras could get far, far worse. On September 26 the BBC published a photograph of a stadium in Tegucigalpa in which the military and police had detained more than six hundred people, some for four days, and all I could think about was Chile in 1973, when Augusto Pinochet's US-backed government detained seven thousand people in Santiago's National Stadium right after its September coup, many of whom were tortured or killed.[29]

But the counterweight to all the fear and horror was the new solidarity, as I became part of something larger than myself. Relationships with old friends and colleagues in Honduras took on a new and deeper meaning. In the United States I now worked with dozens of activists—Hondurans, Americans, Canadians, and Salvadorans—all of us trying to stop the coup.

My steepest learning curve was about the media. The Honduran newspapers, entirely owned by the elites, loved the coup—with the exception of *El Tiempo*, which held back somewhat. They were full of fantastic, alarmist fictions: Zelaya is a drug dealer! The Venezuelan and Nicaraguan armies are amassed at the Honduran border, ready to invade to restore him! The papers published big spreads on minuscule demonstrations in support of Micheletti but ignored Resistance protests numbering into the hundreds of thousands. To its eternal shame, *La Prensa* even ran a doctored photo of the men at the airport carrying the body of Isis Obed, the young man killed by government snipers, in which the blood streaming down from his head had been airbrushed out.[30]

At the same time, the post-coup regime continued to crack down on opposition media. On July 16, twenty military officers again invaded the Jesuits' Radio Progreso and ordered it off the air. On September 28, acting on an executive decree from the new government, police and military forcefully entered the offices of three radio stations and of television Channel 36, seized their equipment, and carted it off to an army facility.[31] Those in the Resistance started referring to the *cerco mediático*—the media siege (literally, "fence")—by which they meant the combination of raw repression of opposition media outlets and the lies and silences in the pro-coup television stations, radio, and papers.

In the United States, I ran head-on into our own *cerco mediático*. The gap between what was going on in Honduras and what the mainstream US media were reporting was breathtaking. They regularly reduced almost everyone who opposed the coup to "Zelaya supporters," although at least half of those protesters had been ferociously opposed to Zelaya while he was in office, and most took to the streets to defend not Zelaya himself but the constitutional rule of law—so hard fought-for in Honduras, as throughout Latin America. On September 26, the Associated Press even referred to "die-hard supporters of ousted President Zelaya," implying that the opposition was merely fanatical groupies who should have politely given up long before.[32]

More baldly untrue was the assertion that Zelaya had precipitated the coup by trying to obtain a second term. The coup perpetrators' fabrication quickly hardened into fact; *Newsweek* even uncritically quoted Jorge Castañeda of Mexico claiming Zelaya was illegally trying to get a *third* term.[33] The silences were even more stunning. Despite reports from Amnesty International, Human Rights Watch, and dozens of international observers, as far as the mainstream US papers were concerned, it was largely as if the repression wasn't even happening.[34]

In July and August 2009, as signals increasingly suggested that President Obama was going to deliberately allow the coup regime to stabilize, many liberal US observers were caught off guard. Obama had been in office only five months at the time of the coup; many still harbored hopes he would be progressive; surely he wouldn't support a military coup in Latin America?

Many potential critics, still starstruck, couldn't quite believe he would be allowing the coup to stabilize. Moreover, scholarly and other experts on Honduras were few and far between, in contrast to long-time and widespread academic interest in neighboring Guatemala, Nicaragua, and El Salvador. Of those few academics who did have knowledge of Honduras, even fewer stepped in to challenge the administration's narrative, leaving a vacuum in the public conversation about the coup.

On November 3, a reporter named Martha Mendoza called me from the Associated Press in Mexico City. I'd heard of her; she had graduated from UC Santa Cruz and worked for my local newspaper. As we chatted casually about the negotiations between Zelaya and Micheletti, I let drop that "the US negotiators may have underestimated the sheer nutso chaos of Honduran politics." She got real quiet after that; I could hear the clickety-clack of a keyboard at the other end of the line. Sure enough, the next morning there was my rather wackily phrased (if potentially accurate) quote in an AP story, broadcast to every paper in the United States and all over the world.[35] Embarrassed, I regretted not having instead landed a precisely crafted, one-line critique of US policy; I learned my lesson and was more careful with reporters after that.

After the first week, when I got a piece into the *San Francisco Chronicle*, I could never get op-eds accepted by any mainstream papers, except once in the *San José Mercury-News*, no matter how many I sent off; nor could others critical of the coup. Meanwhile, obscure characters who supported it got published all over the place. Happily, alternative and online media outlets did take my pieces—*Common Dreams*, the *Huffington Post*, and an op-ed news feed run by *The Progressive*.[36] Alternative radio, too, was a wonderful, open space. On television, Amy Goodman's *Democracy Now!* came through beautifully and regularly, covering the repression, US policy, and Honduran voices of the resistance.[37]

On September 21, President Zelaya, in a complete surprise, popped up inside the Brazilian Embassy in Tegucigalpa, joined by three hundred supporters. The military and police immediately surrounded the embassy, launched tear gas inside, cut off most supplies, and began psychological harassment that lasted for months—blasting loud music, horns, and the sounds of animals screaming, for example. Micheletti declared another state of siege in the rest of country. A new wave of repression swept through.[38]

All fall it was clear that the United States was playing for time, waiting for the presidential elections on November 29. In late October, the endgame fell into place. Zelaya, captive now in the embassy, weaker and weaker in his position within US-manipulated negotiations in San José, Costa Rica, agreed on October 30 to an accord with Micheletti, brokered by the US. President Zelaya would be restored to power briefly until the end of his term in January, serving as part of a "unity government," that would also form a truth commission to address the coup and its aftermath. The only catch was that the Honduran Congress had to approve Zelaya's return.[39] And it never did. On November 3, Thomas Shannon, Assistant Secretary of State for Western Hemisphere Affairs and the architect of the US post-coup strategy, told CNN that the United States would recognize the outcome of the election even if Zelaya were not restored—by so doing giving the *golpistas* a green light to thwart the president's return.[40]

The late November elections were a foregone conclusion. Ongoing repression of basic civil liberties made a free and fair election clearly impossible, while the very same army that had perpetrated the coup controlled the physical ballots. All international bodies—including the United Nations, the Carter Center, and the OAS, with the exception of the US Republican Party and a few delegates from the Democratic Party—refused to observe the process.[41] Carlos H. Reyes, a left-wing independent candidate for president who, in the view of some observers, might have gotten 25 percent or more of the vote, and who had just been hospitalized after the police broke his arm in a demonstration, pulled out of his candidacy, as did candidates from the small, left-leading Unificación Democrática (UD) party and many from Zelaya's traditional right-wing Liberal Party who had stayed loyal to him.[42] With only the blatant coup perpetrators left in it, the Liberal Party largely crumbled; only a token candidate remained on the ballot. The last man standing was

Porfirio "Pepe" Lobo, from the other traditional right-wing party, the National Party, who had supported the coup, but less blatantly, and he claimed the election victory.[43]

On November 29, the State Department released a statement praising the election process—in effect blessing its outcome: "We commend the Honduran people for peacefully exercising their democratic right to select their leaders in an electoral process that began over a year ago, well before the June 28 coup d'etat."[44] Through a completely illegitimate election, Porfirio Lobo would be the new president of the Republic of Honduras. The coup perpetrators had won.

The day of the election, Assistant Secretary of State Thomas Shannon wrote to Secretary of State Hillary Clinton advising her how to respond to it: "As we think about what to say, I would strongly recommend that we not be shy. We should congratulate the Honduran people, we should connect today's vote to the deep democratic vocation of the Honduran people, and we should call on the community of democratic nations (and especially those of the Americas) to recognize, respect, and respond to this accomplishment of the Honduran people."[45]

For all I learned in those five terrible months, my learning curve was never steep enough. I didn't know anything about human rights groups, whether in the US, Honduras, or Geneva, nor anything about nonprofits and think tanks in Washington. I never found the faith-based activists, who I knew had to be out there, somewhere, given their long history of fighting for social justice in Central America. I knew nothing about the State Department or how to influence Congress. I still had no strategic plan. I was working closely with Stephen Coats, Lupita Aguilar, and Rebecca Van Horn of USLEAP, based in Chicago, and I was in contact with the AFL-CIO, but I barely knew about the new world of solidarity with Honduras that came together in Washington, D.C., after the coup—people who generated letters of protest from members of Congress, invited Zelaya to speak, mobilized human rights defenders, and began to construct the building blocks of a national-level network of allies: Jenny Atlee and Tom Loudon, then with the Quixote Center;

Alexander Main, Mark Weisbrot, and Dan Beeton of the Center for Economic and Policy Research; Lisa Haugaard of the Latin America Working Group; Annie Bird, then of Rights Action; activists with School of the Americas Watch. I knew little or nothing of the painstaking, heartbreaking work those people did in the first six months after the coup (and others I still don't know to name). Nor did I know the people who traveled to Honduras with fact-finding missions, or to accompany those at risk, bear witness, or show solidarity, such as the Sisters of Mercy of the Americas, Tom Loudon, the World Council of Churches, Alianza Americas; nor the dozens of people from all over the world who joined President Zelaya in the Brazilian Embassy. It would take years for me to discover all that.

But despite my ongoing ignorance at the time, I nonetheless had new tactics to deploy—talking to reporters and on the radio, writing op-eds, reaching out a little bit to Congress—and my limited contact with new networks and all their tactics. I had all my Honduran friends, with their new tactics and networks. We were all new people now, down to the bones.

Two weeks after the election, on December 13, 2009, drive-by shooters assassinated Walter Trochez, the most prominent LGBTI leader of the National Front of Popular Resistance and a member of its Executive Committee, and it was clear that the hideous violence wasn't over by any means.[46]

Great Awakenings

With a blue-and-white sash across his chest, and with all the hoopla of a legitimate presidency, a big-eared, grinning Porfirio "Pepe" Lobo was sworn into office on January 27, 2010.[47] He immediately appointed to top positions in the government the very military figures who had perpetrated the coup. General Romeo Vásquez Velásquez, who had led it, was awarded Hondutel, the state-owned telephone company, which he promptly announced would be used for intelligence purposes. A show trial lasting only a few days exonerated three top military leaders of the coup. On the day before the Inauguration, Congress declared a general amnesty for the entire coup and all the atrocities committed in its aftermath.[48]

Once elected, Lobo shamelessly announced that his administration was a "government of national reconciliation and unity."[49] Up north, throughout the year to come, the Obama Administration trotted that idea out in official communications *ad nauseum*. The State Department also promoted Lobo's promise to form a new Truth Commission, as had been mandated by the San José accord of October 2009 that had attempted to resolve the coup.[50]

But within days of Lobo's reign, violent repression of the opposition accelerated once again, and with complete impunity. On February 3, 2010, a young woman named Vanessa Zepeda Alonzo, who was active with the Resistance and with her union at the national health service, was found dead, her body dumped from a car in a remote neighborhood of Tegucigalpa. On February 15, a masked gunman on a motorcycle shot dead another union activist involved in the Resistance, Julio Fúnez Benítez, on the sidewalk in front of Benítez's house. A pattern continued from the post-coup months: with the exception of Walter Trochez, the LGBTI activist, the victims targeted were never top leadership but, rather, ordinary people, active in the struggle, whose deaths were harder to pinpoint as having been politically motivated. The strategy was brilliant—everyone got the message, but the deaths were hard for the opposition to spin as repression when reporting to international observers in the human rights community.[51]

Repression of independent media revved up again, too, beginning shortly before Lobo took office. Late on the night of January 6, in Triunfo de la Cruz, an Afro-Indigenous Garifuna community on the north coast, for example, a group of men stole the transmitter and two computers from the community's Radio Coco Dulce, then burned the station.[52] Most chilling was a pattern, drawing from Central America wars of the 1980s, of killing children to get to their parents. In mid-February Dara Guidel, the seventeen-year-old daughter of a well-known opposition radio broadcaster in Danlí, was kidnapped for two days, harassed, released, and then a few days later found hanged.[53]

Two weeks after the inauguration, on February 12, 2010, I finally flew back to Honduras for the first time since the coup. I knew full well it would be terrible and depressing and scary. I had no idea how safe or unsafe anything was for me personally, given the op-eds I'd written denouncing the regime, so I set up a meticulous security system with my friend Stephen Coats at USLEAP, in which he'd know where I was at every minute. Don't talk to cab drivers, a friend cautioned; watch your every word in public. I swore to myself I wouldn't go to demonstrations, talk on the radio, take regular streets cabs, or wear anything that signaled I supported the resistance.[54]

But when I got there, instead of being depressing, it was exhilarating. I returned to an entirely new country in which everyone I knew was full of excited energy, and a new culture of resistance was bursting out all over.

The biggest change was with the young people. When I arrived at my friends' house from the airport, the twentysomethings I knew who had not been politically involved before the coup were falling all over each other to tell me stories about their new lives: what they'd done the day of the coup; how they'd squeezed time off from work to make it to marches; how they'd escaped being grabbed by police; how they were boycotting fast food outlets because coup perpetrators owned them. They sat up in their chairs differently. Cell phones at the dinner table kept going off with ring tones of songs from the Resistance: *Traidores* (Traitors), *Nos Tienen Miedo Porque No Tenemos*

Miedo (They're afraid of us because we're not afraid), or the four bold chords that open the *Himno de la Resistencia* (Hymn of the Resistance) that I heard everywhere that week. A fifteen-year-old girl from next door arrived wearing a red T-shirt that read "I [heart] Honduras Without *Golpistas*." They loved the story of a five-year-old boy who, when each child in his class had been asked to stand up and sing a song, had chosen *Nos Tienen Miedo*, which he'd learned from Radio Progreso and from going to marches with his mom.

The kids told me that all over, people had bought cheap cell phones with radio reception so they could listen to Radio Progreso, the Jesuits' station, and Radio Uno, a low-wattage opposition station that broadcast within San Pedro Sula. When you walked into a store or passed a street vendor or walked down the street you could hear everyone listening, all over, and know who was on your side. Both stations were of full excited opinions on call-in programs and local news reports produced by ordinary people.

Driving from La Lima into San Pedro Sula, twenty minutes away, we passed over a polluted river that stank like raw sewage, known popularly as "*Rio Tufoso*" (Stinky River). The kids pointed out an official-looking green sign that had mysteriously appeared renaming the river "Rio Micheletti," after the post-coup de facto president. When we got into the city, political graffiti was everywhere. Most messages were straightforward: "*¡Golpista!*," the all-purpose epithet marking a coup supporter or perpetrator; "*Militares Asesinos*" (Killer Soldiers); "*¡Eleciones No!*," protesting the November 29 elections that had been boycotted by almost all opposition candidates. I saw "*Micheletti Pinochetti*," equating Micheletti with Augusto Pinochet, the dictator of Chile after its 1973 coup, and long streams of blood-like red paint dripping down the sides of the city's municipal building, where Micheletti had deposed the mayor and installed his nephew.

A sophisticated critique of the media was exploding everywhere, evident in the kids' favorite chant from the marches: "*¡No somos cinco, no somos cien, prensa vendida, cuéntanos bien!*" (We're not five, we're not a hundred, sold-out press, count us well!) In front of the cathedral facing the Plaza Central, in the very center of downtown San Pedro Sula, a giant white banner replicated the logo of one of San Pedro

Sula's leading dailies, promising "Get Stupid in Three Days. Read *La Prensa.*" Another transposed "TeleviCentro" (Central TV) into "TeleviCerdo" (Pig TV). The park itself had been renamed Plaza Libertad, as had parks and plazas all over the country, and the Frente had painted the ballustrades, streetlights, and benches of its front corner red and black.

The older people I talked with were on a high, too, but with a sober look in their eyes. They'd been through the Central American wars of the 1980s. They knew quite how terrible things could get. But as veterans of those battles they also had a clear sense that this maybe, maybe was the main chance for fundamental change they'd been waiting for their whole lives. "All these years I've been involved in the struggle, but I've never felt that change so close," Efraín Aguilar, a lifelong union activist, told me in low, firm tones. I could feel a cautious, but entirely new hope.

Resistance feminism was flourishing, too. "*Ni golpe de estado ni golpe a mujeres*" (neither blows to the state nor blows to women) was ubiquitous on T-shirts, posters, and in chants. My friend's three-month-old granddaughter had a little tie-died onesie emblazoned with "*Feminista in Resistencia*" that she sported in her stroller when she joined marches with her mom, grandmother, and great-grandmother. I took a picture of them all sitting together on a couch—four generations of women in resistance. Everyone told me that the demonstrations were full of old people, babies, and toddlers, even though the tear gas and beatings were continual.

Soon after my arrival, my friend German from the banana unions talked me into an interview on his radio show on Radio Uno in San Pedro Sula. I agreed, already abandoning one of my pre-trip vows. He added that I would be interested in meeting his co-host, who turned out to be Pedro Brizuela, a wily and witty life-long Communist whom I'd interviewed two years earlier as part of my historical research on the labor movement in Honduras. Both of us enjoying the surprise, we trundled upstairs to the studio through three floors of Radio Uno's journalism and broadcasting school, populated by eager teenagers in crisply ironed white shirts, navy blue pants, and blue-and-white plaid skirts, seated in classrooms at decrepit school desks. In the topmost corner of the radio's building, an adolescent girl with shining black hair and a plaid skirt ran the controls. Out the window we could see graffiti on the building across the street that proclaimed in giant letters: "Radio Uno We're With You."

German, Pedro, and I scrunched into our seats, elbow to elbow around a circular table, and lined up the microphones. Once on the air, Pedro promptly announced: "This is Dana Frank, and she's here in Honduras looking for Communists." Ack! I couldn't exactly make him take it back. He asked me what I'd observed so far during my visit. I made a few encouraging comments about the new spirit of struggle and how the country felt so different, then launched into a virulent denunciation of both the Honduran government and my own.

I could feel myself make the choice to say those things, choose to take the risk. It was like I was inside a dynamic I'd only read about in books, in which activists in social movements responded to the repression of their fellow activists by themselves stepping to an even higher level of risk-taking. I'm not saying I did anything heroic, like the things my Honduran friends were doing all day, every day—just that I could feel, in my own small way, new choices I was making from deep inside, inspired by the higher level of commitment and the bravery all around me.

For all the spectacular new hopefulness, though, an undercurrent of terror flowed everywhere, and the older people were particularly aware of it. Daily life was dangerous. "Now I always look both ways before I step into the street," Iris, my other friend from the banana unions, told me. In El Progreso, a teacher active in the Resistance and her union told me the long story of the country's huge teachers' unions and their decades-long militancy, which was now directed at fighting the coup and trying to block the privatization of education. Like the other older folks, she was in it for the long haul. "The terrorism is going to continue," she said. And the potential for violence haunted her every day. "I can leave here and be killed on the way to my house." The stress took its toll: Efraín, the labor educator who told me he'd never felt change so close, had a stroke the day of the coup.

Zoila Lagos, an old friend and a veteran of the women's and labor movements, came to meet me at the banana union office in downtown La Lima. We talked in the scorching hot labor education center upstairs, empty except for a few chairs and a plastic-covered table. Zoila told me that in her poor neighborhood in Choloma—the maquiladora district in the suburbs of San Pedro—the police fired shots and set off sirens in the middle of the night, every night, over and over again, "like it was a war. They do it so we get used to war as part of daily life. So we're afraid, so we stay shut up in our houses. So we don't participate in the Resistance." She said the police knocked on people's doors at dawn and raided their homes with no legal orders, falsely accusing them of having drugs or arms, in what were known as *"madrugados"* (dawn raids). They'd come to her brother's house at four o'clock in the morning, torn up the whole place, and stolen money the family had saved. He'd never been involved in anything.

But the Resistance in Choloma countered by organizing demonstrations in the neighborhoods at night with big bonfires. One or two hundred people would come. The terror didn't keep Zoila at home. "I feel *worse* when I stay home," she said. The teacher I talked to at Radio Progreso said the same thing: "We feel like a family. When we're alone, we feel afraid. When we're together, we feel powerful. We turn that fear into bravery and strengthen ourselves with it."

I also interviewed a middle-class lawyer in her twenties who'd been a Liberal Party loyalist and sided with the Zelaya wing of the party when it split over the coup. Excited and energized just like the other young people, she said that most of her school friends, including Micheletti's son, had cut her off, de-friending her on Facebook. But she had a sea of new friends now in the Resistance. "I got used to sleeping on top of benches during demonstrations," she told me proudly. "I got used to eating sitting in the streets." Listening to her, I could feel how the Resistance had brought together people from wildly divergent class and cultural backgrounds into a new community.

But I also heard stories of families that had been completely torn apart. A line in the sand split the country, *golpistas* on one side, *Resistencia* on the other, driving right through the middle of families—husbands and wives, parents and children—and producing brutal heartache. I heard, too, that thousands had lost their jobs because they'd participated in the Resistance, like a young man I heard of who had gotten official permission for a personal day off from his job in a factory, so he'd be able to go to a demonstration. When a television station ran a close-up of him in the central plaza of San Pedro carrying a can collecting money for the Resistance, he was fired.

This new Honduras, full of struggle, joy, and pride, as well as new heartache, was so different from the one I'd last visited a year and a half before. During the 1980s, Honduras had always been the uncool place—it never produced the huge struggles that emerged in Guatemala, El Salvador, and Nicaragua. In the United States, progressive activists largely viewed Honduras as sort of the armpit of Central America, a US puppet that wasn't cool to visit or study. "Hondurans always had the reputation of being cowards," a Honduran sociologist I talked to confirmed. He, too, had been completely surprised: "I never imagined that Hondurans had the ability or disposition to struggle like this," he said. "It's been terrible, and a great awakening."

The ability of ordinary Hondurans to fight back so bravely and on such an immense scale and to create a new culture of the resistance was a huge surprise to everyone. It was as if the Honduran people collectively surprised themselves. Now they were proud of who they were, not just individually, but as a people. Now they carried stories inside them about what they'd done. Now they had a new culture—humor, art, music, T-shirts, chants—that no one could take away. They knew that people all over the world were visiting Honduras and celebrating the Resistance for its spectacular ability to bridge so many sectors in a common movement. The chorus of "Hymn of the Resistance" that my friend's son, ordinarily so very shy, sang for me at the dinner table that first night, meant something very real: "*Honduras, El Pueblo Está Contigo*"—Honduras, the people are with you.

When I got to Tegucigalpa the trip got dicier. My afternoon flight was delayed for hours and hours. I sat in the waiting room amidst a couple of dozen prosperous-looking people, the whole time thinking: "Which ones are the *golpistas*?" My best guess was an elite-looking family of two older adults and a woman in her late twenties with a sour look on her face, who was busily ignoring a toddler minded by a young nanny. About twenty minutes before the plane finally left, a new passenger appeared and started chatting with them. She was tall, long-legged, blondish, maybe a well-preserved fifty-year-old, dressed like she spent a lot of time in Miami. I heard the word "Micheletti" at one point and had to suddenly look down when she cast her eyes around the room to see if anyone was listening.

By the time our plane finally landed in Tegucigalpa it was ten at night and the airport was shutting down. I called my small hotel as soon as I landed, and they promised a driver. Gradually the airport thinned out, even the people waiting for checked bags, but no driver was in appearance. I got more and more nervous and called the hotel again; they said he'd be there in eight minutes. "Do you need help?" the Miami-looking woman came up to me and asked in English, spotting a white, middle-class *gringa* from fifty feet away. She offered me a ride, but I declined and just asked if she'd mind waiting until the driver showed up. While we waited she told me she was a *diputada*—a congresswoman. I asked her name. "Marcia Villeda," she replied. Then the driver showed up, and I thanked her profusely as he rolled my bag off through the door.

When we were settled into our cab I casually mentioned to the driver, "That woman who was helping me is a diputada. Her name is Marcia Villeda." "*¡GOLPISTA!*" he spat out with ferocious venom. She was Micheletti's right-hand woman, he said, who'd reportedly forged Zelaya's signature on false resignation papers the day of the coup; she was part of *the* most elite family—the Facussés; a big, big shot. He'd seen three or four big SUVs with darkened windows full of bodyguards there to pick her up at the airport.

The driver told me more about Villeda, then about his own life in the Resistance. He was middle-class. His good technical job in a government agency had been cut down to half time by Zelaya's neoliberal predecessor—hence the cab-driving gig. He told me he'd been organizing in the poor neighborhoods of Tegucigalpa, helping to build the Resistance at the grassroots. Since we were at the airport, I asked him about the snipers who had killed Isis Obed on September 21, the day Zelaya had tried to return in his plane. He said he'd been at the demonstration himself, although he had not been one of the people protesting next to the tarmac, where the worst repression had come down.

Yes, I'd vowed I wouldn't reveal my politics to taxi drivers. But I knew that my detailed questions about the Resistance had already made clear which side I was on. Just before we arrived at the hotel I fessed up. We reveled a bit, then arranged for him to take me to the airport when I flew out a few days later. "Aren't you afraid to be so open with a passenger about your politics?" I asked. "No," he said, "they already know who everyone is. So many things have happened, we're not afraid anymore." He was fearless, strong, completely sure of himself and what he was saying.

The next afternoon I got a free graffiti tour of downtown Tegucigalpa from yet another eager twentysomething active in the Resistance. He was like a gutter rat in those streets. The Resistance slogans he showed me were more sophisticated than those I'd seen in San Pedro Sula. My favorite was "*Nadie Ama a Cristo como el Cardenal Ama Al Pisto*" (No One Loves Christ like the Cardinal Loves Cash), a reference to Cardinal Óscar Rodríguez Maradiaga, who had blessed the coup on its sixth day. I saw a lot of walls with fresh, blank paint, which my escort told me was the work of schoolkids who'd been organized by the police to get rid of graffiti. At the bottom of one of the blank walls, someone had taunted back in red spray paint: "*¡Bórrame, Golpista!*—FNRP" (Erase Me, Coup Perpetrator!—National Front of Popular Resistance). My guide said he'd seen another painted-over wall that had been subsequently amended with: "Thanks for cleaning the chalkboard—FNRP."

On my last morning in the country, my taxi-driver friend showed up promptly. When we got to the airport he showed me a low monument between curving off-ramps that had been renamed in spray paint, "Plaza Isis Obed." He showed me the exact spot on a median strip where Obed had been shot in the head.

Deep in the airport gift shop, among artisanal items, I discovered a series of painted ceramic wall plaques, cream-colored with blue and red flowers. Among the classic "*Mi Casa Es Tu Casa*" (My House Is Your House) and the feminist "*Cocinera en Huelga*" (Cook on

Strike)—which I bought—I also saw one that read *"Este Gobierno Ama al Pueblo, Pero Hay Amores Que Matan"* (This Government Loves the People, but There Are Loves That Kill).

That was Saturday. On Wednesday, armed, masked men knocked on the door of Claudia Brizuela, the daughter of the wily old Communist who'd interviewed me on Radio Uno. They opened fire and killed her in front of her children, four blocks away from where I'd been staying in San Pedro Sula.[55]

By early summer, as the June 28 anniversary of the coup approached, it was clear that under President Lobo, repression of the opposition and of independent media had reached levels matching the post-coup period. Killings mounted: according to Reporters Without Borders, eight journalists, all working in radio and TV, were killed during his first six months in office.[56] In February alone, the Inter-American Commission on Human Rights counted two kidnappings, two rapes, eight torture incidents, and fifty detentions, on top of the assassinations.[57]

Much of the violence was perpetrated by state security forces with complete impunity. The most terrible story involved Irma Villanueva, the young woman who, in August 2009, had been grabbed out of a Resistance demonstration in Choloma, kidnapped, and gang-raped by police, and then testified over the radio about what they had done, naming names she'd seen on their badges. On February 9, 2010, two weeks into the Lobo Administration, armed men in ski masks again kidnapped Villanueva, along with her husband, sister, and sister's husband, drove them to a remote site, tied the men to trees, and gang-raped both women in front of their husbands. We'll "see if you'll report us this time," they told her.[58]

As criminal behavior of all sorts skyrocketed, Lobo oversaw the near-complete disintegration of the Honduran criminal justice system, already thrown out the window by the coup. Assassinations, threats, kidnappings, destruction of broadcasting transmitters, rapes, drug trafficking, extortion—whatever the crime, it was almost never investigated, let alone brought to justice. Four judges who had opposed the coup, including Tirza Flores Lanza, an appeals court judge, were summarily deposed without legal recourse.[59]

The Honduran elites' deeper economic agenda underlying the coup began to play out as well. Congress began debating a new mining law, which would legalize open pit mining and forced evictions while providing for consultations with impacted communities only *after* mines had already been approved.[60] A much-touted Law of Temporary Employment, eventually passed in November 2010, broke up full-time, permanent employment and for the first time allowed the legal creation of part-time, temporary jobs—in the name of supposedly creating new jobs. Workers in those new posts would not be eligible for the national health and pension system, nor have the right to organize unions. In an early version, employees under the program would even receive 30 percent of their pay in company-issued scrip, not real money.[61]

For all that—so deliberate, so terrible—the Obama Administration continued to celebrate Lobo and act like everything was fine in Honduras now. It pointed to the Truth Commission Lobo had formed, headed by Eduardo Stein, a former Vice President of Guatemala. The commission had a very narrow mandate, though: it did not investigate the coup's repression of the opposition or journalists, for example, and did not interview victims. "The only purpose of [the commission] is to support the Honduran regime's continued efforts to whitewash those responsible for the coup and its violent aftermath," declared Bertha Oliva, the director of COFADEH.[62]

In accordance with US wishes, in February and March the World Bank and International Monetary Fund reopened the spigot of loans to Honduras for a total of $430 million that had been suspended after the coup, and sweetened the pot with an additional $280 million. On March 16, the Inter-American Development Bank announced it was restoring another $500 million.[63]

But leading governments of Latin America, including Argentina, Brazil, Ecuador, Nicaragua, and Venezuela, held firm in refusing to recognize the Lobo government, and would not readmit Honduras to the Organization of American States. At a March 4 news conference in Costa Rica, Secretary of State Clinton chastised them for not welcoming Honduras back into the fold. "We think that Honduras has taken important and necessary steps that deserve the recognition of relations," she scolded. "We saw the free and fair election of President Lobo," she insisted, and extolled the Truth Commission. "We share the condemnation of the coup that occurred, but we think it is time to move forward and ensure that such disruptions of democracy do not and cannot happen in the future." Of course, by recognizing, funding, and praising Lobo's ongoing coup regime she was signaling that precisely such "disruptions of democracy" in other countries would be rewarded, not thwarted, by the United States. Clinton took the occasion to announce that $31 million in US funds that had been withheld from Honduras after the coup would now be restored.[64]

Street Fashions

By the late spring, I had settled into a more or less permanent state of panic, worrying about whether my friends or their kids would be killed or tortured, worrying about the whole country. I channeled my anxieties into obsessive work around Honduras. New doors opened in the media, especially at *The Nation*. Dan Beeton, the Communications Director for the Center for Economic and Policy Research (CEPR) in Washington, D.C., gradually started educating me about US reporters who covered Honduras, and taught me how to reach out to them. I was now also working closely with the network of US and Canadian activists that had settled into place, coordinated in large part through a new listserve, *Honduras-presente*. Groups including Chicago's La Voz de los de Abajo (The Voice of those from Below), the Chicago Religious Leadership Network on Latin America, and the Alliance for Global Justice now regularly organized delegations to Honduras and arranged tours for Hondurans to speak in the United States.

I arrived back in Honduras two days before the first anniversary of the coup, June 28, 2010. The morning of the anniversary, a Monday, about ten of us met up in the office of COSIBAH, the Coalition of Honduran Banana and Agroindustrial Unions, in the center of La Lima, twenty minutes southeast of San Pedro Sula. Everyone was in a jovial mood: we were off to a big demonstration, then a march. These union activists and their family members and friends were veterans now of a year of resistance to the coup, while counting among them decades of work in the labor, women's, and other social movements.

The room popped with energy and the bright red of impressively elaborated fashion elements that had been accumulated during a year in the streets: crimson T-shirts printed with "FNRP" (National Front of Popular Resistance) or a silhouette of Francisco Morazan, the founder of the country; red FNRP baseball caps or wide-rimmed straw hats with red strips wrapped around them inscribed "*Mujeres en Resistencia*"; and burlap bags slung across their chests, stamped with "*¡FUERA GOLPISTAS! FNRP*" (Coup Perpetrators Out!), made for carrying lunch, a water bottle, and a bandanna for the tear gas.

Someone had brought a pink plastic bagful of foil-wrapped *baleadas,* the basic Honduran breakfast made from a flour tortilla folded in half over refried beans, scrambled eggs, and maybe some cheese or a slice of ham. We sat around the table eating and clowning around until a couple of stragglers arrived. Then we piled into and onto a small, two-seater Nissan pickup truck and took off to the north for Choloma, the maquiladora factory center—where the big four-lane highway between San Pedro Sula and Puerto Cortés passes through a strategic bottleneck, perfect for protest blockades stopping traffic. As we traveled along a back route, through green fields with high tropical trees along their edges, everyone riding in the back whooped it up, waving giant red-and-black flags on sticks with "FNRP" in black letters. Inside the cab we did our own whooping, too. I got regaled with war stories from the twenty or so times they'd blocked the road in Choloma in the months right after the coup, especially August 9, 2009, when the police and military had swooped down with unrelenting brutality, chasing protesters into houses in the poor neighborhoods nearby, launching tear gas inside, beating people with batons. Gloria Guzmán, a former maquiladora worker now organizing for COSIBAH, told me how they'd hidden in the back of a house whose residents had courageously let them in, then escaped out the back door and through the streets.

While we rolled along, news reports on Radio Progreso announced that protesters from the FNRP had already arrived in Choloma at dawn and successfully blockaded the highway, halting all traffic. Other protesters had successfully blockaded every key highway in the country.

Halfway there, though, the announcer reported that police were amassing in Choloma and about to move in on the protesters blocking the highway. It suddenly got quiet in the car. Everyone, including me, was thinking about what we might be walking into up ahead. Later that morning I asked a young man in his late twenties, whom I'll call Pablo, how he handled it. "*Tenemos preparación psicológica*" (We're prepared psychologically), he said firmly and confidently. I heard the same phrase from three different people that day.

The night before, on Sunday, I'd had a test of my own *preparación psi-cológica*—or rather lack thereof. I'd ridden with Iris Munguía, my friend from the Honduran banana workers' unions, to the Plaza Central in downtown San Pedro Sula, for an FNRP cultural celebration at four-thirty in the afternoon. When we arrived, giant anti-coup banners spanned the streets up high, including one announcing "*BIENVENIDOS JORNADA CULTURAL*" (Welcome to Cultural Day). The benches, balustrades, and streetlights in the front right quadrant of the park had all been painted red and black. Along the sidewalk on the right side of the park, in front of the old Grand Hotel Sula, a line of men held up ten-foot-high black crosses with the names, painted on in white, of members of the Resistance who'd been killed: Roger Bados. Anastacio Barrera. Roger Vallejo. Claudia Brizuela, my friend's daughter. More. Too many more.

I schmoozed with friends, listened to unbelievably histrionic speeches, chatted with journalists, and took notes in Spanglish into one of those four-by-eight-inch spiral-bound notebooks journalists carry around, the kind you can hold in one hand. The crowd, maybe three thousand strong, was laid-back. The people I randomly spoke to were, as often as not, middle-class—lawyers, teachers, judges, professors, government workers, in addition to the trade unionists and campesinos that filled the ranks of the Resistance.

Before the coup no one I knew went into the Central Park. It was way too dangerous; you only dared it if you needed to change dollars to Honduran *lempiras* in the days before ATMs. Now, when I arranged meetings, people said "meet me at the Plaza Central." They meant its front corner occupied by the Frente, which blasted songs from the Resistance through monster speakers twenty-four hours a day, the lyrics rumbling far back into Hotel Sula rooms facing the streets—"*Honduras, El Pueblo Está Contigo,*" over and over again.

I'd noticed, too, that people were now using the *vos* form with me a lot. Hondurans generally use the formal *usted* with almost everyone and don't use *tu* at all. They sometimes utilize an informal *vos*, but it's pretty rare, and like a gift conferred on the listener. On this visit, though, I caught *vos* all over the place, often embedded in the way friends accentuated the command forms of verbs when they addressed me. Radio Progreso's punning slogan, "*La Voz que Está Con Vos*" (The voice that is with you), which appeared on stickers all over town now, captured that conferred intimacy and affection.

It got dark. Suddenly, I realized that everyone was moving away, past the Hotel Sula and farther into the middle of the city, toward the hills. Iris announced that she was going to a march, and started quickly walking away, too. I had no warning, fifteen seconds to decide: stay in the park, which was rapidly emptying out in the dark, or take off with her deep into the streets of San Pedro Sula, one of the most dangerous cities in the entire world, *at night*.

At the time I was angry with her for not telling me in advance about the pre-planned march. But I later came to realize that she only had so much bandwidth for my privileged anxieties. This was what she, and my other friends, just did now. This is what they'd done for a year. Take it or leave it.

I made my choice and raced off with her into darkness. At the end of the park we entered a narrow sidewalk sandwiched between the Palacio Municipal (City Hall) on the left and a solid line of huge army transport trucks, bumper touching bumper, parked along the street on the right. There was no exit to either side. I was truly, deeply scared. "This is what I'm doing," I remember incanting to myself, so I wouldn't flip out, although today I have no idea what I meant by that.

In the next block we spilled into the open street, hundreds of us surging forward. I saw a wholesome-looking family with three little bitty children and older people filling homemade tiki torches with gasoline, one for each of them, including the kids. Farther along we passed the men carrying the black crosses with the names of the dead. Beyond them, oversized black coffins had been laid out in a row in the street, one painted with "*Corte Suprema* RIP" (Supreme Court RIP) with a swastika on top, a second with "*Procuraduría General*" (State Attorney's Office) and a bigger swastika, and a third with "*Iglesia Golpista*" (Coup Perpetrator Church) across on top, next to an arrow pointed toward a dollar sign.

After about ten blocks we stopped at the intersection of two boulevards, beneath a statue of Francisco Morazan, the father of the country, painted all white. He was standing proudly in a long frock coat, leaning slightly against a cut-off tree trunk, his hand now hold-ing a red FNRP flag featuring himself in black silhouette. I realized that our rush down the streets hadn't been the actual march but just a walk to join a proper march, which was now about to begin.

Through those world-famous dangerous streets of San Pedro Sula, torches held high to cast a golden glow around us, in four or five long parallel lines of brave ordinary people chanting, we marched slowly back toward the park. I was not afraid.

We all halted when we got to the Radio Uno building. The night before, between midnight and one in the morning, seventy-five to a hundred policemen had amassed on the sidewalks in front of the station, taunting, shouting expletives, and threatening the broadcast-ers high upstairs in the corner studio. In response, the announcers in the studio had pointed a video camera back down onto the cops and denounced them live on the air, streaming the video through their website. On those same sidewalks we marchers now sang and chanted upward at the studio for twenty minutes, chasing the police ghosts far away into the deep darkness.

The next morning, arriving at the Choloma road blockade, we parked our pickup in the same neighborhood where Gloria and the others had hidden in the houses the August before, and walked quickly out to the highway. It was four lanes wide, with a thin median strip along its middle. Off to the right, a few blocks down, I could vaguely make out large groups of protesters standing in front of a couple of burning tires, and in the black smoky distance beyond them a lineup of thirty or forty police. To my left, in the two oncoming lanes of the highway, a line of huge, halted semi trucks was backed up as far as I could see. In front of the trucks, across all four lanes, a hundred or so more police were loosely clumped, in black bulletproof vests and blue or white riot helmets, carrying plexiglass riot shields with thick scratches etched in them. Along the four blocks of highway in between were four hundred or so protesters, loosely arrayed. A Radio Progreso sound truck was parked across the street. On the sides of the highway vendors sold chips and sodas in their usual booths, watching the show. It was all very low-tech.[65]

I admired additional T-shirt statements on the ladies: *"Nosotras Mujeres Exijimos Democracía en el País y en la Casa"* (We Women Demand Democracy in the Country and in the Home); *"La Salud es Nuestro Derecho"* (Health Care Is Our Right); *"Mujeres Recuperemos La Patria, FNRP"* (Women, Let's Reclaim the Country, FNRP). After half an hour I noticed that fist-sized pieces of broken concrete had materialized all over the roadway around me; I watched one young woman set down a ten-inch wide chunk. I noticed twenty-five or thirty men and women with bandannas tied over their mouths, now sitting down in the road across from me in front of the police, placed at five- or six-foot intervals, leaning back onto their arms, their legs splayed out in front. These Choloma demonstrators seemed more hard-core overall than the ones I'd marched with in downtown San Pedro Sula the evening before, more working-class and campesino; they included lots of old, deeply wrinkled men and women bedecked in protest regalia.

A police truck with an enormous tear gas tank mounted on it appeared next to the police lineup on the left. In the middle of a big group of cops I could see a woman I knew from the labor and women's movements talking rapidly to what appeared to be a commanding officer. "They're going to repress us in thirty minutes," she announced when she returned.

I called Stephen Coats of USLEAP and then another human rights activist friend in the United States and described what I was seeing. Stephen told me I should call the US Embassy in Honduras and ask for Silvia Eiriz, the Political Officer—the third-highest-ranking official—whom he'd spoken to before. I took a deep breath and called the embassy for the very first time ever and asked for Eiriz, who took the call. Identifying myself as from the University of California, I summoned a professional tone and I told her a dangerous human rights situation was possibly unfolding, with the potential for violence and brutality by security forces. I knew that the embassy would then know I was there, watching whatever might unfold. She politely apologized that she couldn't talk, and said she'd call me back.

Fifteen or twenty minutes later the tear gas truck backed up, turned around, and left. Some of the police dispersed; others huddled in the median strip like cattle under the trees, sweltering in the ninety-five-degree, humid weather. I looked back and realized that the people seated in the road had all gotten up. Had there been some kind of negotiated end to the blockade? Did my phone call to the embassy make a difference? I don't know.

Slowly, casually, everyone pivoted left, moving toward San Pedro Sula, and the whole mood changed. Now the protesters were jolly and playful. The next stage was supposed to be a car caravan in which we all rode in our cars the nine miles into the center of San Pedro Sula, but people spontaneously decided to walk as much of it as possible. Off we went in the two right-hand lanes, advancing slowly in cars, motorcycles, small pickup trucks, and on foot, while in the left lanes oncoming cars and trucks began slipping forward past us.

People pranced beside the cars; hopped on and off the motorcycles; strode arm in arm ten across in front of our bumper; struck sexy, dramatic poses for my camera, flags wrapped round their shoulders like shawls or folded up over their heads to make a bit of shade. It was one of the most beautiful and joyful things I've ever seen.

I rode in our air-conditioned pickup because of a foot problem, just hopping out once in a while to walk with friends as we inched past small industrial parks, an old union housing development, a labor education center, and eventually reached shaded residential neighborhoods where high trees loomed over the road from both sides. I watched Gloria García, one of the highest-ranking women in SITRATERCO, the biggest Chiquita workers' union, and at the time coordinator for environmental issues for COSIBAH, contentedly walk at least half the way into the city in a pair of black-heeled sandals with three-inch heels, laced onto her ankles with pale pink and baby blue ribbons. I watched two young men carrying spray paint, thin as rails and wearing little string backpacks and makeshift facemasks made out of T-shirt fabric, dart alongside us, lacing graffiti onto the walls.

When we got into the center of San Pedro we turned left along a leafy boulevard. The march was getting thicker and thicker, I realized. I got out of the truck's cab and rode in the back, so I could watch the scene and take pictures—including of the two trucks full of cops following us. A high school marching band stepped into the march, their white T-shirts emblazoned with "Honduran Champions 2009." I saw a long red banner reading *"Feministas in Resistencia,"* one end held up by a man in a blue dress shirt, the other by a woman in a short black dress and black leggings and a red scarf with the face of Che Guevara tied artfully at an angle across her hip. I saw a small young man, alone, in a thin red hoodie that carefully framed his beatific and slightly ironic smile, carrying a sign in rainbow colors on white that read *"DIVERSIDAD EN RESISTENCIA."* I wonder, now, who he was, and if he is alive today.

I could also see the infrastructure of the Resistance in action. In Choloma and now in San Pedro Sula, helpers offered me little sealed plastic bags of water, which you chewed a corner off of and sucked the water out of. As we passed through San Pedro, a man ran alongside us carrying a cardboard box and handing out free white-bread-and-ham sandwiches wrapped in baggies. Others, farther ahead, handed out leaflets to the thousands of observers lined along the route. I've been in my share of demonstrations, but never in my life have I seen people not only take the leaflets but also stand there in rows and actually *read* them afterward. One line of men wearing bright yellow uniform shirts from an auto parts store stood all in a row with pamphlets in hand, reading them. As we passed a concrete, four-story office building under construction, dozens of men looked down from the different floors, bracing their arms into empty window frames to lean out and watch us, some of them waving lengths of plastic PVC pipe in support.

The march got bigger and bigger. By the time we turned left and toward the Plaza Central, it looked like there were around fifty thousand people. I was told the march would have been much larger but it was a weekday, and people couldn't get off work or they'd lose their jobs. Once in the park we half-listened to *very* long speeches, sang along with the rock band, summoned the energy for a last round of schmoozing, then drove home. Happy anniversary.

The next night Iris and I lolled on our beds watching television in a motel room in Sabá, way far away in the Aguán Valley, where we'd driven for a workshop with workers from Dole plantations. The mainstream stations, continuing to run stories on the anniversary, were full of sanitized official discussions of the "crisis"—still refusing to call it a coup—or sycophantic interviews with Roberto Micheletti. We switched to Cholusat Sur, the opposition station, and spent the next two hours silently watching a new documentary film about the Resistance, *¿Quién Dijo Miedo?* (*Who Said Afraid?*), riveted.[66] In between interviews, it featured footage of the police and military chasing down, brutally beating, teargasing, shooting, and killing demonstrators, over and over again in what to me felt like an endless gray blur of repression.

"What a year you've been through," I said to Iris when it was over, touching her foot as I passed by on my way to the toilet. "It was beautiful," she replied. In the bathroom, I realized I didn't know which she meant, exactly. "Did you mean the movie, or the year?" I asked when I came out. "The year," she said.

Graffiti on government sign in the Lower Aguán Valley, "Cops Out of the Aguán–MUCA, MCA (Moviemiento Unificado Campesino del Aguán, Movimiento Campesino del Aguán); Military Out of the Aguán." Photo Credit: Radio Progreso.

CHAPTER TWO

Locked Down:
Campesinos, Police,
and Prisoners

Independence Day

By the fall of 2010, the Resistance was still locked in struggle. The wonderful highs of that first year continued—people's new pride in how they'd risen up, their daily joys of comradeship, the creative flourishing of Resistance culture—but now in a harsher context, as repression escalated again and the full reality of long-term struggle sank in, both individually and collectively. Facing a still chilling reality, tens of thousands of ordinary Hondurans active in the Resistance dug deep, then deeper still. In the big cities, people kept protesting.

Far away in the valleys of northwest Honduras, campesinos, too, stepped forward and demanded land rights—paying a price in blood. For Hondurans in the Resistance, the next year and a half would be brutal, and would conclude with a new horror almost beyond human comprehension. It would also see the formal Resistance make a choice about basic strategy that would play out for years to come.

Soon after the coup's June 28, 2010, anniversary, Lobo's government signaled that repression would not relent. First to bear the brunt were the teachers. Throughout August 2010, sixty-three

48

thousand members of six public school teachers' unions, allied in FOMH (Federación de Organizaciones Magisteriales de Honduras, Federation of Honduran Teachers' Unions), continued demonstrations to protest, among other grievances, the wholesale robbery of two hundred million dollars from their pension fund by the post-coup government. On August 20, during a peaceful march, police suddenly attacked four union leaders and then detained them for twelve hours without medical care. Six days later, during a large, peaceful demonstration of teachers and their allies in front of the Presidential Palace in Tegucigalpa, police and soldiers fired an estimated one hundred tear gas canisters into the crowd and injured four teachers—who were then denied treatment at the public hospital.[1]

Teachers at Francisco Morazan National Pedagogical University, in the capital, had been on strike since early May. On Friday, August 27, as they peacefully demonstrated in front of their university, joined by campesino activities and supporters from other unions, the police and military suddenly started attacking them. When the protesters sought safety inside the university, security forces surrounded them and started firing tear gas while beating and detaining people who tried to run away, injuring seven people, including a journalist. Outside, in front of the university, someone inside a black SUV fired a gun on protesters. The vehicle turned out to be registered to the Honduran Congress.[2]

While this repression barreled forward, Honduras remained a pariah state as far as many of the governments of Latin America, the Caribbean, and beyond were concerned. The Organization of American States still refused to readmit it as a member.[3] In the United States, by contrast, the mainstream media was largely silent about the ongoing resistance and the human rights abuses unfolding in Honduras, and throughout 2010 and the first half of 2011, it was almost like the country didn't exist.

In mid-September 2010, two weeks after the repression of the teachers, I took a trip with my mother to Yosemite National Park, high up in the Sierra Nevada, where I gratefully slipped out of cell phone contact for the first time since the coup took place, fifteen months earlier. After three days in the mountains, as we dropped back down the dry golden foothills into cell range again, I checked my messages. Two days earlier, on September 15, my friend Iris had called and left a desperate message: "Help! Do something! They're attacking us with tear gas and clubs!"

September 15 was Independence Day in Honduras. In Tegucigalpa that day, fifty thousand marchers from the Resistance filled the streets in a crowd stretching two miles long, laughing and cheering and carrying big banners while the police and military stood by and watched and didn't touch them.[4] In San Pedro Sula, another fifty thousand marched equally peacefully toward the Plaza Central. As they passed the three-story building that housed Radio Uno, the independent radio station, the police and military suddenly broke the station's windows and launched tear gas into its narrow passageways, surging in afterward to destroy a life-sized statue of Manuel Zelaya. Inside, they grabbed Ernesto Bardales and broke his limbs and teeth, then continued on a rampage to the Plaza Central, two blocks away, where most of the demonstrators had already arrived. With terrifying booms they shot tear gas canisters everywhere, including at a high school marching band. They turned water hoses on the crowd. They ran up onto the stage and trashed or stole thousands of dollars' worth of musical instruments belonging to the rock band Café Guancaste, which was about to perform. An old man, a street vendor, died of asthma from the tear gas. Iris's small pickup truck was parked nearby with a speaker mounted on top of its cab and a Radio Progreso sticker on its back window. During the rampage security forces broke all its windows.[5]

As a seventy-five-page investigation by an alliance of Honduran human rights groups would document in 2012, the man responsible for unleashing all that repression, along with others, was Hector Iván Mejía, the director at the time of the San Pedro Sula police. A year before, on August 20, Mejía had also been in charge of the San Pedro police when they brutally attacked the Resistance demonstration in Choloma—chasing peaceful protesters through the streets, shooting tear gas inside houses, and gang-raping Irma Melissa Villanueva, all with impunity.[6]

That same Independence Day morning, September 15, Secretary of State Hillary Rodham Clinton addressed the people of Honduras with a clear declaration of US support for the regime:

> Honduras is emerging from a very difficult period. Your resumption of democratic and constitutional government this year has been a testament to the resilience of the Honduran people, and we will work with you to strengthen safeguards for human rights and the rule of law.
>
> The United States supports Honduran efforts to win international recognition for the progress you have made to fully reclaim your rightful place in the inter-American community. . . .
>
> I wish all Hondurans a safe and happy Independence Day.[7]

That week the International Monetary Fund announced it was granting the Government of Honduras a new $196 million loan, another message that the United States was enthusiastically continuing its support.[8]

Twisted, Or: Into the Eye of the Storm

Back in San Pedro Sula three months later, on the night of December 14, I joined my friends German Zepeda and Ruy Díaz on their Radio Uno news and interview show. German was by that point a top leader of the National Front of Popular Resistance for the north coast, while also still president of the Coalition of Honduran Banana and Agroindustrial Unions. A serious, brilliant strategic thinker, German came off as the straight man to his buddy Ruy, a substantially wacko but equally brilliant math professor who, eighteen months into the vicious coup regime, always wore a flaming red FNRP baseball cap and carried a big red banner on a stick slung over his shoulder, with "FNRP" in black letters on it above a silhouette of Francisco Morazan, the founder of the country.

After the show we hopped into a pickup truck and drove to a classic Honduran open-walled restaurant serving *platos típicos*, where eventually three or four other friends joined us; I think they'd come from a meeting of the Radio Uno collective. Around 8:30 p.m., one of them got a phone call: the military had just announced that in the morning it was going to evict the campesinos from the road.

For the past three weeks, two thousand campesino activists from the town of Guadalupe Carney had been occupying the main highway through the Lower Aguán Valley, in the country's north. They were demanding bridge repairs, immediate withdrawal of troops occupying the zone, and, most importantly, justice in the case of five campesinos who had been killed by a landowner's security guards three weeks earlier; no one had been arrested.[9]

For about eight minutes little wheels went around in my head. "How long does it take to get to the Aguán?" I asked. German knew what I meant. "Five hours." Pause. "Do you want to go?" I asked him. "Yes," he said, without hesitating. Ruy wanted to go, too. I agreed, but reluctantly. "Only if you don't bring the red cap. I mean it. I'm serious. It's like waving a red flag. And don't bring the big red flag, either." He said okay.

We went into logistics overdrive. We needed to rent a car—German's was broken. We called Hertz. The car rental places at the airport closed at ten. I didn't have my credit card with me. Ruy went off home to explain to his wife why he wouldn't be going to work the next day. German and I drove to the house where I was staying, got my Visa card, and made it to the airport by 9:45. While the agent filled out the forms we paced nervously, already pumped up as each of us privately began to process what we were doing.

I knew what was potentially ahead. I knew it could be bad. At that point after the coup, we could easily be in the middle of tear gas attacks, brutal beatings, and gunshots when we got to the town. I also knew that witnesses mattered: if a white, middle-class professor like me from the United States were seen observing whatever the Honduran military and police might do to the campesinos, it might diminish the repression; and if there were in fact repression, I could report it afterward. German and Ruy, too, could broadcast what they'd seen, using Radio Uno and other outlets in San Pedro Sula and El Progreso. They had already been working on building bridges between the Resistance world of the big city and the more isolated but daringly militant campesino movement far away in the Aguán.

Honduran campesinos were by this point deep in struggle. Years before, in the 1970s and 80s, in response to powerful campesino organizations, the Honduran government had carried out substantial agrarian reform, granting lands to campesino collectives, especially in the Lower Aguán Valley. But in the 1990s new neoliberal governments in service to elite local landlords had unleashed a counteroffensive. Through shifty deed transfers, a new law allowing sale of collective lands, a corrupt judiciary, and armed terror, approximately twenty thousand hectares of land—including the lands of thirty-five campesino cooperatives—had been seized by big landholders by the time of the coup. Much of this territory had been planted with African palms, which dramatically reduced the need for labor, sucked out the water table underneath, and required poisonous chemical inputs, while supplanting the staple crops that had sustained campesinos and been important for the domestic market. By far the biggest culprit was Miguel Facussé, the richest, most powerful person in the country and a prominent backer of the coup, who, through his Dinant Corporation, commanded both an empire of palm plantations in the Aguán and across the north coast, and his own private army of over a hundred security guards (the exact number is unclear).[10]

In the months before the coup, campesino organizations in the Lower Aguán finalized an agreement with then-President Zelaya for a high-level review of the corrupt land transactions. But that process ended when the campesinos' representative, Fabio Ochoa, was shot the same day. The post-coup regimes of Micheletti and Lobo then threw the negotiating process out the window altogether. In response, with amazing audacity, campesinos organized in the MUCA (Movimiento Unificado Campesino del Aguán, United Campesino Movement of the Aguán) and the MCA (Movimiento Campesino del Aguán, Campesino Movement of the Aguán) began staging what they called land "recuperations" in the Aguán, occupying lands belonging to the state and eligible for land distribution, or illegally claimed by elites. They continued to try to achieve justice in the courts as well, as did other campesino groups.[11]

The November 2010 massacre of five campesinos that prompted the road blockage took place at a plantation called El Tumbador, on the site of a former military installation near the town of Guadalupe Carney, an independent community of twelve hundred campesino families. The government had promised El Tumbador to the campesinos several years before the coup, but Facussé's Dinant corporation had subsequently acquired it through nefarious illegal maneuvers. Government officials then told the campesinos that in order to receive their titles to the land, they would need to occupy it. So that fall, the campesinos in the MCA started attempting to enter El Tumbador to establish possession.[12]

On November 15, 2010, two hundred to three hundred armed security guards working for Facussé's Dinant Corporation surrounded a group of campesinos working in their own fields next door to El Tumbador and shot and killed five men, members of the MCA. When it became clear that no one would be arrested for the killings, three weeks later on December 7, two thousand campesinos from the MUCA and MCA began an unarmed blockade of the highway that connects Puerto Castilla and the city of Trujillo to the rest of the country, where the road passes in front of the town of Guadalupe

Carney. Security forces poured in to occupy the lower end of the valley. By December 14, when we got the call at the restaurant, between five hundred and one thousand police, military, and private forces had surrounded Guadalupe Carney, their guns pointing inward.[13]

Those security forces were trained, and their equipment funded, in part, by the United States.[14] In 2010, after a very partial suspension of security aid right after the 2009 coup, US funding for the Honduran police and military had increased.[15] In fact, the very same week that the campesinos' blockade began, US forces from Joint Task Force-Bravo had just been deployed for a training mission with the Honduran military at Puerto Castilla, a few miles away, right down that same highway.[16]

German picked me up at 4:30 a.m. Ruy was in the passenger seat, capless, and in the pitch dark I didn't even recognize him—he was all cleaned up in a light blue dress shirt and neatly ironed khaki pants, every inch the upstanding math professor. I crawled into the back seat to sleep while they talked politics in low tones up front.

When we stopped for breakfast a couple of hours later, they got out of the car ahead of me, and there on the passenger seat, all smooshed from being sat on, I could see Ruy's red FNRP baseball cap. So much for his sacred promise. From then on, the three of us joked continuously, the laughs fueled by our awareness of the unspoken dangers ahead.

Two hours later we curved south and east through the mountains into the Aguán Valley, turning left before the river to head toward the Lower Aguán. To the right stretched Dole territory, a sea of banana plantations and their workers; to the left, African palms, campesino collectives, and drug traffickers. At around 8:00 a.m., we got a call telling us that the campesinos had withdrawn from the road at the very last minute, just before the military and police were about to unleash their tear gas and batons. So we relaxed a bit. Just a bit.

I called my USLEAP friend Stephen Coats to check in with him as my security backup and to let him know we were about to move out of cell phone range for the next four hours. He told me he'd just called Jeremy Spector, the human rights and labor attaché at the US

Embassy in Tegucigalpa, and informed him that a member of the
Board of Directors of USLEAP (that is, me) was in the Lower Aguán
on her way to Guadalupe Carney, and that he, Stephen, would appre-
ciate it if the embassy paid every attention to my safety.

I found this preposterous. A member of the board of directors?
Every attention to my safety? But of course Stephen, a clever pro,
knew what he was doing—casting me to Spector as an import-
ant-sounding observer and warning the embassy that I was out there,
watching. He knew that the message would probably get through to
the Honduran military, fast.

As we headed into the eye of the storm, we got quieter and quieter. Fifteen minutes later we passed the army's headquarters, where
we slowed down to pass four olive-green troop transport vehicles, a
military van, and a giant truck carrying a tear gas tank with "Policia
Nacional" on the sides. The joking stopped altogether. I started taking pictures out the window of everything I could, my homemade
press pass dangling around my neck like a string of garlic. Down the
highway we passed a billboard with "FUERA MILITARES DEL
AGUÁN" (Military Out of the Aguán) spray-painted on it, signed
by the MUCA.

Finally, around ten, we arrived at Guadalupe Carney. The
asphalt on the highway in front was brand-new black, still steaming
from earlier rain, with piles of ashes left over from protesters' fires.
Soldiers in camouflage and assault rifles were lined up at intervals
up and down the road, and beyond them a second tear gas truck.
We pulled up next to the town's entrance, a low-railed bridge over
a creek, where a clump of fifteen or twenty important-looking uni-
formed men were consulting or standing around. On the other side
of the highway, down a bit, a guy wearing a blue-gray poncho, who
might have been in charge, was talking on a cell phone. I could smell
the rain, the asphalt, the ashes, and the raw power.

We watched as a few people began to leave town on bicycles—the
first residents allowed to leave since the security forces had sealed the
town three hours before. German got out of the car and went to talk
to the guy in charge of the clump, who granted us permission to enter
the town. Meanwhile Ruy had hopped out of the car and was yapping

on his phone in an official tone. He, too, talked to the men in uniform. I asked him what he'd said. He said he'd told them he was a journalist. "From where?" I asked. "Radio Uno." So much for our cover. He spent the next three hours reporting live on the radio from his phone.

I went around to the back of the car to stash my purse in the trunk, and there, tucked inside, was Ruy's big crimson FNRP flag on a stick.

Across the bridge, the town opened up into a maze of yellow dirt roads, crisscrossing between houses tucked between trees in the most beautiful little valley imaginable—nestled between slanted hillsides that rose up on either side, speckled with bright green banana plants. Ahead of us we could see groups of seven to ten soldiers and police trotting briskly up and down the roads, supposedly conducting "inspections" of the houses in search of arms and drugs, while they themselves were armed to the gills. They wore an array of uniforms I quickly gave up on trying to decode—from regular army and regular police to COBRAS and other special forces. I started calling them the Mixed Flock, after the birds who arrive in my yard at home every mid-morning. Some wore camouflage outfits in classic olive-drab; others in shades of light to medium blue. Almost all boasted thick black bulletproof vests, helmets, and assault rifles clutched across their chests. Some carried long blue batons.

When we got to the center of town, wide green fields spread out, with a few scattered horses and a white church off to one side and a large army tent pitched in the middle. Off to the left was the town's collectively-run restaurant, now seized by the security forces, where a bunch of apparently higher-ranking officers were overflowing out of its thatched entryway. I mostly concentrated on taking photographs of every single thing I could, while taking a few breaks to talk to the townspeople. They said the soldiers had deliberately urinated in the church, and that that morning the military had stopped a bus on the highway outside town and taken away the batteries in all the passengers' cell phones, injuring two people. While we talked, a helicopter started thwack-thwack-thwacking above us, circling low in the gray skies. German told me he'd seen snipers on the hillsides when we came in.

Gradually, various soldiers and cops started returning to the field in the middle. They sat down on low benches in pairs, napped under the trees, or wandered in and out of the tent, while two of them trotted back and forth bringing lunch in cardboard cartons and a cooler, one carrying a big bottle of orange soda tucked into his left arm and an assault rifle cradled in the right. By this point, journalists and other observers had started to arrive in town from outside and were interviewing people.

The raids weren't over, though. At a house by the entrance, I could see ten policemen "inspecting" a silver pickup truck. I got as close as I could—the campesinos' very real concern was that drugs or arms would be planted. Three weeks earlier, President Porfirio Lobo, with zero evidence, had charged that there was an arms cache containing a thousand AK-47s and M-16s in the Lower Aguán, where subversives, he claimed, were being trained to attack the government.[17]

Other men, not all in uniforms, were beginning to pull out of town in pickup trucks. Several residents identified *sicarios* (hired assassins), who they said worked for Miguel Facussé. I'd already seen other men in plainclothes among the mixed flock, including an especially authoritative one wearing a knit cap pulled down to just above his eyes, who'd ended up at the restaurant with the big shots.

Before we left, I tentatively asked a young woman I was chatting with if she would allow me to see the inside of her home near the entrance. She said yes; she was very friendly and warm. Inside were two gray cinder-block rooms almost entirely bare except for a hammock. She told me her husband had been one of the five campesinos killed by Facussé's guards four weeks before, and that the newborn baby cradled in her arms had never met his father.

At around 1:30 or 2:00 p.m., German, Ruy, and I finally crossed back over the bridge to the car. All the long way home, we barely shared a word about what we'd just seen, even when we stopped for fried fish by the sea. After that, as the light gradually died along with the rental car's power, I nodded off again in the back while Ruy entertained German with raucous stories of his antics when he was studying abroad in his youth. German fixed the car, more or less, and we slowly puttered into El Progreso in time for me to make it onto the Wednesday night women's show on Radio Progreso.

The next morning German called to tell me that the road outside Guadalupe Carney had been blockaded again. Only this time, it was two hundred of the campesinos' children who had sat down in the highway. After two hours, two thousand adults joined their kids, and then they all withdrew together.

We are not afraid of your repression, the campesino parents were saying. We are not going to stop. We are teaching our children to struggle. They have no other choice.

I can't remember if German asked me to, or I did it on my own, but I decided to call the US Embassy and warn them about the kids in the road. I somewhat uncertainly asked to speak to Jeremy Spector, the human rights and labor attaché Stephen Coats had contacted the day before. It was only the second time I'd ever talked to anyone at the embassy myself. Spector took my call, but only very briefly; I just said that the children were in the road now, and that it was a dangerous human rights situation, and that the embassy should caution the Honduran troops not to use tear gas or violence.

The next day I took a five-hour, fancy bus to Tegucigalpa, the capital. Twenty minutes out of San Pedro Sula, the film *Twister* popped up on nine video screens throughout the bus, full blast. It featured a team of scientists trying to launch an extra-special instrument that can produce pathbreaking research but only if it's landed at the exact right moment in the eye of a roaring tornado. The action largely consisted of a concerned Helen Hunt leaping in and out of pickup trucks among Midwestern cornfields while looking terrific in khakis. The scientists were driving deliberately into the center of danger and getting a high off doing it—just like German, Ruy, and I had. Alas, just as I got sucked happily into the vortex of trying to figure out the exact relationship among Hunt, her vaguely handsome, nice, but ultimately forgettable ex-husband, and his new wife, my phone rang. It was Jeremy Spector from the embassy.

I tried to explain to him that I was on a bus with *Twister* roaring full blast, but he was undeterred. Right off he wanted to know if I was safe; then he said he'd been reading my articles. It was clear that he hadn't known who I was the day before and had now done his homework. "Are you writing something?" he kept asking. "Will you send it to me?" I kept saying I didn't know.

We chatted for half an hour about various human rights and labor issues. I tried to keep our conversation on a track where I could communicate concern without providing any exact information about what I knew or what I was doing—all the while wondering which of my fellow passengers could understand English. He told me he was "promoting dialogue between the human rights community and the Honduran government." Since he was the embassy's official for labor as well as human rights issues, I conveyed my concerns about a proposed labor law reform being debated at the time, the one that was going to turn good, full-time jobs into part-time jobs ineligible for unionization. The whole time I kept trying to avert my eyes from Helen Hunt leaping into the trucks.

Half an hour later, a friend from the United States called to tell me that the State Department had denounced the campesinos of Guadalupe Carney for putting their kids at risk in the road.

I'll now confess I felt secretly guilty for years. Had my first phone call to Spector produced that response—in which the State Department, after not a peep condemning the massacre of five campesinos with complete impunity, after silence about the giant show of military intimidation I'd just witnessed, and given the clear collusion between US-funded state security forces and private thugs, chose to blame the campesinos for being *bad parents?* Should I not have called Spector, thus tipping off the embassy as to what was going on in the road? I was mortified, and never told German I'd made the call.

Four months later, a colleague dug up Jeremy Spector's profile and posted it to her blog. The aptly-named Spector had a master's degree in Strategic Intelligence from the US Joint Military Intelligence College, had been a Lieutenant Colonel in the Navy and a Program Manager at the National Geospatial-Intelligence Agency, and spent time at the Joint Military Intelligence Operations Center in Afghanistan. There was no evidence he had any background or training in labor or human rights.[18]

I had known for years, from my historical research on Honduras, that labor attachés who worked in the United States's embassies in Latin America during the 1950s and 60s had been close to the CIA, and sometimes had actually been CIA operatives themselves.[19] But rubbing up so close to an actual person with an intelligence career was something else.

Four years later, still unsure about my phone call, still feeling guilty, I decided to track down what the State Department had actually said that day about the kids. It turned out that the State Department hadn't denounced the parents through a public statement, but rather during a phone call with a US colleague. She had called its Honduran desk in Washington, D.C., that morning to express her own alarm about the human rights situation in Guadalupe Carney. A man named Greg Maggio had taken her call. He had been oddly aggressive, she recounted when I contacted her. "Instead of just taking my statement and getting rid of me, he went on and on basically trying to convince me how irresponsible the parents were—that they had their children up front," she recalled. "I wasn't sure if he was truly just upset and concerned about the children or if he was just trying out the State Department's new line on me about how the children were being used. Or maybe he was just worn out from dealing with the issue," she speculated, "and was blowing off steam."[20]

I searched the internet for Greg Maggio at the State Department, and, in addition to various ambiguous postings for him in Washington, D.C., found him in a March 15, 2006, Wikileaks cable in which the US Embassy in Guatemala asked the US Embassy in Nicaragua to approve a transfer: "Post would like Greg to spend three weeks in Managua to work on some high-profile human rights issues that have considerable election year significance."[21] In other words, the State Department had apparently sent Maggio to dig up potential dirt on the left-wing Sandinista government before the elections.

I stopped feeling guilty altogether. Of course, I now realized thinking about it, the State Department would have known full well about the kids in the road the minute they'd stepped onto it. And

Maggio had taken the campesinos' bravery and twisted it back as bad parenting.

Three years later, in 2014, when the media erupted in an uproar about the arrival of fifty-seven thousand undocumented, unaccompanied minors at the US border, and instant experts sought to explain why parents would do something so seemingly irresponsible as sending their children on a dangerous trip to a foreign country by bus and train and car in the company of strangers, I thought about those campesino parents in the Aguán Valley and their kids. Those parents had known exactly how brutal the alternatives were at home. Just like the parents who sent their kids north, they were trying to imagine, and build, a future for their loved ones.

Pushing Forward, Pushing Back

That winter and spring of 2010–11, while the campesinos were beginning to take matters of social justice into their own hands, the National Front of Popular Resistance was grappling with its own, big-level strategic choices. The *golpistas* controlled state power; that was all too clear. But the Resistance still had formidable powers of its own. The question was how to take the truly massive grassroots energies that had been unleashed during the immediate post-coup period and translate them into fundamental structural change. And live to tell the tale.

The summer and fall before, during 2010, the FNRP had focused its demands on a constitutional convention, or *constituyente*. A constituyente had, of course, been the straw at which Zelaya had grasped in June 2009 with the Cuarta Urna ballot measure the day of the coup, in which he'd asked voters whether they wanted to elect delegates in November 2009, as part of the presidential election, to a constitutional convention to be held in the future, presumably in 2010 or 2011, after Zelaya was out of office. Zelaya had been trying to replicate the successful conventions that had revised the constitutions of Bolivia (2009), Ecuador (2008), and Venezuela (1999) granting new powers to Indigenous people, recognizing human rights, and promising environmental protection, while symbolically marking a new, more democratic era for their countries.[22]

In 2010, the FNRP picked up the demand for a constitutional convention and now used it both to underscore the need to completely re-establish the nation from below—as the only way out of the elite's lockdown on economic and political power, and as a concrete vehicle to help produce that transition. In the summer of 2010, thousands of regular people involved in the Resistance, including campesino activists and members of COPINH, the Council of Popular and Indigenous Organizations of Honduras, circulated a petition calling for a constituyente. By November, its supporters reported that it had garnered over one and a quarter million signatures—out of a country of eight million people.[23]

By that point the National Front of Popular Resistance still held together an extremely diverse group of political actors. On the one hand were the social movements: campesino, Afro-Indigenous, and Indigenous organizations, all fighting tooth and nail for land rights; the women's movement, through established groups like the Centro de Derechos de Mujeres (CDM) as well as new, overlapping formations like Feminists in Resistance; and the labor movement. STIBYS, the bottling-plant workers' union, especially, provided the infrastructure for the Resistance, with its large union halls in Tegucigalpa and San Pedro Sula where the FNRP could hold big assemblies. An array of professional groups, including Lawyers in Resistance, Journalists in Resistance, and the Association of Honduran Judges for Democracy, also took part. In the other camp stood FNRP members who came from the branch of the Liberal Party loyal to Zelaya. More middle-class, more wedded to the formal political process and, in many cases, its patronage benefits, many of these Liberal Party veterans moved in uncomfortable alliance with the messy world of the grassroots social movements and their more radical demands.

In between were left-leaning trade unionists who had long been committed to the political process, largely through alternative parties but also in the two traditional parties. In November 2009, some had been candidates for Congress and local office through the tiny, progressive Union Democrática (UD) party, but had withdrawn from the ballot in protest. More potentially threatening to the powers-that-be that fall had been the independent candidacy for president of Carlos H. Reyes, the president of STIBYS and the grand old man of the Honduran labor movement; Reyes was joined by Berta Cáceres, the General Coordinator of COPINH, the Civic Council of Popular and Indigenous Organizations of Honduras, as his vice-president running mate. Cáceres's presence on the ticket next to Reyes symbolized the new alliances that were emerging between the dynamic rural social movements that had blossomed in the 1990s and 2000s and the traditional urban, labor-based left. Both Reyes and Cáceres had pulled out of the election in protest.[24]

Crucial to the broader opposition were also longstanding independent human rights groups. COFADEH, the Committee of Families of the Detained and Disappeared of Honduras, the most prominent, maintained professional distance but took tremendous risk to be there at every step to document, publicize, and challenge human rights abuses, especially by state security forces. Other independent progressive institutions played essential roles, most importantly the Jesuits' Radio Progreso and ERIC (Equipo de Reflección, Investigación, y Comunicación), its affiliated research center in El Progreso, half an hour southwest of San Pedro Sula.[25]

Trying to hold all this together and move forward, the FNRP began in 2010 and 2011 a much-needed process of formalizing its internal structure and defining its strategic plan. First was a decision to move geographically outward from the structure centered in the capital and San Pedro Sula. In February 2010, the FNRP held an assembly in the small city of Tocoa, smack dab in the middle of the campesinos' struggle in the Aguán Valley and hours away from the two big cities.

Once in Tocoa, though, the FNRP's internal tensions erupted fast. The Liberal Party faction walked out, potentially for good, when an attempt to add additional delegates from its camp failed. To appease them, the remaining leadership brokered a deal and suddenly named Manuel Zelaya—who was still out of the country, far away in the Dominican Republic—as General Coordinator of the FNRP. The Liberals marched back in, their man at the helm, even if not present. That decision to place Zelaya in charge of the FNRP would have enormous long-term effects. Manuel Zelaya now in many ways supplanted the *junta directiva*—executive board—of the FNRP, which represented the full diversity of the Resistance, especially its social movements. Most immediately, the decision officially ensconced Zelaya as the cult figure around which the Resistance revolved. For many in the FNRP, especially the urban poor, Zelaya was already viewed as a savior, a saint who would lead the Honduran people to the promised land. Acolytes in San Pedro Sula had even constructed a resplendent red-and-black life-sized statue of Zelaya, arm raised in greeting, that was housed in the Radio Uno offices and carried out to the Central Plaza for demonstrations, at which people crowded forward to have their pictures taken with the surrogate Zelaya. Now that Zelaya was General Coordinator, his cult status would be fused with the institutional chieftainship of the FNRP.[26]

On February 26 and 27, 2011, the FNRP held another big assembly in Tegucigalpa, with fifteen hundred delegates shaking the big STIBYS union hall to the rafters with their songs and chants. They made two additional large, important decisions. First, they agreed to implement a new, more formal representational structure, with delegates from each of the country's eighteen different departments plus a new "Department 19," embracing Hondurans outside the country active in the Resistance. Second, they decided that the FNRP would not enter electoral politics. "The conditions for participating in the electoral process are not in place; we want the return of the general coordinator and all those who are in exile and we want the national constituent assembly," declared Xiomara Castro, Zelaya's wife, who had emerged as an important symbolic leader in her own right in the previous year. In the battle over the strategic soul of the FNRP, the social movements had won out over the ex-Liberals, who believed that the FNRP should become a political party. The social movements countered that the power of the Resistance came from its diverse base, and it should remain independent. While alliances could be made, they argued, the unified social movements needed to remain separate. Many were also concerned that any move into electoral politics, in the context of the country's entrenched patronage tradition, would degenerate quickly into opportunism.[27]

The high-water mark of the formal Honduran FNRP came in mid-March, when the FNRP once again left the capital, this time to hold an assembly in La Esperanza, Intibucá, high up in the mountains in Indigenous Lenca territory. Berta Cáceres gave a magnificent welcoming speech that Radio Progreso broadcast live. Far away in my study in Northern California, her words shivered into my toes and my heart and embodied the deepest virtues and vision and feminism of the Resistance at its very best, as she spoke of the women whose hands had carefully and lovingly grown the beans, made the tortillas, and cooked the beans that would now feed the delegates. (Alas, the exact text of her speech appears to have disappeared from the historical record.)[28]

The Resistance hadn't, though, abandoned its all-important tactic of using mass protests in the big cities to try to disrupt business as usual, thwarting the normalization of the post-coup regime and challenging its ability to rule, while conveying concrete demands. In March and April of 2011, at the same time that the FNRP was establishing its formal structures and strategies, the teachers, especially, were again taking to the streets, in the most frontal and brutal clash between the state and social justice activists since the immediate post-coup period.[29]

The Honduran teachers' unions had a long, pre-coup history of powerful grassroots militancy, which they had used to obtain the Teachers' Statute (Ley de Docentes) in 1997, which guaranteed them salaries and benefits not available to other government employees. When the coup hit, the teachers were the first to protest in the streets, well aware that control of the state would be crucial to their fate. Sure enough, the Micheletti post-coup regime swiftly and completely robbed their enormous pension fund, and the Micheletti and then Lobo governments frequently did not pay them at all. So the teachers poured into the streets, and throughout late 2009 and 2010, went on strike repeatedly and for lengthy periods, to demand back pay and the restoration of their pensions (for example, in the August 2010 protests that had been so repressed by the police). The teachers in some ways kept their distance from the FNRP, however. After achieving the Teachers' Statute twenty years earlier, the majority of the teachers' unions—though not all—had stood aloof from the rest of the labor movement. In the post-coup political cauldron, some activists criticized the teachers for being narrowly self-interested. But the teachers nonetheless were widely admired for being spectacularly brave and militant in their post-coup protests.

The stakes for all rose in March 2011, when the Honduran Congress debated a new law that would open the door for privatization of the entire country's public school system. The law would transfer control of education to municipalities, which would then be free to establish for-profit schools. Looming behind the law was a pilot program organized by former neoliberal president Ricardo Maduro (2002-2006), in which teachers would work on ten-month contracts, be paid as little as one-third of their current salaries (thus below the minimum wage), and receive no pensions. The model was developed with funding from the Inter-American Development Bank (IDB), as a part of a larger global program of educational "reform" aimed to undermine teachers' unions.[30]

On March 17, a whopping ninety percent of all the sixty-eight thousand public school teachers in Tegucigalpa went out on strike, pouring into the streets in protest. In response, the police and military teargassed their demonstrations for almost three solid weeks. The government suspended three hundred five teachers for two to six months for demonstrating and, when negotiations with the unions broke down, threatened to suspend another five thousand.[31]

On March 31, two weeks into the strike, the Honduran Congress passed the privatization law. In solidarity, the FNRP launched a nationwide *paro cívico* or "civic strike" the day before, protesting the law and the repression, while also demanding a higher minimum wage; lower prices of food, fuel, and public utilities; and calling for a constituyente.[32] That day and the day that followed, resistance in the streets escalated, as Hondurans used one of the few weapons they had left and placed their bodies directly in front of amassed state security forces, in a steely wall of defiance.

In these demonstrations, as throughout the post-coup period, the Resistance continued to present itself as a *movimiento pacífico*, a peaceful movement. In practice, that meant an overwhelmingly nonviolent, unarmed movement. One very tiny subset of protesters did consistently follow its own rules of engagement: if the police or military began to attack violently, they would fight back, but only by throwing rocks and using sticks.

Ilse Ivania Velásquez Rodríguez was one of the nonviolent teachers who went out on strike on March 17. A fifty-nine-year-old elementary school teacher and former principal in Tegucigalpa, she had rushed to the Presidential Palace to defend Zelaya on the morning of the coup. For months and months after that, she took to the streets. Throughout the summer of 2010 she circulated petitions for the constituyente. "My sister wanted to retire this year," her sister Zenaida, who lives near me in San José, California, told me in early April 2011. "But they told her she needed to be on a waiting list" behind two thousand others, because the pension fund had been looted.[33]

The morning of March 18, 2011, the second day of the big strike against the passage of the new law, Ilse joined other teachers at a demonstration in front of the Tegucigalpa office of their state-run retirement agency. As police and soldiers stormed down the streets and aimed tear gas at them, the teachers, to signal their nonviolence, raised their hands up high. The police started launching tear gas anyway, fast. At 10:44 a.m., as Ilse tried to run away, a policeman deliberately shot a tear gas canister directly into her face, at close range. She fell to the ground, unconscious, in an asphyxiating cloud of gas. The driver of a passing television truck, himself affected by the fumes, ran over her right side. She lay face down in a pool of blood seeping out of her body. She died in a hospital three hours later.[34]

Ilse Velásquez's stunning death anticipated the violence that security forces rained down against protesters two week later on March 31, the day of the nationwide civic strike against the education bill. In the town of Nacaome, in the country's south, police suddenly launched tear gas at teachers and their allies as they gathered in the morning in the street, getting ready to blockade it. When a group of protesters fled into a nearby house, police shot several canisters of gas inside. At least five children were present in the house, and a two-month-old baby, Christopher de Jesús Bonilla García, was asphyxiated. When he stopped breathing, his father gave him mouth-to-mouth resuscitation. The police continued to blast tear gas canisters as the father tried to run away with the baby. Finally, he climbed over a wall to pass the baby to its grandfather, who escaped on a motorcycle and reached a medical facility. The baby survived, but potentially with long-term damage to his lungs.[35]

At six-thirty that same morning, during a demonstration in Triunfo de la Cruz, a community of Afro-Indigenous Garífuna people on the north coast, police moved in and selectively grabbed Miriam Miranda, Coordinator of OFRANEH (Organización Fraternal Negra Hondureña), the most prominent Garífuna group. Spitting racist insults, they hit her, shot tear gas at her abdomen at close range, and threw her onto the asphalt and then into jail where, her lungs burning, her chest turning purple, she was refused medical attention and not read her legal rights for over two hours—then charged with sedition.

"Despite state functionaries' plastic smiles and eagerness to obtain international recognition," Miranda declared the next day, after an international outcry freed her, "under the regime of Porfirio Lobo the criminalization of dissent has sharpened."[36]

That morning, campesino activists also successfully blocked traffic in Planes, at the entrance to the Aguán Valley, in solidarity with the teachers. Just after noon, as they were about to disperse, police fired tear gas and live ammunition at them, injuring at least twelve and killing one, whose body was grabbed away by authorities so quickly that he or she couldn't be identified.[37]

By this terrible spring of 2011, Honduran security forces had mastered the art of using gas canisters as deadly weapons, not just against protesters but against journalists identified with the Resistance. That same day in Tegucigalpa, police surrounded and closed in on reporter Lidith Diaz, jerking the cable of her microphone, with its blue, red, and yellow logo of TV Globo, an opposition station. When she objected, they shot a tear gas canister straight at her feet. Two days later, police shot a tear gas canister directly into the face of Salvador Sandoval, a cameraman for the opposition television station Cholusat Sur, fracturing his septum. "The police have all the media identified as 'resistance' or 'not resistance,'" he charged from his hospital bed.[38]

State repression of demonstrations in March and April came on top of an unrelenting daily bombardment of death threats, harassment, and assaults by paramilitaries and others extralegal agents, directed against all sectors of the opposition, broadly defined to include not just the formal FNRP but anyone working for human rights, social justice, and the rule of law, or reporting about them. In the capital, rocks rained down on cars in the parking lot of the STIBYS union hall. In San Pedro Sula, an unmarked car routinely lurked outside the office of the Centro de Derechos de Mujeres (Center for Women's Rights), shadowing María Elena Sabillón, an attorney who represented victims of domestic violence. Transgender women showed up dead in alleyways and garbage dumps.[39]

When Honduran security forces attacked and seized Miriam Miranda, multiple human rights activists from the United States wrote to Jeremy Spector, the same human rights and labor attaché in the embassy in Honduras that I'd spoken with myself, to ask for his help in protecting Miranda. In a reply to them, Spector reported very briefly that the Honduran government had released Miranda. He then followed that with four paragraphs in which he virulently criticized the teachers for being violent, while saying nary a word about the violence perpetrated by Honduran state security forces that day, or for weeks before it. Spector went out of his way to criticize the teachers' decision to strike, dismissed their alarm over the privatization law as "unfounded" and "complaints," and called on the teachers to return to their classrooms—although they weren't being paid. While he wrote that it was a "tragedy" that the teacher, Ilse Velásquez, had been "run over by a press vehicle," he made no mention of the police having fired a tear gas canister straight at her face, causing her to fall to the ground near the vehicle.[40]

Victory Laps

Repression by Honduran police and military, under Lobo's command, wasn't just about raw power, though. Like the coup, it was about taking over the Honduran state in order to implement an economic agenda in service to the Honduran oligarchy and to transnational corporations. Their economic project was designed to suck money out of those very same teachers, factory and plantation workers, and land rights defenders that were pouring into the streets, and to direct those funds into the pockets of elites. That spring of 2010, the Lobo Administration began launching not just tear gas canisters but economic initiatives those canisters served.

High on the list was a scheme so farfetched it seemed unthinkable, known as the Model Cities or Charter Cities. Ostensibly modeled on Hong Kong and Singapore, the proposed Model Cities would be special zones, known as ZEDEs, *Zonas de Empleo y Desarrollo Económico* (Zones of Employment and Economic Development), in which outside investors would be free to invest and develop entire cities as they saw fit, and into which Hondurans could migrate if they chose. Existing Honduran labor, environmental, and other laws wouldn't apply; the Honduran Constitution wouldn't apply; Model Cities could even sign treaties with foreign governments and military forces. The mastermind behind the original Honduran Model Cities proposal in 2010 was US economist Paul Romer, joined in an initial advisory group by Ronald Reagan's son Michael and by Grover Norquist, the man who invented the far-right, grassroots, Tea Party movement that brought ultra-conservatives to power in the US Congress.[41]

The Model Cities proposal was neoliberals' wildest fantasy come down to earth. In the Honduran context, it flowed out of a long history of economic enclaves controlled by transnational corporations.[42] Throughout the twentieth century, the United Fruit and Standard Fruit companies had ruled over entire zones of Honduran territory with their banana plantations. Beginning in the 1970s, transnational corporations moved into new "export processing zones" or maquiladoras, inside which apparel and electronics manufacturing plants exploited

Honduran workers—more than a hundred thousand at the time of the coup—with little interference from the Honduran government.[43]

While the Model Cities proposal lurked in the wings, the Honduran government began to make way for lower wages, fewer basic labor rights, and a weaker labor movement. The Employment Law passed Congress in September 2010, breaking up full-time jobs and turning them into part-time, temporary employment ineligible for unionization or the government's system of health care and pensions.[44]

In early May, to much fanfare, the government held an investment extravaganza called "Honduras Is Open for Business," with Mexican entrepreuner Carlos Slim, at the time the richest man in the world, and Paul Romer, the Model Cities advocate, as speakers (Bill Clinton was originally scheduled, too, but canceled). The conference was designed to reassure investors that Honduras was once again safe to invest in, and promised a golden future. "We are the most attractive investment destination in Latin America" the conference's glossy pamphlet promised on its first page. Whether the event generated any actual investments was unclear, but it certainly generated a host of mocking parodies in the solidarity world up north: "Honduras, Open for Repression." "Honduras, Busted Open for Business."[45]

Then, suddenly, seemingly out of the blue, on May 22, 2010, Presidents Juan Manuel Santos of Colombia and Hugo Chávez of Venezuela announced that they had brokered an agreement with the Honduran government allowing former president Manuel Zelaya to freely return to the country. The Cartagena Accord, as it was known, contained three key provisions: first, all criminal charges against Zelaya and his top ministers, still in exile as well, would be annulled. Second, the government of Honduras would commit itself to protecting human rights. Third—and here the plot thickens—a legal path would be made clear for the National Front of Popular Resistance to become a political party.[46]

Many members of the FNRP leadership apparently didn't even know about the pact before it was signed and made public. Within the Honduran Resistance more broadly, there was no democratic decision-making process involving its negotiation or approval. The

FNRP had in fact voted democratically three months earlier *not* to enter into electoral politics. In Cartagena, Zelaya and his inner circle, knowing full well the Liberal-Party camp within the FNRP was chomping at the electoral bit, had cut a deal that in effect threw the Honduran social movements off the Resistance bus. The powers in the hemisphere that backed the pact—Venezuela, Colombia, Nicaragua—for their part, wanted a resolution to the "problem" of Zelaya's ongoing exile and Honduras's ongoing status as a pariah state. The United States, especially, wanted recognition of Lobo's government by the countries that still held out, and Honduras's return to the Organization of American States.[47]

On May 28, 2011, almost two years after the coup that had deposed him, Zelaya landed triumphantly at Toncontín International Airport in Tegucigalpa. The joyous crowd that poured out to welcome him spread far up and down the boulevards, farther than the eye could see; even pro-coup, ultra-conservative newspapers and television stations counted it at nine hundred thousand to one million two hundred thousand—perhaps one-eighth of the entire Honduran population. The US mainstream press, largely silent about Honduras for a year and a half, throughout all the repression, assassinations, top-level thievery, and destruction of the rule of law, now announced that Zelaya was back, and that Honduras could re-enter the international community.[48]

On June 1, four days later, the Organization of American States indeed voted thirty-three to one to readmit Honduras.[49] In late September, President Porfirio Lobo flew north for his own victory tour. At the United Nations he gave a big triumphant speech in which he acknowledged past wrongdoings by the Honduran government, promoted his Truth and Reconciliation Commission, and reassured the world that human rights in his country were improving. He launched a new theme that would drive US and Honduran policy discourse in the years to come: gangs and drug traffickers, he warned, were escalating in Honduras, and were now "serious threats" to the Honduran people.[50]

But crime, violence, and drug trafficking—all, indeed, dangerously shooting up in post-coup Honduras—had flourished, of course, in the ripe climate of mass poverty fostered and further promoted by Lobo and the Honduran elites. If crime were the issue, the first and foremost criminal act threatening the Honduran people had been the coup, which remained in complete impunity, and the ongoing coup regime's near-complete destruction of the rule of law in its aftermath. And Lobo himself, not the gangs, oversaw the police who in turn attacked peaceful demonstrators and countenanced extrajudicial killings.[51]

Lobo followed his United Nations speech with dinner at the White House.[52] In a photo op at the Oval Office, he was all jolly and charming, side-by-side with a relaxed-looking President Barack Obama, the two in matching armchairs. Obama proclaimed,

> Today begins a new chapter in the relationship between our two countries. In part because of pressure from the international community, but also because of the strong commitment to democracy and leadership by President Lobo, what we've been seeing is a restoration of democratic practices and a commitment to reconciliation that gives us great hope.

Lobo echoed back: "We have reaffirmed our democratic vocation. We have reaffirmed the road to democracy that we are on and that we will be continuing on. We will be opening even more spaces for our people to be able to express themselves."[53]

Honduras in Flames, I: Rigor Mortis

On June 24, a month after Zelaya's return, the Honduran police and military destroyed almost the entire campesino community of Rigores, in the Aguán Valley, turning a seven-room cinderblock schoolhouse, three churches, a community center, and more than a hundred houses into burned-out rubble in a single afternoon. The nearly five hundred residents had an hour's notice to pull out their belongings, then watched as their homes were torched by security forces and crushed by a bulldozer.[54] In footage taken by documentary filmmaker Jesse Freeston, who happened to be in the area at the time, and who posted it to the Honduras solidarity email list, I could see walls of flame consuming the thatched roofs, rising high up in a macabre dance, billowing sideways in the wind.[55]

Six weeks later, back in Honduras, I asked my friends German and Ruy if we could again drive the five hours from San Pedro Sula out to the Aguán Valley to visit Rigores. Once in the Aguán, we turned left before the big bridge and twenty minutes later pulled off the highway onto a dirt road and parked in an open area near some trees. We sat down under a small shelter made of four metal poles holding up a bright green plastic tarp as a roof over three benches, six or seven small orange school chairs, and a chalkboard. Hanging from a tree, an eight-by-ten-inch sign with an arrow pointing toward the shelter read RUTA DE EVACUACIÓN ("Evacuation Route"). I still can't decide if that was a joke or for real, in case the police, military, or private thugs reappeared.

German and Ruy had called ahead, and several men and a woman were there to meet us. Gradually more people showed up, including several children. They told us that the shelter was the town's new schoolhouse. The first to talk was Santiago Maldonado, an older man wearing a loose gray short-sleeved button-down shirt with the tails out, jeans, black rubber boots, and a brown leather cowboy hat above silver hair and a narrow face. He was warm but very serious and looked us right in the eye when he got to the hard parts.

Rigores had been settled since 2000 by members of the Campesino Movement of Rigores (MCR). At the time of the eviction, they were obtaining final legal title to the land through the Agrarian Reform Institute (INA), in a process that included the land's expropriation from Eric Rivera, a large landholder alleged to be a drug trafficker, who had illegally claimed ownership. In the face of aggressive demands from Rivera that the campesinos leave, Cesar Ham, the Director of the Agrarian Reform Institute, repeatedly reassured the campesinos that there would be no eviction. But private actors repeatedly attempted to evict them nonetheless, over and over, beginning in 2005. Threats and intimidation escalated.[56] On May 15, 2011, an eyewitness reported that Dinant Corporation security guards working for Facussé shot Francisco Pascual Lopez, a farmer from the Rigores Community, while he was tending his cattle, and then dragged him onto Facussé's Panama Plantation nearby. He was never seen again, despite great pressure for an investigation.[57]

As we sat there on the benches, the residents told us that at nine o'clock in the morning on June 24, 2011, between five hundred and a thousand police, military, and plainclothes men had shown up at the entrance to the Rigores without warning. The officers commanded the campesinos to leave but had no eviction order, so the campesino men put up a barrier at the entrance to the community, while the women stayed at the houses with the children. At around 1:00 or 2:00 p.m., the security forces produced what they claimed was an eviction order from a judge. Human rights investigators have since established that the order was illegal, because no judge was present at the site, nor had there ever been the requisite investigation by the Public Ministry into the legitimate land rights of the families.[58]

The residents told us that the officers informed them they had one hour to remove their belongings. The women started pulling things out of their houses, stuffing them into plastic bags, fast, while their children stayed inside, crying, afraid; some kids ran crying into the streets. If the men tried to go near the houses or the children, security forces grabbed them. (At least sixteen men and one woman were detained by the police during the course of the day.) The women tried to get some of their furniture out but couldn't move most of it fast enough. One young woman told us that she and other women had tried appealing to the police and soldiers. "You're poor people, too!" they cried out. But the police just replied, "Hurry up, it doesn't matter to us if we are, too."

After an hour, the police and military forces started burning the thatched houses with cigarette lighters. Residents later told investigators that security guards working for Facussé's Dinant Corporation participated in the attack.[59] A bulldozer plowed through, slamming into the cinder-block buildings and crushing what was left of the burned thatch structures. The town's three churches—one Catholic, one "Iglesia de Dios," one Protestant missionary—were destroyed early on, and there was no time to remove anything from inside them. Eric Rivera, the man who illegally claimed the land, led the cops through the ups and down of the dispersed community, in and out of the trees, showing them where the houses and structures could be found.

The residents called human rights officials, labor unions, campesino federations, relief agencies, everyone they could think of. Eventually, allies from the Fundación San Lorenzo and COPA, the Coordinación de Organizaciones Populares del Aguán (Coalition of Popular Organizations of the Aguán) arrived, and the police allowed them to enter the community and help take away belongings in four pickup trucks. Other friends and cars arrived, too, and helped get the children—terrified, traumatized—safely away from the scene. They'd watched the whole thing. One woman recounted, "I said to the oldest, get your stuff out! Get the papers out!" Her son Eduardo, who told me he was thirteen, recounted: "I was afraid they were going to grab me." "I was afraid," said Ruth, age ten.

Police and soldiers from the military destroyed twenty-four more structures in addition to the houses, the school, a kindergarten, and the churches. They also deliberately tore down the fences around the houses—so that animals could get into homes and gardens—and burned down and destroyed crops that had just been planted. Two women miscarried that day. Another had a stroke and was taken to the hospital.

After the meeting at the shelter, Eduardo, the thirteen-year-old boy, offered to lead German, Ruy, and me on a tour through the community. It was midday by then and at least a hundred degrees and humid as we walked around in the glaring hot sun. It smelled like smoke everywhere. It looked like a war zone. It was a war zone.

We followed yellow dirt roads and paths splayed across a low, rolling landscape of green fields, clusters of forest, spiky tropical plants, and crows, with here and there a broken fence or a cow. Mostly we saw pile after pile of low rubble and sticks that I kept trying to imagine, almost impossibly, had once been beloved homes. One pile had a rusted-out, burned bicycle lying on its side out in front. Near another I could see a small cooking structure with a newly thatched roof over a concrete cooking stove and a table with a few dishes and pots. In its back section a piece of red plastic tarp was wrapped around four wooden poles. The whole structure had three rows of barbed wire twisted tautly round its side. That structure was a family's rebuilt home.

After half an hour, German and Ruy decided to walk back toward the car and the schoolhouse-shelter, warning me about the sun. I'm fine, I said, I'm used to it, and I kept walking with the boy. As we got farther out from the entrance a gorgeous view opened up to the west, of broad fields across the plain, glowing gold and green. The boy showed me a piece of cinder-block wall that had once been the seven-room schoolhouse, and more rubble that had been a church. We ran into a man and boy who said they were just back from hunting, carrying a machete and a dead two-foot-long iguana hanging slack from a stick. We passed through a bit of woods where a group of women were washing clothes in a creek that can't have been more than eight inches deep.

Circling back, near the shelter and the car, alone by this point, I met a tiny, hunched-over old man, who told me he was on his way back from working in the fields. He pointed out the miniscule thatched structure that he and his wife were now living in, maybe two and a half feet high, five feet long at most, just a little triangular roof against the thundering rain and ferocious sun. He told me that when the police and soldiers started to burn down the houses, the men had been laughing, "presumably on drugs." But one of the policemen, when he saw what was about to happen, had left.

Back at the shelter, Ruy, German, and I said goodbye and thank you to our hosts and promised our solidarity, then drove away in our pickup with the air conditioning blaring full blast. Once we were back on the main paved road, German and Ruy stopped at a neighborhood store for sodas. I didn't get out of the car. I felt nauseous in my whole body and couldn't really talk. It must have been all that heat and sun, I told German. I think now that was only part of it.

No one was ever charged for what the police and military did to Rigores that day. No one ever went to jail. José Antonio Maradiaga, coordinator of public prosecutors for the lower Aguán Valley, told Human Rights Watch in late 2013 that he had never ordered any investigation of those who carried out the eviction in Rigores. According to Human Rights Watch, Maradiaga insisted that "no houses had been burned, and so no investigation was warranted. When he was told there was a video of the apparent destruction, he said the peasants were to blame for the violence, if there was any."[60]

In 2012, as knowledge of atrocities committed by the post-coup Honduran government finally seeped out to the international press, some commentators talked about Honduras as a "failed state," because the rule of law had so completely collapsed, and the judiciary, police, and prosecutors were so overwhelmingly corrupt.[61] But it wasn't a failed state. The Honduran state worked great for those who controlled it—for the landowners and drug traffickers and oligarchs and transnational corporations and US-funded and trained military, and the corrupt public officials who served them. The destruction of Rigores was just one tiny example of the post-coup maelstrom of greed, torching any semblance of legality and justice.

Later, I decided to look up *rigor* to see what the name of the town, Rigores, might mean. My Spanish-English dictionary translated it as "severity" or "rigor." It provided an example: "*con todo el rigor de la ley*—with the utmost severity or full rigor of the law."

A Slow-Moving Massacre

But even the destruction of Rigores and the massacre at El Tumbador, which had prompted the campesinos' road blockade outside Guadalupe Carney, were just droplets in the wide river of horror in the Aguán. Between January 2010 and November 1, 2011, a total of at least sixty-one campesino activists, their family members, and their allies were killed, one by one, two by two, in a slow-moving massacre that turned the beautiful rolling farmlands of the Lower Aguán Valley into a twisted plantation of terror and death. By the middle of February 2013 another thirty-three would be dead, along with five security guards. Three and a half years later, the total number of dead campesinos and their allies would be more than a hundred and fifty.[62]

Before the coup, campesino cooperatives in the MUCA had been engaged in legal processes through which they sought to regain rights to twenty-eight farms that had been illegally taken from them. But the coup threw that approach out the window. So, after the coup, they chose to recoup their land losses of the 1990s and 2000s by advancing classic tactics through which campesinos had utilized Honduran agrarian reform law for thirty years: reoccupy the land through "recuperations," then file legal papers to establish legal possession, as allowed by the law—as they had, for example, in Rigores. The law stated clearly, moreover, that no one landholder could own more than a limited amount of land in a single region. Yet Miguel Facussé, the famous, superrich *golpista*, had, through coercion, terror, and fraud, claimed twenty-two thousand acres in the Bajo Aguán by this point, at least one-fifth of the entire zone, and planted it in African palms for his expanding biofuel empire. In December 2009 and January 2010 thousands of MUCA members occupied twenty-six of the twenty-eight farms for which they had been negotiating for a decade. Separately, other campesino activists in the MCA had earlier pursued legal processes and recuperations to establish rights lands on a former military base, the CREM (Centro Regional de Entrenamiento Militar, Regional Military Training Center), which the government had agreed to distribute to campesinos.[63]

An exhaustive sixty-four-page report compiled in February 2013 by Annie Bird, at the time Co-Director of Rights Action, enumerates what happened next. Throughout the next years, security guards and others allegedly working for Facussé's Dinant Corporation and for other elites hunted down campesinos like animals up and down the roads, rivers, and pathways of the valley. On August 17, 2011, for example, as Victor Manuel Amaya (#15 in her report), Rodving Omar Villegas (#16), and Sergio Magdiel Amaya (#17), members of the MUCA, were driving from Tocoa to the occupation at Las Marañones, Dinant guards in a blue pickup truck reportedly opened fire with an AK-47, killing them all instantly. On October 11, 2011, six security guards, along with police and military forces, reportedly shot and killed Santos Serfino Zelaya Ruiz (#57) and opened fire on fifteen women spreading salt on fields claimed by Facussé. The women hid for hours afterward in the trees. On January 11, 2008, Resistance activist and journalist Juan Chinchilla was kidnapped in the Aguán Valley, tortured, and interrogated. He escaped after two days and reported that his captors "almost all wore uniforms of the police, and private guards of Miguel Facussé."[64] A July 2011 report from a joint fact-finding mission of the International Federation for Human Rights, World Council of Churches, Foodfirst Information and Action Network (FIAN), and other international human rights groups concluded of the killings in the Aguán: "In all cases, according to witnesses and members of the peasant movements, the security guards working for Miguel Facussé and René Morales [another rich landowner] are seen to be the primary actors."[65]

Bird compiled broad evidence establishing, moreover, that Honduran state security forces were responsible for a great number of the killings and atrocities in the Aguán, acting both independently and in collaboration with security guards. On June 5, 2011, a police pickup truck opened fire on José Recinos Aguilar, Joel Santamaría, and Genaro Cuesta (#38-40), all MARCA members, while they were standing on the San Esteban farm, then loaded up their bodies for delivery to the morgue. Three weeks later, police and members of the military burned down Rigores. In mid-September, six weeks after my visit, they returned to the community and rampaged through it again, randomly grabbing and detaining people, including children. One of those was a sixteen-year-old boy who testified that police put a bag over his head, sprayed him with gasoline, and threatened to kill him.[66]

The line between private and public security forces was permeable. "Military, police and private security forces are reported to exchange uniforms depending on the context, to mobilize jointly both in police patrol cars and automobiles that belong to private security companies employed by the African palm planters," Bird wrote. Men wearing the uniforms of Facussé's security firm, Orion, reportedly shot and killed Roney Diaz (#31), for example, but observers recognized them as members of the Honduran Armed Forces' Fifteenth Battalion. COFADEH, the prominent Honduran human rights group, underscored: "The relationship between the military and the private security guards demonstrates clearly that the security guards are acting as paramilitary forces."[67]

In many cases, though, the identity of the assassins was never known. On May 12, 2011, Olvin Gallegos (#35) and Segundo Gómez (#36), members of the MARCA, another campesino rights group, left on a bicycle to travel from one campesino-held farm to another. They were seen entering the section of highway in between, that passed through a disputed property called El Mochito. They were never seen again. The bicycle was found on El Mochito but family members who searched for the two men were threatened and chased out. On July 16, 2011, MUCA members Luis Alonso Ortiz Borjas (#41) and Constantino Morales Enamorado (#42) were on their way from the occupation at Marañones to buy food in the nearby town of Ilanga. Gunmen with AK-47s opened fire on them, then put their bodies in the back of a pickup truck and drove away.[68] The two men were never seen again. When I visited Marañones a month later, members of the fourteen hundred campesino families living and working there told me they hadn't left the farmlands for a year; their children hadn't been to school; they hadn't been to doctors; three women had given birth in the encampment. "If we leave here we'll be killed," they told me.

The numbers next to each name help us grasp both the specificity and the scale of the killings. But they distance us from the torture, the pain felt by loved ones and colleagues, the state of permanent terror, and the ongoing anguish, both individual and collective, as the cases remained in impunity indefinitely. And these killings were only the tip of the iceberg in terms of the threats, illegal detentions, excessive use of force, torture, and harrassment in the legal system, experienced up and down the Bajo Aguán, day after day, month after month, year after year.

As the crisis grew, the Honduran government answered with a sequence of mass militarizations of the entire lower Aguán Valley. In April 2010, President Lobo sent in seven thousand police and military in Operación Trueno (Operation Thunder), which publicly promised to end violence in the region but in fact was designed to raise the level of terror. The government did very publicly negotiate the sale of five of the twenty-six farms to MUCA cooperatives, but with onerous terms impossible to meet. In November 2010, when campesinos protested the killings of five campesinos at El Tumbador, Lobo again sent a thousand troops. In August 2011, Joint Task Force Xatruch II again occupied the valley, and stayed for good this time. "With the militarization of Xatruch II they are trying to convert our zone into Iraq," COFADEH and the MUCA declared in a joint statement. "Our settlements are being submitted to a permanent state of siege."[69] The direction of the military forces in the Aguán Valley remained largely under the Fifteenth Battalion, which bore responsibility for at least thirty-four criminal acts in the region over the course of three years, Bird documented.[70]

The Honduran government forces of Xatruch II, which were camped out in the Bajo Aguán through all these years, were part of the problem, by no means the solution. Killings, disappearances, and terror continued, perpetrated by state security forces as well as security guards. On September 17, 2011, I called the police station in Tocoa, the largest town in the Bajo Aguán, to inquire about the condition of more than thirty campesinos that had just been rounded up and detained. "Tell her they've killed all the campesinos," I heard an official in the back clearly say; then they hung up. I called another colleague in the United States immediately and asked her to call, too. She called right after that and asked how the detainees were being treated. "Like dogs," the official who answered replied. "Are they being tortured?" my colleague asked. "I hope so," replied the official.

On October 6, members of Operation Xatruch II captured, detained without charges, and tortured Walter Nelin Sabillón Yanos, a MUCA member, FIAN reports. Sabillón testified to FIAN that while he was in detention at the Tocoa police station, authorities beat him, repeatedly placed a hood on his head, and three times applied electric shock to his hands, abdomen, and mouth while interrogating him about the campesino movement.[71]

US dollars helped pay for this. In the two years after Lobo's election, US funding for the Honduran military and police shot up sharply. Police and military funding, at least $6.7 million for 2010, rose to at least $9.8 million in 2011. Funding under the Central American Regional Security Initiative, supposedly to combat drug trafficking in Central America, rose to $135 million for 2012, a one-third increase over the previous year. The US also allocated $45 million in new funds for its own military construction in Honduras, including expansion and improvement of the jointly operated Soto Cano Air Force Base at Palmerola, and opened three new military bases.[72]

Honduran military operations in the Lower Aguán Valley, including joint operations with Facussé's guards, benefited from these funds, as well as from equipment and special training. That summer of 2011, as so many campesinos were being slaughtered, seventy members of Honduras's Fifteenth Battallion received a special thirty-three-day training course from the US Rangers. Members of the Xatruch Special Forces group in the Aguán Valley, in a September meeting with representatives of US-based Honduras Solidarity Network, confirmed that they had received training from the United States military.[73]

In the middle of all this, cables released by Wikileaks on September 30, 2011, shed light not only on Facussé's activities but on the roles of the US military and the State Department in the Aguán Valley and in Honduras more broadly.[74] A cable dated March 19, 2004—five years before the coup—from the US Embassy in Tegucigalpa to Washington, entitled "Drug Plane Burned on Prominent Honduran's Property," reported that "a known drug trafficking flight with a 1,000 kilo cocaine shipment from Colombia ... successfully landed March 14 on the private property of Miguel Facussé." According to the cable's author, US Ambassador Larry Palmer, sources informed police that the plane's "cargo was off-loaded onto a convoy of vehicles that was guarded by about 30 heavily armed men." The plane was seen burned and its wreckage then buried by a "bulldozer/front-end loader." Palmer wrote that "Facussé's property is heavily guarded and the prospect that individuals were able to access the property and, without authorization, use the airstrip is questionable." One source, he reported, "claimed that Facussé was present on the property at the time of the incident." Ambassador Palmer also reported that "this incident marks the third time in the last fifteen months that drug traffickers have been linked to this property owned by Mr. Facussé." In a subsequent cable on March 31, 2004, Palmer noted the confiscation by Honduran authorities of "approximately 700 kilos of cocaine" and conveyed the belief that the drugs may have come from the burned plane on Facussé's property.[75]

Further evidence linked Facussé to drug trafficking the year of the coup. On February 22, 2009, *El Heraldo*, a right-wing Tegucigalpa newspaper, reported that, according to an official of the Honduran government's anti-narcotics office, a Cessna aircraft with fourteen hundred kilos of cocaine had been found in Farallones, east of the Aguán Valley in the department of Colon, "on a landing strip that according to our information belongs to Miguel Facussé."[76]

Precisely as US funding for the Honduran military and police escalated under the pretext of fighting the drug war, then, US-supported troops were conducting joint operations with the security guards of someone the United States knew was a drug trafficker, in order to violently repress a campesino movement on behalf of his illegal claims to vast swaths of the Aguán Valley.

But, amazingly, despite all that violence, all that death, all that military intimidation, the campesinos stayed on many of their recuperated properties. In the years to come, as they were evicted repeatedly, they would nonetheless return over and over, and even occupy new farms. "They think with this they can weaken the group, stop the fight," Eliseo Pavón, a campesino activist who had been wounded when a motorcyclist shot and killed another activist, told the *New York Times* in September 2011. "But it won't happen."[77]

"It is better to die here," a leader at the Marañones encampment told the *Times*. "We don't have anywhere else to go. We can't give up on the struggle. Where would that leave the deaths of our comrades. In vain?"[78] The MUCA signed off its communiques: "We are not fish living on water; we are not birds living on air, we are campesinos and campesinas who need to live on the land. No More Blood Baths in the Lower Aguán!"[79]

Honduras in Flames, II: Body Counts

People in the cities weren't spared death at the hands of the police, either.

Saturday night, October 22, 2011, Alejandro Rafael Vargas, twenty-two, the son of Julieta Castellanos, the rector of the biggest university in the country, the Universidad Nacional Autónoma de Honduras (UNAH), and a friend of his, Carlos David Pineda Rodríguez, passed through a police checkpoint in Tegucigalpa after they had left a party at the home of Zelaya's former top minister. After they drove past the checkpoint, police shot up the car from the rear four times. One of the bullets passed through the car into Pineda Rodríguez's back. Forensics later established that the two men were then captured alive, transported out of the city to the south, and then executed with shots to their heads. Their bodies were found that afternoon in a dump.[80]

When the news hit the media, government officials admitted that the likely culprits were at least four members of the police. Public investigators descended on the police station, impounded three police vehicles, and found blood matching that of one of the victims. The government announced that it had arrested four policemen. Lobo fired five top police directors. A week later, though, it was revealed that the head of the Tegucigalpa police had released the four arrested men from custody soon after, telling them to take a few days off and then report back. Naturally, they disappeared. Two weeks after the killings, the Minister of Security announced with great publicity that one hundred seventy-six police officers had been arrested for connections to other murders, drug trafficking, and robberies. But it soon it turned out that those one hundred seventy-six weren't actually arrested after all, only that fifty to seventy-two members of the police force—the number kept varying—had been reportedly called before a new hastily composed police commission. Only four men evidently remained in custody in the original case of the killings.[81]

The prominence of Julieta Castellanos, the university rector—herself a member of the ruling National Party—and the clear involvement of police precipitated a huge scandal. Throughout that fall, Hondurans threw open the floodgates that had been holding back their protests against police corruption, as people stepped forward to denounce the police, provide evidence of criminal activities, and call for international intervention.[82] The police, they charged, were riddled with death squads, drug traffickers, and members of organized crime up to the very highest level. "It's scarier to meet up with five police officers on the streets than five gang members," declared former police commissioner María Luisa Borjas.[83] Police corruption had long predated the coup, but the post-coup rotting out of the judiciary and attorney general's office, and the general destruction of the rule of law, had created the conditions for vast corruption among the police. By the next spring of 2012, COFADEH, the Committee of Families of the Detained and Disappeared of Honduras, reported that more than ten thousand complaints had been filed about abuses by the police and military since the coup, none of which had been addressed.[84] The Vice President of Congress reported that police chiefs had told him that up to forty percent of all police were tied to organized crime.[85] Castellanos herself, who emerged as an outspoken, outraged public leader, famously demanded in November 2011, that the international community—including the United States—cut off funding for the Honduran police: "Stop feeding the beast," she declared.[86]

The floodgates opened, too, about criminal drug traffickers and their allies embedded in the government. Prominent critics and even government officials, including Marlon Pascua, the defense minister, talked of "narco-judges" who blocked prosecutions and "narco-congressmen" who ran cartels. Alfredo Landaverde, a former congressman and police commissioner in charge of drug investigations, declared that one out of every ten members of Congress was a drug trafficker and that he had evidence proving "major national and political figures" were involved in drug trafficking.[87]

Throughout November, Landaverde spoke out against police corruption, not just in the case of the rector's son and his friend, but throughout the force. He denounced, for example, the documented "disappearance" that season of thousands of confiscated weapons, many of which later showed up on the black market. Two years earlier, in December 2009, General Julián Aristídes Gonzáles, the former director of the government's anti-drug-trafficking office, announced that he established that police were connected to extensive drug trafficking. He had been swiftly assassinated. Landaverde, in turn, announced he had evidence proving that police had killed Gonzáles. On December 7, 2011, two years to the day after Gonzáles's death, Landaverde himself was shot up in his car, along with his wife, who survived. It was the most prominent assassination in Honduras in two years, and it sent shock waves into the bones of the entire broad Honduran opposition—and all of us up north, too, in solidarity: if they would kill Landaverde, they'd kill anyone.[88]

Six years later, in 2016, the *New York Times* would report evidence that both Gonzáles's and Landaverde's murders were ordered by the topmost officials of the Honduran police.[89]

On the morning of February 15, 2012, I slept in long past 6:30 a.m. for the first time in months, exhausted from tracking and responding to so much. I didn't look at my email right away, like I usually did. At 9:15, I answered a phone call from Adrienne Pine at American University, who also worked on Honduran human rights issues. "Don't you know about the prison fire?" she asked.[90]

The night before, Valentine's Day, at least three hundred fifty-nine people (all men except for one woman, who was visiting her husband) had died in a fire at La Granja penitentiary in Comayagua, Honduras, in the one of the worst prison fires in all modern history. When the fire broke out, the prisoners were locked into spectacularly overcrowded cells, in some cases sixty to a room. "Bodies were found piled up in the bathrooms, where inmates apparently fled to the showers, hoping the water would save them from the blistering flames," reporters found. "Prisoners perished clutching each other in bathtubs and curled up in laundry sinks."[91]

In Honduras, prison guards are regular police. After the fire started, many of the guards didn't have keys, or refused to use them and fled, abandoning the screaming prisoners. Rubén García, a survivor, testified that guards shot at the prisoners before fleeing. Outside, firefighters rushed over from their station two minutes away, but the guards held them back for thirty minutes before allowing them to enter. US military firefighters, fifteen minutes away at Soto Cano Air Base, were never called in. Family members living nearby rushed to the prison only to be met by bullets and tear gas. They could hear the screams.[92]

The public spokesman for the police about the fire was Héctor Iván Mejía, the same man who had been director of the San Pedro Sula police on August 20, 2009, when Irma Melissa Villanueva was gang-raped by police, and on September 15, 2010, when the San Pedro police rampaged through the Independence Day rally.[93] At the time of the fire, another police spokesman insisted at first that the inmates were dangerous gang members and hardened criminals. But the Comayagua penitentiary was in fact a second-tier prison, housing ordinary criminals from that region. The Associated Press soon discovered, moreover, that over half of those in the prison had never even been charged. Many were awaiting court dates that would never arrive, in a country with no functioning judicial system.[94]

Former police commissioner María Luisa Borjas, by this point a target of ongoing death threats because of her criticisms of police corruption, charged the next morning that the fire was a "criminal act" by the Honduran government. Attorney Joaquin Mejía called it "the institutionalized violence of the state."[95] José Miguel Vivanco, director of Human Rights Watch for the Americas, told the *New York Times*: "This horrendous tragedy is the result of prison conditions that are symptomatic of the country's larger public security crisis."[96]

By mid-morning after the fire, *The Nation* had emailed me asking for an article to post early the next day.[97] By early afternoon, *Democracy Now!* wanted me on the show via Skype at 5:00 a.m.[98] In shocked overdrive, all the rest of the day I listened to the Jesuits' opposition station, Radio Progreso, as its announcers read out the names of the dead over and over, their incantation of those classic Honduran names underscoring the magnitude of the blow to the Honduran people. I interviewed Óscar Estrada in Boston, a Honduran who had made a documentary film about a 2003 prison fire, in which police deliberately set a fire that had killed sixty-nine alleged gang members. A year later, another prison fire had killed another one hundred four inmates who were unable to escape. Each time, the government promised to address the horrible, overcrowded conditions in the prisons; it would never happen again, they said. Mourning the new victims, Estrada said to me, "At least I know now I can still feel."[99]

At six o'clock that evening, I forced myself to start writing the *Nation* article. Right before midnight I sent it to my editor then tried to sleep. At 3:00 a.m., I got up and put on television-worthy clothes and makeup, and at 5:00 Skyped live onto *Democracy Now!* from my study, stumbling on my words and looking hideous but landing my points well enough.

Afterward, I made a huge mistake. Adrienne, the colleague who had called me to tell me about the fire, had by this point reported extensively about it on her blog, Quotha.net. When I looked at it again, she had posted photographs. She warned readers that if they scrolled down, the pictures would be upsetting. But I clicked onward anyway. There appeared the most horrible and terrifying picture I have seen in my entire life: the brown charred bodies of twenty or thirty men piled and curled up on top of each other in a desperate huddle, trying to escape through a metal grate.

Totally sleep deprived, overwhelmed with the stress of trying to learn about and grasp the fire, write about it fast, then talk on television, I went down a psychological rabbit hole in a way I never had before and never have since, through eight years of post-coup atrocities. How could human beings do such horrible things to each other? How could the police have thrown away the keys, held back the firefighters, shot at the families? What did that say about the world? What did I do now with my thoughts, imagining what the dying men in that pile had gone through? I was losing it.

I had to drive south down Highway 101 toward Los Angeles that afternoon, so on the way there I turned off the freeway at Pinnacles National Monument and drove the half hour east into the park, then hiked two miles up a low valley to some rocks where I could sit and look back at the ridge of brown rock outcroppings high across from me, just as the late afternoon sun hit them.[100] I sat there and summoned every power of good I could think of in the entire world and channeled it into my deepest soul.

On the way down, I passed a great horned owl up in a pine tree, watching me and doing that thing that owls do when they mysteriously turn their heads 360 degrees. Once I was back on the freeway a big white owl swooped by at dusk right across in front of my car. On the smaller road I took to the coast, just before dark, a third, grayish-brown owl swept by. I'd driven those routes for decades and never seen an owl. In many cultures, owls are a symbol of death.

Hondurans and US allies at a briefing in the US House of Representatives, November 2009, L-R Jessica Sánchez (Feministas en
Resistencia), Mery Agurcía (COFADEH), Jennifer Atlee (Friendship Office of the Americas), Bertha Oliva (COFDAEH), Jean
Stokan (Sisters of Mercy of the Americas). Photo Credit: Sisters
of Mercy Institute Justice Team.

CHAPTER THREE

The Struggle Up North: Media, Solidarity, and the US Congress

Northern Exposure

Then the darkness lifted a bit in the United States, if not within Honduras. Suddenly, and astonishingly, at the beginning of 2012 the US media wall blocking out news about Honduras shattered, then crumbled down altogether. That spring the US Congress pushed back against the administration's policies again and again, too. Very quickly the State Department was on the defensive. By the summer it became much clearer to the US public not only what was going on inside Honduras but also that the atrocities were in many cases at the point of a US-funded gun, and even a gun in the hands of US forces.

One clear light had already pierced through the US media wall during the previous fall. Elisabeth Malkin from the *New York Times* went to the Aguán Valley and came back with a beautiful story published on September 15, 2011: "In Honduras, Land Struggles Highlight Post-Coup Polarization."[1] But when the police killed the rector's son and his friend in October, and the uproar over police corruption tore through Honduran media all day every day, nary a word appeared in the mainstream US papers. When Alfredo Landaverde, the prominent police inspector and critic of the police,

95

was killed in December, only a brief mention made it into a few papers two days later.[2]

If the media didn't notice, Congress did. On November 28, 2011, Representative Howard Berman, the Ranking Democrat on the House Foreign Affairs Committee, sent a flaming three-page letter to Secretary of State Clinton, enumerating human rights abuses in Honduras and challenging US support for Honduran security forces. "Madam Secretary, the most chilling aspect of this rather gruesome set of problems is that US government assistance is flowing into the thick of it."[3] Paraphrasing Castellanos's call to end US security aid, he concluded: "We owe it to her and all Hondurans, as well as US taxpayers, to evaluate immediately United States assistance to ensure that we are not, in fact, feeding the beast." In mid-December, Congress for the first time placed human rights conditions on twenty percent of the funding for Honduran security forces in the new State and Foreign Operations Appropriations Act for 2012, and Obama signed it into law.[4] Under pressure from Congress, the US-controlled Millenium Challenge Corporation that same month cancelled as much as two hundred million dollars in funding scheduled for the Honduran government.[5] No one in the mainstream media covered any of this at the time.

But with the new year, the crisis in Honduras finally started breaking through. On January 18, 2012, the Peace Corps announced it was pulling all its volunteers out of the country because of growing danger, and the media picked up the story nationwide.[6] United Nations statistics from October, reporting that Honduras had the highest murder rate in the world, and that San Pedro Sula was the city with the highest murder rate—even surpassing Ciudad Juárez, Mexico—started popping up in articles at CNN and other mainstream outlets.[7]

A few days before Christmas, Dan Beeton, the Communications Director at CEPR (Center for Economic and Policy Research), the progressive think tank in Washington, D.C., contacted an editorial writer at the *Los Angeles Times* and talked to her about Honduras, part of his regular work sending information to US reporters and editors who covered Latin America. On December 21, at Dan's suggestion, she called me, and we had a thirty-minute phone conversation about Honduras. I held my breath for ten days. Finally, on January 2, the *Los Angeles Times* published an editorial in the official voice of the paper: "Holding Honduras Accountable: President Porfirio Lobo Must Demonstrate That He's Taking Measurable Steps to Prevent Human Rights Abuses."[8] It opened with the murder rate and a report from Human Rights Watch, referred to the Berman letter and to Landaverde's killing, cited congressional concerns, and called on Lobo to be accountable for human rights abuses if he were to receive continuing US assistance.

For the first time, a US newspaper—and a major one, to boot—had named the problem, questioned US aid to Honduras, and publicized the congressional pushback. Other prominent papers started publishing long news stories reporting parts of the crisis in Honduras, especially the escalating violence but also police corruption: the *Washington Post* on December 27, the McClatchy News Service on January 20, then the *Miami Herald* on January 23; the next day the *Herald* ran its own editorial questioning US security aid to Honduras.[9]

This new, cascading coverage was amazing. But almost none of it mentioned the coup or US responsibility for the Honduran meltdown in its aftermath. Furious that both could just disappear from history like that, at two o'clock in the morning on Sunday, January 22, I wrote the opening lines to an op-ed in my head, then got up and scribbled them down on the kitchen table. The next afternoon, in three hours, I wrote up an article and sent it to the *New York Times*. I knew the iron was hot. Maybe, finally, after two and a half years of rejections, I could get published in a mainstream paper. Twenty-four hours later, the *Times* wrote back that they were interested. By Thursday, the article was officially accepted and edited. To my complete surprise the *Times* didn't change the politics of my argument one whit.

Friday morning, on my way to Connecticut, I pulled into a park-and-fly lot near the San Francisco airport. I picked up that morning's *New York Times* from a rack, sat down inside the shuttle van, slowly opened the paper, and found my article splayed across the middle of the right-hand editorial page: "In Honduras, a Mess Made in the U.S." There was my opening line: "It's time to acknowledge the foreign policy disaster that American support for the Porfirio Lobo administration has become." A boxed subhead in the middle of the text declared: "After a coup and rigged elections, a wave of state-led repression." There it all was in the authoritative *Times* font, not just the coup, but the illegitimate elections, Landaverde, the police killing Castellanos's son and his friend, her call to "stop feeding the beast," and my criticism of the Obama Administration for funding state security forces that were killing campesinos in the Aguán.[10]

The article hit a vein. Over the next two weeks, I got two hundred emails that ran two to one in my favor, including moving letters from Hondurans in the United States and all over, thanking me for naming clearly what was going on. Hostile letters from other Hondurans began by telling me that my facts were all wrong, but almost always ended by insisting that Zelaya was an agent of Venezuelan President Hugo Chávez and had had to be removed "by any means necessary." The print edition of the *Times* ran one letter to the editor, supporting me. Soon after, it ran two longer, hostile letters online. The first, from James Creagan, a former US ambassador to Honduras, insisted: "It may be gratifying to attribute Honduras' problems to generals with sunglasses or to rigged elections. But it is not true. This is not the 1970s with Central American coups, contras and revolutionaries." (Unfortunately, he got the 1980s Contra War in Nicaragua war off by a decade.) Rather, Creagan asserted, the violence in Honduras "is caused by drugs, gangs and corruption . . . all driven by the market for coca leaf products." The second, from the Honduran ambassador to the United States, Jorge Ramón Hernández Alcerro, attacked my "insinuations" about the elections as "offensive," blamed the violence on the US demand for drugs, then lauded the progress of the Honduran government in addressing security issues. His language matched almost word for word a State Department press statement issued two weeks before.[11] In Honduras, *El Tiempo*, the one center-right newspaper, published my article in Spanish as a lead story. *El Heraldo*, the prominent right-wing Honduran paper, then published both of the hostile letters with the headline "Ofensiva Diplomática Hondureña en el *New York Times*" (Honduran Diplomatic Offensive in the *New York Times*).[12]

I had planned to fly to Honduras two weeks after those letters came out, but cancelled my trip—no way would it be safe to enter the country at that point. I thought: will I never be able to visit my beloved Honduras again? For all my anguish, I knew it was just one tiny sliver of what all the thousands of Hondurans in exile since the coup were experiencing.

Three things happened with that op-ed and the new media coverage: first, they brought down the media wall altogether, both in terms of publicizing the crisis in Honduras, and in terms of naming US responsibility for it. Second, in a way I hadn't been before, I became a public actor in the debate about US policy in Honduras. Third, and most importantly, the articles legitimated what hundreds of activists in the United States had been saying for three and a half long years since the coup, ourselves repeating what we'd learned from those in Honduras. We weren't the fringe anymore.

On Valentine's Day, February 14, two weeks after my op-ed, the Honduran prison fire that killed three hundred fifty-nine people made big headlines worldwide. At that point a new, major factor in the transformation of US media coverage of Honduras began to kick in. In early 2012, the Associated Press (AP) assigned two new investigative reporters to cover Honduras, Pulitzer Prize–winner Martha Mendoza, an American living in California; and Alberto Arce, a Spaniard who moved to Tegucigalpa. The impact of their work hit immediately, as, along with others, they covered the prison fire with moving depth. It was AP's reporters who discovered, for example, that most of those who died in the fire had never even been charged.[13]

In early March, ninety-four members of Congress, led by Representative Jan Schakowsky of Illinois, sent a letter to Secretary of State Clinton demanding that all US assistance to Honduran security forces be suspended until human rights concerns were addressed.[14] It wasn't the first such letter; Representative Sam Farr had led on a similar letter in October 2010 with twenty-nine cosigners. On May 31, 2011, eighty-four members had signed a letter led by Representative James McGovern, also requesting that aid be suspended.[15] The McGovern letter, though, went public three days after Zelaya returned to Honduras and had been buried altogether in the celebratory coverage reporting that Zelaya was back and justice had been restored. The new, March 2012 Schakowsky letter didn't make headlines immediately either, but news of it started to spread, and it got picked up in subsequent stories about Honduras. On May 22, Representative Sam Farr put out a statement expressing alarm over human rights abuses in Honduras, and *El Tiempo* reported on it in San Pedro Sula with the headline "*Congresista Estadounidosense Denuncia Ataques Contra Periodistas y Gays*" ("US Congressmember Denounces Attacks Against Journalists and Gays").[16]

It's difficult to articulate quite how powerful it was to experience the media transformation and congressional pushback that winter and spring, after so much horror, so much silence. Those of us up north could feel that our work of solidarity was finally paying off, in ways we'd never imagined possible. Hondurans in the opposition, who saw the articles and letters and statements begin to appear in their own press, began to feel less isolated, less like the terrors were happening under the cover of darkness, and more like somebody powerful in the US government might be not only paying attention but also speaking out. For me personally, in the middle of it all, that spring was an extraordinary experience of empowerment and hope.

But that whole spring was also always punctuated by new horrors in Honduras that made daily life a roller coaster, full of both gut punches and high points. The killings of campesinos in the Aguán Valley continued. On January 20, two masked men on a motorcycle shot and killed MUCA member Matías Valle while he was waiting by the side of a road for his bus. On March 29, Edilberto Flores of the MUCA was shot and killed while traveling home from work. On April 10, Arnoldo Trochez of the MUCA was shot and killed while working on the Las Marañones farm that had been recuperated by campesinos.[17] When campesinos launched a new wave of land occupations in the Aguán and Sula Valleys on April 24, the Honduran military and police, at the behest of the landowners, moved in to force them off the properties brutally.[18]

The horrible news wasn't just about campesinos. On May 5, prominent LGBTI and Resistance activist and journalist, Erick Martínez, who was running for Congress, disappeared and was found strangled to death two days later. Honduran human rights groups reported that at least seventy LGBTI people had been killed since the 2009 coup.[19] On May 9, Alfredo Villatoro, a famous conservative radio host, was kidnapped and then found dead six days later.[20] When asked what the police were going to do to protect journalists against attacks, police spokesman Héctor Iván Mejía blamed the victims: journalists, he said, should perform their work "responsibly, professionally, without much emotion that threatens the rights of another person, to avoid the likely consequences of revenge."[21]

In early May, as the criticisms of US policy escalated, the *New York Times* launched a clearly coordinated, sequential counteroffensive that it seems safe to assume was prompted by the Obama Administration. On May 5, a page-one news story entitled "Lessons of Iraq Help US Fight a Drug War in Honduras," celebrated three new "forward operating bases" working through Foreign-Deployed Advisory and Support Teams (FAST) in Honduras, through which US security forces, including personnel from the Drug Enforcement Administration (DEA), were working with the Honduran government to fight drug traffickers, doing so with a "discreet footprint," given what it called the "messy" history of US military support for the Contra war during the 1980s.[22] Three days later, the *Times* ran an online debate, "Should US Troops Fight the War on Drugs?" Of the six opinions solicited from experts, five answered yes, albeit counseling care in deploying troops.[23] That same day, Sunday, May 8, the *New York Times Magazine* ran a slick spread celebrating the Hondurans' Model Cities proposal, entitled "Who Wants to Buy Honduras?" complete with an outrageous cartoon that depicted a broad green jungle, punctuated only by a tiny city in the middle, rising amid construction cranes. A yellow plane flew over the city carrying a banner reading "THE NEW HONDURAS, EST. 2010." In front, a sign poked up out of the jungle reading "GOOD HONDURAS," with an arrow pointing toward the city, and "BAD HONDURAS," with an arrow pointing off the page. A second sign read: "WELCOME TO THE NEW HONDURAS (DON'T WORRY, IT'S NOT REALLY HONDURAS)."[24] (As the columnist Dave Barry loved to say, I am not making this up.)

A week later, it all blew up in the Obama Administration's face. At two in the morning on May 15, 2012, two State Department helicopters carrying Honduran security forces and US "advisors" from a DEA FAST team shot and killed four Afro-Indigenous Honduran civilians—two of them pregnant—and injured four others. The victims had been traveling peacefully in a long narrow boat up the Patuca river, near Ahuas, in the Moskitia region of northeastern Honduras. At first, Honduran papers reported the incident as a successful joint DEA-Honduran raid that had killed drug traffickers. But local villagers, including the mayor of Ahuas, soon insisted that the victims were not drug traffickers at all, rather just ordinary people using the cool hours of the middle of night to travel home with their purchases from the coast, as locals did regularly.[25] After Honduran human rights groups raised an alarm, Bloomberg News and the Associated Press picked up the story; the AP started reporting on it extensively; the *New York Times* sent someone down to interview victims, and quickly it was big news that the DEA had killed innocent civilians in Honduras.[26] On May 22, the AP further reported that US and Honduran forces had not only shot up the victims in the boats but, in a terrifying commando raid afterward, had also gone on to terrorize and interrogate local people on the ground in the town of Ahuas.[27]

Faced with repeated questioning at its daily press briefings, the State Department insisted that the DEA agents had participated in the attack only in an advisory capacity, that the victims were drug traffickers, and that the victims had fired on DEA agents seated in another boat. It denied US responsibility for the deaths and injuries. In a famous exchange at the May 17 briefing, the AP's Matt Lee threw question after question back at spokesperson Victoria Nuland. "The US DEA was involved only in a supporting role.... We were involved purely supporting and advising," declared Nuland.

> QUESTION: Well, does that mean that they advised them to open fire on a canoe carrying civilians with a pregnant woman and—
>
> MS. NULAND: Well, I highly—
>
> QUESTION: Well, I don't understand—you say they're in an

advice and support role. So what did they advise and support? Did they—

MS. NULAND: Well, again, I—

QUESTION: Did they tell—did they say, hey, this looks like a good target; shoot it?

MS. NULAND: Well, first of all, as I understand it, the Honduran authorities are taking—are doing a broad investigation of this incident to evaluate what exactly happened and how it happened. So I think we need to let that go forward.[28]

In the aftermath, rather than conduct its own, in-depth investigation of the entire incident, the State Department deferred to the corrupt Honduran government's own investigation. But that investigation was incompetent, corrupt, and extremely limited. In the most glaring example, a month after the incident, Honduran authorities conducted a botched autopsy on one of the victims, during which her rotting body parts fell out of the tomb onto a plastic tarp. The Honduran government then used its autopsy report to insist that the woman wasn't in fact pregnant—an argument obviously irrelevant to the issue of how she was killed, but designed, rather, to impugn the surviving victims' testimonies.[29]

In August, Annie Bird, then of Rights Action, and Alexander Main of CEPR, with help from Karen Spring, published a fifty-eight-page report, extensively documenting the victims' stories and the available evidence. They confirmed the victims' version while underscoring the Honduran government's vast incompetence in handling the case. Nonetheless, the US State Department continued to deny responsibility and stuck to its version of events. When high-ranking senators and members of Congress continued to question what had actually happened, State Department officials trotted around Congress showing truncated parts of a surveillance video that had been taken from an accompanying airplane. They claimed that the video showed the victims deliberately ramming their boat against a second boat with US agents aboard, while shooting at them. Insisting the video was classified information, the administration never allowed the public to see it.[30]

Five years later, in May 2017, the Offices of the Inspector General of the Departments of Justice and State would issue a four-hundred-twenty-four-page report that blew the administration's response out of the water. It vindicated the victims' version forcefully: they weren't drug traffickers, the Inspectors General reported. DEA agents had in fact been in the helicopter yelling at the Honduran forces to "FIRE, FIRE" on the victims in the boat. The video, the investigation reported, didn't show any fire from the victims' boat at all—but it did show shots from the other boat, aimed at the victims. The Inspectors General concluded that both the DEA and the State Department had misinformed and misled Congress and the public and then obstructed the subsequent investigation.[31]

When the news broke in May 2012 about the DEA incident, the administration's spin control couldn't black out media coverage of what had happened, nor the outrage at what the United States had done. Not only was US support for repressive Honduran security forces widely challenged by this point, but now US direct forces were implicated in killings within Honduras.

In August, I got an email from an editor at *Foreign Affairs*—as mainstream and upstanding a publication as you can get—asking me to write an article about US policy in Honduras for its website.[32] At that point I knew for sure that the public debate over US policy in Honduras had changed altogether. But, again, the dark side loomed: in response to my *New York Times* article and a cover story I wrote for *The Nation*, Miguel Facussé, the Honduran palm oil magnate, wrote me three formal hostile letters, in the third of which he threatened to sue me for character defamation. In the Honduran context, that was close to a lethal threat.[33]

Houston, We've Got a Problem

For the first time since the immediate post-coup period, this exploding media coverage and congressional pushback about Honduras put the Obama Administration on the defensive. As early as mid-January 2012, you could almost hear the alarm bells whooping inside State Department Headquarters in Foggy Bottom: "Houston, we've got a problem."

On January 18, President Lobo flew on short notice to Miami, where the United States Southern Command is headquartered, to meet with "senior US officials" in order "to review security cooperation and acknowledge the leadership and efforts that President Lobo and the Honduran Congress have taken to improve citizen security," the State Department announced. Its press release was all praise for Lobo: "Over the past several months, Honduras has strengthened its legal framework to better combat organized crime, appointing judges with national jurisdiction, approving a security tax, authorizing wiretapping, and establishing a police advisory board, among other reforms," as well as planning to reform and strengthen the police. In this missive, the administration did acknowledge—for the first time—that Honduras in fact had a security crisis necessitating reform. But it also blessed two new, dangerous measures that had just been passed by the Honduran Congress, both of which had been roundly denounced by the Honduran human rights community: first, a new security tax, through which all electronic financial transactions within the country, including credit card payments and account transfers, would be taxed five percent, with proceeds from the tax going into a new, centrally controlled security fund that had zero transparency; and second, a wiretapping law that authorized increased surveillance by the very same security forces that were committing human rights abuses.[34]

Next began a parade of US officials down to Honduras. On February 7, Oliver Garza, a high-level official in the State Department's anti-narcotics bureau, appeared in Honduras for meetings with President Lobo, the US Ambassador, and other officials, and took up office in the embassy. He had a murky past: in 2001, Garza had been implicated in an incident in which three thousand AK-47s were shipped from Central America to Colombian paramilitaries.[35] In late February, the White House announced that Vice President Biden would be traveling to Mexico and Honduras March 4 through 6. It framed Biden's visit within an exploding debate about the drug war. Guatemalan Otto Perez Molina had just announced his support for decriminalization, challenging US policy overtly, while criticisms of the destructive impact of the US-funded militarized drug war in Mexico escalated.[36] In the Honduran context, Biden's visit, combined with other administration initiatives, sought to adeptly reframe the police corruption scandal, the murder rate statistics, and alarm over human rights abuses by US-funded security forces, all within the rubric of the drug war: police killings were subsumed under a generic "security crisis," and the "security crisis" was in turn the result of drug trafficking. Therefore, the US needed to continue, even increase, security assistance to Honduras, rather than suspend it. In late March, William Brownfield, Assistant Secretary of State for International Narcotics and Law Enforcement Affairs (the Honduran papers referred to him as "*El Zar Antidrogas*"), flew down to reaffirm US support for Honduras and address issues of organized crime, citizen security, and human rights.[37]

After the letter led by Representative Schakowsky went public, though, the State Department did newly admit to human rights concerns. Julissa Reynosa, Deputy Assistant Secretary of State for Western Hemisphere Affairs, traveled to Honduras and struck a more critical tone in her public comments, expressing concerns about impunity, human rights violations, and especially the killings of LGBTI people and journalists.[38]

At the same time, the State Department was moving quickly behind the scenes to encourage the Honduran government to reform its police. Two new Honduran commissions, designed ostensibly to clean up the Honduran police after the killing of the rector's son and his friend, had already failed utterly. By August 2012, though, after several months of work, only eighteen members of the force had been prosecuted nationwide.[39] In early 2012, the United States promoted the creation of a seemingly more powerful body, the Commission for the Reform of Public Security (CRSP, Comisión de Reforma de la Seguridad Pública), to which the Honduran government granted a broad mandate: investigate corrupt police and members of the military, and recommend deep changes to the country's police training and education systems. Its members were apparently handpicked by the State Department. The chair, sociologist Victor Meza, was a former Communist with complex centrist politics, viewed by the embassy prior to the coup as generally friendly to the United States. The other members ranged from left to right: Matías Funes, a historian at the UNAH with progressive leanings; Adam Blackwell, a mainstream Canadian diplomat at the Organization of American States; Jorge Omar Casco, a conservative Honduran judge and law professor; and Achilles Blu, a Chilean general who had been linked to money laundering and drug traffickers.[40]

President Lobo's own answer to the policing crisis, though, was to send in the military to conduct domestic policing, first in sporadic forays, then through increasingly broad mobilizations that gradually extended into months and months. In November 2011, the Honduran Congress voted to interpret the Constitution to allow an expanded role of the military into policing. On April 24, Lobo extended the military's new mandate for a second six weeks.[41]

Meanwhile, congressional criticisms of US policy continued to mount. On March 5, Senator Barbara Mikulski of Maryland, the second-highest-ranking member of the Committee on Appropriations, led seven colleagues on the first letter to issue from the Senate questioning human rights and US policy in Honduras. On May 31 Representative Jan Schakowsky and sixteen other members of the House sent President Lobo a letter expressing their alarm over attacks on human rights defenders, especially in the Aguán Valley. First-term Representative Jared Polis led on a June 26 letter to Secretary of State Hillary Clinton, raising concern about the rash of killings of LGBTI people with impunity. That letter included among its eighty-four co-signers several top-level figures who hadn't yet appeared on sign-on letters about human rights in Honduras, including Representatives Howard Berman, Adam Schiff, and Deborah Wasserman-Schultz.

On May 21, the Honduran government, as the centerpiece of its commitment to cleaning up the police, announced the appointment of a new National Director of Police, Juan Carlos Bonilla, known as "El Tigre" (The Tiger). US Ambassador Lisa Kubiske welcomed him in a tweet.[42]

Rumors had been circulating about "El Tigre" Bonilla for years. In 2011, Bonilla had been the subject of an internal investigation, which established his oversight of death squads inside the Honduran police, that killed alleged gang members as part of "social cleansing" campaigns between 1998 and 2001, while he was a regional police chief. One witness testified to investigators that he had informed Bonilla on the phone of the capture of an alleged gang leader, and Bonilla had instructed the witness: "You've got him. You know what to do." While on the phone with Bonilla, the witness heard loud gunshots, which he then reported to Bonilla, who said, "It's done. Let's go take a look." The victim's body was found right after that in a car that had crashed into a wall. As a result of the investigation, Bonilla had been placed on leave for two years, beginning in 2003, while he supposedly received treatment for mental health issues. María Luisa Borjas, the police inspector who was running the investigation—and who in 2011 and in later years be so outspoken in her criticisms of police corruption—charged at the time that her work had been shut down by top officials, including then-Minister of Security Oscar Álvarez. She herself was suspended after she called a news conference to protest the investigation's closure.[43]

When Bonilla was later named National Director of Police, in 2012, the Associated Press got its hands on Borjas's report, confirmed its validity, and, on June 1, broke the story about his death squad past.[44] Now the news up north and around the world wasn't just that the United States was funding repressive Honduran security forces and killing civilians with its own security agents; it was also in bed with a death squad leader at the very top of the entire Honduran police force. The US role in Honduras was sounding more and more like the 1980s.

But Bonilla stayed on at the top of the police nonetheless. A 1998 US law known as the Leahy Law specifies that if the US government receives credible evidence that a US-funded individual or unit has committed gross violations of human rights and is not being brought to justice, it must immediately suspend all aid and cooperation with that individual or unit. It also requires that US-funded forces be vetted for criminal backgrounds before receiving assistance.[45] On May 22, the day after Bonilla was appointed, an AP reporter at the State Department's daily press briefing asked spokesperson Victoria Nuland a question about Leahy Law enforcement regarding the Ahuas DEA killings. Nuland replied that she had no knowledge of the Leahy Law being currently applied in Honduras.[46] With that reply, the State Department thus ignored the documented evidence against Bonilla—on top of the vast, documented evidence by this point of human rights abuses by Honduran security forces in hundreds of other cases. We can also ask, moreover, whether US Ambassador Kubiske knew about the evidence against Bonilla at the time she tweeted to welcome his appointment.

Congress had placed human rights conditions on twenty percent of security aid to Honduras in the 2012 State and Foreign Operations Appropriations Act, holding back funds until the State Department could certify that advances had been made in freedom of expression, freedom of association, the rule of law, and other fronts. To its shame, in the second week of August the State Department certified that those conditions had been met. But deep in the middle of the certification document was one small paragraph:

> The Department is aware of allegations of human rights violations related to Police Chief Juan Carlos Bonilla's service a decade ago, and has established a working group to investigate thoroughly the allegations against him to ensure compliance with the Leahy Law. While this investigation is ongoing, we are carefully limiting assistance to special Honduran law enforcement units, staffed by Leahy-vetted Honduran personnel who receive training, guidance, and advice directly from US law enforcement, and are not under Bonilla's direct supervision.[47]

The AP got its hands on the document, and on Saturday morning, August 11, broke the news that the US had withheld money from Bonilla because he was an alleged death squad leader. On Sunday, El Tigre Bonilla went on *Frente a Frente*, the most prominent political TV show in Honduras, and said it was all lies invented by the AP and that anyone who repeated the charges against him was a criminal and should be treated as one. The show's host, Edgar Melgar, assured the audience that official US government sources had confirmed that at no point had the US decided to suspend aid to El Tigre. The US Embassy itself remained silent. Finally, on Monday afternoon, it confirmed that the State Department's certification document was real and that the funds for Bonilla had indeed been withheld. But it made no further comment. The Associated Press reported that day that Senator John Kerry, at the time the Chair of the Senate Foreign Relations Committee, "said it was 'prudent' to limit aid until questions about Bonilla are resolved."[48]

The US-funded and US-fought drug war in Honduras continued to degenerate that summer. On June 23, during a drug interdiction incident, Honduran forces working with a DEA FAST team member killed a suspect who was lying on the ground, allegedly after the subject reached toward a gun. On July 3, when another suspected drug plane crashed near Catamacas, Honduras, US and Honduran authorities took a pilot into custody. When a second pilot allegedly began to move back into the plane, US FAST team members then shot two rounds into him; he later died of his wounds. The Inspectors General's investigation five years later reported that Bonilla had allegedly ordered that a gun be planted among the evidence. The DEA knew at the time but covered it up.[49]

The situation spiraled farther and farther out of control. On July 28 and 31, the Honduran Air Force shot down two alleged drug planes that had been flying over the Caribbean, in violation of international protocols and using intelligence obtained form the United States through Colombia. In mid-August, the United States stopped sharing radar intelligence with Honduras—the first public admission that things were going terribly, terribly wrong there.[50] The basic premises of the militarized drug war nonetheless remained largely unchallenged. In the administration's logic, killing drug traffickers was okay, implicitly; the only problem was if innocent "civilians" were unjustly hurt or if international protocols about shooting down planes were not properly followed. Due process, a trial, orderly punishment—all of that dropped by the wayside if the victim was indeed transporting drugs.

The climax of that arc of scandal, corruption, death, and congressional challenges came on October 12, when the *New York Times* ran an extensive page one story, "U.S. Rethinks a Drug War After Deaths in Honduras"—a long, long way from its celebratory stories the prevous spring. The article opened with the Honduran Air Force shooting down the two planes in late July, and prominently reported that the United States, in response, had stopped cooperating with the Honduran authorities: "All joint operations in Honduras are now suspended," the *Times* reported. That was bombshell enough. But the bigger news followed: Senator Patrick Leahy,

> expressing the concerns of several Democrats in Congress, is holding up tens of millions of dollars in security assistance, not just because of the planes but also over suspected human rights abuses by the Honduran police and three shootings in which commandos with the United States Drug Enforcement Administration effectively led raids when they were only supposed to act as advisors.

Tens of millions of dollars suspended.[51] For the first time, Congress had not just advocated stopping the flow of money to Honduras, but actually done so.

By that fall of 2012, the US role in Honduras was all over the news; Houston did, indeed, have a really big problem. Once the media started covering Honduras thoroughly, the horrors popped out one after another. People I knew in the Honduran Resistance would sometimes remark after the coup, "They do our work for us," meaning that the ongoing repression and corruption by the government was so blatant, it made the case against the regime easy. That season of 2012, between the prison fire, the appointment of El Tigre Bonilla, the DEA massacre, and the shooting down of the drug planes, the US and Honduran governments indeed did much of the work for us. Without the new media coverage in the north, though, much of that would have remained under the cloak of darkness.

Climb Every Mountain

Congress roared back at the Obama Administration. But it didn't just wake itself up and decide on its own to speak out about Honduras policy. Behind the curtain, hundreds, even thousands, of US activists educated, cajoled, and pressured individual members of Congress, senators, and their staffers. Those staffers in turn chose to take on the project of human rights and US policy in Honduras. A hive of invisible labor made possible every statement, every letter to the Secretary of State, every human rights condition placed on aid.

The curtain in front of who actually did the work inside Congress can only be pulled back part way, however. An array of Byzantine rules mandates silence about the processes that actually go on inside Congress and perpetuates the collective myth that it was the congressperson or senator who produced an outcome seemingly singlehandedly. Breaking those rules can destroy an aide's career or mean that aides refuse to work with outsiders who don't respect the rules. Much of the labor that produced congressional action is necessarily confidential for entirely different reasons, moreover: the Department of State, White House, Department of Defense, an array of intelligence agencies of the US government, the Honduran government and its oligarchs, and many other actors would all like to know more about how, exactly, Congress came to challenge them, often successfully. Moreover, being identified as having communicated with the US Congress is extremely dangerous for Hondurans who come to Washington to speak out about human rights; they have been repeatedly and publicly attacked by Honduran government officials, including President Juan Orlando Hernández, as "bad Hondurans" who lie about their country and cause it damage. Even if it were safe or acceptable to tell all, much of which happened in Congress about Honduras policy still remains unclear. There are curtains beyond curtains, but I can only draw back a few.

Before the coup, to be honest, I was one of those people who thought that writing to your member of Congress was largely a waste of time. I thought Congress was so bought off by corporate money that there was little purpose in trying to move it. In my political life, and in my teaching as a history professor, I largely put my faith in grassroots social movements that change the world from below. But two years into the coup, I started seriously rethinking my attitude toward congressional work. I couldn't see how anything I was doing so far was going to translate into a change in US policy—the Obama Administration wasn't exactly heeding the advice I doled out in my articles. I still kept asking myself: what powers do I myself have to stop this? So, I decided to try Congress.

In February 2011, I made a first serious foray to Washington. I had no idea what I was doing. My knowledge of concrete political processes was close to nil. (My niece helpfully passed along an animated clip from *Schoolhouse Rock* about how a bill becomes a law.)[52] I honestly thought that I should just go in there and simply ask congressmembers and senators to roll back the coup. And they would figure out how to do that—what did I know, after all? Instead, I found out, you were supposed to have an "ask," a specific, concrete request of an aide, that you had decided on yourself in advance. In meetings, I knew I was often being an idiot and was always nervous. But as I started flying back and forth to D.C. regularly every few months, I learned ropes fast, in a second big post-coup learning curve.

The congressional office buildings were like giant rabbit warrens, inside which I usually lost all sense of direction. Meetings with aides might take place in the office's front reception area, perched on the edge of little black leather couches in front of other visitors; or standing up in the hall outside, making it impossible to take or read notes; or in the congressperson's or senator's spacious, high-ceilinged personal office, tastefully decorated with artwork representing the virtues of his or her home district. Some of the offices had snacks arrayed on the receptionists' desks, purveying further delights of the district—Jelly Bellies from Illinois (Senator Richard Durbin), Raisin Bran from Michigan (Senator Deborah Stabenow), peanuts from Georgia (Representative Hank Johnson).

Specialized language expanded infinitely. The aides had a finely tuned hierarchy of job titles, often used in abbreviated form, which I learned to decode, more or less, in order to assess the measure of power each held, like LC (Legislative Correspondent) and LA

(Legislative Assistant but also Legislative Aide, one of which is higher than the other, but I can't remember which). In the Senate there was the Committee on Foreign Relations (SFRC) but in the House it was called Foreign Affairs instead. Most important was the Appropriations Committee ("Approps") and especially its Subcommittee on State and Foreign Operations (known as "State and Foreign Operations" or SFOPS, pronounced Ess-Fops). Representative Nancy Pelosi, the Democratic Minority Leader, was referred to as The Leader—which to me sounded like "Fearless Leader," the Russian conniver in Rocky and Bullwinkle cartoons of my childhood. Hillary Clinton was "The Secretary," the State Department was "State," while the Defense Department was DoD (pronounced dee-oh-dee), Labor was DoL, and Justice was DoJ. My favorite was when aides referred to the reprsentatives they worked for as "the member," regardless of gender. Otherwise they referred to "my boss" and I reciprocated by calling "the member" "your boss." I was taught not to speak of "power" but instead of "the ability to get things done."

I was walking into—and flailing about in—a welter of seemingly ancient but unwritten rituals, codes, and etiquettes. The basic rule underlying everything was that I had zero "ability to get things done" and had to defer to every single aide I met with. I was, by definition, begging. Almost all of us, in turn, tippy-toed around the members and senators much of the time, as if they were gods come down to earth, in so doing perpetuating a culture of hierarchy and deference that should have no place in a democratic society, let alone in the buildings where that supposed democracy is concretely enacted.

It turned out I loved the thrill of the chase: searching every byway and gradually moving deeper and further upward to meet with higher-ranking aides or even, eventually, representatives and senators themselves. I confess I also loved those pretentious build-ings, despite the fact that they were designed to legitimate and celebrate a Congress that has historically been the playing field of moneyed powers. Just like everyone else, I fell for the symbolism, the glamour, the star-watching, while simultaneously keeping a running critique in my head the whole time: of the architecture that delib-erately evoked the Roman Empire; of the glossy paintings of slave-holding founding fathers, senators and cabinet officers; and of the army of working-class people of color, especially African Americans, working as security guards, cafeteria servers, and room cleaners for a Congress that was largely white, male, and elite.

I did like that it was okay to be a strong, smart, older woman—an acceptable and even somewhat respected category on the Hill, the legacy of the powerhouse women in the Senate and House who were now in their seventies and even eighties in some cases. I watched them on CSPAN to see how they dressed and how they carried themselves. I had a bright turquoise polyester blazer with flat black plastic buttons down the front that I called my Hillary Clinton jacket. I joked that I was going to be Hillary for Halloween. One afternoon I was sitting on a granite bench in the atrium inside the Hart Senate Office Building, my face turned rightward to talk with a colleague. A voice from the left suddenly inquired, "Hillary?" I turned to see a highpowered-looking white man in his forties, in a well-cut suit. "No, I'm sorry, my name's not Hillary," I replied. As he saw my face, he apologized, mortified, and started to run away. It dawned on me, "Did you mean Hillary *Clinton*?" But by the time I asked, he was already headed for the exit like a bat out of hell.

But the whole thing had a formidable and chilling downside. I was disturbed to learn that much of the foreign policy of the United States Congress is developed by twenty-six-year-olds who, however well-trained or well-meaning, are each responsible for US relations with the entire world (although in the Senate they might only have half the world)—with the exception of committee staffers, who are more specialized and who just have entire regions. Those aides answered, in turn, to Legislative Directors and Chiefs of Staff, but in these early years I rarely had access to high-ranking staffers, let alone the members and senators themselves. Although maybe a third of the aides I met with were caring and helpful, another third would listen to what I had to say for half an hour with a blank stare without asking a single question, not take a single note, and do nothing afterward. Another third would be outright hostile or contemptuous. A good many of the younger aides were swelled up with their own power and the sheer volume of people kissing their feet.

In 2011, before the media coverage of Honduras changed, the great majority of aides gave me looks that said, "No way is what you're saying true"—that the US-funded military and police were killing people with complete impunity or beating the pulp out of peacefully demonstrating teachers. Even some of the more engaged aides—and we're only talking about a handful of people in the entire Congress at that point—might subtly communicate that while they now believed what I'd told them in our previous meeting, what I was currently reporting was too farfetched to be true.

Some aides actually worked for the State Department itself, in a clear violation of the constitutional separation of powers. The State Department offers year-long "fellows" as free labor to key Senate and sometimes House offices. These staffers return to careers at State once the fellowship is over. Some of the State Department fellows were extremely supportive, even though my projects were overtly critical of the administration. Others promoted the State Department's line exactly—I could tell that they'd be on the phone to State within minutes of our meeting, recounting my arguments and activities. All of them, however sincere their concerns about the issues, ultimately had to serve two masters.

I was constantly reminded that much of what took place around me within those halls of power was loathsome. I could feel the cold currents of money flowing all round me. Once, waiting for a staffer for the House Committee on Labor and Education, I watched three white men in beautifully cut gray suits tell the receptionist they were from Apple. What exactly were they selling—or, rather, buying? All through the big wide halls I saw clusters of three or four middle-aged lobbyists, usually white men, with maybe one white woman or one African American man, in that same kind of gray suit, conspiring before their meetings, especially on days when the members and senators were in town. I thought of them collectively as The Oil and Gas Lobby. One day I picked up a crisp business card from the floor of the Hart building, and it was actually from a representative of ExxonMobil.

The halls swelled with military men, too, pedaling who-knows-what murderous war in uniforms so dripping with medals and broad gold epaulets that their jackets looked like they could stand up by themselves. And, of course, there were scary Republicans lurking in every corner and behind more than half the office doors. Representative Ileana Ros-Lehtinen, the Cuban-American from Florida who flew to Honduras after the coup to support de facto President Micheletti, smiled at me once outside an elevator, clueless as to who I was.[53]

But I wasn't so clean myself, either. As I climbed that Hill, I could feel the dark side grow inside me, too, like the evil snake deep inside Harry Potter. I bowed and scraped before the senators and members just like everyone else; I name-dropped, eavesdropped, calculated, connived. I enjoyed laughing at that clueless smile from Ros-Lehtinen—even though she was actually quite progressive on LGBTI issues. I loved the battle a little too much. In many ways I was no different from those corporate lobbyists, whom I could sometimes see clutching my same spiral-bound congressional directory. Was I warm and charming because I sincerely liked an aide and wanted a human connection? Or because I wanted his or her boss to sign a letter questioning US support for Honduran security forces? Where did one stop and the other begin? I could pull heartstrings for hours with concrete stories of my Honduran friends and horrible things that had happened to them and their children. But as I deployed every tool of persuasion I had in order to try to keep them alive, I felt tainted myself. Was that the price of the ticket?

Nothing I experienced was unique—half the world was watching *House of Cards* obsessively during those same years, after all—but this was me it was happening to. At the end of every week of five or six meetings a day, I'd get on my plane to faraway California, battered from the contempt and the moral compromises, from repeating all those Honduran atrocities and, most of all, from the seeming impossibility, still, of actually changing US policy, and I'd swear to everyone I knew that I was never coming back.

Tools of the Trade

The whole point of going to the Hill was to use congressional pressure to influence Honduran policy at the White House and the Department of State. To my endless surprise, my colleagues and I did, in fact, unleash a measure of power; or, as they say, we got things done.

The first task was educating aides and members, continuously. We spent an enormous amount of tedious, unromantic time on email, forwarding and translating news articles, reports from human rights groups, and State Department missives; framing the latest news in bullet points; and analyzing developments in Honduras and in US policy. It usually took two or three requests—sometimes five—to an aide to obtain a meeting. Maybe a third of the aides queried never replied to requests. We also helped Honduran human rights activists who traveled to Washington meet with aides and members themselves. The Hondurans, of course, could speak with a direct authority far beyond ours. In order for those meetings to happen, colleagues in D.C. did the quotidian, invisible work of setting up the appointments, arranging the visitors' housing and meals, translating for them, and shepherding them around not just on the Hill but to meetings at the Inter-American Commission on Human Rights, the World Bank, the State Department, and to brown-bag lunches and receptions with nonprofit groups (NGOs) in D.C.

If we could then get an aide to care, our easiest ask was that his or her boss contact State and express concern about reports the member had received regarding human rights abuses in Honduras. We asked members to sponsor briefings, usually organized and chaired by NGO activists who lived in D.C., at which Hondurans and US experts presented analyses of the human rights context in Honduras. Committee hearings would have been the next step above that, but we never got that far, since Republicans controlled the House beginning in 2011, and we weren't strong enough in the Senate, where the Democrats were in the majority at the time. The one exception was the Tom Lantos Human Rights Commission, which is bipartisan. It was co-chaired by Representative James McGovern, Democrat from Massachusetts, a decades-long, dedicated champion of human rights in Latin America, and Republican Representative Frank Wolf of Virginia, of that rare, and dying breed of Republicans who seriously cared about human rights.

On July 25, 2010, Padre Melo (Reverend Ismael Moreno Coto, SJ), the Jesuit intellectual and Director of Radio Progreso, spoke at a hearing of the Tom Lantos Commission on press freedom, at the invitation of McGovern.[54] Representative Sam Farr, from my own district, attended the briefing himself, and was deeply moved by what Padre Melo said. After Padre Melo returned to Honduras, he and Radio Progreso got death threats, presumably in response to his testimony. Desperate to make something happen, I hunted down Farr at the annual Labor Day picnic of the Monterey Bay Central Labor Council. I finally nailed him for ten minutes at a picnic table, under the shadow of the redwood trees, while he ate his barbecue-grilled chicken and garlic bread, and told him about the death threats since Padre Melo's testimony. I could see him visibly shudder. "Send me something," Farr said. The next day Alexander Main of the Center for Economic Policy Research (CEPR) and I worked on letter from Farr to Secretary Clinton. Twenty-nine additional members signed that first letter from Representatives, which requested a suspension of police and military aid to the Honduran government until human rights abuses had been addressed.[55]

By the spring of 2011, when I started traveling to D.C. and working more centrally in Congress, a team of us working on Honduras had begun to coalesce: Alex from CEPR, Annie Bird of Rights Action, and myself, soon joined by Jean Stokan, Justice Director of the Sisters of Mercy of the Americas, and Jenny Atlee, of the Quixote Center and then Friendship Office of the Americas—both sophisticated veterans of Central America solidarity work during the 1980s. All four had been doing work on Honduras in Congress since right after the coup, long before I jumped in. We were joined by expanding circles of other activists, especially from School of the Americas Watch and Witness for Peace. It was never a formal grouping, more like fluid partnerships formed ad hoc to work on specific projects.

As we started eliciting letters and other initiatives in the House, I was definitely still groping in the dark about how to work Congress.

I made all kinds of mortifying mistakes, to which I will not here confess. We played a thousand guessing games with no clear answers. How often could you bother an aide who'd promised something but not gotten back to you? When were you supposed to call, when did you email? Sometimes a staffer would agree enthusiastically to do a letter or publish an op-ed, and we'd write drafts—which took long, arduous days to produce, including factchecking—and receive an encouraging response, but the project would never come to fruition. The offices were just too overwhelmed with other issues. The average time from request to actually emitting a letter or statement from a member was maybe six months, although the individual letters from members, press statements, statements for the *Congressional Record*, and floor speeches that we helped shake loose often happened within a week, especially in urgent situations. At least half the projects we worked hard on never saw the light of day.

By 2012, a nationwide system was in place for harvesting signatures on sign-on letters. At its center was the Honduran Solidarity Network (HSN), a loosely organized network of national-level peace and social justice groups, regional Latin American solidarity groups, and faith-based coalitions, including Witness for Peace, School of the Americas Watch, Rights Action, the Chicago Religious Leadership Network on the Americas, Chicago's La Voz de los de Abajo, the Alliance for Global Justice, the Marin Interfaith Task Force on the Americas, and other groups all over the United States and Canada, organized almost entirely online through a discussion list, its members in regular contact with Hondurans in the opposition. Solidarity activists included Hondurans living in the United States, Honduran Americans, Salvadorans and Salvadoran Americans, and an array of other Americans and Canadians. In contrast to some other prominent organizations working on US Latin America policy, the Honduras solidarity world was horizontal in its internal structure, informal in its coordination, and not based on Washington, D.C.; it extended, moreover, far beyond the organizations formally affiliated with the Honduras Solidarity Network to include all kinds of individuals like myself. That made possible an engaged, nationwide base of activists who themselves had their own direct communications with

Hondurans activists and organizations within the country, often in long-term partnerships.

When the congressional work really took off, in 2012, members of the HSN already had three years of dedicated grassroots work under their belts. They hosted weeks-long speaking tours by Honduran activists such as Miriam Miranda and Luther Castillo of OFRANEH, educating a sea of local activists about Honduras. They put in the equally painstaking work of organizing and leading delegations of US activists from the peace, labor, social justice communities, who traveled to Honduras to meet with Honduran human rights defenders, campesinos in the Aguán, Afro-Indigenous and Indigenous land rights defenders, and many others.[56]

Members of the HSN also regularly organized emergency action alerts when individuals or groups were illegally detained by authorities, threatened, or otherwise at grave risk. Those alerts, in turn, were made possible by international solidarity activists in Honduras doing the work of accompanying at-risk Hondurans in their daily lives. A tight system was in place: within minutes of an alert being issued, dozens, sometimes hundreds of people in the network would then call the State Department, the US Embassy in Tegucigalpa, Honduran authorities, or all three. Somehow members of the network from time to time got their hands on the direct phone numbers of topmost figures in the Honduran government, such as the Minister of Security or the head of the Armed Forces, who would actually answer their phones and talk to activists at length, in some cases fabricating elaborate lies—like insisting that no one had been detained. By 2014 the network had a full-time staffer in Tegucigalpa, Karen Spring, who by that point brought years of experience as a researcher and advocate.

When a congressional letter began to circulate for signatures, a formidable get-out-the-vote machine drawing on this base kicked in. Gary Cozette, a longtime faith-based activist with the Chicago Religious Leadership Network on Latin America, built a district-by-district list, matching representatives with local activist constituents. Working with a committee of the Honduras Solidarity Network, he kept up a barrage of personalized emails encouraging people to ask their members to sign a letter, then cheer-led to the whole HSN list as each new signature rolled in, goading us to pull in higher and higher numbers. In later years, Elise Roberts of Witness for Peace Midwest took on the task. It was a great, collective joy to watch the congressional signatures roll in over the course of a three-week, hard-fought campaign, in which each of us could feel the power of hundreds of others we'd never met in most cases, all pulling together.

Powerhouse national organizations also endorsed the letters and helped garner signatures. In the years following the coup, the Sisters of Mercy of the Americas made Honduras their top foreign policy priority in their social justice work and were essential in encouraging Catholic and other faith-based congressmembers and senators to question US policy in Honduras.[57] From the day of the coup onward, the AFL-CIO was adamant in publicly condemning US policy and in supporting the resistance. On September 13, 2009, the AFL-CIO passed a resolution at its national convention denouncing the coup and calling for an end to all US assistance to the Honduran government, the withdrawal of the US ambassador, and revocation of the visas of the top coup leaders. In November 2009, AFL-CIO President Richard Trumka put out a public statement condemning the illegitimate elections. Its Solidarity Center continuously lent support to trade unions in Honduras, especially in the maquiladora and agricultural sectors. In October 2014 top-level leaders of the AFL-CIO went on a delegation to Honduras in support of a complaint filed with the US Labor Department about labor violations under the Central American Free Trade Agreement (CAFTA). Its report condemned not just the lack of basic labor rights, but militarization and the destruction of the rule of law.[58]

Other nongovernmental organizations in Washington did extremely important advocacy work on Honduras as well, especially the Latin America Working Group (LAWG), which persistently publicized human rights abuses and helped originate some of the earlier letters from the House—although it more hesitantly endorsed the "suspend the aid" demand and was less comfortable than my friends and I were with overt criticism of US policy on some fronts. LAWG, along with the HSN, also originated multiple sign-on letters from NGOs and other groups to the State Department, especially from faith-based groups.[59]

The Washington Office on Latin America (WOLA), by contrast, in 2009 remained famously aloof from the Resistance and those who vigorously opposed the coup. Although WOLA did condemn the coup and criticize the November 2009 elections, it worked to construct a third-way leadership group within Honduras that was neither Zelaya nor Micheletti, undermining the goal of Zelaya's return as legitimate president. When President Lobo came into office in early 2010, a representative of WOLA testified before the House Committee on Foreign Affairs that the United States should restore security aid that had been partially suspended after the coup because a new government of "national reconciliation" was in place, echoing the State Department's phrasing. In the years since, WOLA never supported suspending security aid, although it supported conditioned aid. (Only in December 2017, in the aftermath of the post-election repression, did WOLA for the first time call for security funding to be suspended.) In 2012 and 2013, after the police scandal broke, WOLA worked with the State Department to help coordinate over $200 million in new aid to the Honduran police— for the purpose of reforming the police—while El Tigre Bonilla was the national director.[60]

Many activists in the United States who were deeply committed to combating US policy on Honduras, and who agreed with the demand to suspend security aid, chose nonetheless not to do work pressuring Congress, preferring to focus on other strategies. It's important to note, as well, that serious barriers blocked many people from doing congressional work, should they have wanted to. To visit the Hill, you needed to live in Washington, D.C., or have access to travel funds or time away from paid work and family responsibilities. Once there, conversations and emails with aides usually happened in fast-paced, high-powered English (with the exception of meetings with visiting Hondurans, which we translated). Those factors alone prohibited most Hondurans living in the United States from engaging directly with Congress. Much grassroots constituent pressure did take place at the district level, where the barriers to entry were somewhat lower. But even there, undocumented Honduran immigrants—a big hunk of Hondurans in the United States—would think twice about walking into a local government building and speaking truth to a representative of US governmental power.

By mid-2012, as Representatives Schakowsky, Farr, and McGovern stepped forward to take leadership roles on Honduras, and our demands coalesced around suspending police and military aid, we turned to building a broader base of leadership by focusing on specific issues that could help reach out to wider constituencies. In June 2012, we worked with Representatives Jared Polis, Barney Frank, and the Equality Caucus on a letter to Clinton signed by eighty-four congressmembers about LGBTI repression in Honduras.[61] We worked with Representative Hank Johnson of Georgia, a member of the Congressional Black Caucus, on a letter to new Secretary of State John Kerry about Afro-Indigenous land rights and the DEA's killings of Afro-Indigenous people in Ahuas, and we got fifty-eight signers. Thanks to the tireless and meticulous attention to Honduras on the part of his aide, Sascha Thompson, Johnson emerged as long-term leader on progressive Honduras policy.[62]

By late 2012, every office I'd met with, every letter-signer, every recipient of my informational emails was a Democrat. I really thought I'd do more harm than good if I tried to reach out to Republicans, although I knew the power of bipartisanship and knew Republicans in the House generally wouldn't sign a letter unless it was co-led by members from both parties.

In November 2012, I got a meeting with an aide to Representative Frank Wolf, the Republican co-chair of the Tom Lantos Commission on Human Rights. I was nervous about how this would go. Knowing that Wolf cared about religious freedom, I dragged Jean Stokan of the Sisters of Mercy with me. At the beginning of the meeting I handed the aide my *Foreign Affairs* article, which had just come out. She was surprised and told me that it had just circulated among the congress-member's staff; it turned out she herself was interested in the crisis in Honduras. At the end of the meeting, I casually threw in, as I did in all my meetings, "I'll be in town still for the next three weeks, if your boss would like to meet with me himself," knowing full well he wouldn't. In those years, I almost never obtained a meeting with a member. "Yes," she said, "he would. Are you free in an hour when he comes back from lunch?"

An hour later, the aide pulled us down the hall to meet Representative Wolf, one of the highest-ranking Republicans in the House and a former chair and current member of the all-important Subcommittee on State and Foreign Operations (SFOPS) of the Committee on Appropriations. She made clear we were just going to meet him, and that was it. When we shook hands, though, Wolf demanded: "Which one of you wrote that article?" and pulled us into his office for twenty minutes. He had a large, full-body photograph of Ronald Reagan on the wall. "I read your article and I'm outraged!" he declared. It turned out his daughter had lived in San Pedro Sula for two years, and he'd visited her, and cared about the country. He asked us what we wanted him to do. "Support human rights conditions on police and military aid to Honduras," I said quickly. "Tell Anne Marie that Wolf is on it," he instructed the aide, who tapped out a message to Anne-Marie Chotvacs, the top staffer to the Republicans on the SFOPS subcommittee, right as we sat there. He looked up at a world map above the couch Jean and I were sitting on. "It's going to hell down there. We've lost Ecuador. We've lost Bolivia." As Jean and I finally slipped out, he put his hand on my arm and queried: "Are there any Contras down there now?" Wolf stood by his word and, as far as I can tell, continued to support the human rights conditions on Honduran security aid until, to our loss, he retired in early 2014.

Powers That Be

I'd figured out by this point that success on the Hill depended on the commitment of individual aides who cared. The magic formula, I realized, was first, an aide who cared about the issue; who, second, worked for a congressperson who also cared; and third, if that member gave the aide a green light to pursue the project; and finally, if the member was high-ranking, served on one or more of the relevant committees, and had a lot of constituents communicating with him or her within the member's home district. The representative's Legislative Director and Chief of Staff had to be on board, too. The more those factors lined up, the more we could achieve. At the top of the heap among aides were staffers to committees and to the congressional leadership who were much more specialized in their political purview and who had access to higher levels of knowledge and power through their bosses.

In the spring of 2011, I heard there was an important, high-ranking Latin America expert named Peter Quilter who worked for Representative Howard Berman, at that point the Ranking Member of the House Committee on Foreign Affairs. But Quilter sounded far above my reach, so I forgot about him. I did know that, in early September 2009, Berman, the committee's chair at the time of the coup, had written a terrific op-ed in the *Los Angeles Times*: "Honduras: Make It Official—It's a Coup," calling on the Obama Administration to admit that it was a military coup and suspend almost all assistance, as legally mandated. "This one looks, walks and quacks like a duck. It's time to stop hedging and call this bird what it is." In June 2011, the House Foreign Affairs committee was about to hold a hearing about whether to restore the visa of coup perpetrator and post-coup de facto President Roberto Micheletti, along with other leaders of the coup. Going out on a limb, I called Berman's office cold and asked to speaker to Peter Quilter. I was a bit stunned that he took my call (even the most helpful aides usually didn't), knew who I was, and talked to me right then and there for an hour about the question of Micheletti's visa and Honduran politics in general. From then on, we worked closely together for two and a half years, until he left the Hill for another job as Minister of Finance and Administration at the Organization of American States.

Argentinian and American, he had black hair, a goatee, and was sharp as a tack and even faster-talking than I am, which is saying a lot, with a spectacular sense of humor and an impressive ability to land a metaphor. For every meeting I'd arrive ten minutes early at the Foreign Affairs committee's reception area and inform the staff I was there, and they'd ding him. Every single time he'd fling the door open at precisely the second the meeting was scheduled to begin. We'd meet at the same table by the window in the basement cafeteria of the Rayburn building. After precisely one hour, he'd leave.

Our first meeting was in October 2011, three or four days after the rector's son had been killed by the police in Honduras. When I told Peter about it, he jolted in his chair at the news—he already knew an enormous amount about Honduras and understood immediately what the killings meant. He told me President Lobo was trying to do a good job but under tremendous pressure from the Honduran right. I replied that I thought that was b.s. and that Lobo was himself the Honduran right and was working him. I had the sense that not a lot of visiting experts talked to Peter that way, but that he wasn't offended; he was listening hard. I could tell, too, after that meeting, that something had changed in my ability to get things done in Congress.

That November, Peter asked me to send him talking points for a letter from his boss to President Lobo about human rights in Honduras. I did the best I could, while apologizing that a letter criticizing a foreign head of state was pretty much a new genre for me. That draft morphed into Berman's November 28 letter to Hillary Clinton, the one that ended by asking "Madam Secretary" to "evaluate immediately United States assistance to ensure that we are not, in fact, feeding a beast."[63]

Peter almost never told me what he was working on about Honduras, or what he was saying to the administration or the Honduran government. We never discussed any country except Honduras. I never saw inside his office. I learned where the boundaries were, and we stayed precisely within them. But he mentored me, consciously, about the ways of the Hill, the State Department, and the administration. He read my long, weekly bullet-point summaries of Honduran political developments. In October 2012, he wrote another, flaming letter from Berman to the Secretary of State, this one three pages long, that took on US policy in Honduras, questioned State's certification of the human rights conditions, and insisted that "it is time to stop pretending the coup never happened." "US policy needs a re-set," Berman declared. "We can view the terrifying human rights situation through the lens of 'threats to citizen security' . . . or we can understand the same human rights violations through the prism of the coup and indeed a lockdown on the political process by long-entrenched elites."[64]

Years later, discussing our respective roles in trying to advance Honduras policy, Peter underscored the labor that was going on behind the scenes, which I could barely glimpse at the time. There were "people who cared enough to push," he stressed. Their bosses mattered enormously, too. Representative Berman had to care. "Berman had to say, 'I really like that letter, let's go with it.'" Berman had to be willing to use up some of his political capital on the Honduras question. I could see that the members had to be committed: if they led on a letter, they had to been able to talk about the issues on television, the radio, with the State Department and the White House. Over the years, I could see how Representative Jan Schakowsky, in particular, was always deeply committed to our work on Honduras and keenly on top of the issues, always eager to meet with visiting Hondurans and take their stories deep into her heart.

In writing this account, I struggled hard to strike a balance between depicting the work I did as part of my own story and crediting the ways in which that work was always embedded in and dependent upon the work of thousands of other activists all over the United States and the world and, most importantly, the work of tens of thousands of Hondurans, many dying in the struggle, who were always the most important actors. Peter helped me put it in perspective: "Everyone could tell a story; the journalists, too, have stories to tell. They all advanced the ball somehow. All had some skin in the game. There were people who cared. Everybody's a bit of a hero."

We were cooking with gas in the House. But the Senate was a much more formidable challenge—more formal, more forbidding, but also more powerful.

I was told by a longtime NGO activist in D.C. that it was impossible to get a letter out of the Senate; they just didn't do letters, and, in any event, the senators were more conservative. But working closely with the Sisters of Mercy, and thanks to the committed work of a constituent in Maryland, we elicited a letter to Clinton from Senator Barbara Mikulski, at that point the second-ranking Democrat on the Committee on Appropriations. Six other senators signed. Released in March 2012, right after the big Schakowsky letter, it questioned US support for Honduran security forces that had committed human rights abuses. It stopped short of asking for a suspension of the aid— but it was from the Senate. One aide who'd worked in both houses told me that a single phone call from a single senator to the State Department was worth calls from fifty members. Later, in 2014, Senator Benjamin Cardin would lead on an even stronger letter signed by twenty-one senators.[65]

I'd heard that there was another, almost mythical man out there in the Senate, who'd been there forever, who cared about Latin America and human rights and who, supposedly, had the power to suspend police and military aid all by himself if he wanted to. I wasn't sure that was true. His name was Tim Rieser; he worked for Senator Patrick Leahy, chair of the Committee on the Judiciary and of the Subcommittee on State and Foreign Operations of the Senate Committee on Appropriations, for which Rieser was his top aide.

Congress has three key powers in relation to the executive branch: passing legislation, confirming appointments, and controlling funding. Of these, the power over the purse strings is the most important, given that Congress has to approve an annual budget not just for the US government—including the State Department itself—but for US projects in foreign countries, including foreign military funding and development aid. That funding is controlled by legislation written by the Committees on Appropriations of the two houses, and especially the subcommittees on Defense and on State and Foreign Operations. In addition, the chairs of these committees, and of the Senate Foreign

Relations Committees, and, in the Senate, the ranking members, also have the power to individually place appropriated funds on temporary hold if they choose.

In February 2011, I wrote to Tim Rieser and got an appointment— a rarity, I realized much later. When my colleague Alex and I came in the door, Tim was seated at a computer in the back left corner. He waved us over to a small couch and a couple of chairs in the other back corner, finished whatever he was working on, then came over to sit down across from us. He was in his late fifties, small, thin, with silver hair parted on one side, falling down at an angle above a narrow face.

I nervously rattled off my by-then-standard, ten-minute speech delineating the horrors of the Honduran government in the aftermath of the coup. Tim didn't say a word or smile the whole time. When we finished our spiel, he asked, "Do you know how much the US funding is?" I had no idea. Alex rescued me with some general remarks. Tim delineated what he could and couldn't do to help us, flashed a deep smile, and the meeting was over.

That spring I started emailing him once a month or so with brief information about Honduras. By the summer, my emails had grown into regular summaries, with bullet points and news clips, sometimes daily, as the assassinations of campesino activists in the Aguán Valley accelerated, one by one, two by two. By this point, Annie Bird of Rights Action was sending him information from her meticulously documented investigations into the Aguán as well. Finally, getting no response, I worried that I was bothering him and should stop. In August, I called him for the first time, asking if my information was too much. "Keep it coming," he said, while apologizing that he couldn't do much because "I have to deal with all the terrible places in the world," not just Honduras. "But this is my terrible place," I pleaded.

Like Peter, Tim almost never told me what he was doing. I came to understand I shouldn't ask. I never had any idea who else he was hearing from about Honduras—although I knew that, in 2010 and 2011, there wasn't much advocacy going on beyond what came from my colleagues and me. I kept the emails to him flowing. When I hit the crack-up point from the relentless assassinations that fall, I wrote: Please make it stop.

On October 3, 2011, out of the blue, he emailed: "The Senate version of the FY12 foreign aid bill eliminates funding for the military (it does not affect DoD funded programs), and conditions aid to the police. However, the House version does neither, so I can't predict what the final outcome will be."[66]

Six years later, I still have that email on my wall in Santa Cruz. I couldn't believe it. At that point, I had no idea what it meant to put conditions on foreign aid; I barely even know there was a foreign aid bill in process. But I did know that after over two years of terrible atrocities, sobbing powerlessness, and unbearable grief, someone I barely knew, far, far away, someone who possessed real power, had done something enormous.

A few days before Christmas 2011, Congress passed the final State and Foreign Operations Appropriations bill for the following year, which placed the first conditions on aid to Honduras—albeit only on the portion allocated under the State and Foreign Operations Appropriations Act:

> (d) HONDURAS.-Prior to the obligation of 20 percent of the funds appropriated by this Act that are available for assistance for Honduran military and police forces, the Secretary of State shall report in writing to the Committees on Appropriations that: the Government of Honduras is implementing policies to protect freedom of expression and association, and due process of law; and is investigating and prosecuting in the civilian justice system, in accordance with Honduran and international law, military and police personnel who are credibly alleged to have violated human rights, and the Honduran military and police are cooperating with civilian judicial authorities in such cases: Provided, That the restriction in this sub-section shall not apply to assistance to promote transparency, anti-corruption, and rule of law within the military and police forces.[67]

It was the law. Tim did it. I suspect, though, that in most contexts, if thanked for what he did, he himself would state that it was "Congress" who placed the restrictions.

It was also Tim Rieser who, in October 2012, told the *New York Times* that Senator Leahy, with the support of other Democrats, had placed tens of millions of dollars in US security aid to Honduras on hold.[68]

No question: by the end of 2012, I finally had the strategic plan that I had been utterly missing the day of the coup. Congressional briefings, letters to the administration, public statements, human rights conditions enacted in an actual law involving actual funds—my beloved colleagues and I learned about all these tools and learned to deploy them through complex planning and a national grassroots get-out-the-vote machine. We knocked on a hundred doors, literally, until we learned which offices cared and would come through; we learned to triangulate constituents, members and senators, and organizations they would listen to. We learned which members were friends with which, and who followed whose leadership. Other powerful tools nonetheless stayed beyond our reach: resolutions, official congressional delegations (known as CODELS), legislation other than the SFOPS bill. But the trend of our work was nonetheless upward, however endlessly frustrating, and we were always astonished that we pulled off any of it.

The essential question remained, though, of the interface between all this congressional work and the Honduran opposition. Who, exactly, were we accountable to in Honduras as we made our demands in Washington—especially as the National Front of Popular Resistance splintered in these same years? The whole congressional process was spectacularly secret, moreover. We could barely discuss the letters until they went public, for example, lest our enemies pounce. We ourselves only remotely understood the tools and processes inside Congress—how, then, did we share that with the Hondurans? As I began working in Congress, I tried to explain to Hondurans as much as possible what we were trying to do up north. The response was always enthusiastic, and eventually would produce organizational endorsements of our work. But the technicalities of the different congressional committees, their jurisdictions, and the subtleties of conditioning in the SFOPS bill were formidable to explain, especially in Spanish. To a certain extent, we had to make a leap of faith up north, knowing also that it was our own taxes that were paying, in part, for the atrocities in Honduras, and that we had to answer for those dollars ourselves.

Hurricane Sandy

In the fall of 2012, while I was teaching in D.C. for the quarter, I rented an apartment on the corner of 17th Avenue and T Street Northwest, near DuPont Circle. The best thing about it was its wall of small-paned windows looking out at the trees growing in a little triangular park in front of the building. I loved watching those high, leafy trees sway in the wind as they gradually changed colors during September and October.

On Monday, October 29, the whole city of Washington, D.C., was shut down for two days because of the imminent arrival of Hurricane Sandy. That meant not just that the entire federal government was closed, but most other offices and institutions, too, and the buses and Metro weren't running. It also meant that a group of Honduran judges I knew, in town to testify at the Organization of American States (OAS), at a big hearing in support of the Inter-American System of Human Rights, were stranded in the city for two extra days, waiting around for their rescheduled event on Wednesday.

There were six of them: Tirza Flores Lanza and Luis Chévez, two of the four judges who'd been illegally deposed for opposing the coup and never reinstated, and Mandell Pandy and Mario Díaz, both sitting judges. They were leaders of the Association of Honduran Judges for Democracy, seeking support from the Inter-American Commission for reinstatement of the deposed judges and for judicial independence in Honduras. A journalist and a lawyer came, too, from Radio Progreso and ERIC, the Jesuit-run research center.

Their hotel was close to my apartment, and I invited them over so we could meet. They trotted over through hard rain and now-swirling golden leaves and plopped into the couch and chairs in my tiny, triangular living room. All of them looked like ordinary mortals, wearing jeans or sweatpants or other hanging-out-in-a-hotel-room-style clothing. I was thrilled to have a captive roomful of serious Honduran experts whose brains I could pick, and I started grilling them about the status of the supposed police cleanup under way in the country. After forty-five minutes Luis asked meekly: could we have some music? It was around eleven in the morning. I produced Juan Luis Guerra's classic merengue hit, *Buscando Visa Para un Sueño* (*Looking for a Visa for a Dream*), already primed. Luis and I started dancing a bit. Then everyone else did. That was it for the meeting.

I started worrying about lunch. The proverbial cupboard was literally bare: I was hardly ever home, and hadn't been shopping lately, and there was nothing stocked up because it was just a short-term rental. I managed to unearth a can of tuna, a can of chickpeas, a single package of spaghetti, and a jar of red sauce. I blinked, and Tirza produced a tasty lunch for seven out of that.

We laughed our way through lunch, plates on our knees. Then suddenly, at around two o'clock, I blinked again, and they were all whisking out, their overcoats and scarves already on, more than half-way through the door. By this point it was clear from the weather reports that Sandy wasn't going to do that much in Washington; it produced a fair amount of wind swishing the trees up and down and some respectable rain, but nothing to write home about. These were Hondurans, though, and they knew their hurricanes and were super-cautious, I realized, while still begging them to stay a bit longer. After they left, I carried something into the kitchen, and discovered that everything had all been perfectly cleaned up.

The next day I walked back to their hotel. It was peaceful and quiet now outside, and all the leaves were gone from the trees except for five or six brave yellow stragglers. The city was still officially shut down. The Hondurans had nested into one of the judges' hotel rooms that had a litle kitchen and were working on the collective statement that they would read at the hearing the next day. Two more people showed up, from the Center for Justice and International Law (CEJIL), an NGO that helps Latin Americans and Caribbeans interface with the Inter-American Commission. Earlier, the Hondurans had made a foray to a nearby store to stock up their own kitchen. We made another, better lunch. (Well, we women made another, better lunch.)

Wednesday, I got up bright and early, dressed to the gills in my Hillary look-alike blue blazer and my best silver jewelry, and took a cab to the OAS building at the end of the Mall. It was a big, heavy-looking, gray thing with three arching doorways (deliberately evoking a French imperial bureaucratic palace, I suspect). Next door sat the headquarters of the Daughters of the American Revolution, with its own white imperial columns, sort of a cross between the Roman Forum and a slave plantation; and beyond that lay the Red Cross's own white-columned edifice.

I ascended the long steps to the main entrance of the OAS, into its lobby where more grand stairways swept up either side to the meeting hall upstairs. Not sure about my bad knees, I found an elevator tucked away in the lefthand corner. Lo and behold, I found myself alone in the elevator with José Miguel Insulza himself, the Secretary General of the OAS. I got to make an actual elevator speech in 1.8 minutes. He remembered meeting me a few weeks before; I encouraged him to do more on Honduras.

Upstairs in the giant meeting hall, with its soaring ceilings, a big U-shaped table took up more than half the length of the room, facing a dais across the top of the U, where the commissioners lined up. The rest of us sat five-deep in rows of black chairs at the bottom of the U or along its side by high windows.

When Tirza, Mario, Luis, and Mandy arrived, they had been miraculously transformed into august personages, the men in their best suits and ties, Tirza in a bright regal red suit, all of them every inch the judicial presence. When it was their turn, Mandell Pandy, seated at the U-table, read their statement, and it was beautiful and passionate and forceful and moving. He concluded:

> The Association of Judges for Democracy hopes that IACHR
> [Inter-American Commission on Human Rights] bears in mind
> this participation and that it considers the millions of victims that
> could not be here and that need a commission that responds genu-
> inely to the challenges of those human rights, and not to pressures
> of the oligarchs that hold power in the Americas.[69]

I was so proud to know them, proud to be sitting with the rest of the group in the chairs behind along the side.

I also couldn't help noticing that during a long, in many ways tedious, day of presentations from dozens of countries, attended by allies and observers from all over the hemisphere, it was the Hondurans who seemed to be having the best time, gossiping a little, giggling, wiggling from time to time. Just a tiny bit. I was happy, too, to know that these were my people.

John Kelly, US Secretary of Homeland Security at the time (L) and Juan Orlando Hernández (R), Washington D.C., March 2017. Photo Credit: United States Department of Homeland Security.

CHAPTER FOUR

A Dictator Rises: Juan Orlando Hernández and His US Friends

The Space Closes In

On June 29, 2012, a lawyer named Antonio Trejo Cabrera achieved something both extraordinary and unprecedented: He won a legal case against Miguel Facussé, the palm oil magnate whose security guards had been accused of killing dozens of campesinos in the Aguán Valley. The ruling restored land rights to members of the MARCA (Movimiento Auténtico Reinvidicador de Campesinos de Aguán). While other campesino groups had pursued direct land recuperations, the MARCA had chosen to keep fighting in the courts—although campesinos who'd tried the legal route had lost over and over again.[1]

Trejo received multiple death threats in the months that followed. Campesinos from the MARCA, on their now legally mandated lands, reported that Facussé's Dinant Corporation security guards shot at, menaced, and tortured them. In late August, in response, Trejo and over two dozen campesinos and their families tried to pursue legal redress at the Supreme Court. But Honduran authorities retaliated by illegally detaining them. The Inter-American Commission on Human Rights mandated protection for Trejo. But the government provided

137

it for only three days. Trejo declared publicly that if anything should happen to him, he held Miguel Facussé responsible.

Saturday night, September 22, Antonio Trejo had just finished officiating at a wedding in Tegucigalpa when he received an urgent phone call from a stranger. He stepped outside the church and onto the sidewalk to answer the call, and two shots hit him in the head, two in the torso, and one in the leg. He died soon after in the hospital.[2]

Before the killing of Antonio Trejo, all the assassinations of campesinos had taken place far away from the capital, in the Aguán Valley or other rural areas of struggle; none of the campesinos' lawyers had been touched. Now the level of threat escalated, fast. Now, too, the legal pathway to land rights closed down even more sharply.

During the fall of 2012, repression of the Honduran opposition escalated once again, taking new forms while closing in on the social movements, media, and human rights defenders alike. While light finally shone in the north on US policy, darkness continued to fall within Honduras itself. The democratic space contracted at the grassroots. Yet, ironically, formal democratic spaces newly opened up in the electoral sphere, as national attention shifted to the primary elections of November 2012, ramping up to the November 2013 presidential election. Now the formal Resistance transformed itself into a new political party—but with a cost. And a new actor marched onto center stage, entering from the wings on the right, wearing boots: Juan Orlando Hernández, the rising dictator.

President Porfirio Lobo helped build that stage, little by little advancing further the militarization of domestic policing. The Honduran Constitution, written in 1982 in reaction to two decades of military dictatorship, specifies that the job of the armed forces is guarding the borders. But Lobo lacked the political will to clean up the corrupt and murderous police. His answer, instead, was increasingly to send in the military. Beginning in November 2011, Lobo authorized soldiers to engage in domestic policing for longer and longer periods, expanding their mandate from brief forays, to three months, to six months and longer, extending well into 2014. More and more checkpoints staffed by the military popped up along highways throughout the country. Soldiers moved in on the bus stations, airports, and prisons, and stayed. They stopped buses along their routes, mounted them, and demanded all passengers' IDs. To pay for all this, the Honduran Congress passed a new, controversial Security Tax in June 2011, placing a three percent tax on financial transactions—including ordinary bank account transfers and credit card payments—that created an enormous slush fund for security forces, with no transparency.[3]

By March 2013, swarms of soldiers began to suddenly occupy neighborhoods, especially poor ones, and harass people. When residents asked the reason for the takeovers, no answer was given. One observer from the Honduras Accompaniment Project, a US citizen, reported that, while he was walking down a wide pedestrian pathway in Tegucigalpa, he witnessed six or seven soldiers as they picked out men passing by, lined them up against a wall, demanded that they spread their legs, and searched them. Meanwhile, headlines in the government-allied newspapers celebrated the military's vigorous assault against gang members and drug traffickers.[4]

In addition to extending the regular military into domestic law enforcement, Lobo and the Honduran Congress also began creating entirely new units to further militarize policing. First proposed in July 2012, the TIGRES (Tropas de Investigación y Grupos de Respuesta de Seguridad), a hybrid police-military investigative and rapid-deployment special forces unit, raised alarms immediately, because of its parallels to the infamous Battalion 3-16, the Honduran military's death squad unit of the 1980s. The TIGRES proposal was widely protested, delaying its approval.[5] On a larger scale, in August 2013, Lobo announced that a new police group within the military, known as the Military Police of Public Order (PMOP), would undertake domestic policing and that five thousand of its troops would be immediately trained and launched into the streets.[6]

The dangers of all this militarization were clear. Soldiers are trained to track and kill a hostile enemy. Successful policing, by contrast, depends on respect for local communities and citizens' legal rights, careful handling of evidence, and the use of minimal force. In the United States, military involvement in domestic law enforcement has been banned since 1878 through the Posse Comitatus Act, although exceptions since have been myriad, including the deployment of the National Guard.[7]

In Honduras, the military's involvement in law enforcement swiftly proved deadly. In Tegucigalpa, on May 26, 2012, fifteen-year-old Ebed Yanes, who had never left his house alone at night, snuck out on his father's motorcycle in search of a girl he'd met on Facebook. Without stopping, he passed through a checkpoint staffed by the military. Soldiers swept out of the checkpoint, hunted him down in an alley, and shot him up, killing him. The Associated Press would later establish that the unit that killed him was US-trained, equipped, funded, and specially vetted, and that a colonel who covered up the incident afterward had been trained at the School of the Americas in Fort Benning, Georgia, and at the Naval Postgraduate School in Monterey, California.[8] In another incident, on July 5, 2013, members of the Engineers' Battalion of the Honduran Armed Forces shot and killed Tomás García, a Lenca Indigenous activist, while he was nonviolently protesting a hydroelectric dam in Intibucá.[9]

Lobo also began transferring administrative authority over the regular police to the military. In March 2013, he merged the ministries of security and defense into a single unit under Arturo Corrales—who'd been one of the two top negotiators for Micheletti after the coup.[10] The new Vice Minister of Security came from the military, as did three top appointees to management positions within the National Police.[11]

Repression of campesino activists and their allies continued with impunity. On November 10, 2012, Jhonny Rivas and Vitalino Álvarez, leaders of the MUCA, were ambushed while working in the La Confianza settlement; as they ran away, they could hear high-calibre arms going off.[12] On October 23, three men kidnapped Karla Zelaya (no relation to the deposed president), a journalist working with the MUCA, and held her blindfolded for three hours while torturing her and interrogating her about the locations and travel plans of MUCA members. "Only with killing the leaders will this movement end," they told her. In the first seven weeks of 2013 alone, nine campesino activists were killed.[13]

Right before that, in December 2012, Tracy Wilkinson of the *Los Angeles Times* flew to Honduras and interviewed Miguel Facussé at length. He was unrepentent. When she asked him about allegations of his involvement in the killing of Antonio Trejo, the lawyer, he replied. "I probably had reasons to kill him . . . but I'm not a killer."[14] Two months later, on February 26, José Trejo, Antonio's brother, was shot and killed on a motorcycle, a day after he had traveled to Tegucigalpa to pressure authorities and speak to media outlets about his brother's case.[15]

Restrictions on freedom of the press tightened. Dina Meza, a journalist for COFADEH, the human rights group, reported receiving repeated, sexualized death threats, for example. Strangers began following her and her son throughout 2012 and early 2013. She filed report after report with the authorities but got no response.[16]

On Saturday morning, December 15, 2012, I had breakfast near the San Pedro Sula airport with Padre Melo of Radio Progreso. At the end, I suggested we take a five-minute stroll through the airport, for his protection—so he'd be seen with me, a relatively well-known professor from the United States. He agreed, and we took our walk, as I checked in for my flight a few hours later. Padre Melo pointed out to me a man in his sixties who was seated up in a shoe-shine chair, watching everyone in the high-ceilinged main room. Padre Melo said that during the 1980s the man had been the Battalion 3-16 officer in charge of the San Pedro Sula airport, and the one who identified the leftists to kill.[17] He said that the man now worked for the businessmen of the city, "watching the airport for anyone who threatens their interests." The man was very clearly observing us. I went up to a newsstand across from him, deliberately, looked up (he was maybe fifteen feet away), and our eyes met. Maybe he thought I was just another North American accompanying Padre Melo for his protection. Or maybe he knew who I was. Padre Melo said that every time he came to the airport to fly, the guy followed him all the way to the gate. For me, it was one thing to know that 3-16 members were out there. It was another to see one of them face to face and exchange a look.[18]

At a broad, strategic level, Lobo also continued to take on the teachers' unions, which had been the backbone of the Resistance in the streets. Brilliantly, in February 2012, he named a new Minister of Education, Marlon Escoto, an agronomist who had himself demonstrated against the coup and spoke openly about having done so. Escoto proceeded to systematically harass and repress the teachers and their unions. For example, he disciplined, fined, and fired rank-and-file teachers if they persisted in demonstrating on schooldays—even though the government still owed them several months in back pay. He did purge many of the "ghost teachers" who remained on the payroll but didn't show up. But Escoto also raised school fees—in a country rent by mass poverty—and extended school hours into the late afternoon, putting schoolchildren at tremendous risk on their way home from school after dark.[19] In January 2014, after radio journalist Marvin Ortiz questioned him assertively about the school fees, repression, and other issues, Escoto tweeted: "I'm coming after you, so you can tell me why you're insulting me and if I owe you anything."[20]

All this took its toll on the opposition, both organizationally and psychologically. In February 2013, a group of US human rights observers who returned from Honduras reported that activists they'd just met with in the human rights community and social movements were terrified and isolated in new ways. Infiltrators and spies were everywhere, so people trusted each other less and less. Systems that had been in place to identify and contain provocateurs were no longer in place. People were exhausted, and the problems too complex and huge, so they predicted more provocateur activity in future demonstrators. Psychological manipulation—the famous "psy-ops" pursued by intelligence agencies—was pervasive.

Slowly, surely, deliberately, and lethally, the space closed in around each of the social movements and their allies. Symbolically, in December 2012, security forces evicted the National Front of Popular Resistance from the corner of the Central Plaza of San Pedro Sula, which its members had occupied since the coup.[21] For three and a half years members of the FNRP had passed out leaflets all day, every day, blasted out Resistance music from a sound system, and kept the corner's balustrades, benches, and streetlights painted red and black. At the same time, the connections among the social movements that had woven them into a unified, coordinated body, however loosely organized, began to disintegrate, leaving the grass-roots projects like islands in a sea of snarling wolves. "The social movements are becoming disarticulated," numerous Hondurans told me in this period.

The formal FNRP took itself apart, in fact, in late 2011 and 2012. When he returned to Honduras in May 2011, Manuel Zelaya had announced that the Resistance would now found a political party as part of the Cartagena Accord—although at their February 2011 national assembly, FNRP delegates had voted democratically and emphatically not to enter into electoral politics. The rest of that year after Zelaya's return, the leadership of the Frente proceeded to trans-form it into a new party, Libertad y Refundacíon, known as LIBRE. The formal Resistance split into two camps: on one side LIBRE enthusiasts—a coalition of long-time Liberal Party activists and left-ists, some of whom were trade unionists—and on the other side the social movements and their closest allies, including the Indigenous coalition COPINH, the Afro-Indigenous organization OFRANEH, and the Jesuits' Radio Progreso. Many activists did bridge the two approaches, such as banana worker unionists in COSIBAH, who had long advocated third-party electoral activism but remained deeply committed to the campesino struggle in the Aguán and elsewhere. Many activists central to the social movements, such as Wilfredo Paz, a prominent campesino leader who would be elected to congress from the Aguán Valley, ran as LIBRE candidates. But as official FNRP energies swarmed toward the upcoming elections, it quickly became clear that the LIBRE camp had, in effect, largely thrown the social movements out of the formal Resistance, where they would remain outsiders, searching for new connections among each other and for new avenues to keep their vibrant grassroots activism alive. After this point, it works best to refer to the "opposition," a broad category that includes the grassroots elements of the previously unified Resistance, but also a great range of other actors, including those in the electoral sphere, who bravely opposed the ongoing coup regime.[22]

Nonetheless, LIBRE emerged as a new, powerful force in Honduran electoral politics in 2012 and 2013. It was the first large,

independent party of the center-left in all Honduran history.
Xiomara Castro, Zelaya's wife, became its presidential candidate,
her face plastered on walls, hills, bus stations, as LIBRE sought to
draw on her friendly, charismatic presence and the popularity she
had built during the years when Zelaya was absent. The party's new
power, in turn, drew a murderous response. Between May 1 and the
November 18, 2012, primaries, eleven LIBRE activists or candidates
were assassinated, especially as the primary candidates' names
became clear. On November 3, for example, Edgardo Adalid Motiño
Flores, a LIBRE lawyer and candidate for mayor in Morazan, Yoro,
was gunned down at 9:30 p.m., right after leaving a meeting with
Castro at a LIBRE rally.[23]

   As the primaries approached, the government turned overtly
and publicly against human rights defenders as well. At the end
of October 2012, Bertha Oliva, the Director of COFADEH, and
Victor Fernández, an attorney and leader of the Movimiento
Amplio por Dignidad y Justicia (MADJ, Broad Movement for
Dignity and Justice) traveled to Washington, D.C., met with a range
of congressional offices and others, and spoke at a briefing in the
House of Representatives about the Honduran primary election in
November. A week later, on November 5, Renato Álvarez, the host
of the most popular national talk show, read on television from what
he alleged was a diplomatic cable from Jorge Ramón Hernández
Alcerro, the Honduran ambassador to the US, to President Lobo.
"The participation of Bertha Oliva and Victor Fernández proves
the conspiracy of NGOs and Honduran people against the electoral
process in Honduras," it charged, and enumerated exact information Oliva had provided at the briefing about LIBRE's challenge to
the two-party system and widespread impunity, corruption, and
human rights abuses. Álvarez, the host, then turned to four guests
on the show, including two congressional candidates, and they all
condemned Oliva for what she'd supposedly said about the elections; the speakers went on to charge that she was doing all this
to promote her "business" and that COFADEH was lying all over
the place. Later, congressmembers attacked her on the floor of the
Honduran Congress, including charging that she had spoken in the

US Senate against the military police. In the Honduran context, these were lethal threats—and in the case of the cable, from the top of the government itself.[24]

There was one bright light, if few caught its rays. In early October, the Comisión de Verdad (known in English as the True Commission, as opposed to the government's Truth Commission), organized by independent civil society, finally issued its extensive report. The commission had been formed in response to the Honduran government's own Truth and Reconciliation Commission, formed in 2010, which, in July 2011, had issued a report renouncing the coup as indeed a coup, but blaming both sides. The government commission's recommendations, many of them excellent, were roundly ignored by Lobo's government at the time.[25] The second, civil society commission, by contrast, analyzed and condemned almost two thousand accounts of human rights violations committed between the coup and August 2011 by state security forces. It documented widespread repression of the opposition, a dysfunctional judicial system, and the criminalization of protest. Its recommendations focused on an end to impunity, especially through reform of the judiciary and sanctions on the coup perpetrators.[26]

Judicial Powers

The November 18 primaries confirmed LIBRE's new strength, as the party drew 594,531 votes, compared with the Liberal Party's 719,583 and the ruling National Party's 1,444,444. None of the actual vote totals were clear, however, since the election process itself was controlled by President Lobo's National Party and, as per the Honduran Constitution, overseen by the armed forces. Fraud was widespread, and the outcomes widely understood to be fictional. In a hotly contested Liberal Party race, the winner was declared to be Mauricio Villeda, a conservative, lackluster party loyalist, over the somewhat more centrist Yani Rosenthal, the son of Jaime Rosenthal, the oligarch who owned *El Tiempo*—the one newspaper that had stayed somewhat neutral during the coup. In an even more scorching race within the National Party, Ricardo Álvarez, the mayor of Tegucigalpa, ostensibly lost to Juan Orlando Hernández, the President of Congress.[27]

Handsome, smiling, a formidable charmer, relatively young at forty-four, Hernández looked like he was born wearing a clean white shirt—and was a dangerous thug.[28] Known popularly as "Juan Orlando" (his compound first name) or, in writing, "JOH," he already had a track record of overthrowing the rule of law, having voted for a congressional statement that approved the 2009 coup.[29] He grew up in the province of Lempira, high in the western Honduran mountains. According to a US Embassy cable issued at the time Hernández became President of Congress in January 2010, he was the fifteenth of his parents' seventeen children. (When I mentioned that to a top Honduran diplomat I once sat next to on a plane, he said no, no, Hernández's father had at least forty children.) Hernández attended a military academy through high school. He never quite fit in, though—he wasn't from a military family and was shorter than the other students. An older boy, whom Hernández, while president, would later promote within the military, had stepped in to protect him. Thereafter, the Honduran armed forces remained Hernández's safe, go-to place, as he waded into higher and higher political waters and deliberately roiled them.[30]

Ricardo Álvarez, who "lost" the National Party primary to Hernández, was a formidable figure himself, allied with a powerful elite group to the right of Lobo and Hernández that included Jorge Canahuati, the mega-rich oligarch who owned *La Prensa* and *El Heraldo*. After the results were announced, a clash of the titans ensued. I was in Honduras in early December as all this played out, and my interviewees were abuzz with talk of a looming constitutional crisis—in what form, no one knew, just that a really big storm was most definitely brewing. One theory was that a bogus constitutional convention was about to be launched, at which the military would step in and take over. Much speculation centered on a series of decisions that previous fall, in which the Supreme Court had ruled against Lobo. Although the court had unanimously backed the coup in 2009, some of the justices had later publicly regretted doing so, and they had gradually begun to exercise a degree of independence. In mid-October, the court rejected the Model Cities law—not a difficult decision, since the law threw out the Honduran Constitution's jurisdiction inside the proposed new zones.[31] In late November, the court's Constitutional Branch rejected a new law ostensibly cleaning up the police, in part because it mandated the use of polygraph tests, which international norms widely condemn for their violation of the right to not self-incriminate.[32] After the contested primary, Ricardo Álvarez, Juan Orlando Hernández's rival, filed a request to the Supreme Court for an entire, vote-by-vote recount of the National Party results. It decision was due December 12.[33]

At three in the morning the night of December 11, 2012, the Honduran Congress, chaired by Hernández himself, voted to depose four out of five members of the Constitutional Branch (Sala Constitucional) of the Supreme Court. (The other ten members are the equivalent of appeals court judges in the US.) The fifth, Oscar Chinchilla, was loyal to Juan Orlando. The next day Congress named four new justices to take their places. It was all completely illegal.[34]

And with that, Hernández took power. All the reins of official power would now be at his disposal, if not immediately: Congress, the Supreme Court, the attorney general and prosecutors, the police, and the military, to which he remained close. One Honduran oligarch told a friend of mine that week that, in fifty years of Honduran politics, he'd never known a more Machiavellian, dangerous figure that Juan Orlando Hernández. And this source knew whereof he spoke.

The events quickly became known as the "technical coup." Humor abounded: Honduras now not only had "*golpistas*," but also "*re-golpistas*" and "*doble-golpistas*." In the next few days three different people told me the same joke: "Why are there no coups in the United States? Because there is no US Embassy."

By December 20, Congress swore in the four new Supreme Court justices and then, within days, reconsidered the Model Cities law that had earlier been rejected, and this time passed it.[35] Meanwhile, the case of four judges who had been illegally deposed in 2009 for opposing the coup moved forward in the Inter-American Commission on Human Rights (IACHR). On April 2, 2013, the commission ruled in favor of the judges, mandated that the Honduran government restore them and pay restitution, and forwarded the judges' case to the Inter-American Court. But Lobo still refused to reinstate them.[36]

That summer Hernández continued to grab new reins. In late June 2013, Luis Rubí, the attorney general, and his assistant, Roy Urtrecho, both resigned amid charges of mishandling funds and rumors of connections to drug traffickers.[37] According to Honduran law, Congress could then choose to promote the third-ranking prosecutor to be the new attorney general, or it could name a new one. Either way, the successor legally serves out only the remainder of the original appointee's five-year term—which, in order to ensure the balance of powers, deliberately bridges the four-year presidential term. In this case, the new attorney general's term should have ended in March 2014. In August, Congress considered applications for a new attorney and assistant attorney general. Oscar Chinchilla, the one Supreme Court justice in the Constitutional Branch loyal to Hernández who hadn't been deposed, applied, but didn't make the cut to the final group of candidates, for lack of qualifications. Congress reopened the search; then named Chinchilla attorney general for an illegal new five-year term, along with his assistant.[38] It was Juan Orlando's doing. He'd resigned as President of Congress that June, supposedly in order to concentrate on his campaign. But he was running the show more than ever.[39]

In October, Chinchilla transferred twenty-one prosecutors off their cases and into different regional jurisdictions. They had been pursuing cases against high-ranking police and military officials for their involvement in human rights abuses, and other volatile cases. Edy Tabora, a prosecutor for human rights, charged, "They are condemning me to death in sending me to Tocoa [in the Aguán Valley] without any protective measures, because in that sector there is a strong presence of military police against whom there are precedents of duly registered accusations of violations of human rights."[40]

Our Men in Honduras

Where was the United States, as all this played out? It quickly became clear that the administration supported Hernández, albeit with qualifications. What wasn't so clear was how US congressional pushback in precisely this period was impacting US policy. No question, it mattered. But how, exactly, took a lot of guessing.

In September 2012, María Otero, Under Secretary of State for Civilian Security, Democracy, and Human Rights, traveled to Honduras, and issued public statements that appeared to strike a new tone of concern for the human rights crisis; she insisted that no one was above being investigated, including top government officials, and announced the creation of a new US-Honduras Bilateral Human Rights Working Group.[41] But she sent a far different, and ominous, message by signing and publicly celebrating a new security pact with the Honduran government during that same visit.[42] A pattern emerged: the United States would bow to pressure and up its public commitment to human rights. But it would simultaneously solidify its commitment to Honduran security forces and those who controlled them.

At the embassy level, US officials continued to send mixed messages, often undermining State's public commitment to human rights or subtly sowing confusion about US actions that had been compelled by Congress. On November 12, 2012, Ambassador Lisa Kubiske gave a big interview to the Honduran media in which, according to *El Tiempo*, "She denied that the US aid to combat drug trafficking had diminished, to the contrary it had been greater this year than the one before." Speaking about the Honduran military's interception of airplanes that previous summer, she insisted: "It can't be said that we've cut the aid." Although it was six days before the primary election, she didn't say a word about the recent wave of repression and killings of LIBRE candidates and activists and of campesinos.[43]

As the primary fraud unfolded in late November and early December, Ambassor Kubiske went silent. The entire week of the Technical Coup, she was conveniently out of the country. After it, as Hondurans of a wide range of political stripes raised public alarms about the destruction of the rule of law, the US put out a mealy-mouthed statement:

> We are monitoring the situation closely, in coordination with partner nations and international organizations, and urge all actors to respect democratic norms.
>
> The United States is deeply interested in the success of democracy in Honduras and the strengthening and independence of its institutions. We strongly support the rule of law and respect for the constitutional separation of powers, as well as a fair and transparent democratic process.
>
> We look to the Honduran people to resolve this matter peacefully and democratically.[44]

In other words, the State Department was saying: We're going to look the other way. We're okay with this. We support Juan Orlando. Inside sources within Honduras told me in this period that the State Department loved Hernández: he was young and could stay in power for a long time. He was a strong man, in contrast to Lobo's reckless clownishness and weak ability to control his opponents on the right. He fit the long, tragic pattern of Latin American dictatorships supported by the United States. In its January 2010 cable evaluating Hernández, the embassy had reported to Washington: "He has consistently supported US interests."[45]

US military support for Honduran security forces continued to grow in 2012 and 2013, although actual funding totals are not entirely clear. The total for 2012 was at least $27 million; the actual figure is probably much higher. In the category of "Foreign Military Financing," US funds shot up from $1 million in 2012 to $2,848,000 in 2013; totals in some other categories dropped.[46] Much of US security aid was channeled through the Central American Security Initiative (CARSI), a largely non-transparent package into which the administration increasingly folded segments of its development and "humanitarian" aid, including training for security forces, making it harder for critics to object to CARSI funding, since those who did so could then be accused of holding up monies for other, benevolent purposes. Other funds flowed in from a variety of spigots. At the beginning of February 2013, Martha Mendoza of the

Associated Press (AP) reported that, in 2011, the US Department of Defense had spent "a record $67.4 million on military contracts in Honduras," as well as eighty-nine million dollars on the US's own unit of six hundred troops stationed at Soto Cano Air Base. She also found that "Neither the State Department nor the Pentagon could provide details explaining a 2011 $1.3 billion authorization for exports of military electronics to Honduras—although it would amount to almost half of all arms exports for the entire Western Hemisphere."[47]

In November 2012, the United States restored the radar intelligence cooperation it had suspended in the summer when it had become concerned over corruption and the shooting down of planes.[48]

Congress continued nonetheless to put brakes on part of the flow of US money to Honduras. Because of pressure from top congressional figures, in December the Millennium Challenge Corporation, a US-funded slush fund for foreign governments, turned down up to $200 million in infrastructure funding to the Honduran government.[49] Senator Leahy (and perhaps others) continued to place temporary holds on large sums of money, although they could not do so indefinitely. Yet for every dollar held up by Congress, whether through these processes or potentially through the new conditions placed on aid to Honduras in the December 2012 State and Foreign Operations Appropriations Act and in subsequent years' appropriations bills, perhaps five other dollars flowed in from international financial institutions controlled by the Obama Administration—such as a $60 million loan from the US-controlled Inter-American Development Bank to the Honduran police, announced on June 21, 2012.[50]

On March 13, 2013, the Associated Press dropped a new bomb, reporting that current death squads were operating within the Honduran police, still under the leadership of Juan Carlos "El Tigre" Bonilla, the National Director of Police who had been established to have led death squad activity in 2003. The AP's Alberto Arce documented two cases in 2013, in which young men associated with gang activity were detained by the Tegucigalpa police and then disappeared and were presumed dead. He uncovered at least one hundred fifty official complaints of additional death-squad-style killings that had been filed in the capital and fifty in San Pedro Sula.[51]

The previous August, in 2012, the State Department had declared in its certification document that it maintained zero contact with Bonilla while it was investigating the evidence against him. In the meantime, State insisted, it would be "carefully limiting assistance to special Honduran law enforcement units, staffed by Leahy-vetted Honduran personnel who receive training, guidance, and advice directly from US law enforcement, and are not under Bonilla's direct supervision."[52] On March 23, the AP broke a second story establishing clearly that the entire Honduran police were in fact under Bonilla's jurisdiction—therefore no such independent units existed.[53]

The AP's revelations set up a series of evasions, flip-flops, and shameless lies on the part of the State Department, as it sought to address challenges while wiggling over to support Bonilla. At a March 25 State Department press briefing in Washington, the AP's Matt Lee asked the agency's spokesperson, Patrick Ventrell:

> We had a story about the U.S. support for Honduran police ... which you'd long said had nothing to do with the police chief Bonilla, and we're saying that every single one of the units you claim was vetted reports directly to Bonilla. How do you square that with what you told Congress and what you've said publicly about this?

Ventrell replied: "I can tell you right now that there is a review process," but he couldn't comment on internal deliberations. "Are you urging the Honduran Government to relieve Mr. Bonilla of his duties?" Lee countered. Ventrell answered: "I'm not aware that we've taken a position before this review is finished, so I think we're going to conduct a thorough review and then take a look and be back in communication not only with Honduras but with the US Congress." Two days later, at the briefing, other reporters kept pushing the issue, while unsuccessfully trying to get Ventrell to specify exactly how much the United States was funding Honduran security forces. One reporter wondered out loud whether the United States had decided to place "larger national security" and other issues above concerns over funding Bonilla.[54]

It turns out that the State Department had known about the evidence against Bonilla, and even acted on it, ten years before—ever since María Luisa Borjas first filed her report documenting his death squad activity in 2003. In a February 26, 2003, cable to Washington, US Ambassador Larry Palmer wrote:

> In his meeting with Minister of Public Security Oscar Alvarez, Fisk [Dan Fisk, Deputy Assistant Secretary of State for Western Hemisphere Affairs] urged Alvarez to take action against corrupt police, to send a strong signal about impunity by arresting fugitive policeman Juan Carlos "Tiger" Bonilla, and to act carefully against whistle-blowers, such as ex-Chief of Police Internal Affairs Maria Luisa Borjas.[55]

In other words, for all its later assertions of a long review process beginning in August 2012 and extending into the spring of 2013, State had known about Bonilla's terrifying human rights record all along. After Ambassador Palmer wrote his 2003 memo, though, Oscar Álvarez hadn't fired Bonilla. Nor did Álvarez protect Borjas as the embassy had requested. Instead, he fired her and shut down her investigation.[56]

At the top of the US drug-war heap in the spring of 2013 sat William Brownfield, Assistant Secretary of State for the Bureau of International Narcotics and Law Enforcement, known as INL. By that time, he was a formidable, experienced pro, adept at managing foreign governments, their security forces, the US media, and, especially, the US Congress. He'd previously served as US Ambassador to Colombia, Chile, and, most famously, Venezuela, from which, in 2006, President Hugo Chávez had publicly threatened to expel him.[57] On March 28, 2013, right after the new AP death squad story broke, Brownfield gave a long, dial-in press conference to reporters in Spanish, in which he discussed the Bonilla case extensively. In a key section, he laid out a new interpretation of the Leahy Law:

> What we've done in this moment, is accept that the government of the United States, in accordance with its obligations under the law, we are not going to work with the director general of the National Police, we don't have relations with him, we're not offering even a dollar or a cent, and also, we've eliminated the

level immediately below, the twenty officials or functionaries that
work directly with the director general, neither do we work with
them, to give two degrees of separation to whatever program that
we support the National Police with, to assure that there is not
contact with the director general.[58]

I came to call this Brownfield's "two degrees of separation" speech.

Soon, though, State pivoted to directly blessing El Tigre and
pushing aside the evidence against him. "Ten years ago there were
allegations and accusations against him; I know that he underwent
a judicial procedure that had a good result for him, of not guilty,"
assured Ambassador Kubiske on April 3.[59] Brownfield himself insinu-
ated on May 12: "I haven't seen that any conclusion has been reached
that supports the accusations of some groups about the record of the
leadership of the Honduran police," then announced, "I respect the
work that El Tigre Bonilla is doing, I admire him and believe that he
is good for Honduras, but I am restricted by US law in terms of who
I can work with."[60] Together, it appears that Kubiske and Brownfield
were subtly seeking to undermine those who criticized Bonilla, while
sending deliberately mixed signals about their own positions versus
those legally mandated by Congress.

You could almost see the US officials squirming. As Senator
Leahy continued his hold on the funds, as the human rights conditions in the 2012 Appropriations Act kicked in to potentially restrict
still more US funding, and as the US media rained down its new
revelations about who, exactly, the US was supporting in Honduras,
the State Department played a slippery dance, trying simultaneously
to shore up the ongoing coup regime and, in order to evade congressional pressure, clean it up a bit.

Cause and effect were rarely clear for those of us observing from
the outside. But timing and correlation did suggest plenty. In April
2013, a flurry of announced "reform" activity in Honduras followed
the Associated Press's new revelations, and we can assume that US
pressure elicited it. Luis Rubí, still the attorney general at the time,
reported that eighty percent of all criminal cases remained in impunity.[61] Lobo announced the creation of more criminal courts. Charges
were finally filed in the high-profile, May 2012 killing of Ebed Yanes

by soldiers at the checkpoint.[62] Honduran government officials engaged in a round-robin of public finger-pointing about who was to blame for the failed cleanup of the police. A story in *El Tiempo* about Chepe Handal, accused by the US Treasury Department of being a drug trafficker, suggested openly that government officials and businesspeople were widely implicated in drug trafficking.[63]

At the beginning of June, the US itself cut funding for the Honduran government's police cleanup office, the DIECP (La Dirección de Investigación y Evaluación de la Carrera Policial), in an implicit—if only implicit—admission of the organization's spectacular ineffectiveness. In April the DIECP had reported that in the entire previous year only twelve of fourteen thousand total members of the police had been accused of corruption or criminal acts.[64]

Other US actions, though, suggested further conscious pushback against the pressure up north. In his May 12 speech praising El Tigre Bonilla, Brownfield made an apparently deliberate reference to the US Congress holding up funds for Honduran aviation.[65] The next day—by seeming coincidence—René Osorio Canales, the head of the Honduran armed forces, gave a big interview to the Honduran media, in which he spoke at length about how the planes of the Honduran Air Force were old and dilapidated and needed $200 million to bring them up to date.[66]

Under US pressure, the Honduran government wavered between willful incompetence, announcements of "reforms" that were only for show, and dramatic actions that ostensibly demonstrated great political will but in fact often had destructive impacts, such as reckless layoffs that gutted the rights of public employees. On June 6, Lobo suspended the entire twenty-two-hundred-member staff of the DNIC (Dirección Nacional de Investigación Criminal), the criminal investigation division of the police.[67] In May, in response to Honduras's international notoriety for having the highest murder rate in the world, the local police in San Pedro Sula told reporters from *El Tiempo* that they had been ordered not to report violent crimes, presumably so that the statistics would go down.[68]

While the US Embassy was working its ways with the Honduran government—or attempting to—it was also continuing to construct and support an alternative "civil society," funded by USAID and allied US foundations, that would seek to represent the Obama Administration's interests in Honduras while appearing to emerge independently from within the country. In this period, most prominent of these groups was the Alliance for Peace and Justice, headed by Julieta Castellanos, the rector of the National Autonomous University of Honduras (UNAH), who emerged as a major public figure after her son was killed by the police. The Association for a More Just Society began to take a more prominent role as well.

Amid all this squirming, weaseling out, behind-the-scenes squeezing, and routine deception of the public, the real forces behind positive outcomes in US policy, let alone changes in the behavior of the Honduran government, were ultimately impossible to decode accurately from the outside. Some of the worst abuses were evidently curbed a bit; but at the same time the administration's larger goal of supporting JOH in the long term appeared to harden.

On June 18, 2013, the US Senate upped the ante: Twenty-one senators, led by Benjamin Cardin of Maryland, sent a letter to Kerry expressing "concern regarding the grave human rights situation and deterioration of the rule of law in Honduras." The senators recounted the reports they'd received of police death squads, of the failure to clean up the police or prosecute human rights violations, and of "a pattern of violence and threats against journalists, human rights defenders, members of the clergy, union leaders, opposition figures, and LGBT activists." They concluded by asking the Department of State to provide a "detailed assessment" of current efforts by the Honduran government to protect human rights and investigate extrajudicial killings by security forces, and to "conduct a thorough review to ensure that no US assistance is provided to police or military personnel or units credibly implicated in human rights violations." They stopped just short of saying, "suspend the aid." But they were senators, they counted almost half the Democrats, and they included top leadership—not only Leahy, Chair of the Committee on the Judiciary, but also Assistant Democratic Leader and Whip Richard Durbin and committee chairs Barbara Mikulski, Tom Harkin, Deborah Stabenow, and Barbara Boxer, along with future Vice Presidential candidate Tim Kaine.[69] Working on that letter with Algene Sajery, the top foreign policy aide in Cardin's office, my colleagues and I thought we'd be lucky, and thrilled, to get five to seven names signed on. We were mostly stunned that we'd helped produce something so powerful from the Senate, and had been happy to be working with Algene, a sophisticated and sharp senior aide with a long history of working on human rights issues effectively.

As usual, we couldn't put our finger on the letter's exact impact. Two weeks after it went public, though, I met with a top-tier official at the Department of State in Washington who told me he'd just been in three solid days of meetings about Honduras. He gave me two hours of his time—and that of three others—and took what I said seriously. He offered that "we did cut the money for the DIECP," the semi-defunct police cleanup office. I asked him if he could please specify exactly where the Central American Regional Security Initiative (CARSI) funds were flowing inside Honduras. "We don't really know," he replied. "We barely tell Congress that!" He promised to follow up with information. He never did.

Testimonio

In July 2013, I was asked to testify before the Tom Lantos Commission on Human Rights in the US House of Representatives, about human rights and US policy in Honduras. In theory, testifying in the US Congress should have been exciting and empowering, if still mildly terrifying. In practice, it took place in a wave of real terror and registered like a tiny, well-dressed blip on a radar screen of fear and anguish.

A month before the hearing, to the day, on June 25, 2013, my friend Chema started receiving death threats. The first call told him to "stop talking shit on the radio because if you don't we're going to shut your mouth. You should get your white clothes ready, so they can bury you, because we're going to kill you." His wife took the second call a few days later: "Señora the problem isn't with you. Tell your husband that if he doesn't shut his mouth on the radio we're going to kill him." On July 5, for the second time, a darkened car circled over and over again around Radio Progreso, the Jesuit station in downtown El Progreso, during Chema's nightly show, "Sindicalista en el Aire" (Trade Unionist on the Air). Padre Melo, the director, had to drive him home.

His full name was José María Martínez, shortened to "Chema," but everyone called him "Chemita" because of his height—or, rather, lack thereof (although I'd never noticed myself because, at five and a half feet, I'm often a good six inches taller, at least, than many people in Honduras anyway). He had spiky black-and-gray hair slicked back from his forehead, a thick mustache, and a big grin. He was the Communications Director for FESTAGRO, the Federation of Honduran Banana and Agroindustrial Unions. He liked to spend his lunch breaks sending out silly visual jokes to his friends—I remember one with a mock-up photo of Hugo Chávez clutching Mel Zelaya by the waist as they faced forward on the prow of the Titanic. Everyone knew and loved Chema because of his radio show, which he'd run five days a week for nineteen years. He organized workshops for rank-and-file banana workers, too, teaching them how to produce radio shows themselves, and every night regular workers would be on the air with him discussing labor conditions on their plantations or how the latest contract negotiations with Chiquita were playing out. At the end of the show, one of them would announce the exact times workers on the local Chiquita plantations had to show up at work the next morning, in a rhythmic recitation of pre-dawn daily life cutting and packing bananas: "Finca Omonita, men numbers seventy-five to ninety-three, 5:15; women numbers twenty-two to fifty-eight, 5:45."

The exact source of the threats to Chema was not entirely clear—in part because the corrupt police never followed up with an investigation, despite the clear evidence—but it was speculated they were probably connected to an organizing campaign by the unions at the Tres Hermanas banana plantation, which Chema had been talking about a lot on his show.

Those threats tore me up inside. Chema and I had worked together for a dozen years. There's a picture of him in my book on the banana unions; he's the guy on page 59 working on a pink sign celebrating women's projects. I didn't know him personally at all, but once, just once, maybe two years after the coup when he was driving me to the airport, he put his hand on my forearm for a half a second, and said, "Thanks for everything you're doing." It was a beautiful, fleeting thing.

The year before, in 2012, after it had gotten dicier for me to be in Honduras myself, Chema twice came with me as a sort of bodyguard when I traveled from San Pedro Sula to Tegucigalpa—not armed or anything like that, but just so that if I got whisked away somehow, or worse, there'd be a witness. Of course, he could be whisked away, or worse, too. I got him a room in my same hotel, and he helped with the cabs and the appointments and claimed he actually enjoyed listening to me say the same things over and over again in the meetings. We never talked about personal issues and never once flirted, in a country where flirting is generally elevated to a very high art form among many people.

When the threats against Chema accelerated in July 2013, I already had a trip to San Pedro Sula planned, so I offered to stay in his house for a few nights to help protect him and his family. He said yes quickly. Meanwhile, he was working with human rights groups to try to find someone to pay for a plane ticket to the United States—

where he had relatives he could stay with—and had contacted the US Embassy for help getting a visa. But the embassy's response was sluggish, to say the least, despite considerable pressure from the AFL-CIO, human rights groups, and the US Congress.

Three days before the Saturday when I was supposed to leave for Honduras, I got the email asking me to testify before the Tom Lantos Commission. I would need to be in Washington the following Thursday, July 25, 2013. I'll admit that by that point I had privately fantasized about some day testifying in Congress—although once I began to play out the fantasy in my head, it quickly degenerated into a bad dream of drooling incompetence, accessible forever on CSPAN.

Should I cancel the visit to Honduras and go to Washington instead? Or give up testifying and come through for Chema? Deep inside me, I knew there was no way I could tell Chema I wasn't going to stay with him after I'd said I would. I decided to split the trip. I'd fly to Honduras on Saturday as planned, then fly to D.C. on Wednesday to testify, and then fly home from there, giving up the remainder of the week's trip I'd planned in Honduras.

I loved seeing his house and staying there. It was on the corner of two dirt roads, in the peaceful outskirts of El Progreso, with a broad view out the living room window of a soccer field and the hills beyond. I loved watching Chema and his wife, a nurse, banter back and forth affectionately next to each other on the couch; I loved meeting his son, a dental technician, who lived there too; Chema was building an extra room for him around the back. I felt honored to be in their house. The whole time I was there, I kept thinking about that phone ringing with the voice telling Chema to buy his burial clothes.

On Monday, at Radio Progreso, I met up with Tirza Flores Lanza, the former appellate judge who'd been one of the people with whom I'd spent Hurricane Sandy. Sleek and glamorous, with straight black hair cut to artfully curve just below her chin line, Tirza was the highest-ranking of four judges who had been deposed for opposing the coup, and who had a big case moving forward in the Inter-American Commission on Human Rights.

On Wednesday morning, Tirza and I rendezvoused again in the San Pedro Sula airport for our flights together to Miami and then D.C. As we passed through security and then filed onto the plane, I relaxed, figuring hey, I'm with a former judge, no one's going to mess with me or detain me this time. We settled into our seats, Tirza about ten rows back from me in the next section. Just before the plane was going to leave, an official from American Airlines approached me and asked if I were Dana Frank and could I please come with her. I stood up to signal to Tirza what was happening, waving at her dramatically and semi-desperately with an array of hand gestures. She smiled back happily—not decoding that I was signaling trouble—and waved "Hi!" The official told me I'd need to come back with her to the airport to personally observe an inspection of my suitcase, because something suspicious had been identified. I stepped into the aisle and called back to Tirza again and waved my arms even more dramatically. She smiled back happily and waved "Hi!" again.

The official led me all the way back inside to the check-in counter and down a long glassed-in hall that ran behind it, then into a small room where two police officers were staring at a screen showing luggage moving past through a metal box. She was apologetic as she explained that I needed to wait until the inspecting officer arrived. I could see my bag sequestered over in the corner. I was well aware that drugs might have been planted in it. The entire time all this was going on, from the moment I walked off the plane, I stayed on my cell phone talking loudly to an American friend, a human rights activist with decades of experience in Central America, describing every single thing I was seeing and hearing and the nametags of every official I met. Above the luggage-screening machine a large sign declared "No cell phones."

After maybe twenty minutes, a young man showed up wearing camouflage, black army boots, a rifle across his chest, and "Air Force" sewn onto his shirt. He was very nice, as he unzipped my suitcase and saw there was almost nothing inside—it was an old, extra bag I'd brought in full of presents. We agreed that the whole alarm was probably prompted by dogs sniffing a dried-up mystery blob on its outside, which was probably food.

But I don't really know, still. Was it harassment?

I got back onto the plane, where Tirza remained innocently clueless about my having been whisked-off. In the Miami airport, we bounced around in jeans, looking for snacks and the *New York Times*, while I polished the final draft of my testimony. She turned out to be the perfect source for fact-checking: "Was it four or five judges who were deposed by Juan Orlando Hernández in the Technical Coup?" "Four."

When we got to D.C., we heaved our suitcases up three flights of stairs to a sumptuous room at the very top of the Tabard Inn, near DuPont Circle. (I'd offered Tirza half my king-size bed so that she could afford to come testify.) I settled onto the bed with my back to its brass frame, Tirza into a wingback armchair in the opposite corner.

Fifteen minutes after we got there, her phone rang. As she listened to the call, I could see her face drop from happiness to horror to devastation in seconds, just like something out of a movie—but this was the real thing. The call was from her husband, Guillermo López Lone, also a former judge who, like Tirza, had been deposed for opposing the coup. He told her that another judge, Mireya Mendoza Peña, had just been assassinated, shot up twenty times while driving in the middle of El Progreso, where Tirza and I had both been two days before. Mireya was a colleague of Tirza's; she was a member of the Executive Committee of the Association of Honduran Judges for Democracy, of which Tirza and Guillermo were leaders; she'd met with Tirza just the week before. She was the first judge assassinated since the coup. Of course, it could just as easily have been Tirza, or her husband, who'd been assassinated.[70]

The next morning, we ironed our clothes and Tirza dried her hair; then she left for an early meeting. At 9:45, we met up again in the hall outside the hearing room in the Rayburn House Office Building, each in our best, most tasteful outfit—Tirza in a gray jacket with black piping over a matching grey dress, I in a dark blue brocade jacket over black pants.

While we waited for the hearing to start, I got an email from the acting human rights officer in the US Embassy in Tegucigalpa, responding to a request from the AFL-CIO for an escort from the embassy to help Chema get safely to the airport, once he got a ticket and visa. No, the official replied in the email, the embassy couldn't help escort him, but he'd be glad to ask the Honduran National Director of Police to help out, if we'd like.[71] I realized immediately that the email in my hand was a volatile smoking gun, proving that the embassy was, in fact, working with El Tigre Bonilla, despite its denials and Brownfield's vow of "two degrees of separation." I couldn't begin to decide at that moment what to do with the evidence I now had. But I knew what it meant.

This was supposed to be the glamorous part, the testifying in Congress, but between the assassination, the sleep deprivation (I'd tossed and turned the night before and only gotten two hours of sleep), the threats against Chema, and the email, I was in a flipped-out blur the whole time and could barely grasp any of it, as we milled about, greeted friends and reporters and aides, met prestigious Hondurans, chatted with the two other colleagues who were testifying, shook hands with Congressmembers and with new Senator Tim Kaine, who was also testifying, and lined up in our seats. I did absolutely fine when I read my prepared statement. Then Representative James McGovern, the committee's Democratic co-chair, gave a speech, and I could tell he was warming up to ask me a question. He was talking about the continuation of US foreign aid to the corrupt Honduran police and military, despite ongoing abuses: "They are going to think we are a cheap date, . . . that the money will keep coming no matter what they do." Cheap date? I was so dumbstruck—and starstruck—that this tall, handsome, jovial man, who was an actual United States Congressmember, had just said something so wonderfully forceful and comic, that I could barely answer the question that indeed followed, about what I thought would happen if the US did, in fact, suspend the money. I did manage to not drool or stumble or be a total idiot in my answers (but I don't think I was great, either).

After that, Tirza and I went off in a cab to two meetings at the State Department. It was like walking into an imperial force field, into that big cold concrete building in Foggy Bottom, all chrome and shiny black surfaces inside, with its giant lobby featuring flags from the countries of the world waving from the ceiling as if to say, "We are all Good Neighbors here." Right before we entered our second meeting, with the Director for Western Hemispheric Affairs of the Bureau of Democracy, Human Rights, and Labor, I checked my email again in the hall and found an emergency alert announcing that two observers from the Honduras Accompaniment Project had just been kidnapped in Honduras by forty men armed with rifles and machetes. They had arrived the day before at the community of Nueva Esperanza, to help protect Indigenous residents protesting a mining project. The observers had been released after two hours, but their safety still wasn't at all clear.[72] When the director arrived, I told him about the kidnappings immediately and with great alarm and explained that the Honduras Accompaniment Project was a US-based NGO and that the two people who'd been captured were possibly US citizens. He said, "Send me the information later" and strode into the meeting room.

How do I explain that that was perhaps the worst moment of all those twenty-four hours surrounding the hearing? Two people, possibly US citizens, who certainly worked for a US-based organization, had just been held captive at gunpoint for two hours and weren't necessarily safe, and the response from a high-ranking official in the US State Department was that I should send him the information later—which would be after at least an hour, possibly two. The cold, willing obliviousness of it stunned me.

I stumbled through the meeting in an even deeper stupor. Afterward Tirza had one more meeting, at the Inter-American Commission on Human Rights a few blocks away, and I tagged along. When we finally got back to the hotel, we dumped our stuff in the room, staggered back down to a couch in the hotel bar, and quickly went for a beer each, and then another, and then some bar food.

Back in our room afterward, Tirza was in the wingback again and I was on the bed, both of us lost in our laptops. Out of the blue, in perfect English, each word enunciated clearly one by one, still looking down at her computer, she announced: "I do not want to die."

The next morning, Tirza left for the airport before dawn to make it home in time for Mireya's funeral. I slept in a bit longer, then caught my own flight home to my safe, comfortable life in California.

Chema left soon after for Nicaragua and stayed two months but was heartbroken with loneliness and couldn't afford to pay for a hotel or rent, and returned home. He stopped doing his radio show—other brave souls from the unions kept it going—but continued with an online interview program called "*Sindicalista en el Web*" (Trade Unionist on the Web). On November 29, an unmarked, dark car parked in front of his house next to the soccer field. His wife took pictures of the car, including its plates, but the police did nothing. On January 8, he got a call saying he'd escaped in November but wouldn't escape again. He started sleeping in a different place every night. In March 2014, eight months after he'd first asked the US Embassy for help getting out of the country, the United States finally approved his visa, and a human rights group paid for a plane ticket. He made it safely to the airport with no help from either the embassy or from the Honduran National Director of Police, instead escorted by carfuls of his friends and comrades from the labor movement and Radio Progreso, and he flew far away from home. He hasn't been back since.

A month later, I officially queried the US Embassy as to whether it did, indeed, have contact with Bonilla, quoting the email I'd received about Chema and citing Brownfield's assertion that "we [the US government] have no relations with him." The Public Affairs Counselor responded: "In the statements you quote, Assistant Secretary Brownfield was referring to the fact that the US Government provides no training or material assistance to those individuals. The Embassy does discuss law enforcement matters with the Honduran National Police, including its leadership."[73]

Three months later, the Associated Press conducted a long interview with Bonilla, in which Bonilla discussed his regular contact and close cooperation with the US Embassy.[74] He had been seen coming in and out of the embassy daily.

Demonstration Election

The closer it drew to the November 24 general election, the tenser it got.

LIBRE activists fanned out into the neighborhoods. Xiomara Castro, the party's presidential candidate, promised to re-found Honduras from the bottom up, with a new constitution, a referendum law, and laws protecting Indigenous, African-descent, and LGBTI people.[75] From the earliest polls at the beginning of 2013, through the very last ones a month before the vote, she steadily tracked between three and ten percentage points above Juan Orlando Hernández, with the exception of one poll at the last minute, of dubious provenance (Honduran law doesn't allow electoral surveys in the last month before an election). Nothing remotely like this had ever happened before in Honduran history. There had never even been a successful opposition party of the left or center-left, let alone one that was in first place in the polls. For all of 2013, the question loomed: could Xiomara actually win? Would President Lobo and the military allow her to? Would the United States countenance that? If she did in fact win in a free and fair election—which no one expected was possible—what would happen afterward? A military rebellion? Deliberate chaos in the streets provoked by the oligarchs? Another coup? It was hard to imagine any positive outcome. But a tiny, tiny sliver of hope glinted high up in a corner of the Honduran sky.[76]

The other surprise in the polling data was the rise of a second new party, the Anti-Corruption Party, led by television sportscaster Salvador Nasralla. Composed largely of middle-class and upper-class refugees from the traditional Liberal and National Parties, who were conservative but fed up with their parties' corruption and alarmed about the security crisis in the coup's aftermath, its adherents had in many cases supported the coup and weren't about to come near LIBRE. Nasralla steadily drew ten to eleven percent in the polls, suggesting he could be an effective spoiler.[77]

Hernández, for his part, came on strong; he played the fear card and aggressively promoted further militarization to stem the security crisis. On July 15, he famously promised to put "a soldier on every corner."[78] In the late summer and early fall, he was the engine behind creating five thousand new members of the military police, amid much media celebration. The newly launched troops had only three months of training and eighth-grade educations.[79] By this point, he had allegedly bullied and bribed all the newspapers, even the Liberals' *La Tribuna* and *El Tiempo*, into enthusiastic support for his candidacy. Jaime Rosenthal, the patriarch of *El Tiempo*, was rumored to have capitulated in part because of a $49 million no-bid contract he was awarded in March 2013, in which his company got to provide cement for the nation's highway construction for the next five years.[80] Amid media coverage that gushed forth day after day, Hernández's law-and-order fearmongering did appeal to some poor people in the cities, as did his National Party's new *Bono de Diez Mil* (Bonus of Ten Thousand), through which the very poor were given cash payments in what was widely understood to be a vote-buying operation.[81]

For decades, the oligarchs who ran the Liberal and the National Parties had traded power back and forth in backroom deals, locking down control over the state. They were deeply threatened by LIBRE and responded viciously. The terror directed against LIBRE activists and candidates, which had begun during the primaries, continued. So did the long, post-coup pattern of killing mid-level or rank-and-file leaders, never the top figures, in order to make it harder to pin down the assassinations as targeted political violence. Between May 1 and October 15 alone, nine LIBRE activists and candidates were assassinated, as well as three from the National Party and one from Nasralla's Anti-Corruption Party (PAC). Lest we attribute these to "random violence" or "common crime," the killings of political figures continued for two weeks after the November 24 elections, then stopped.[82]

The US Congress was paying attention to all this, however. On October 14, Representatives Raúl Grijalva, Hank Johnson, and Mike Honda sent a letter to Secretary of State John Kerry, expressing concern over the elections. "We fear the country currently lacks conditions to guarantee a free and fair election process," they wrote, citing the continuing human rights abuses threatening civil liberties, the lack of a level playing field, and the "increasingly central, and ominous role" of state security forces. "We are concerned that the Embassy has not spoken forcefully about the militarization of the police under the impetus of one of the candidates."[83] On November 13, two weeks before the election, Senator Tim Kaine led on a letter from thirteen senators raising concerns: "Honduran journalists are regularly the targets of violence and threats, and political candidates have been killed as a result of running for office. These challenges raise serious concerns over the Honduran government's ability to conduct free and fair elections."[84]

That same day Representative Eliot Engel, ranking member of the House Foreign Affairs Committee, gave a speech at the Council of the Americas in Washington, D.C., about the upcoming Honduran and Salvadoran elections. He criticized "an overly militarized US relationship with Honduran security forces and the human rights perils that this creates with security forces that have become politicized." Engel wrapped up his speech dramatically by referring to the "the unfortunate baggage left by some past US administrations that have historically been nakedly partisan in Central American politics....[B]y words and deeds, the burden is on us to actually persuade our Central American friends that we do not have a finger on the electoral scale, and that we will work with whoever is elected."[85]

The State Department itself had no problem waving that finger. Dripping with arrogant paternalism, on November 3, Ambassador Kubiske told the Honduran press that after the elections, "We are going to see if a person is chosen who represents the will of the people, then we are going to begin to see the convergences between the United States and the desires of that government."[86] Five days later Kubiske cautioned that the results might not be available the night of the election, and that unfounded rumors would be moving about. "That's why Hondurans are worried about this issue of whether there will be violence or not." In raising this alarm about potential violence, Kubiske was exactly echoing charges by Hernández's National Party that LIBRE would somehow rebel violently if it didn't win. "It's important to know the candidates, what vision they have," she catechized, then stressed ending insecurity and building a more prosperous economy—Juan Orlando's exact campaign themes.[87]

When the elections finally arrived on November 24, violence and armed terror did erupt, but directed against, not caused by, the opposition. In the Colonia Kennedy neighborhood of Tegucigalpa on November 22, two blocks full of military police surrounded a meeting of LIBRE members with its congressional candidate Gilberto Ríos, pointed rifles at the faces of the people arriving, and, in the words of one eyewitness, "looked up at the headquarters with terrible eyes filled with hate." The troops left when some of the participants who were international observers put on their official vests.[88] That night in La Unión, Lempira, armed men moved about intimidating people, including Noé Alvarado, a city council candidate for LIBRE. In the town of El Paraíso, Danlí, a hundred armed, masked men surrounded fifty people in a hotel who had credentials as official election observers of the *mesas* or voting tables. The masked men threatened to burn down the hotel if the observers went to the tables for the elections.[89] The night before the election, María Amparo Pineda Duarte and Julio Ramón Maradiaga, affiliated with a rural workers' cooperative, were returning home from training as election observers when they were ambushed and shot by masked men with high-caliber weapons. They both died immediately.[90] That night military authorities took over and shut down the antennas for Radio Globo and Channel 11.[91] The list goes on and on.

The Honduran government also harassed international election observers. Two days before the election, migration authorities arrived at ERIC, the Jesuit research center in El Progreso, and demanded the identification and immigration papers of members of a US delegation from the Honduran Solidarity Network who were in town for election training.[92] That morning in Tegucigalpa, six people wearing ski masks and three wearing T-shirts of the immigration authorities arrived at the reception desk of a hotel where international observers were staying, and demanded that all the observers come to the lobby. When they arrived, the masked men and women interrogated them, went through their passports, and seized the passports of two Brazilian observers. When the two asked why, they were told, "Because, yes, we can." The observers were deeply shaken and terrified.[93]

Although turnout on election day was high, international observers in their post-election reports documented a nationwide maze of irregularities, apparent fraud, and intimidation. A team from the International Federation for Human Rights (IFHR), for example, encountered booths placed in front of widespread voting sites; at the booths, National Party voters were given credit cards providing discounts on medications, food, phone bills, and other products. The federation's delegation documented people who weren't allowed to vote because they had been declared dead, noted the lack of transparency as the ballots were transferred from polling places to the electoral commission, and reported that official poll-watchers from some of the smaller parties were selling their credentials.[94]

The official delegation from the European Union put out a preliminary report expressing concern over lack of transparency in campaign finance and "serious signs of trafficking in credentials and other irregularities." But it largely blessed the electoral system's reliability and transparency.[95] According to Leo Gabriel, an Austrian member of the delegation, though, there was a fierce debate within the delegation. In an interview at the airport as he left town, he was scathing: "I could see from the start that this electoral process was compromised." Echoing the IFHR, he spoke of dead people who voted, live people who were declared dead and couldn't vote, bold vote-buying by the National Party, and collusion over the sale of poll-watching credentials. "During the transmission of the results there was no possibility to find out where the tallies were being sent, and we received reliable information that at least twenty percent of the original tally sheets were being diverted to an illegal server that they kept hidden." He said that evidence indicated that many of the results were pre-arranged. "To speak of transparency, after everything that happened last Sunday, is a joke."[96]

The vote count took forever. On the Friday after the Sunday election, Xiomara Castro and LIBRE gave a press conference demanding a vote-by-vote recount and an investigation by the attorney general, citing a range of irregularities.[97] But, of course, Hernández's party controlled the electoral commission, the attorney general, the Congress, and the Supreme Court, so there was no one to appeal to. On Saturday, the Supreme Electoral Tribunal (Tribunal Suprema Electoral, TSE), the official electoral commission, announced that ninety-five percent of the votes had been counted, and that Juan Orlando Hernández was winning clearly with thirty-six percent to Xiomara Castro's twenty-eight percent.[98]

As all this played out, much of the US mainstream press was surprisingly strong in reporting criticisms of Hernández, electoral fraud, and intimidation. The previous two years' drumbeat of congressional pressure and grassroots education had paid off. The *New York Times*, for example, ran a largely supportive story about Castro challenging the results.[99] The *New Yorker* posted a story the day before the elections that quoted Rafael Alegría, the Honduran director of Via Campesina and LIBRE candidate for Congress, warning of National Party machinations with potential US backing.[100] Two weeks before the election, *Foreign Affairs* even allowed me to opine: "The stakes are high: either Honduras will plunge deeper into its vortex of violence and repression, or it will have a fighting change to begin to re-establish the rule of law and construct a viable economy."[101] The *Washington Post*, though, carried the torch for the Obama Administration under the headline "Honduras Election Brings Risks of More Instability." According to the *Post*, the risk was that "Castro, Zelaya and their supporters could send Honduras into another downward spiral if they cry fraud after a loss and take it to the streets."[102]

The next Thursday, December 6, US Ambassador Lisa Kubiske visited the electoral commission's computer center for a lengthy period. Upon her exit she declared that all was "normal and transparent" and that "inconsistencies have been verified." "In general it has been a transparent process, beginning with the representation of the persons at the electoral tables, later the public scrutiny, the representation of all the parties in the computer center."[103] President David Matamoros of the electoral commission thanked her: "She has always been very close to the process."[104] We have no further evidence of how the embassy might or might have had "a finger on the electoral scale," to quote Representative Engel. But, certainly, Kubiske blessed the scales that Lobo, Hernández, and the National Party had so efficiently tipped.

On December 12, the Supreme Electoral Tribunal finally declared Juan Orlando Hernández to be President of the Republic of Honduras. It never allowed the recount Castro had demanded. Hernández allegedly received 1,149,302 votes (36.89 percent), Castro 896,498 (28.78 percent), Villeda of the Liberal Party 632,320 (20.30 percent) and Nasralla of the Anti-Corruption Party 418,443 (13.43 percent) in the final count.[105] The election was over, and Juan Orlando had taken charge.

But the opposition's enormous electoral push of the previous year nonetheless produced one political earthquake. The composition of the Honduran Congress was transformed altogether. For decades and decades, the National Party and Liberal Party had split up the Congress between themselves. In the aftermath of the coup and the 2009 elections, after the Liberal Party split and then largely fell apart, the National Party for four years enjoyed a strong majority in Congress. In the final 2013 results, though, the entire Congress was reconfigured. Of one hundred twenty-eight total seats, the National Party was in front, but now counted only forty-seven seats—losing its majority. LIBRE had thirty-night to the Liberal Party's twenty-six, the new Anti-Corruption Party picked up thirteen, and two tiny older parties held one each. Without question, the two-party system was indeed shattered. Other surprises abounded, too. LIBRE picked up multiple mayorships in small towns and cities. In San Pedro Sula, where LIBRE was assumed to be strong, the PAC got almost all the congressional seats. The city's mayoralty, though, was awarded to the National Party's Armando Calidonio. How had he won as mayor, people asked, when the PAC had gained the city's congressional vote?[106]

Ignoring all the horrible violence leading up to the voting, the State Department issued a public statement the day after the elections announcing, "The United States congratulates the Honduran people for their peaceful participation." Once again intimating that LIBRE was itself somehow about to explode into violence, it asked Hondurans to "await the completion of the counting of official results and to resolve election disputes peacefully through established legal processes"—although those processes were all controlled by Juan

Orlando. When the final official results were announced on December 12, Secretary of State John Kerry immediately congratulated Hernández: "The Honduran people turned out in record number to vote on November 14, and we commend the Honduran government for ensuring that the election process was generally transparent, peaceful, and reflected the will of the Honduran people."[107]

The Obama Administration thus got the demonstration election it presumably wanted.[108] The ongoing coup regime now had the face of a seemingly democratic process that it hadn't had after the 2009 Lobo election. The United States, for its part, could now clean up its own image as a supporter of the regime and pretend that Juan Orlando and his National Party cronies, responsible for much of the vortex of violence and impunity into which Honduras was increasingly plunged, were now going to heroically ride in and solve the crisis they had themselves provoked, promoted, and exacerbated. Once again, the State Department was willing to support even the most egregious of dictatorial leaders in order to promote US power in the region.

Fathers and Children

What would President Hernández do with all his new power? And would anyone be able to stop him?

A week after the election results were certified, Lobo and Hernández finally fired Juan Carlos "El Tigre" Bonilla, the documented death squad leader, as National Director of the Police—presumably the price of the ticket for the US Embassy's support.[109]

Then things went nuts. In what was referred to as the "*hemorrágia legislativa*" (legislative hemorrhage), Congress, in its last two weeks before the outgoing session closed on January 20, passed over a hundred twenty laws, more than it has passed in the previous two years altogether, and supported over eighty executive orders. Some of the laws had reportedly been written in less than twenty-four hours; some passed in two or three minutes; the content of most was never known publicly until they were weeks later published in *La Gaceta*, the official publication, at which time they would be officially enacted. New legislation awarded almost a hundred new contracts, for garbage collection, water, highway construction, passport issuance, and energy production. As it had been itching to do since before the coup—Mel Zelaya's refusal to agree on this had been one of the precipitating events behind his ouster—Congress passed laws allowing the privatization of Hondutel, the state-owned telephone company, and the ENEE (Empresa Nacional de Energía Eléctrica), the electric power system. Other laws raised the government's private debt limit by $30 million, froze government salaries, and reformulated administrative functions. A new Law of Secrecy walled off government activities from transparency. A new Mining Law ended a moratorium on mining without consultation with the neighboring community. And the *paquetazo* (package scandal) placed fifteen percent taxes on the consumption of a broad basketful of consumer goods, including food. The National Party congressmembers were making the most of the last days of their outright control of Congress, simultaneously out of control, feeling their oats, and grabbing up government wealth and power for themselves and the cronies in every way possible, while also setting up the framework for future control and profits.[110]

The outgoing Honduran Congress also abolished the prominent Committee on the Review of Public Security (CRSP), known as the Meza Commission, although the committee's legal mandate extended into 2015. I visited the CRSP office in Tegucigalpa on January 30, 2014, days after it was terminated, to interview one of its five members, Matías Fúnes. With white floor tiles and blank white walls, the office already felt empty, as if someone were about to come for the furniture. Fúnes, in his late sixties, amiable and chatty, wearing a long-sleeved white *guayabera* shirt, told me the commissioners had learned about the shutdown on television.

The CRSP was promoted in the spring of 2012 by the US Embassy as a response to the previous fall's police scandals. During 2012 and 2013, the State Department and its affiliated NGOs in the United States also helped manage as much as $300 million that flowed into the Honduran police to pay them to reform themselves—precisely as El Tigre was running the show. The CRSP's legal mandate gave it powers to investigate not only the police but also the Public Ministry and the judiciary, with the right to look into individuals' bank accounts and to develop broad proposals for the reform of the police. On October 26, 2012, Fúnes told me, the commission had completed a set of seven proposals, including constitutional reforms setting up a meritocratic system in which civil society participated in reviews, a depoliticization of many functions of the judiciary and prosecutors' offices, a new organic law of the police— "It had to be a fundamental change"—that created a new community policing system from scratch throughout the country, and new career rights for individual police officers, including health care for their families so the police could afford to live on their salaries and not be tempted into corruption. Fúnes said the commission had consciously worked closely with many within the police in developing its proposals, so the force would have a sense of ownership over the project and not be blindsided.

Fúnes told me that when the commission completed its report, the US Embassy asked to see it before it was sent to President Lobo. No, the commissioners said, they were done, and they presented their proposals to Lobo. Two months later, they met with him, and he hadn't read it. After the CRSP sent off its report, the commissioners were made to understand that the embassy did not support them any more. The US didn't want a broad, nationwide, top-to-bottom reform of the police, Fúnes told me. Instead it wanted small, "vetted units," loyal to the United States and controlled by it (in theory, at least).[111] During 2013 the CRSP continued to present its proposals to the Honduran Congress and other governmental bodies; the United States continued to cite the commission as evidence of the successful advance of police reform in the country. But it was, in effect, dead long before they came for the furniture in January 2013.[112]

On January 27, in Honduras, I watched Juan Orlando's inauguration on television for hours, stuck to the screen, nauseated. It was like watching a horror movie in which a large smiling and waving insect with a blue-and-white satin sash across his chest devoured his children, while erect military men at his back maintained impassive stares. I watched hours and hours of military contingents marching by the podium in lockstep and saluting, in what later photographs revealed to be a half-empty stadium filled by supposed supporters, who had reportedly been paid $2 and a sandwich to show up in the hot sun and cheer.[113]

Young people threw it right back, though, with a new surge of popular culture. I saw college students in sleek black T-shirts with white letters reading *"No Es Mi Presidente"* (Not My President) or, playing off Hernández's initials, *"Presidente? No Me JOHdas"* (President? Don't Fuck with Me).

When the new Congress opened in late January, the National Party needed eighty-six out of a total of one hundred twenty-eight votes to rule. It needed the Liberal Party's twenty-nine members—who hesitated for about thirty seconds, then cut a deal to remove several items from the much-maligned Paquetazo of consumer taxes, in exchange for voting for Mauricio Oliva of the National Party as president of Congress—thus becoming from then on, as one Honduran I interviewed at the time put it, "a parasite on the National Party."[114] Once Oliva was then ensconced as president of Congress, the National Party could manipulate the congressional rules and internal machinery as it saw fit. Right off, Liberal and National Party members were provided with offices, but the PAC and LIBRE members weren't.

On the congressional floor, it got nasty fast. The PAC swiftly lined up to vote alongside LIBRE, but their combined total wasn't enough to counter the National and Liberal delegates. The Honduran Congress had no history of real parliamentary opposition or debate. LIBRE congressmembers weren't allowed to even present candidates for the presidency of Congress; they were often prevented from introducing legislation or even speaking. As a result, they faced a difficult choice: be silenced or protest. Of widely variant antecedents and political approaches, LIBRE congressmembers vacillated between attempting parliamentary actions and, when they were thwarted, acting like a protest group, even demonstrating on the congressional floor. The newspapers then painted them as unstable animals, incapable of rational governance.[115]

Hernández quickly delivered on his promise to put "a soldier on every corner." In his inaugural speech, he announced that twenty-five thousand new forces would be launched in a giant security operation. "The party's over" for criminals, he declared in the speech's most famous line, and announced that the TIGRES special forces would begin operating that day.[116] On January 6, during the hemorrágia legislativa, National Party congressmembers introduced an amendment to the Constitution that would expand the mandate of the military police. Perhaps most chillingly—and most illustrative of the elite's long-term strategic thinking, as well as of Juan Orlando's closeness to both the military and Evangelical Protestants—on March 29, Hernández launched a new program called *Guardianes de La Patria* (Guardians of the Homeland), in which children as young as five would spend time being indoctrinated in the values of the armed forces, working closely with evangelicals. "Every Saturday, more than 25,000 children at a national level will receive civic and religious formation that will allow them to shape feelings of love for Honduras." The Guardianes program would be all over the papers and television for years, with pictures of happy children learning to salute, plant trees, and wiggle on the ground under barbed wire in the woods.[117]

Hernández's political program also included a range of carrots and sticks designed to simultaneously seduce poor voters, threaten the opposition, and deflect international critics. He launched a new economic program, *"La Chamba,"* that paid maquiladora factory owners fifty percent of workers' (outrageously low) salaries for three-month jobs.[118] He announced the "Unidad Especial de Investigación de Muertes Violentas en el Bajo Aguán," a new Special Task Force that would investigate crimes in the Aguán Valley.[119] Congress passed two hostile laws requiring more than ten thousand nonprofit organizations to file complex paperwork and disclosure requirements; if ruled improper, the NGOs could be immediately shut down and their assets seized. The organizations affected included a big laundry list of opposition groups working on women's, environmental, and human rights issues, such as C-Libre (no relation to LIBRE), an important group and website that documented violations of press freedom.[120]

To justify his domestic militarization, Juan Orlando needed an internal enemy. LIBRE and its adherents served that function—as did anyone who dared question his authority and policies. That spring, Guadalupe Ruelas, the upstanding, highly respected director of Casa Alianza, a children's advocacy NGO, emerged as a key, public critic of the Hernández Administration. Ruelas was the sweetest, nicest man imaginable. In early May, he charged that because of corruption and impunity, the government was failing to protect children. "The killings of children have increased since the new government took office," he declared, and said that the militarization had only made things worse. On May 8, while Ruelas was driving a car bearing Casa Alianza's logo, he was stopped by the military police at a checkpoint in downtown Tegucigalpa. While his vehicle was stationary, two men on a police motorcycle rammed it. The military police then pulled him out of the car and beat him up ferociously, kicking him and dragging him face down all the way to the entrance to the Presidential Palace. They then took Ruelas to a police station. He was refused medical care until 4:30 a.m., when he was hospitalized. It took an international campaign to get him free that next day. "His injuries were the result of a traffic collision," the police stated to the media, and said he'd failed alcohol tests. Newspaper stories ran photos of him in a hotel right before his arrest, allegedly drinking a glass of wine with a woman who was not his wife. He'd been at the hotel for a forum on children.[121]

On May 13, five days after all that was sinking in, LIBRE congressmembers inside the main congressional meeting hall became concerned about the use of police and military violence against demonstrators outside the building, who were protesting the party's exclusion from the Supreme Electoral Tribunal (TSE), which oversees the electoral process. As LIBRE members began to object from the floor, observers spoke out loudly from the gallery, and demonstrators outside allegedly attempted to move upstairs toward the chamber, suddenly around three hundred members of the military police, COBRAS special forces police, and the regular military surrounded the LIBRE congressmembers, beat them up, launched tear gas, and drove them brutally out of the building. Mauricio Oliva, the president of Congress, gave the order to charge. That night, Univision, the international Spanish-language television network, showed clips of Honduran security forces aggressively deploying batons inside the chamber. You could see clearly as they drove one congresswoman against a wall with batons, then knocked Congressmember Claudia Garmendia, in a bright red blazer, stockings, and heels, onto the floor and surged over her. Five LIBRE congressmembers were hospitalized, including Garmendia. Honduran newspapers and television reported it as a criminal riot unleashed by LIBRE, that had been heroically quelled by Juan Orlando's security forces.[122]

US support for the regime surged on, too. On June 2, General John Kelly, head of the United States Southern Command (Southcom), met with Honduran authorities and then effused over Hernández's work fighting organized and transnational crime. "The commitment on these fronts is impressive," he said, "and to see the work that this government has carried out in these recent months, it's incredible."[123]

Inroads in US policy could be identified, though. At the end of April, the embassy sponsored a forum on human rights, with military leaders lined up in a row. Outgoing Ambassador Kubiske struck a new, more critical tone in her remarks: "The government has good intentions, but there is no human rights policy; the system could strengthen itself for the benefit of Hondurans themselves." She granted that there were cases in which members of the military committed abuses of power "but after one or two years nothing happens." She acknowledged that she'd heard concerns raised about the Guardianes de la Patria program.[124]

As that spring's orgy of militarization, repression, and unrequieted admiration played out, criticisms in the US Congress of the regime and of US support for it reached their highest point since the coup. On May 28, Representative Janice Schakowsky led on another letter to Kerry, questioning US police and military aid to Honduras. We went over the top on that one and garnered signatures from a hundred eight congress-members. This time, the *New York Times* gave the letter its own story—the first time any paper had done so about Honduras: "Lawmakers Ask State Department to Review Support for Honduras."[125]

On June 11, the Senate Foreign Relations Committee held a hearing to confirm the new US ambassador to Honduras, James Nealon. Nealon had previously served two years as right-hand man to General John Kelly at Southcom. His appointment signaled a new upper-hand for the Defense Department regarding Honduras policy, in relation to State and the White House. Nealon produced the usual list provided by the State Department of the Honduran government's commitments and achievements, but it was thin and only perfunctory. In their questions to Nealon, the senators on the committee struck a new tone. Tim Kaine, who had studied with the Jesuits in Honduras in 1980 and '81, asserted: "When I was there it was a military dictatorship. It was a very brutal place. . . . But it's worse now than then." Miraculously, even Cuban-American Senator Robert Menendez, the committee chair—a ferocious opponent of US-Cuban detente and Venezuela's Hugo Chávez—acknowledged that in order for the United States to stay engaged in Honduras, "We need partners with the political will to address the situation," thus admitting the possibility that Juan Orlando might not have the requisite political will.[126]

That moment, June 2014, was our mountaintop in the congressional and media work. It seemed possible, just possible, that a tipping point in US policy had finally arrived. I held my breath. Like the Hondurans during the 2013 elections, I dared to hope. It was dangerous.

Birthday Parties

January 25, 2014, two days before Juan Orlando Hernández's inauguration, was my birthday. It also happened to be the birthday of women's
suffrage in Honduras, celebrated as Honduran Women's Day.

The afternoon before our birthdays, I took off for the Aguán Valley
with my friend Iris Munguía, Secretary of Women for FESTRAGRO
(Federación de Sindicatos de Trabajadores de Agroindustria), the
newly expanded federation of Honduran agricultural workers'
unions, joined by Chema Martínez, at the time still FESTAGRO's
Communications Director, and Gloria Guzmán, one of its organizers.[127] Chema was quiet the whole trip; it was like he had a new
personality, living with the death threats. At least while he was with
me he was less likely to be killed and could breathe a bit. This time
we turned right after we crossed main the bridge in Sabá and drove
away from the campesino collectives and palm oil estates and toward
the opposite end of the valley. The Upper Aguán, along with chunks
of land throughout the rest of the valley and the north coast, has been
Dole territory ever since it was conquered in the early twentieth
century by its predecessor, Standard Fruit. In 2014, over twenty-four
hundred people worked for Dole in Honduras, a third of them women
laboring in packinghouses. For complex historical reasons, their biggest union, SUTRAFSCO (Sindicato Unificado de Trabajadores de la
Standard Fruit Company, Unified Union of Standard Fruit Company
Workers), still had an excellent union contract with Dole, dating
back to the famous Honduran General Strike of 1954. The contract
included small bits of paid time off for union education.[128]

The next morning, we drove out along a dirt road near the top of
the Aguán and wound back and up and down into a smaller, rolling
valley, where a classic banana corporation enclave opened up. It was
like going back in time. White, two-story buildings with green trim
were arrayed among well-coifed lawns and tall, wide trees—a magic
imperial kingdom managed for a hundred years by North American
bloodsuckers. In 1950, Ramón Amaya Amador called its banana
plantations a green prison, in Honduras's most famous novel, *Prisión
Verde*. He grew up in Olanchito, right nearby, on the main road.[129]

We pulled up in front of a small building on the right and trudged up an exterior stairway to a large room upstairs. Thirty-one smiling women banana workers from SUTRAFSCO awaited us—round-faced, round-bodied women in their twenties, thirties, and forties, wearing brightly colored T-shirts or green polo shirts with the union logo, and high-heeled sandals, a few in sleek dresses. Four male leaders greeted us, in jeans and their own matching red polo shirts with union insignia.

Iris took charge and ran a workshop about women's empowerment. She started with a speech, about everything from supporting women's self-esteem to gender politics in the family to the importance of women educating themselves about political issues so they could understand their union contracts, the company's practices, and the broader political world—"So we can sew it all together," she concluded, deliberately using a metaphor from women's work in the home. After each of the participants stood up and introduced herself, Iris gave a PowerPoint talk about the history of Women's Day, helped out by rank-and-file women who took turns standing up and reading parts of the text. "Men didn't give us suffrage; it was the product of struggle," she stressed. Then, to liven things up, Gloria led everyone in a loud—really loud—chant she'd heard at a forum of labor women we'd attended in San Pedro Sula the day before. *"Vea vea vea. Que cosa mas bonita. Nosotras las mujeres. Luchanda por justicia"* (Look, look, look. What a beautiful thing. We the women. Struggling for justice). She and Iris talked about the devastating new Paquetazo, the fifteen-percent tax on consumer goods, just passed by the Congress. *"No hay paz, no hay paz. Los frijoles valen más,"* we shouted (There's no peace, there's no peace. Beans cost more.). One woman stood up and proclaimed: "This about the Paquetazo is public robbery." Then all the parctici-pants broke up into small groups to discuss questions about barriers to women's self-esteem and reported back.[130]

The process politics of the workshop were as important as its content. Iris emphasized that the women needed to learn all this actively, so they themselves could go on to teach others who weren't present. She'd been terrified, she said, when she first started doing work in her union. "My whole body shook." As I watched her speeches, I could see she was knocking their socks off as an empowered female role model. At the end of the workshop, as each woman got up and shared her reflections, I watched with awe. They, too, were self-possessed, articulate, ferocious, and tremendously engaged. "I work twelve hours a day, seven days a week," one of them declared. "And the best thing is to have this time off to learn." Then the male leaders concluded with their own slide show about a recent trip they'd made to Florida, courtesy of Dole, and promoted the company's new strategies for raising production standards.

Downstairs, a cluster of men and women sat watching a television set with rabbit ears in the corner, on which a scratchy, irregular image showed the new mayor from LIBRE being sworn in in nearby Olanchito—wearing his own blue-and-white satin sash, just like Juan Orlando's—in a grand moment for a town with a hundred-year history of challenging the banana corporations and their elite allies.

Upstairs, the workshop ended around noon. A sheet cake appeared, with *"Feliz Día de la Mujer"* (Happy Women's Day) spiraling across it in transcluent red letters over white frosting. Suddenly everyone stood up, cheered, and started singing Happy Birthday—to me, and to my complete surprise. I was handed a giant knife to cut up the cake. It got a bit messy, what with the fluffy frosting, producing more humor and cheering. Someone cranked up music and for two hours we all danced *merengue* and a bit of *cumbia* and once or twice a *punta*—the dance of the Afro-Indigenous Garifuna people of Honduras. This, of course, was my idea of a great time. Even Chema danced and laughed.

In the early afternoon eight or ten of us, including women activists from the union—rank-and-file as well as leadership—piled into two cars and drove back to Olanchito, half an hour away. We pulled up at local television station and filed into its studio, where we took turns talking on a local program called *Tribuna Sindical* (Labor Tribune). When it was my turn, toward the beginning, I just stayed on for five minutes, not wanting to take up more than my share of time. It turned out the show went on for two hours. The woman who was the head of the union's new women's committee spoke, then Iris, and then each of rank-and-file women. They talked eloquently and bravely about their workplaces issues, their union activities, and their unique concerns as women. Again, it was an empowerment project: these women were simultaneously developing their skills at public speaking and raising their self-confidence as women and as activists, while serving as role models for others.

Iris, Chema, Gloria, and I checked into our hotel, rested, then took off again at dusk for another Women's Day event with a different union of Dole workers, SITRABARIMASA. This gathering was more of a pure party, in a wooded outside restaurant with alcoves around the sides. Gradually about two dozen women arrived and arrayed themselves around a big long table, with a few male union officials at one end. We drank sodas and ate chunks of roasted meat and thin strips of fried bananas, known as *tajadas*, red salsa dribbled over the top of both. After some hours, the men gave speeches recognizing the work of the women. To much whooping, they awarded raffle prizes wrapped in yellow cellophane—a blender, a microwave, and for the grand prize, a stove, all tools of women's work in the home, I noticed, donated by a regional chain of hardware stores. Then everyone danced, hard, for two or three hours at least, late into the night.

I collapsed back into my hotel room. There I spent the entire night throwing up and crawling to the toilet, with a fast fever. By mid-morning I resorted to antibiotics. All the five hours in the car home I hung on, gradually feeling better, but exhausted. "Only another hour and I can sleep," I whimpered to my car-mates as we got closer to home. "Only twenty minutes more and I can sleep." When we returned the rental car at the airport, near Iris's house, "Only ten minutes and I can sleep."

We finally pulled up in front of the house. "Surprise!" erupted twenty friends and loved ones from Iris's family and the banana unions, packed into Iris's garage, complete with balloons, festoons, and a big round birthday cake with lemon-yellow frosting flowers, decorated by Iris's daughter. I went up to each person and gave them a hug, went to sleep for an hour, apologizing, then woke up and danced some more.

That was the day before Juan Orlando's coronation. Through all the assassinations, through all the vicious police corruption, through all the degeneration of the rule of law, in the middle of it all, Hondurans were still organizing at the grassroots, still moving their political projects forward, still advancing women's empowerment and the labor movement. Honduras wasn't a continuous river of horror, as the US press liked to suggest. All kinds of activism continued, and community media spaces were still open, too, like that local television station. And everyone was still dancing. We didn't go out at night the same ways we used to; it was too dangerous. But we filled those garages. On Iris's birthday, the previoius December, there were even mariachis.

Indignados anti-corruption protest, Tegucigalpa, June 26, 2015. Photo Credit: Reuters/Jorge Cabrera.

CHAPTER FIVE

Borderlands of Good and Evil: Immigrants and Indignados

Gang Activity

Precisely as congressional criticism of US support for the Honduran regime achieved its potential tipping point in late May and June 2014, a news story flamed across the US media and stayed at the top of the headlines for weeks: fifty-seven thousand undocumented, unaccompanied minors from Central America had swarmed across the border from Mexico and more were on their way.[1] Signal flares shot out that the children were invading US territory and posing a dangerous threat to the country's sovereignty, economic life, and national identity. Although the children came from El Salvador and Guatemala as well, the largest numbers were fleeing Honduras.

National alarm over those children reframed the entire debate in the United States about Honduras policy for years to come—not just in the media, but in Congress, the White House, the State Department, and the Washington NGO world. Honduras was suddenly back in the news, that was for sure. But it was now conceptually fused with two other Central American countries, and a punching bag in a new, panicked, national conversation about immigration and border practices.

188

The story first developed when the United Nations put out a one-hundred-twenty-page report in March 2014, *Children on the Run: Unaccompanied Children Leaving Central America and Mexico and the Need for International Protection*, investigating the reasons why minors were leaving their countries in increasing numbers. The UN found that fifty-seven percent of the children were fleeing violence, especially from gangs, and called for international measures to protect them.[2]

On June 5, picking up the story and flinging it rightward, Breitbart News—the racist, ultraconservative website that would later underlay President Donald Trump's election—posted a series of photos under the headline, "Leaked Images Reveal Children Warehoused in Crowded U.S. Cells, Border Patrol Overwhelmed." Breitbart's coverage, seemingly cast initially as humanitarian concern over the children, swiftly expanded to fan the flames of immigration hysteria, with a rapid-fire series of stories about hordes swarming into the United States: "8 Reasons to Close the Border Now," shouted a July 8 story, listing among them "Disease," "Threat of Terrorism," "Safety of US Citizens," and "American Culture Is Under Attack." Another story that same day warned: "Report: More than Half of Central American Immigrants on Welfare." Central American children were suddenly a weapon in Breitbart's hands, apparently deployed to disrupt Obama's ability to push through immigration reforms in his last months in office.[3]

Then mainstream media picked up on the story, similarly spinning out the children as an imminent danger to the nation. CBS News reported, for example, "experts agree, Central Americans who are deluging the southern border with tens of thousands of their children are breeding not only a humanitarian crisis, but a serious national security threat to the United States"—its language seething with classic nativist phrasing: "deluging," "breeding," "threat."[4]

More sympathetic outlets, though, began to focus supportively on the danger the children faced once they had arrived in the United States, as it became clear that they were being housed in overflowing, inadequate detention facilities, lacked legal counsel, and were terrified refugees, not invading threats. "Children Crossing Border Alone Create 'Urgent Humanitarian Situation,'" wrote the *Los Angeles Times*, for example.[5] Most of the children, it turned out, were not sneaking onto US territory and then being apprehended by the Border Patrol, but, rather, arriving at the border and throwing themselves into the arms of immigration authorities, seeking asylum.[6]

Under the 2008 Trafficking Victims Protection Reauthorization Act, immigrant children traveling alone and not originally from Canada and Mexico are guaranteed a legal hearing before immigration authorities and required to be placed in the "least restrictive setting that is in the best interest of the child," and, if possible, with family members.[7] Yet as journalists and activists soon documented, thousands of immigrant children were not in fact being reunited with family in the United States, but instead were huddled in crowded, substandard, repressive detention facilities near the Mexican border, terrified, sobbing, paralyzed. In interviews and other reports, it became clear how deeply traumatized they had been by the trip north on "*La Bestia*" (The Beast), the freight trains atop which migrants traveled, preyed on by rapists, thieves, and drug cartels. Some of the children had traveled with their undocumented mothers, with whom they were being held in horrifying "family detention centers."[8]

Sympathetic journalists also flew to Honduras to examine the roots of the migration. Gangs, violence, and drug traffickers were the problem, they reported, and flew home—with little or no mention of the corrupt, dangerous Honduran government and its ongoing destruction of the rule of law, or of its role in perpetuating and expanding crime, violence, and poverty. Worse, many of these stories celebrated the heroic work of Honduran security forces which, they reported, were bravely fighting gangs and drug traffickers. On August 1, the *Washington Post*, for example, ran a slide show displaying "Harrowing Images of Police Battling Gang Violence in Crime-Stricken Honduras." The *Post*'s photographer "spent almost three weeks in the Honduran capital of Tegucigalpa traveling with an investigative unit of a Honduras police force and watching them tackle violence in one of the world's most dangerous regions."[9]

Other articles even went so far as to speak positively of Honduran police and military forces that were preventing children from leaving their country. NBC News reported on July 25, for example, "Honduran Special Forces Work to Keep Kids from Fleeing Country." "Clad in flak jackets and bearing automatic rifles and side arms, elite forces are scouring the ragged countryside that straddles this border between Honduras and Guatemala."[10] These stories didn't emerge by coincidence. US Embassy officials actively reached out to offer reporters inside access to guides, tours, and Honduran officials, to try and control the narrative.

Overall, this transformation of the public conversation in the United States about Honduras was stunning, and rapid—it only took around three weeks. In the right-wing version, children were taking advantage of lax border enforcement to invade the country, posing a national security threat. In the liberal version, gangs and drug traffickers were producing terrifying violence in Honduras, making children flee northward, where they were met with scary conditions within the US border enforcement system.

Yes, the gangs in Honduras were indeed terrifying by this point, proliferating in poor and working-class neighborhoods. Young men without jobs or hope were threatened or seduced into the gangs, which treated young women like sexual prey. Bodies littered the streets and empty lots as a result of the gangs' broad range of criminal activities, their attacks on those who refused to cooperate, and inter-gang warfare. Honduran migrants, asked why they had left home, told harrowing, detailed stories of gangs and their predations.[11]

Drug traffickers and their attendant violence had metastasized, as well, in the aftermath of the coup. Working both with the gangs and in competition with them, drug traffickers carved out their own territories and left their own piles of plastic bags of victims with slit throats, eyes gouged out, missing limbs. If the *narcos* wanted you to do something, you said no at your peril.

As the gangs spread, they started expanding into new income-generating activities, especially extortion of small businesses and transportation operators. Working hand-in-glove with local police who took their own cut of the proceeds, gang extortionists were operating throughout the big cities by 2014.[12] That year, Hondurans paid an estimated two million dollars to extortionists.[13] In 2013, a friend of mine started working in a small business his cousin had recently opened in San Pedro Sula. The cousin's whole family had pooled its savings to buy the business. My friend finally had a good job. One day a gang member showed up to demand a weekly "tax," or extortion payment. The cousin said no. Three days later the gang came back and shot her up, killing her on the spot. My friend only survived because he'd been away from the store that morning and not at the counter, where he usually worked. Both the psychological and the economic impacts on him were enormous.

But let's be clear: those gangs and drug traffickers took over a broad swath of daily life in Honduras in part because the elites who ran the government permitted and even profited from it. Who was the gang, in this story? By 2014, the full effects of the coup regime's ongoing destruction of the rule of law were manifest. The judiciary was largely corrupt; the criminal justice system functioned to protect the crooked and the murderous. The police were deeply interwoven with the gangs and drug traffickers. In August 2013, one Honduran government official overseeing police cleanup admitted that seventy percent of the police were "beyond saving." In its 2013 human rights report for Honduras, the State Department itself spoke of "widespread impunity" caused by a weak justice system.[14] Human Rights Watch concluded in 2014, "Perpetrators of killings and other violent crimes are rarely brought to justice."[15]

Public alarm especially increased over the killings of women, in what were spoken of as "femicides." By 2016, ten women in Honduras were killed every week, eighty-five to ninety percent with impunity, making the country one of the most dangerous places in the world to be female.[16]

All of this largely disappeared from mainstream media stories in the United States about the roots of the immigrant children's migration, although a few journalists did quote individuals who were afraid of their local police. Astonishingly, the previous years' reporting about death squad killings by the Honduran police was largely invisible, although in many cases it had been published by the very same newspaper or news service. Absent, too, in the coverage, for the most part, were the extensive reports about human rights abuses committed by the Honduran military, and the alarms raised by so many, including the US Congress, about militarization of the police.

Many of the news stories did point to economic factors behind Hondurans' emigration. But again, it was as if the Honduran economy were just a natural disaster, not the product of five years of deliberate economic policies. Pre-coup Honduras had never been a golden age, economically. But the country did have a functioning state that had provided basic services to large numbers of Hondurans. It had an economy based on agriculture, maquiladora export production, and services. Most people were seriously poor. But there were niches, and hopes, and thriving small businesses, and a middle class—albeit tiny—and manufacturing enterprises serving a regional and sometimes broader market.

The post-coup regime destroyed much of that functioning state and modest economy. Right off, under Micheletti, the coup perpetrators robbed much of the country's coffers blind, such as the teachers' pension fund. Thereafter, the elites stole broadly from the Honduras state in rampaging corruption. Sarah Chayes documented that corruption in a one-hundred-sixty-one-page report for the Carnegie Endowment for International Peace, *When Corruption Is the Operating System: The Case of Honduras*, released in May 2016. Chayes described Honduras as a "kleptocracy." "It is no longer possible to think of corruption as just the iniquitous doings of individuals," she concluded. "Corruption is the operating system of sophisticated networks that link together public and private sectors and out-and-out criminals—including killers." She linked Honduran migration explicitly to corruption—and to US support for the regime: "Urban violence and out-migration . . . are by-products of the corruption of the very government that enjoys US (and European Union) support to combat those ills."[17]

With the government close to bankruptcy because of so much theft, Presidents Lobo and Hernández then turned to international lenders to sustain their operation, in the process driving up the national debt while using the new funds to shore up their long-term reign.[18] In 2010-12 the International Monetary Fund (IMF) lent $202 million to Honduras.[19] The World Bank lent $75 million in 2013 alone. In December 2014, as the border kids debate was playing out, the Inter-American Development Bank (IDB) granted $110 million for Hernández's *Bono de Diez Mil* (Bonus of Ten Thousand) program of small cash transfers to the very poor, widely understood as a vote-buying operation.[20] The IMF simultaneously approved $189 million in loans to Honduras with still more funds for the *Bono de Diez Mil.*[21] With these loans, both the IDB and the IMF, controlled by the United States, were signaling their long-term endorsement of and support for Hernández. The World Bank also funded "development" projects that destroyed rural livelihoods, such as Facussé's Dinant Corporation—which replaced campesino collectives with African palm plantations that employed few workers—or hydroelectric dams, which wrecked Indigenous ways of life.[22] The bank's support for Facussé would be challenged in early 2014 when its own internal compliance body, under pressure from seventy organizations that had protested abuses, reported that Dinant had failed to follow ethical standards.[23]

The price the IMF demanded for its funding of the government was the continued dismantling of the Honduran state.[24] This was the neoliberal model that President Ricardo Maduro (2002-06), Zelaya's predecessor, began imposing; Zelaya's resistance to neoliberalism had been one of the reasons for the coup.[25] After the coup, Lobo and especially Hernández pushed through the neoliberal privatization of Hondutel, the state-owned telephone company, and of the ENEE, the national energy company, in the process obliterating good, unionized government jobs with healthcare benefits and pensions. In October and November of 2014 alone, two thousand employees of the ENEE lost their jobs. On almost the same day as the IMF and IDB loans were announced in December 2014, Hernández's top aide announced that seven thousand government workers would be laid off in the next year. Earlier, on June 13, 2014, the IMF Executive Board explicitly promoted "reducing the wage bill of the Honduran government." By February 2015, José Luis Baquedano, president of the Confederación Unitaria de Trabajadores de Honduras (CUTH, United Federation of Honduran Workers), the nation's largest labor federation, reported that ten thousand public employees had lost their jobs as a result of the IMF.[26]

The elite's robbery of government funds and its ongoing elimination of public-sector jobs in turn eviscerated social services.
According to the Center for Economic and Policy Research, in the
two years following the coup alone (2010-12), spending on public
housing, health, and education all dropped, while extreme poverty
rose by 26.3 percent.[27] By 2014, the economy began to break down at
the most basic level. The most glaring example of the government's
raw inability to manage it erupted in early June 2014, when neoliberal programs in the agricultural sector, along with a drought,
helped produce a nationwide shortage of beans—the essential
protein source in the Honduran diet. It was so dire that the government arranged for the importation of beans from Ethiopia, although
Honduras ordinarily produced a surplus of beans. The Ethiopian
beans, though, were not going to arrive until mid-September, precisely when Honduran bean crop would be harvested. Their arrival,
however nutritious, would thus compete with domestic beans, dam-
aging the Honduran farmers who grew them.[28]

Meanwhile, the US-promoted Central American Free Trade
Agreement, (CAFTA), implemented in Honduras beginning in
2006, forced small- and medium-sized Central American producers
of milk, corn, and other products to compete with far more powerful US agribusiness producers, and with those from other Central
American countries as well. "CAFTA has only exacerbated the des-
peration and instability in Honduras," a top-level delegation from
the AFL-CIO concluded after a fall 2014 visit.[29]

In November 2017, the Center for Economic and Policy Research
summarized the economic devastation of Honduras since the coup.
GDP dropped from 3.8 percent to 1.8 percent. Unemployment rose
from 3 percent to 7.4 percent; women's underemployment rate, in
particular, more than doubled.[30]

What the news stories about the kids missed, then, was the role
of the Honduran government, international lenders, and the United
States government in actively destroying Honduran livelihoods.
Again: who, exactly, was the threatening gang here?

As the "gangs" disrupted their lives, Honduran parents sold
their houses or borrowed thousands of dollars to pay a *coyote* who

might, just might, carry their beloved children away to some mea-sure of safety in the United States, however traumatized they might be psychologically by the passage. The parents who took this risk were usually single mothers; they were hoping, just hoping, that they could save their loved ones from torture, rape, a sure death, or starvation within Honduras. When those terrified children arrived begging at the border, the US right then transformed them into a national security "threat" to the United States.

On August 19, 2014, I was asked to testify before the Judiciary Committee of the California Assembly about a proposed resolution calling on the United States to "ensure that these unaccompanied children have access to due process, lawyers, a judge, and justice" and to address root causes in the sending countries.[31] In the elevator of the State Capitol building that morning, I chatted with a group of eight or ten friendly and excited middle-aged and older people, mostly white, some evidently Latino. An hour or so later, upstairs outside the hearing room, I saw the same people again, surrounding Assemblymember V. Manuel Pérez, the Judiciary Committee chair who had introduced the resolution. It turned out my elevator-mates were among those who had organized virulent anti-immigrant protests in Murrieta, in Riverside County, California. On July 1, as many as three hundred people had blocked three buses carrying undocumented detainees and forced them to turn back, earning one of the protest leaders an appearance on Fox News.[32] In the hall, I watched as they started shouting hostile remarks at Pérez and his aide. "You're un-American, you're not American, because you were born in Mexico," one man spat out.

After I read my statement in the hearing, the Murrieta people stepped up to the microphone to speak against the resolution. Patricia Lyons, who identified herself as the leader of Concerned Citizens of Southwest Riverside County who had organized the Murrieta protests, denounced "this tyrannical resolution." "We stopped the buses and stood up for national sovereignty," she declared. Others accused the committee of being un-American and "trying to destroy this country by bills such as this HR 51." Robert Dalton, a member of the National Coalition for Immigration Reform Action, said that it was logistically impossible that the kids had traveled to the United States on trains and buses; it was all made up, he said. "The idea of children or adults riding on the top of the train is ludicrous." "It took aircraft to transfer, to move fifty thousand people. . . . Obama's goal is to crash our economy, create chaos, then fundamentally transfer America into a Communist state."[33]

When the public comment ended, Assemblymember Christina García spoke movingly in support of the resolution, and said that her parents had been undocumented immigrants. The resolution passed the committee overwhelmingly, and on August 27 the whole California Assembly approved it by voice vote.[34] Breitbart might have unleashed vicious anti-immigrant hostility at the grassroots, but its tsunami of anger ran into a powerful wall of love and compassion, as well.

Alliances for Insecurity

The White House's initial response to the "crisis" was a June 20 "Fact Sheet" announcing its actions to address the children's arrival from Central America. Bowing to both left and right, it promised to provide additional funds to the three sending countries for the reintegration of deportees and support for programs for at-risk youth, while adding far more new funding to security forces, especially through the Central American Regional Security Initiative (CARSI). In order, allegedly, to promote what it described as efficient processing of immigrants and to "allow ICE to return unlawful migrants from Central America to their home countries more quickly," the White House also announced that it would reinforce the Departments of Homeland Security and Justice at the US border.[35]

By early July, the administration's response had solidified into a long-term commitment to the repressive governments of both Honduras and Guatemala, while promising to simultaneously cut off immigration and treat immigrants well. The State Department's spokesperson acknowledged that there was a "humanitarian situation taking place in our—on the border" yet insisted that "we must do whatever we can to stem the tide." The White House announced that the presidents of Guatemala, Honduras, and El Salvador had been invited to the White House to meet with Vice President Biden and President Obama and to have lunch afterward. Together, they would "discuss how to reinforce our ongoing collaboration to stem the flow of undocumented migrants from Central America to Mexico and the United States." The announcement's phrase "stem the flow," like the State Department's use of "stem the tide," implied a giant flood was spilling over the lower part of the country, drowning it in dangerous brown children.[36]

Although the administration expressed a sincere commitment to addressing the issues facing children once they arrived in the United States, its core response was a military one: strengthen police and military in the sending countries, strengthen the United States Border Patrol, and, soon, increase funding for Mexico to enforce its own border with Guatemala. "We are looking at redirecting some of our foreign assistance through the Merida Initiative to help strengthen Mexican interdiction along their southern border," testified Francisco Palmieri, the State Department's Deputy Assistant Secretary for Central America and the Caribbean, at a June 25 hearing of the House Committee on Foreign Affairs.[37]

General John Kelly, commander of the United States Southern Command (Southcom) (later Chief of Staff in Trump's White House) and a longtime admirer of Juan Orlando Hernández, kept the alarmist fires stoked. On October 7, he used the Ebola virrus outbreak in West Africa to spread fantastic—and unfounded—fears about potential movement of Ebola to Central America. "If it breaks out, it's literally 'Katie bar the door,' and there will be mass migration into the United States," he warned in a speech at the National Defense University in Washington, D.C. Kelly later suggested that he had said that in part to try to obtain more funding for SouthCom.[38]

Funding for the Central American Regional Security Initiative (CARSI), which flowed throughout Central America but largely to the three northern countries from which the children had fled, had already continued to increase in the years before the border kids "crisis," from $101.5 million for 2011, to $161.5 million in 2014. We know very little, though, about where exactly it ended up, or for what purposes it was used. CARSI is largely non-transparent, the Congressional Research Service, a bipartisan agency of the US Congress, confirmed to me in 2016. Nor was CARSI's effectiveness proven. In a December 2015 report, *Central America Regional Security Initiative: Background and Policy Issues for Congress,* the research service concluded: "Despite indications of progress in certain communities, most country-level security indicators have yet to show significant improvements."[39]

As the question of the unaccompanied minors loomed large in the United States that June and July of 2014, the government of Honduras rushed to construct its own narrative, in which it was both blameless and heroic. Hernández insisted that responsibility lay with the United States because its appetite for drug consumption fueled drug trafficking through Honduras, which in turn produced violence, causing children to flee. In a speech to the US Chamber of

Commerce on June 13, for example, he explained, "This is a security problem provoked by drug trafficking. . . . This is a problem that we didn't create but originated with drug consumption here."[40] Within Honduras, Juan Orlando cast himself as the benevolent protector of innocent children. His wife rushed to the US border to investigate the situation of the migrants, then rushed home to welcome the planeloads of deported women and children as they began arriving back in Honduras by mid-July.[41] Despite Hernández's nationalistic rhetoric, though, and despite US funding for "reintegration" of the children, when the deportees got off the planes in this period they were evidently only handed a bottle of water, lunch in a white styrofoam container, and a bus ticket. Maybe a blanket. At the beginning of June, as part of neoliberal restructuring, the government had in fact shut down the Honduran Institute for Childhood and the Family (INHFA, Instituto Hondureño de la Niñez y Familia), its children's services office, and laid off all eleven hundred unionized employees.[42]

By early July, the Honduran papers started running celebratory news stories reporting that state security forces had successfully captured Hondurans seeking to flee their country. "Frontier Police Recover in the West of Honduras Eight Minors That Traveled Without Authorization" read a typical headline. The accompanying photos showed clutches of four or five children along with women, sometimes holding toddlers in their arms, their faces blurred or covered with a black strip to disguise their identities, standing next to soldiers or policemen in front of police stations.[43] (Readers could reflect on which, exactly, were the criminals. By February 23, 2016, a Honduran paper would even run an article celebrating the work of dogs in preventing child migration. The article began, "Helped by dogs, this Tuesday a series of police operations began in the entrances and exits of the principal cities of Honduras in search of minors that travel alone or accompanied toward the United States."[44]

In late July, when Juan Orlando visited the White House alongside the other two presidents, the US press published a love fest of articles legitimating him. He landed a long, entirely uncritical interview in *Time*—perhaps the most prominent celebratory story about a Honduran president in the country's history. "Hernández said his government has worked hard to reduce [the] murder rate in his first months in office, but said violence is still a major problem driving the youth migration," it repeated uncritically. "The United States has a responsibility to help Honduras, Hernández says, because US drug consumption is driving the violence." In an accompanying photograph, Hernandez appeared magisterial; amiable but commanding in an expensively-cut suit and tie.[45]

Politico Magazine, in its own interview, showed him laughing in rolled-up shirtsleeves, as he reached out to shake a happy little girl's hand amid a crowd of children and their families. In a complete reversal of an article the editors had solicited from me a mere six months before, which they chose to entitle "Honduras: The Thugocracy Next Door," *Politico*'s editor held back any potential criticisms and served as a mouthpiece for the president's repeated assertion that the United States bore responsibility for the crisis because of its drug habit.[46]

More powerfully, the US Congress rushed to address the "crisis," swiftly moving the policy conversation—and funding stream—rightward. Republicans, including high-ranking figures such as Representative Kay Granger, Chair of the House Committee on State and Foreign Operations of the Committee on Appropriations, and Darrell Issa, Chair of the House Committee on Oversight and Government Reform, flew to Tegucigalpa to embrace Juan Orlando Hernández.[47] Republicans focused on criticizing Obama's border policies, which, they charged, had put national security at risk. They showed little interest in addressing root causes within the countries. The solution, rather, was deportation, fast. Representative Tom Cole charged, for example: "We are essentially incentivizing the flow of this population by not returning the unaccompanied juveniles to their countries of origins quickly.[48] Republicans' longer-term solution was arms, arms, arms, both for US border enforcement and for Central American security forces.[49]

Important Democrats themselves slid rightward, fast, although not as far. On June 19, Senators Robert Menendez, Dick Durbin, and Mazie Hirono and Representatives Luis Gutiérrez and Lucille Roybal-Allard put out a proposal that was in many ways progressive—in naming the immigrants as "refugees" from violence (as had the UN); in calling for comprehensive immigration reform and respect for current laws that provided "special protections for unaccompanied minors, trafficking victims and asylum seekers"; and in asking the administration to seek alternatives to detentions, as well as to increase funding for economic development in the sending countries. Other solutions they offered, though, were more disturbing: "continue intelligence-gathering activities to combat cross-border smuggling," and dramatically increase funding for CARSI. The United States Southern Command, they argued, moreover, "should be appropriately resourced to conduct the intelligence, surveillance, and reconnaissance efforts need to combat criminal activity and narcotics trafficking." Kelly's alarms were paying off. These Democrats also called for more funding to the three northern countries through the Millennium Challenge Corporation (MCC)—although congressional pressure from high-ranking Democrats had helped cut off MCC funding to Honduras since 2012 because of human rights abuses.[50]

Representative Eliot Engel, Democrat and Ranking Member on the House Committee on Foreign Affairs, in late June circulated a sign-on letter calling on the administration to address root causes in the sending countries. In the letter, Engel lauded the effectiveness of previous CARSI funding for the police and military and called for an increase in its funding. Engel's proposed solutions included expanding economic development aid and USAID funding, but missed the big picture, in which the both the United States and IMF loans were supporting a government that was actively destroying jobs and gutting the economy. Sixty members joined Engel on his letter. Of those, twenty-seven had signed previous letters calling for a suspension of US security funding for Honduras because of human rights abuses.[51]

Others balked. Representative Raúl Grijalva and the Progressive Caucus, by contrast, put out an alternative proposal focused on placing "the well-being of these kids first." "Most of all, we must realize that increased enforcement on our border is a solution in need of a problem, and proponents of militarization are using the plight of these kids to achieve their political agenda."[52]

By September, the administration's response had consolidated into a proposal known as the Plan of Alliance for Prosperity in the Northern Triangle, formally presented in September 2014 and promoted by the Obama Administration vigorously all that fall and for years to come. Developed under the auspices of the US-controlled Inter-American Development Bank, its title deliberately evoked President John F. Kennedy's 1961 Alliance for Progress, a multiyear funding program through which the United States had sought to exercise "soft power" throughout Latin America and the Caribbean in response to the 1959 Cuban Revolution.[53]

The more explicit model for the new Central America program was Plan Colombia, which received over eight billion dollars in US funding beginning in 2000, the vast majority of which flowed to Colombia's police and military. The *Washington Post* editorialized as early as July 26, "The Immigration Crisis Solution: A Plan Honduras," echoing a call from Hernández "for a new joint security and development effort for Central America similar to the US-backed, multi-year campaign that stabilized a Latin country once thought to be hopelessly mired in crime and political violence: Colombia." Honduras, though, had no guerrilla war underway, as did Colombia. More importantly, Plan Colombia deepened that country's already bloody and longstanding war; it emboldened its military, already implicated in massive human rights crimes, to commit further assassinations, often in alliance with right-wing paramilitaries.[54]

With its Alliance for Prosperity proposal, the US now merged its policy approaches to Honduras, El Salvador, and Guatemala into a single package, although El Salvador's progressive FMLN party, democratically elected, was a long way from the corrupt regimes of the other two countries. Fusing the three countries made it harder for critics to denounce US support for Honduras and Guatemala's repressive, corrupt regimes without dragging in El Salvador's. At the same time it necessitated a higher level of expertise about all three countries from those of us who wanted to engage in policy debates. As the policy coalesced, the concept of the "Northern Triangle" countries as a bloc, rarely utilized before the United States chose to deploy it to link the three countries, hardened into policy fact. Nicaragua, by contrast, disappeared from the mainstream conversation, although it, too, suffered from mass poverty. But under the leftist government of the Sandinistas, gangs and drug trafficking had not proliferated in the 2000s and 2010s, as they had in its neighbors to the north. Its children weren't fleeing north in terror. *The Economist* dared point out the reason: Nicaragua had thoroughly remade its police during the 1970s revolution into a new, nationwide, community-based model that at this point enjoyed broad public trust and effectively cut down much criminal activity.[55]

Concretely, the Plan of the Alliance for Prosperity in the Northern Triangle focused on infrastructure and supporting the very economic sectors that already led the hyperexploitation of Honduran working people and the country's environment: maquiladora factory export production, tourism, and extractive industries, plus the newly rising sector of power generation. The latter, combined with attention to a new port development in the Gulf of Fonseca on the Pacific coast, hinted at long-term economic aspirations, including the much-fantasized Model Cities, which the plan explicitly supported. The plan also spoke of "improved labor market conditions"—suggesting even further deliberate erosion of labor law enforcement and basic labor rights. It was silent about police corruption, human rights abuses by security forces, and the general human rights crisis, in which human rights defenders, members of the opposition, and journalists were regularly threatened and assassinated.[56]

Overall, the Plan treated the Honduran government as if it were a crystal-clear, pure vessel into which gold could be poured and prosperity would flow outward. In reality, the Plan would further enrich and strengthen the political power of the very same elites whose greed, deliberate subversion of the rule of law, and destruction of natural resources and of Indigenous and campesino land rights, were responsible for the dire conditions the proposal ostensibly addressed. It was like the oligarchs were being rewarded for their post-coup labors, while the children and their mothers huddled in terror at the borders.

The administration's support for the Plan—along with its support for the Hernández regime and its long-term planning for US power and policy goals in the region—climaxed on January 29, 2015, when Vice President Joseph Biden published an op-ed in the *New*

York Times entitled, "A Plan for Central America." Biden endorsed the Alliance for Prosperity, emphasized Plan Colombia as its model, and went beyond the proposal to call for a broad range of funding and reforms—in answer to the previous summer's "dangerous surge of migration."[57]

Responding to a full court press thereafter from the administration, the US Congress appropriated $750 million for Central America in December 2015, more than twice as much as each of the previous two years and equal to the entire CARSI total amount from 2008 to 2014. Funds available for security purposes increased from $161.5 million in 2014 and 2015 to $252 million in 2016.[58] In a complex give-and-take outcome brokered by the two parties, the funding bill did include stronger conditions on a portion of the aid: twenty-five percent of the funding to the central governments of Honduras, El Salvador, and Guatemala could be released only if the State Department certified—and key congressional offices agreed—that the country had taken steps to increase its border enforcement and cut down on emigration by combatting smugglers and "informing its citizens of the danger of the journey." Fifty percent was contingent on human rights conditions, expanding on those in the previous four years' funding bills: the government had to improve transparency, prosecute security forces that had committed human rights abuses, protect human rights defenders, and "curtail the role of the military in internal policing." It also had to increase taxes, support programs to create jobs, fight organized crime, and involve impacted civil society groups in the implementation and evaluation of the Plan for Prosperity.

While the US Congress continued to question security aid to Honduras, alternative funding channels opened up. In July 2016, the government of Israel signed a new agreement for military cooperation with Honduras, building on an earlier deal in which it had provided three new military radars to Honduras—right after the US had suspended radar cooperation with the Honduran military in 2012. The funds, totaling $209 million, would pay for an Air Force war ship and the refurbishing of the Honduran Air Force's helicopters and fighters jets.[59] The ship itself would be built in Colombia.[60] Colombia, for its part, continued to provide regular police training to Hondurans within both Honduras and Colombia. In December 2013, when El Tigre Bonilla, the death squad leader, was deposed as National Director of Police, he was dispatched to Bogotá, to work with the Colombians in training Honduran forces. Was the United States, unable to freely pour money and training into Honduran security forces because of alarm over human rights abuses, thus channeling funds and other resources through surrogates?[61]

Among the funds that Congress appropriated in 2014, '15, and '16 were millions of dollars for public education campaigns to teach Honduran parents about the dangers of sending their kids north. Those efforts shaded over into a consistent theme among many mainstream US discussions of unaccompanied minors traveling to the United States: that somehow it was bad parenting that had produced the crisis, and therefore if the parents were taught by their northern betters how best to protect their children, the "crisis" would end.[62] Visiting Honduras in September 2014, six months after the first funds were allocated for these campaigns, I could see the impact of those funds. I passed billboards on the highway warning people about the danger of *coyotes*. Driving home one afternoon, our car got stuck in the middle of a Children's Day parade put on by local schools in a poor neighborhood of San Pedro Sula. Amid the marching drummers and fleets of kids in their matching school uniforms, I saw a tiny little girl, maybe five or six, twirling along with a baton, a bit dazed-looking, in a silver outfit, with a white sash across her chest that read: "*No Migración Infantil*" (No Child Migration). The newspaper the next morning featured photos of parading ten-year-old boys dressed in black, carrying black coffins on their shoulders next to a black papier-mache train engine labeled "*La Bestia*" (The Train).

The problem, though, had never been that Honduran parents didn't know about *La Bestia, coyotes*, or all the risks of the trip north. They knew them all too well. The problem was they also knew about gang activity at home, on all fronts.

Zero to Axe Murderers in Thirteen Minutes

When, exactly, did I start using the term "axe murderer" all the time? As in, "The president of Honduras is an axe murderer." At first, I was just being flip and only threw it out there every once in a while, in private, to refer in a general sense to the successive governments that took power in Honduras after the coup. "The Honduran government is run by axe murderers," I'd drop, but only with people who already understood what I meant.

But as Juan Orlando Hernández's presidential campaign advanced over the course of 2012 and '13, I got more specific. I needed some kind of shorthand to try to capture his criminal bulldozing of the rule of law and to convey quite how villainous he was. In public, I still held back my epithets, instead building my case slowly but clearly from documented evidence—although when he was inaugurated I did call him a "dangerous thug" in the *Houston Chronicle*. But during meetings in Congress, I was increasingly blindsided by the turnover among aides: every six months I'd meet with a new sea of twenty-six-year-olds who knew nothing about Honduras at all. Over and over, I'd try to explain in a half-hour meeting quite how bad it was down there and who the US was supporting. Afterward, describing those meetings, I'd groan to friends, "It's zero to axe murderers in thirteen minutes." Casting "axe murderer" out there, I flailed in the gap between the horrors I was tracking in Honduras, on the one hand, and my inability to get other people to understand what I wanted to communicate, on the other.

Despite all the atrocities, though, I never deployed the phrase in print. I'd already gotten letters threatening to sue me for character defamation from Miguel Facussé, whose Dinant Corporation was widely alleged to have murdered campesinos struggling for land rights in the Bajo Aguán Valley.[63] Widely *alleged*, I am now careful to insert. So, let me clarify: The president of Honduras is an *alleged* dangerous thug. The president of Honduras is an *alleged* axe murderer.

In June 2014, I ran into a friend in the grocery store. Argentinian, in her fifties. I mentioned my question, "When, exactly did I start using the term axe murderer all the time?" Before I explained further, she announced: "Welcome to the club. You know what I mean, right? Assassins. And in my country, they pardon them." In an email that had arrived by the time I got home, she'd defined who was in that club: "Those of us who carry stories of state atrocities and the states that pardon them."

At a commencement ceremony at my university, I sat next to the provost, Alison Galloway, and casually mentioned my axe murderers fixation. Oh yes, she said. She told me about an article she had just written, in which she tried to convey what it meant to be a forensic anthropologist—that is, someone who examines dead people, and the sometimes violent ways in which they died. It's rough. Most people don't want to hear about your actual work, she writes in the article I read soon after, and there's a club among her colleagues, among those who deal with "the maggots, the smell, the decomposed organs within the body cavity"; they understand each other's isolation and unique challenges.[64]

My wisecrack use of "axe murderer" is also, of course, in part, a joke, drawing on vast references in popular culture. There's the 1993 movie, for example, *So I Married an Axe Murderer*, starring Mike Myers, in which mounting evidence suggests that his character's fiancée and eventual wife is a real axe murderer—but the killer turns out to be her jealous sister, whose axe-wielding they successfully fend off at the end.[65]

The use of "axe murderer" in popular culture is, partly, about latent violence—the idea that a seemingly innocent, mild-mannered person turns out to be someone who can pick up an axe and mercilessly slaughter people.[66] Arguably the most famous axe murderer was Lizzie Borden, who, in 1892, was charged with hacking to death her father and stepmother. ("Lizzie Borden took an axe/and gave her mother forty whacks.") The punch in our usage of "axe murderer" hinges on that phrase *turns out to be*. The amiable guy, or fiancé, might suddenly burst through a door, or pop out of the woods, or drag you into the woods. Surprise is always in there, about both the whacking and the killer's true propensities, as in a July 24, 2014, headline announcing: "Cynthia Nixon Shocked to Learn Her Ancestor Was an Axe Murderer." The actress's ancestress had chopped up her abusive husband in Missouri in the 1840s. "I'm sure we'll make many jokes about it in the years to come, about the axe murderess in the family," reflected Nixon, "but I think we will remain in awe of her."[67]

"Axe murderer" is also deliberately over the top—the perpetrator hasn't just committed murder; he or she has hacked someone up at close range, making them spout blood. The name stands in for the most outrageous crime possible by the least likely person, as when people say, "he could be an axe murderer and no one would notice."

But my own use of axe murderer was different, in part. I needed the joke to handle very real terror. Alison Galloway talks about dark humor among her fellow forensic anthropologists, who need a release from their quotidian examinations of rotting bodies.[68] My axe-murderer cracks, too, are classic black humor. They're in the genre of "things are so bad we have to laugh at them."

I went into deep internet and entered "axe murderers" but the algorithm guy inside Google politely queried back: "Did you mean axe *murder?*" I acquiesced, and got a long, explicit list from Wikipedia of horrific murders throughout modern history.[69] At first, I was repulsed by the list. But then I realized that I wasn't—that this was normal for me, normal because I'd been reading about this kind of atrocity almost every day in the Honduran newspapers for five bloody years. I could feel that I had created some sicko distance deep inside me, between myself and the daily horrors, so I could handle it. But that process just underscored the gap I was trying to bridge with others, trying to get from zero to axe murderers in the thirteen minutes allocated. On the radio or on television I had to do it in four or five minutes sometimes. With print media, it got down to two hundred words.

But I knew I could land it in eight: "The president of Honduras is an axe murderer." Nine, with *"alleged"* in there.

Actual axe murderers in Honduras, however, don't, as a rule, use axes. When it comes to that, they are more likely to use machetes. On March 13, 2012, Fausto Flores Valle, a radio host in the Aguán Valley, was riding along on his bicycle when assassins suddenly killed him with eighteen machete blows.[70] On March 5, 2014, a group of people ambushed María Santos Dominguez, an Indigenous activist with COPINH who had been vocally opposing a dam development, and attacked her with machetes, rocks, and sticks. When her son ran up to help, they cut off his right ear and part of his face.[71] On May 4, 2014, Cándido Rodríguez Castillo allegedly raped a thirteen-year-old girl, then killed her, her ten-year-old sister, her seven-year-old brother, and their eighteenth-month-old baby brother, using a machete.[72]

But those stories are about individual acts, in which you can see the axe/machete-wielder. They don't capture the systemic way in which raw violence is countenanced, encouraged, and committed by the post-coup Honduran government as an institution, and directed especially at social justice activists, land rights defenders, the opposition, and journalists. They don't capture the judges who let off their vicious drug trafficker allies; they don't capture the illegally appointed attorney general transferring out twenty-one prosecutors who had been pursuing high-level cases of organized crime. They don't capture Hernández and his allies in the Honduran Congress abolishing the Commission for the Reform of Public Security in 2013, with a green light from the US Embassy, as the president swept into office.

What's going on in Honduras—the axe murdering—is collective, then. Yet at the top of that government sits a single individual who, to the best of my knowledge, has never physically killed anyone with an axe or a machete, but who bears enormous responsibility for what's going on.

When the supposed "crisis" of children at the border hit the media in June 2014, Juan Orlando's track record was suddenly a hundred percent latent; he was just Mr. Charm, with his glowing interviews. US senators and members of Congress quoted him like he was a heroic figure fighting the good fight against the drug traffickers, protecting his borders against human smugglers, and caring for the little children with nationalistic love.

I went nuts. "You'd never know the president of Honduras is an [alleged] axe murderer," I sobbed.

On July 25, 2014, when Barack Obama rewarded Juan Orlando with a meeting at the White House, the two were joined by then-President Otto Pérez Molina of Guatemala, who has been widely implicated in torture and the "scorched earth" mass razing of entire Mayan villages during the 1980s, and Salvador Sánchez Cerén, the new President of El Salvador, a leader of the guerrilla war against the US-supported regime during the 1980s.[73] It read like a joke: "A genocidal torturer, an axe murderer, a former guerrilla comandante, and the leader of the free world walk into a bar. . . ." (Correction: "An *alleged* genocidal torturer, an *alleged* axe murderer. . .")

Those unaccompanied minors who fled Honduras in the first six months of 2014, like thousands since, were running away from the axe murderers in their woods. What did they find in the northern woods, when they reached the US border? When US government planes, driven by rabid packs of immigrant-haters, deported them back south, into whose arms have they been delivered?

Those kids are members of the club. They most definitely, like my Argentinian friend and myself, "carry stories of state atrocities and the states that pardon them."

In September 2016, I was finishing dinner with a colleague in a small Italian restaurant in Washington, D.C., when suddenly Secretary of State John Kerry came in and sat down at the table next to us, two feet away. My dinner-mate and I exchanged astonished looks for the next hour, prolonging our meal with a second glass of wine and then dessert. When we got up to leave, she introduced herself to Secretary Kerry and chatted a bit. So I decided I would, too. I said my name, then told Kerry that I worked on Honduras policy. "How are we doing down there?" he queried, amiably. I blurted back matter-of-factly: "We're supporting the axe murderers."

I didn't need thirteen minutes, only four seconds and five words. Then the maitre'd and secret service officers swooped in and whisked us away.

What Is the Path?

It was still partly daylight as the marchers showed up at the entrance to the Universidad Nacional Autónomo de Honduras (UNAH, National Autonomous University of Honduras), and everyone kept telling me that the numbers looked smaller this week. Most people carried torches, the bamboo kind sold in the United States for Hawaiian-themed parties. By the time we got halfway to the Presidential Palace, though, the march was clearly huge—later estimated at sixty thousand.[74] While we crested a bridge, just as it was getting dark and the marchers beside me chanted "No to the dictatorship!" and "*Fuera JOH!*" (Hernández Out!), I could see thousands of torches lighting up the boulevard for blocks and blocks, as far as I could see, in both directions. It was spine-tinglingly beautiful.[75]

For six weeks leading up to that night of June 26, 2015, tens of thousands of Hondurans in larger and larger marches throughout the country lit their torches on Friday nights in protest against the government's corruption and impunity. The marches' organizers called themselves the *"Indignados"*—the Outraged. The immediate source of their wrath was a scandal that broke that May, when David Romero, the director of Radio Globo, revealed checks and bank records documenting that as much as ninety million dollars had been siphoned out of the National Health Service (Instituto Hondureño de Seguro Social, IHSS) and into the election funds of the ruling National Party and of Juan Orlando Hernández himself. The scandal implicated not only Hernández but dozens of others, including the president of Congress, Mauricio Oliva, who had chaired the congressional committee that oversaw the IHSS's finances; Gladys Aurora, the vice president of Congress; and Oscar Álvarez, the leader of the National Party bench in Congress, who, along with the president's sister, Hilda Hernández, the minister of Communications, had signed off on the checks. The attorney general, Oscar Chinchilla, was implicated, too, because he was sitting on the evidence. At first Chinchilla denied the checks' veracity but soon he and even Hernández partially admitted that the evidence was real.[76]

Outrage shook through Honduran society. The collapse of the once-respected IHSS in the past two years had been monumental. In 2013, it had already been revealed that over three hundred million dollars had been stolen from the IHSS. Corrupt providers had over-charged for ambulances by tens of thousands of dollars. Contractors delivered medicines that turned out to be false and even dangerous, such as vaginal suppositories filled with flour. By 2015, newspapers reported that medicines were often missing altogether or that there were no dialysis machines or plates for x-rays. Women who arrived to give birth that spring were told to come back with all the supplies they'd need—down to the wrist bracelet—even if it were late at night and the pharmacies were closed. The torches, along with the crosses with names on them that many carried, symbolized the three thousand people, at least, who were estimated to have died because of the IHSS's collapse.[77]

The Tegucigalpa marchers I saw on the night of June 26, and again a week later on July 3, appeared overwhelmingly middle class, many in their twenties and thirties, wearing modish eyeglasses and a lot of crisp black and white. Reports indicated that they spanned the country's entire political spectrum; most of these people were apparently not part of the resistance against the 2009 coup; some had even supported it. My entirely unscientific poll of marchers near me indicated that they came from all four parties. I also saw Doris Gutiérrez, the brave, outspoken lone congressmember from the tiny PINU (Partido Inovación y Unidad, Unity and Innovation Party), being interviewed on the side.

The Honduran middle class, always small, was by this point feeling the full ferocious pinch of the post-coup regime. They lived in the same dangerous sea of violence as all Hondurans and were now paying new taxes that the elites who ran the government had imposed but themselves allegedly evaded. They paid into and used the IHSS system, and paid taxes into it for their employees as well. By 2015, their financial lives were collapsing; marchers told me they were pulling their kids out of college because they couldn't afford the fees.

It wasn't clear, though, who exactly organized and led these marches. The torch protests spread like wildfire all over the country

in many ways spontaneously; no single official organization with formal leadership emerged. The leaders that popped up as "Indignados"
to speak to the media ranged across the political spectrum, from
activists with unclear backgrounds, like Ariel Varela, who soon traveled to Washington regularly to meet with OAS and other officials
and later identified himself as part of a group that in its missives
implicitly supported the coup, to Wilfredo Méndez, the director
of CIPRODEH, the Centro de Investigación y Promoción de los
Derechos Humanos (Center for the Investigation and Promotion of
Human Rights), a longstanding, independent human rights group
with a progressive track record.[78] On June 22, Varela and other
Indignados began a hunger strike outside the Presidential Palace,
soon joined by Méndez. Then seven Tolupan Indigenous people
joined, making clear they were protesting against corruption and
impunity, but also against the violation of their own land rights, and
intimidation when they sought to defend those rights.[79]

Other actions shaded rightward. One group of Indignado leaders
announced that political figures were not welcome in the marches,
making clear they meant leaders from LIBRE, especially Manuel
Zelaya—although LIBRE and PAC members had been in the streets
protesting the regimes for years before the Indignados. Among the
banners and placards in the mainstream torch marches, I noticed few
references to human rights, repression, Indigenous concerns, land
rights, or advancing militarization; when I casually mentioned the
latter to a few fellow marchers, I was met by an awkward silence. Most
ambiguously, for their Friday, July 17, torch protest, the Indignados
in Tegucigalpa announced that their route would end not at the
Presidential Palace or the Congress building, as before, but at the
US Embassy. When they arrived at the gates, they didn't protest US
support for the regime, as expected by many. Instead, a small group
led by Varela asked for the Ambassador's help. Nealon granted them
a two-hour meeting inside the embassy.[80]

Longtime left-leaning activists from the opposition were understandably ambivalent about the torch marches, having suffered years
of repression while many of the Indignados supported the coup or
sat silently by until its effects reached an intolerable tipping point

that pulled them under, too. But Resistance veterans understood that this was a sincere and very powerful moment of uprising against corruption and impunity. They also knew that any viable progressive future for Honduras would need the middle class on board. They, too, were moved by the torches, and jumped into the marches in greater and greater numbers.

The night after that big march in Tegucigalpa I watched another, much smaller torch march, this one overwhelmingly working class, in La Lima, the old United Fruit company town on the outskirts of San Pedro Sula. It started with clusters of ten or twenty weathered-looking men and laughing older women, most of whom had spent decades cutting down banana stems or packing fruit in the packinghouses. We all waited in the weeds for the march to start, while ants climbed our calves and a high school marching band arrived in an old yellow school bus from the United States. As it got darker and the march began, the protesters shouted their way past the old headquarters of the United Fruit Company and over the bridge curving into the center of town. Hundreds of people, from the very old to the very young, joined, including dozens of tiny girls—some on their mini-bicycles, some in strollers, some sandwiched between their parents on motorcycles that passed slowly along the side.[81]

Working people of La Lima had been marching through those exact same streets ever since the 1954 General Strike from which all modern Honduran history flows. That night, they shouted the same slogans as had the middle-class Tegucigalpa marchers—"*¡Fuera JOH!*" (Hernández Out!) and "*¡Cuál es la ruta? Sacar ese hijo de puta!*" ("What is the path? Throw out that son of a bitch!"). I heard the same, rewritten version of *La Bamba* that I'd heard in the capital, opening with "*Para sacar Juan Orlando . . .*" (To throw out Juan Orlando . . .). But their torches were almost all homemade from plastic bottles and duct tape, and they marched along with a practiced ease born of lifetimes of struggle, passed along, now, to yet another generation.

Indignados of all stripes did agree on the same core demands: first, the resignation of President Juan Orlando Hernández, Attorney General Oscar Chinchilla, and Assistant Attorney General Rigoberto Cuellar; and second, an independent commission on impunity sponsored by the United Nations, modeled on Guatemala's Comisión Internacional contra la Impunidad en Guatemala (CICIG, International Commission Against Impunity in Guatemala). Created in 2007, by 2014 the CICIG had been effective in investigating and helping prosecute and convict more than two thousand government officials charged with corruption, extrajudicial killings, and other crimes.[82] During that same spring and summer of 2015, as Hondurans were protesting Juan Orlando's regime, Guatemalans were pouring into their own streets by the tens of thousands and, along with the CICIG, helped produce the September 3 resignation and jailing of Guatemalan President Otto Pérez Molina on corruption charges.[83] Observers began to speak of a "Central American Spring," evoking the 2010 Arab Spring, when mass protests from below had toppled governments throughout the Middle East.[84]

As the demand for a UN CICIH snowballed in June and July 2015, Hernández craftily countered on June 24 with a proposal for a *national* commission on impunity, which he would control, with international advisors and a "dialogue."[85] The protesters weren't at all fooled. How could a corrupt government investigate itself? people underscored to me. It would be like "the rats guarding the cheese," as one critic put it. US Ambassador Nealon tweeted his support for the proposal.[86]

The Obama Administration was understandably worried that the protest situation was slipping rapidly out of its control and could lead to Hernández's downfall. On June 29, the Organization of American States (OAS) and the United Nations told the press that they had signed an agreement with the Honduran government to facilitate a "dialogue" to strengthen democracy in Honduras and combat corruption and impunity.[87] By September 28, the OAS had fully taken charge of the project on its own, and announced the formation of a new Misión de Apoyo Contra la Corrupción y la Impunidad en Honduras (Mission to Support the Fight against Corruption and Impunity in Honduras), known as the MACCIH. The MACCIH would be charged with investigating corruption by government officials and recommending reforms. It would draw on international experts. But unlike the CICIG, it would not have independent power to investigate cases. It would have no teeth; all it could do was recommend reforms, not implement them. It would, though, create the impression that corruption and impunity were effectively being addressed in Honduras. And everyone understood that it would be under the control of the United States.[88]

Prominent Hondurans in the Honduran human rights community quickly underscored the weaknesses of the MACCIH. They noted, too, the lack of public consultation about the project. The Coalition Against Impunity, a broad alliance of independent human rights groups, declared:

> Critical and opposition organizations in our country have been excluded from the national dialogue, which has been conducted with sectors identified with the ruling party, leaving out organizations that promote human rights, real justice system reform, unions, women, peasant movements, indigenous peoples, student movements and other sectors mobilized in social protests that have demanded the changes necessary for the removal of corruption, violence and impunity.

This exclusion, they stated, "forms part of a dangerous emerging trend of reducing the space they have gained through many years of experience demanding the protection of human rights and fundamental freedoms of the more vulnerable sectors." The coalition's members reiterated unequivocally their demand for a CICIH.[89] Even Eric Olson of the Woodrow Wilson Center in Washington, ordinarily directly aligned with the State Department, expressed concern that the MACCIH could be "mere window dressing."[90] The OAS's forceful launching of the MACCIH set up a difficult choice for the Honduran opposition: whether to continue to push for a UN-sponsored commission or to accept the MACCIH and try to get the most out of it. Eventually, by 2017, they would largely pivot to the latter.

The Obama Administration, for its part, faced its own formidable challenge. It had to figure out how to shore up the regime and at the same time discipline its monster, who was more out of control than ever. Increasingly, the United States deployed extraditions (and, perhaps more importantly, the threat of extradition), to try to scare Honduran elites into submission—although it wasn't the State

Department or the White House calling the shots.

In January 2012, the United States pressured President Lobo into accepting an extradition law, the country's first since 1982.[91] Beginning in late 2013, the US Department of the Treasury and the US Attorney General's office in the Southern District Court of New York then began to close in on key drug trafficking figures within Honduras and demand their extradition to the United States. The Department of the Treasury first targeted Miguel Handal Pérez, aka "Chepe" Handal, and members of his family, using the Kingpin Act, which mandates the freezing of US assets and a ban on financial interactions with anyone from the United States. In December 2014, the Honduran government extradited the Valle brothers, two mid-level *narcos* rumored to be close to Juan Orlando, after the DEA had helped capture them in October.[92] Then, in January 2015, two top-level drug traffickers, brothers Javier Eriberto Rivera Maradiaga, and Devis Leonel Rivera Maradiaga, known as the "Cachiros," who had been cooperating with the DEA for at least a year, turned themselves in to US authorities rather than be killed by rivals. The Cachiros, in turn, while in custody in Miami, squealed in meticulous detail.[93]

After that, the Department of Justice went after the big fish. In early October 2015, using the Cachiros's information, the Southern District Court of New York indicted and demanded the extradition of three members of one of the richest and most powerful families in Honduras, the Rosenthals, charging them with money-laundering under the Kingpin Act. Yani Rosenthal turned himself in and was flown to the United States; Yankel was arrested in Miami. Jaime Rosenthal, the aging and ailing patriarch, remained at liberty in Honduras, and the Honduran government did not extradite him. Within a week of the indictment, the Honduran government seized and shut down all the Rosenthals's assets, without any due process, including a cement plant, a sugar refinery, the Banco Continental, the newspaper *El Tiempo,* and other enterprises, laying off an estimated twenty thousand total workers—adding to the ranks of the unemployed.[94]

In one fell swoop, the US Department of Justice struck a huge blow: on one front, it took down a top oligarch family, presumably striking terror into the bones of the rest, who were themselves cozy with drug traffickers and organized crime. On another front, the Rosenthals weren't just random oligarchs. They were Liberal Party; Yani had come in second in the party's 2013 presidential primary and presumably would be running again; he was somewhat more centrist than the other leading candidates. When the IHSS scandal and the Indignados' protests had erupted that spring, *El Tiempo* had taken a clear stand critical of Hernández for the first time since 2013. So when the US Department of Justice took down the Rosenthals, it also took down the one semi-independent newspaper, and eliminated a viable centrist candidate from a future candidacy for the president.

The relationship between the Justice Department's Southern District Court of New York, which was prosecuting the cases, and the State Department, remains murky, although evidence strongly suggests that the Southern District of New York acted independently and that the State Department did not control the process, learning of the charges and extradition requests in these and other Cachiros-related cases only right before they were filed.

The Justice Department pursued National Party political figures as well. In May 2015, former President Porfirio Lobo's son Fabio was arrested in Haiti on drug trafficking charges and sent to the United States.[95] (He would be convicted in 2017 and sentenced to twenty-six years in US prison.) In December 2015, another branch of the Department of Justice charged and extradited former President Rafael Callejas, as part of the FIFAgate soccer corruption scandal.[96] Callejas has been the mastermind of the National Party, the grand old man behind Juan Orlando. Throughout that year and the next, Ambassdor Nealon's tweets and press statements gushed with celebrations of the Honduran government's successful fight against impunity and corruption, in partnership with the United States.[97]

With these and other extraditions, the United States addressed its discipline problem in part by outsourcing the Honduran criminal justice system. If the Honduran government wouldn't prosecute its crooks, the United States would—although it's important to disaggregate who exactly the "United States" is in this instance, given the independence of the Department of Justice from the State Department and the White House. In this new empire by extradition, Honduran sovereignty was pushed by the wayside on yet another front.

The problem, though, was unsolvable, because criminal drug traffickers were interwoven throughout the top levels of the Honduran government, its security forces, its elected officials, and the elite businessmen who controlled them. Yet the Obama Administration wanted to keep Hernández in power, nonetheless, for an array of geopolitical, military, and economic objectives.

Five days after that enormous Tegucigalpa torch march I witnessed, the US Embassy held its annual Fourth of July party, thick with Honduran elites in their best suits and dresses. The walkways were tastefully, and presumably deliberately, decorated with tiki torches.[98] Standing next to Juan Orlando, US Ambassador James Nealon proclaimed: "relations between the United States and Honduras are perhaps the best in history."[99] You could almost hear Tammy Wynette belting out in the background, "Stand by Your Man."

Despite the embassy's clear voice of support for the regime, that season ordinary Hondurans had found new ways of speaking eloquently for themselves. While Hernández blocked almost all formal avenues of democratic input, the middle class was discovering the power that lay in the streets, a power that working-class Hondurans had claimed for decades. In the long, dark, repressive night of post-coup Honduras, the torch protests, with their magical lighting and ferocious outrage, brought a new and completely surprising burst of exhilarating hope—reminding everyone, on all sides, that anything could still happen.

Activists protesting the assassination of Berta Cáceres, Tegucigalpa, March 8, 2016. Photo credit: AP Photo/Fernando Antonio.

CHAPTER SIX

Boomerangs:
Berta Cáceres and
the View from the Backyard

She Didn't Die, She Multiplied

Berta Isabel Cáceres Flores was born in 1971 to the Lenca Indigenous people in La Esperanza, Honduras, high up in the mountains east of the capital. Her mother, Austra Bertha Flores López, was a midwife and twice mayor of La Esperanza. During the 1970s and '80s, Austra Bertha worked with refugees from El Salvador and taught her daughter about social justice and struggle. Berta Cáceres, when she reached college, helped found COPINH, the Council of Popular and Indigenous Organizations of Honduras (Consejo Cívico de Organizaciones Populares e Indígenas de Honduras).[1]

During the 1990s and 2000s, Berta worked hard with COPINH and the Lenca people on a range of activist efforts to protect local Indigeous peoples' rights. Beginning in 2006, Indigenous people of the community of Rio Blanco, affiliated with COPINH, started noticing signs of imminent construction of what soon turned out to be a new hydroelectric dam project known as Agua Zarca, which was being developed as a joint venture by a Honduran company, DESA (Desarrollos Energéticos, S.A), and a Chinese one, Sinonydro, with funding from the World Bank and a variety of European and

Honduran investors. The dam and its construction process would devastate the local Lenca people's traditions, culture, and basic survival by cutting off access to food, water, and medicinal plants. The United Nations Declaration on the Rights of Indigenous People, along with Convention 169 of the International Labor Organization (ILO), mandates that Indigenous people must be given free, prior, and informed consultation on any such project.[2] But the Lenca people formally rejected the Agua Zarca dam.[3]

With increasing tenacity and bravery, the COPINH community of Rio Blanco began challenging the dam. They tried the courts; they talked to UN officials. Finally, beginning in 2013, they started protesting directly where the dam was now being constructed. In April 2013, they put up a roadblock to try to cut off access to the site and kept it up for months. Berta Cáceres, General Coordinator of COPINH at the national level, came to Rio Blanco to support the struggle. All along, she had been helping the community out as their alarm over the dam increased and their campaign escalated.[4]

Then serious repression began. In May 2013, authorities charged Berta with possession of an unlicensed gun which, she countered, had been placed in the bed of her truck by the military at a security checkpoint. Until charges were finally dismissed in January 2014 she had to show up in court every week and live with the threat of extensive jail time hanging over her head.[5] On July 15, 2013, soldiers of the First Engineers' Battalion of the Honduran Armed Forces shot and killed COPINH member Tomás García while he and a hundred others were marching toward the project's gates; the soldiers also injured his son.[6] In August, the government issued further criminal charges against Berta and two other Lenca activists, accusing them of coercion, usurpation of land, and other crimes. The three went underground for months. "Defending human rights in Honduras is a crime," Berta declared. "They are criminalizing the right to our identity and sense of self." The charges had locked her in: "I cannot live my life like before. I cannot go to the office, take part in our campaign, or leave the country to denounce our situation in international forums."[7]

Although she is often described as an "environmental and Indigenous activist," Berta Cáceres was also a committed feminist, a firm supporter of LGBTI rights, and a clearsighted critic of capitalism. In the months leading up to the coup and after, she ran as an independent candidate for vice president alongside Carlos H. Reyes, pulling out of the November 2009 election in protest.[8] She was one of the top leaders of the Resistance, helping organize and inspire the social movement base after the formal FNRP largely became LIBRE. In photographs she had some incredible ability to always look alive and smart and subtly amused. It's as if she knew her time on earth was going to be short and shone into each camera so that in the future she could walk out of pictures and into our hearts, reminding us to keep struggling for social justice—and to keep laughing.

During 2015, COPINH began protesting the dam vigorously again, and by the early months of 2016, repression of COPINH and, in particular, of Berta Cáceres, escalated dangerously. She got at least thirty-three separate threats, which she reported to the government, none of which were investigated. By the end of February, one source was bombarding her almost constantly with text messages, threatening to kill her if she didn't stop organizing against the dam. Berta knew it was bad: she started trying to arrange it so someone else could sign COPINH's checks. Hugging her daughter Laura Zuñiga Cáceres goodbye at the airport on March 2, she told her: "If you hear that something's happened to me, don't be afraid."[9]

All over the world, people tried to keep Berta alive, using every public recognition imaginable. Members of the Honduras Solidarity Network and others brought her to Washington and talked to Congress about her regularly; she was known in Canada, Europe. Most prominently, in April 2015, Berta Cáceres was awarded the prestigious Goldman Environmental Prize. When they handed Berta the prize on the Opera House stage in San Francisco, I watched with Zenaida Velásquez, my longtime Honduran activist colleague, at the front of the top balcony. Berta stepped up to the microphone in a glittering dress on that most upper class of upper-class stages and exhorted:

> Wake up! Wake up, humanity! We have no more time. Our consciences are shaken by the fact that we are only contemplating our own self-destruction based on capitalist, racist, and patriarchal predation. The Gualcarque River has called upon us, as have the

other gravely threatened rivers all over the world. Let us answer their call.

Mother Earth—militarized, fenced in, poisoned, where elemental rights are systematically violated—demands that we take action. Let us build societies, then, that are able to coexist in a just, dignified way, for life.... Let us come together and remain hopeful as we defend and care for the blood of this Earth and its spirits.[10]

A few days later, the Goldman Foundation held another ceremony in Washington, D.C., to celebrate its prize recipients. House Minority Leader Nancy Pelosi held an event in the Capitol in their honor, replete with senators and members, and met with Berta herself at some length.[11] In October, Berta met Pope Francis in Rome.[12]

But even all that wasn't enough. Just before midnight on March 2, 2016—hours after she'd hugged her daughter goodbye—two gunmen burst into the home in La Esperanza where Berta was staying. One shot her up, the other shot a Mexican friend and colleague, Gustavo Castro Soto, who was in another room, wounding him. She died in Gustavo's arms soon after.[13]

Now everyone in Honduras knew that they really would kill anyone, no matter how famous. A shudder passed through the entire opposition: Whoever challenged the regime from then on was among the walking dead. And, of course, an extraordinary, effective leader had now been eliminated from the movement. In the North, unable to stop the train of US policy from tearing through post-coup Honduras, we had measured our success in part by people not killed. Bottom line, we wanted to help keep the Hondurans alive for another day, to fight their struggles as they chose. Now we, too, knew that nothing we could do could keep any given Honduran alive, not even the most celebrated, the most beloved, the most at-risk.

The Honduran government, in classic form, swiftly announced that it was investigating as a culprit the injured Mexican, Gustavo Castro, and two members of COPINH; it implied the assassination had been a "crime of passion." Castro was held in captivity and refused medical care for days, then prevented from leaving the country for a month, although he took refuge in the Mexican Embassy part of that time.[14]

On June 21, though, the *Guardian* revealed that Berta Cáceres's name had appeared on a hit list belonging to the Honduran military.[15] Over the course of the next year, eight men would be arrested in her case, of whom three had connections to the military and one was an active-duty major in the Honduran armed forces at the time of her killing and had been trained by US Special Forces. Evidence further pointed potentially toward the elite owners of the dam project, indicating they could be the intellectual authors of the crime.[16] On May 2, the prominent opposition radio journalist Felix Molina posted on his Facebook page that he was about to reveal information implicating top political figures in Berta's killing. Within hours two strangers jumped into his cab in Tegucigalpa and shot him repeatedly in the legs. He fled the country into exile.[17]

When Berta Cáceres was killed, though, something extraordinary happened. To use the phrase COPINH members proclaimed at her memorial service and in placards and banners at demonstrations thereafter, "Berta didn't die, she multiplied." The *New York Times* reported Berta's assassination prominently the next day; news media all over the United States and the world picked it up and kept reporting about it; Nina Lakhani at the *Guardian* dug deep into the story for months.[18] Environmental activists rose up in horror and moved the news of Berta's assassination around their networks.[19] Indigenous peoples' organizations spanning the Americas traveled to La Esperanza and embraced COPINH's struggle, demanding justice in her case.[20] Berta wasn't just about Honduras any more. In her afterlife, she became a potent global symbol of peoples's struggle from below and repression from above. Her image moved, like Che Guevara's, all over the world. By the beginning of 2017, you could even buy a cell phone cover or a tote bag with her face on it. In early May 2016, two months after her death, I went to a local meeting of the Santa Cruz Climate Action Network to hear a university colleague talk about Latin American perspectives on global justice. Before he spoke, the organizers—whom I didn't know at all—announced that the funds raised at the event would be going to COPINH; the speaker opened with a video clip of Berta's Goldman Prize acceptance speech. That fall, I asked my students in a US history class how many of them had heard of Berta Cáceres (I'd never mentioned her). Of forty-five, nine stuck up their hands.

But there was a downside to Berta's rock-star status. In Washington, Berta and her case became a political commodity, available to many who had not especially cared about her struggles when she was alive, and who promoted policies with which she would have vehemently disagreed.

On the positive side, longtime congressional allies came through beautifully immediately after she was killed. Senator Leahy told the Department of State within hours of her death that he would not approve the release of any further funds for the Honduran government until her case was being appropriately investigated and those responsible for her killing were being brought to justice. He released an eloquent statement that Berta's family read at her memorial service in La Esperanza on March 4, calling for an independent investigation of the crime and the shutdown of the dam. Leahy challenged Honduran leaders to publicly defend the rights of activists like COPINH, journalists, and others, rather than arresting or intimidating them. "Indigenous people, landless people, people demanding a healthy life for their children and relief from hunger, poverty, injustice, corruption, greed and the destructive exploitation of the environment. Instead of respect and support, they have too often been threatened and killed with impunity."[21] Within a few days Representatives Hank Johnson and Keith Ellison began circulating a sign-on letter that had sixty-two total members of Congress on it by March 17, when it went public. They called for an independent investigation by the Inter-American Commission on Human Rights, the suspension of US security funding to Honduras, and a review of US-supported loans from multilateral development banks. Echoing Leahy, they asked the State Department to pressure the Honduran government to stop the dam and guarantee protection of Cáceres's family, COPINH, and human rights defenders.[22] Other members and senators, including House Minority Leader Nancy Pelosi and Senator Benjamin Cardin, put out individual public statements and tweeted; Keith Ellison, who emerged as an important champion in this period and thereafter, gave a floor speech; Representative Betty

McCollum sent a letter to the State Department, forwarding information from US human rights activists about Leahy Law violators in Honduras and requesting enforcement of the Leahy Law.[23]

Then the plot thickened. On Monday, March 6, Representatives Sam Farr and Norma Torres circulated their own, different letter, that merely expressed concern about the case and called on the Honduran authorities to investigate; asked the US government to cooperate in every way possible; and called for protection of human rights defenders. In its requests, it matched almost exactly the statement that the State Department had put out the day after Berta had been killed. Missing altogether was our longtime demand that Farr himself and over ninety other members had supported for years, calling for the suspension of police and military aid to Honduras.[24] Yet the human rights situation was worse now, for all to see. The letter was a giant step backward.

Representative Norma Torres emerged in 2015 and '16 as an increasingly powerful counterforce to the progressive policy on Honduras so many of us had built for years. Born in Guatemala, elected in 2014 from a district east of Los Angeles, Torres was the first member of Congress from Central America.[25] In early 2015, she formed a new Central America Caucus, of which she became co-chair, along with Republican Representative David Valadao of Bakersfield, California.[26] Torres had a long history as a centrist. When she had served in the California legislature before coming to Congress, she often voted with Republicans against bills that had been introduced by liberal Democrats on environmental and labor issues—although California Democrats enjoyed a supermajority and didn't need to work with Republicans in order to pass legislation.[27]

The fall before Berta was killed, in October and November 2015, as the OAS's MACCIH proposal threatened to squash the Hondurans' demand for an independent United Nations commission against corruption and impunity, Alex Main and I worked with Representative José Serrano's office on a sign-on letter in the House, supporting a UN commission modeled on Guatemala's CICIG.[28] I thought it was a no-brainer, a non-controversial theme among progressives, given its mass popularity within Honduras; the letter was eventually signed by fifty-three other members. But Representatives Norma Torres and Sam Farr wouldn't sign the letter, to my surprise. Just three weeks before, I had been in a meeting with Farr in which he had personally promised Bertha Oliva, the director of COFADEH, that he would put out a public statement supporting a CICIH.

In late February 2016, neither Torres nor Farr would sign on to a letter from Representatives Marcy Kaptur and Hank Johnson, expressing concern over threats to Honduran trade unionists.[29] Kaptur, the most senior woman in the House, was a key champion of labor rights in Honduras and a rock-solid supporter of our progressive policy initiatives at every turn. If Farr, with his own strong labor record, wouldn't sign that letter either, something was clearly up. By the time Berta Cáceres was assassinated on March 2, 2016, the terrain in the House had clearly shifted: my colleagues and I didn't just have to battle with the administration and conservative Republicans from then on, we had to deal with an aggressive centrist promoting her own initiatives on Honduras while also seeking to undermine our projects.

So we upped the ante. Working behind the scenes for six weeks, Representative Hank Johnson's aide Sascha Thompson and I, helped by aides to five other members and a few trusted colleagues in the solidarity community, crafted the first congressional bill requiring that security aid to Honduras be immediately suspended and that the United States vote no on any loans to Honduras from international development banks.[30] Entitled the Berta Cáceres Human Rights in Honduras Act, it was modeled on similar bills in the 1980s that had proposed to cut off US security aid to El Salvador. On June 14, 2015, Johnson introduced the bill on the House floor, co-sponsored by Representatives John Conyers, Keith Ellison, Marcy Kaptur, Janice Schakowsky, and José Serrano.[31] Soon after, the six initial cosponsors published a joint op-ed in the *Guardian*: "America's Funding of Honduran Security Forces Puts Blood on Our Hands."[32]

Much to our surprise, the bill had legs. Far more than any letters from Congress in the years before, the bill garnered support and publicity that grew and grew. Like Berta's image—and, of course, building on it—the Berta Cáceres Act, HR 5474, took on a life of its own; or, rather, was breathed into life by the hard work of thousands of activists who beat the bushes pressuring their representatives to sign on. By the end of 2016, a total of fifty-one members had officially co-sponsored it.[33] Endorsers included the AFL-CIO, Sierra Club, Friends of the Earth, American Friends Service Committee, American Jewish World Service, Center for Constitutional Rights, Greenpeace, Latin America Working Group, Maryknoll Office for Global Concerns, National Lawyers Guild, Presbyterian Church USA, School of the Americas Watch, Sisters of Mercy of the Americas, United Church of Christ Justice and Witness Ministries, and Witness for Peace, along with the host of regional Latin America solidarity groups that had long supported Honduras—a total of sixty US and international organizations (but not the Washington Office on Latin America, WOLA, which worked closely with Norma Torres).[34] Within Honduras, twenty-nine prominent human rights and other groups affiliated as the Coalition Against Impunity courageously endorsed it.[35] Journalists around the world cited it in news stories about a range of Honduran themes. It was a gift that kept on giving. When Hank Johnson later reintroduced it on the anniversary of Berta's assassination on March 2, 2017, twenty-four original cosponsors joined on, and, as HR 1299, the total would reach seventy by that fall.[36]

Three weeks after the bill was first introduced, in late June 2016, President Juan Orlando Hernández flew to Washington to defend his nation against what became known in Honduras as the "Ley Berta" (Berta Law).[37] Representative Norma Torres's staffer invited members affiliated with the Central America Caucus to a private meeting with Hernández to learn about the president's achievements improving prosperity and security in Honduras. They could "also" ask Hernández about human rights concerns if they wanted.[38] In March 2017, like clockwork, three weeks after the bill was reintroduced, Torres again invited Hernández to speak to the caucus. This time word got out. The *Guardian* and *Democracy Now!* reported that protesters lined up in the hall outside, holding up a banner reading "BERTA CÁCERES PRESENTE" and photographs of Berta and other social justice leaders assassinated since the coup.[39] Although Torres's promotion of Hernández was chilling, her efforts were effective, as her staff worked vigorously against the bill in both 2016 and 2017. Several members, especially newer ones and those from Southern California, now followed her lead and her assumed moral authority as a Central American and would not sign on to the bill. Before he retired at the end of 2016, Representative Farr did eventually join as a cosponsor of the bill, under pressure from constituents. But even after Berta's family wrote a personal letter to Representative Torres in the spring of 2017 asking her to support the reintroduced bill, she still refused.[40]

Cleanup Acts

While Berta's star shot across the international firmament, social justice activists and human rights defenders inside Honduras paid a heavy price for the new spotlight shining on human rights abuses in their country. Two weeks after Berta was assassinated, Nelson García, a COPINH activist, was killed; in July another COPINH member, Lesbia Janeth Urquía, was killed as well.[41] During the following year, demonstrations by COPINH in front of the Presidential Palace demanding justice for Berta's case were met with tear gas and raging security forces, who in one instance chased old women and children down the local streets. On April 15, a group of COPINH members who were marching to the Gualcarque River were met by twenty-five to thirty people armed with machetes and rocks, who threatened the protesters and their international companions.[42]

Repression steadily beat down on other Honduran social activists and their defenders throughout the country. In May the government shut down David Romero's all-important Radio Globo, claiming its license had not been properly renewed.[43] In October, in the Aguán Valley, José Angel Flores, the campesino leader of the MUCA, and Silmer Dionicio George, another MUCA activist, were assassinated outside their Tocoa office.[44] Threats against trade unionists continued with impunity. The November before, Nelson Nuñez, an organizer with FESTRAGRO, the agricultural workers' union, had received increasing death threats and had to move his home, but despite two congressional letters in early 2016 raising alarm about his case and others, the government failed to provide adequate protection or properly investigate the case.[45]

Still spiraling out of control, the Honduran Congress passed two startling new laws establishing a legal framework for even more powerful future repression of the opposition. Reform 335B to the Penal Code, passed in February 2017, made it possible for journalists and other commentators to be charged with supporting terrorism and be jailed for four to eight years if they were deemed to have written with "apology, exaltation, or justification" about what the government deemed "terrorism."[46] Reform 590, passed in September, allowed fifteen- to twenty-year sentences for demonstrators and others who sought to "subvert" constitutional order or to induce "terror" in the population. Judges could decide the definition of "terrorism." With these measures the government was criminalizing as terrorist both those who sought to demonstrate against it and those who might criticize it in the media. "The current government has done everything possible to restrict dissent as part of the re-election strategy laid out by the Juan Orlando Hernández regime," charged Miriam Miranda of OFRANEH, the Afro-Indigenous Garifuna organization.[47] While tightening the legal noose around its critics, the government gave its security forces a carte blanche to kill protesters. In May, Congress modified Article 25 to grant immunity to security forces who used their weapons while in the line of duty.[48]

Repression also increased against international human rights defenders who regularly traveled to Honduras to accompany at-risk Hondurans or to document abuses. In mid-May, 2015, the Honduran government charged that an Italian-German citizen, Giulia Fellin, had incited violence at a COPINH demonstration, and announced that she was being expelled; Fellin had to take refuge in the Italian Embassy before leaving the country.[49] In late October, a Spanish man who had previously accompanied COPINH members and others was detained in handcuffs at the airport, interrogated for four hours, denied habeas corpus, and put on a plane to El Salvador without his passport.[50]

On September 22, 2016, I published an op-ed in the *New York Times* entitled "End US Support for the Thugs of Honduras."[51] Within hours, right-wing Honduran websites launched articles attacking me. One article on *Nos Queda Claro*, headlined "The Opposition and International Media Continue their Campaign to Damage Honduras," featured a lurid graphic superimposing my face on a sea of flagwaving LIBRE and PAC enthusiasts.[52] Over the next days, *Nos Queda Claro* expanded its targets with a series of slickly designed, poster-style graphics linking me to an alleged international conspiracy of leftists including Amy Goodman and Juan Gonzáles of *Democracy Now!*, Annie Bird, Nina Lakhani of the *Guardian*, Manuel Zelaya, and several Honduran journalists, including Jhonny Lagos, director of *El Libertador*. One advertised a fictional conference entitled *"Gran I*

Simposio, Tema Central Terrorismo Mediático" (First Grand Symposium, Central Theme Media Terrorism): "Learn about teachings in yellow journalism, manipulating information, discrediting a country and its authorities," it promised. Another depicted a spiderweb linking ten of us and declared "*¡AL DESCUBIERTO! Red Izquierda Radical Lanza Campaña de ODIO CONTRA HONDURAS*" (REVEALED! Radical Left Network Launches Campaign of HATE AGAINST HONDURAS"). On Amy Goodman's Facebook page someone wrote in: "They are all sympathizers of the left and of course you should support THROWING THEM OUT. The minute they travel to Honduras."[53] Further targets on hostile websites included Alexander Main of CEPR—attacked originally after he published an op-ed in the *New York Times* in February 2016 critical of Hernández—and Victoria Cervantes and Karen Spring of the Honduras Solidarity Network, along with Hondurans Bertha Oliva of COFADEH and Gerardo Torres of TeleSUR.[54]

On February 2, 2017, a representative of the British NGO Global Witness, which had recently put out a widely cited report documenting that Honduras was the most dangerous place in the world to be an environmental defender, had to be rescued by a UN official during a live television talk show, when Honduran authorities on the show, including the Secretary of Natural Resources, declared that he should be immediately captured and criminally charged.[55]

These campaigns built on terrifying earlier attacks on international human rights defenders in Honduras. On July 24, 2013, two members of the Honduras Accompaniment Project, Daniel Langmeier, a Swiss citizen, and Orlane Vidal, a French citizen, had arrived in Nueva Esperanza, Atlántida, to accompany the community in its struggle against an illegal mining project. The next morning, thirty to forty men surrounded them, held them at gunpoint for four hours, threatened them with death, then literally drove them out of town.[56]

The most prolonged attacks against a US citizen were against Annie Bird, co-director of Rights Action at the time, who, for years and years, investigated human rights abuses by Honduran state security forces, especially those perpetrated against the campesino movement in the Aguán Valley. Her February 2013 report on the 15th Battalion was particularly damning in its documentation of the alleged involvement of Honduran military and police with Miguel Facussé's private security guards in the deaths of campesino activists. On December 12, 2013, the same day the Honduran government certified Juan Orlando's election, Colonel German Alfaro, commander of the Xatruch III Task Force in the Aguán, went on Honduran television and radio to attack Bird aggressively. "We are in the process of investigating a complaint against a supposed American named Annie Bird, who is going around doing destabilizing work here in the Aguán sector, meeting with various campesino leaders," he announced officially. The newspapers picked up the story and ran her photo. *La Tribuna* said she was in the Aguán plotting armed rebellion.[57]

Again, in July 2014, Alfaro—who was trained and funded by the United States—went after Bird, this time joined by the head of the National Agrarian Institute (a cabinet-level minister) and Roger Pineda, Facussé's spokesperson. With zero evidence, they charged on television and the radio that she was plotting armed violence in the Aguán, had entered the country illegally, and was feeding information to Al Queda. It was all over the papers.[58] Someone using a Hitler image as their ID declared on *El Tiempo*'s website that she should be burned to death.[59] Despite pressure from both the US Congress and a wide range of human rights groups, the embassy remained publicly silent, however, about these dangerous attacks on a US citizen by a US-funded officer of the Honduran armed forces.

Top officials of the Honduran government, including Juan Orlando, continued to publicly attack Honduran human rights defenders who spoke to international allies or who traveled to Washington. Those who criticized the government to outsiders were branded as "bad Hondurans" who sought to destroy the country, and were allegedly funded by international leftists and LIBRE.[60] The space for dissent closed in more tightly than ever.

President Juan Orlando Hernández, though, for all the international outcry, still rode high in the saddle. During 2015 and 2016 he set the stage for a permanent dictatorship. Article 239 of the Honduran Constitution, written in response to two decades of military rule, states unequivocally that no president can serve more than one term; it even states that if a sitting president advocates re-election, he or she must be immediately removed from office. But in April 2015, the Honduran Supreme Court—under Juan Orlando's control—simply ruled that the articles weren't valid, because they violated international norms on human rights.[61] It had zero authority to do so; changing the constitution requires a long, complex process. With that ruling, Hernández began a completely criminal march toward re-election. It didn't matter that legal experts, other political parties, and international observers screamed out in objection. In the November 2016 primaries, he won the National Party nomination hands down—although who really knew, since he controlled all the electoral machinery—and sprinted toward the November 2017 final election. Xiomara Castro won the LIBRE nomination again, Salvador Nasralla the PAC's.[62] In May, Castro and Nasralla decided to run as a united ticket, known as the Opposition Alliance, headed by Nasralla as presidential candidate and Castro as his running mate.[63]

In an October 15 public statement, well before the primaries, the US Embassy in Tegucigalpa clarified its position on reelection: "The US Government does not oppose President Hernandez or others from presenting themselves for re-election according to Honduran democratic processes. It is up to the Honduran people to determine their political future through their democratic institutions and processes."[64] Juan Orlando had his official green light. Meanwhile, with tens of millions of dollars in new US aid in hand, the embassy increasingly sought to exercise its soft power agenda in Honduras, especially through the Association for a More Just Society (Asociación Para una Sociedad Mas Justa, ASJ), an evangelical Christian NGO, which, between 2010 and 2017, received at least $5.6 million in State Department funding and $900,000 from USAID, including $2,646,000 in December 2016 alone—enormous sums in the Honduran context. Promoted and cited widely by the embassy and the Honduran papers as Honduran "civil society," visiting the US Congress to ostensibly represent Hondurans, the ASJ closely followed the State Department in its positions—so much so that it became a useful indicator of the administration's line at any given point.[65]

In August 2015, the *New York Times* published a lengthy article by Sonia Nazario spanning several pages of the Sunday paper, headlined "How the Most Dangerous Place on Earth Got Safer: Programs Funded by the United States Are Helping Transform Honduras." The article touted the ASJ's gang prevention program in a neighborhood of San Pedro Sula, Rivera Hernández, where the organization worked closely with the Honduras police, and explicitly countered the Berta Cáceres Act's demand for a suspension of US security aid.[66] It seems safe to conclude that the State Department had a hand in developing and placing the article, to challenge the bill. But as analysts from the Center for Economic and Policy Research (CEPR) and others pointed out, Nazario's arguments were based only on anecdotal evidence and evaded the broader context of corruption, criminal activity, and human rights abuses by the rapidly militarizing Honduran police. CEPR also examined closely the only known quantitative study of the effectiveness of CARSI programs, performed by the Latin American Popular Opinion Project (LAPOP) at Vanderbilt University (and, like the ASJ, USAID-funded), and concluded that LAPOP's rosy portrait of CARSI programs was not borne out by the evidence.[67]

In January 2016, the Honduran government launched yet another commission to clean up its police, the Special Commission for the Purging and Transformation of the National Police (Comisión Especial para el Proceso de Depuración y Transformación de la Policía Nacional).[68] Promoted widely by the adminstration's allies in Washington—especially by the Woodrow Wilson Center—as evidence of the regime's progress, the commission gave new meaning to the idea of foxes guarding the chicken coop. Its members included Vilma Morales, a former Supreme Court judge who had supported the coup and who served as one of two top negotiators for de facto president Roberto Micheletti in its aftermath; Alberto Solórzano, an openly anti-gay evangelical minister tight with Hernández; and, as its supervisor, former general Julian Pacheco Tinoco, the Minister of Security, also a close associate of Hernández's, whose appointment as minister was widely denounced for representing further incursion of the military into controlling the police.[69] Pacheco faded into the woodwork, though, after one of the Cachiros, a top-level narco, testified in March 2017, in a New York drug trafficking trial, that Pacheco had helped oversee drug shipments.[70] Omar Rivera of the Association for a More Just Society—ostensibly representing "civil society" on the commission—stepped up as its spokesperson. Soon he was quoted in the papers almost daily, perhaps more than any other public figure other than Juan Orlando himself.[71]

The membership of the police reform commission illustrated, once again, who the administration's "partners" in Honduras were—and how US alignment had shifted even further to the right. We can contrast this new commission's members with those of the earlier 2012 and 2013 Commission for the Reform of Public Security (CRSP), who were widely understood to have been handpicked by the embassy: a Canadian OAS diplomat, a left-leaning professor, a conservative law professor, a Chilean judge (albeit with a dubious background), and a respected center-left sociologist at the helm.[72]

By early 2017, the new commission claimed that more than 2,959 police had been "separated"; later in the year, the number would climb to more than 4,000. But there was no independent verification of the commission's claims. One set of statistics it released in February 2017 acknowledged that of 377 police supposedly "cleaned up" in the latest round of purges, 171 were in fact "cancelled for restructuring," 149 took voluntary retirement, and only 57 were "cancelled for just cause."[73] In November that year the commission announced that 4,445 members of the police had been separated—as many as a third of the original total on the force. But of that number, 2,997, it said, were let go for reasons of restructuring, 252 abandoned their jobs, 98 were laid off, 58 were convicted, 68 were dead, 29 took obligatory retirement, 889 took involuntary retirements, and 54 were permanently disabled. In other words, what was claimed by the Honduran government and its US allies to be a purge of corrupt, criminal elements, was largely a mass layoff, for reasons apparently unrelated to corruption, disguised as crime fighting. As of May 2017, fewer than a hundred cases of actual criminal activity had been forwarded to the Public Ministry, and only a handful were being prosecuted. Those did not include Juan Carlos "El Tigre" Bonilla, the death squad leader. They did not include Elder Madrid Guerra, accused of authorizing the torture of dozens of resistance detainees in 2009. As observers in the criminal justice and human rights community underscored, the vast majority of the corrupt police who were separated walked the streets—leaving them free to continue criminal activities.[74]

And what of Héctor Iván Mejía, who had been in charge of the San Pedro Sula police in 2009 when they rampaged through a Resistance demonstration and gang-raped a protester, and in 2010 when the Independence Day demonstration had been teargassed? During the first year of the commission's work, Mejía was promoted repeatedly, up to the second-highest position in the National Police. In January 2017, the papers reported that he was about to be named National Director. But in April—presumably because of pressure from Honduran critics and the US Congress—he was suddenly kicked up and out of the country and made a special police attaché to the Honduran delegation at the Organization of American States in Washington.[75]

As the November 26, 2017, elections barrelled forward with Hernández's criminal candidacy as its helm, two supposed "achievements" of his administration hardened into fact in the messages of his allies in the north, the State Department, and the NGO world, and in elements of the media. First was the police cleanup. The second was an alleged drop in the murder rate. Again, though, there was no independent verification—the numbers were based on pure assertion by the regime, backed up by the UNAH's Observatory, which itself was dependent on government statistics.[76] Meanwhile alarms increasingly sounded within Honduras about the accelerating increase in "femicides"—killings of women. In March 2014, the Center for Defense of Women (Centro de Defensa de Mujeres, CDM), announced that between 2010 and 2013, 2,139 women had been killed, an increase of sixty-five percent, and ninety percent of those cases remained in impunity. In July 2017, almost two dozen women's groups denounced the killing of 463 women the year before. Only fifteen of those killings were being investigated. They criticized the government for focusing on organized crime and drug trafficking while looking away from domestic violence.[77]

The administration's close work with so-called vetted units among Honduran security forces further underscores the character of its partners in the country and illustrates US attempts to appear to be observing human rights norms while actually working with the dangerous and the corrupt. Under the 1998 Leahy Law, the United States is required to vet all individual recipients of its security aid to ensure that they have not committed gross abuses of human rights. In most cases that has meant a rapid check in US agency databases and a Google search for reports of human rights crimes. Some special "vetted units" are composed entirely of vetted individuals; those units work closely with US forces, such as the DEA. US officials point to these vetting processes in order to publicly proclaim US adherence to human rights standards.[78]

But special vetted units in Honduras continuously committed human rights violations. The Tegucigalpa soldiers who hunted down and killed fifteen-year-old Ebed Yánes in 2012, when he passed through a security checkpoint, and the colonel who ordered a coverup, had been vetted.[79] The Honduran police who shot and killed four innocent Hondurans in Ahuas in May 2012, on the instructions of the DEA, had been vetted.

Other vetted units were documented to be corrupt or criminal, such as the TIGRES (Tropa de Inteligencia y Grupos de Respuesta Especial de Seguridad), which was launched in mid-2015, the most special of special units. Two months later, a hundred of them participated in a much-publicized raid with the DEA, in which the Valle brothers, alleged drug traffickers, were captured. Two months after that, the government charged that as many as seventy of those TIGRES had stolen $1.5 million of the $21 million seized during that raid. Only nine TIGRES were ever charged; all were later acquitted.[80] Five months after they were exonerated, another group of TIGRES was arrested for allegedly tipping off another prominent alleged drug trafficker, Wilter Blanco, about his imminent capture. Those arrested TIGRES included one recently acquitted in the Valle case.[81] Two weeks before Berta Cáceres was killed, she told a Witness for Peace delegation that the TIGRES had become a "hostile and aggressive presence" in Lenca territory.[82] In other words, the United States's cleanest, most favorite partners in Honduras have been criminals or human rights abusers over and over again.

The View from the Backyard

On Sunday, November 16, 2017, Hondurans finally went to the polls. That night, the Supreme Electoral Tribunal, the commission which oversaw the vote-counting, announced, to everyone's astonishment, that with fifty-seven percent of the ballots counted, Salvador Nasralla was winning; he had forty-five percent of the votes, compared to forty percent for Hernández and thirteen percent for Luis Zelaya of the Liberal Party. Then, abruptly and without explanation, the electoral commision shut down the counting process and didn't announce any more results for two days. On Monday, Luis Zelaya conceded to Nasralla. One member of the electoral commission announced that the trend in the remainder of the results was "irreversible." On Tuesday, the commission—largely controlled by the ruling party—then claimed that the computers had shut down. Over the subsequent week, it gradually released new results five percent at a time, until Juan Orlando was ahead by one and a half percent, with almost all the ballots supposedly accounted for. On December 17, the electoral commission officially announced that Hernández had won by fifty thousand votes, or 1.71 percent of the total.[83]

As it became clear to Hondurans, and to the world, that the ruling party was stealing the election outright, the Opposition Alliance launched enormous peaceful demonstrations all over the country. Militants, drawing on tactics they had deployed at the time of the 2009 coup, put up road blockages nationwide, using burning tires to stop traffic. Hernández responded by declaring martial law and cracking down with repression even more brutal and lethal than that immediately following the coup. For the first time, security forces used live bullets against demonstrators, night after night, in some cases firing indiscriminately into the air toward groups of protesters. In other cases, individual demonstrators were hunted down in their neighborhoods or showed up dead. By December 31, according to COFADEH, thirty people had been killed, of those, twenty-one at the hands of the military police, one by the regular police, and five by unknown perpetrators of "paramilitary character." Two hundred thirty-two people had been injured, 1,396 illegally detained, and 126 demonstrations repressed.[84]

Even more than during the 2013 elections, though, this time international eyes were wide open as to what was happening. By and large, the mainstream media coverage in the United States did a good job of covering widespread evidence of fraud and the subsequent repression. The Organization of American States, usually in complete lockstep with the State Department on Honduran policy in recent years, announced, after being allowed to inspect a portion of the ballot evidence, that it could not guarantee the veracity of the results, and went so far as to call for a new election.[85] International outcry over both the election robbery and the repression grew rapidly. Senators Leahy, Reed, Merkley, and Cardin all denounced the repression and called into question the legitimacy of the election.[86] Representative Jan Schakowsky wrote a superb op-ed in the *New York Times* three days before the election, warning of Hernández's criminal candidacy, and on December 19 put out a joint statement with Senator Jeff Merkley calling for a new election.[87] On December 21, Representative Keith Ellison led on a letter to Secretary of State Rex Tillerson signed by twenty-seven members of Congress calling for a new election and a suspension of all security aid; he also wrote his own powerful op-ed warning that the US and Honduran futures were becoming increasingly and darkly similar.[88] Representative Norma Torres and twenty members, all but one from the House Foreign Affairs Committee of which she was a member, joined onto the call for a new election in a letter that same day, but did not ask for suspension of security aid.[89]

Completely predictably, on December 22, the Department of State blessed Juan Orlando Hernández's claimed victory. "We congratulate Juan Orlando Hernandez on his victory in the November 26 presidential elections, as declared by the Honduran Supreme Electoral Tribunal (TSE)." Its official statement did bow to the controversy, only to call preposterously for "dialogue" so the country could move forward. "The close election results, irregularities identified by the OAS and the EU election observation missions, and strong reactions from Hondurans across the political spectrum underscore the need for a robust national dialogue." Those who challenged the results were urged to "use the avenues provided by Honduran law." All sides were equally exhorted to "refrain from violence"—as if it were the opposition that was killing people with the bullets—and state security forces asked to "respect the rights of peaceful protesters."[90]

Hernández's false inauguration, rocked by mass protests, marked the beginning of a new chapter of Honduran history. If the Trump Administration's support of a vicious dictator has been made crystal-clear, presumably decided by Chief of Staff John Kelly, the illegitimacy of the election remains equally so. Indeed, the coverage of the election and international objections brought to light Hernández's long criminal history in new, powerful ways. That light will hopefully continue to shine, and help the Honduran people achieve democracy and a measure of justice.

The first year of the Trump Administration, so grand and terrifying a rupture on so many fronts, thus brought continuity to US policy in Honduras—even a heightening of the same approach, for the most part. The State Department, under Secretary Rex Tillerson at the time, spent the year paralyzed. Topmost positions, such as Assistant Secretary of State for Western Hemisphere Affairs, remained unfilled. Ambassador James Nealon left in July 2017; as of March 2018 no replacement had been named. But key figures who had long been managing Honduran policy under Obama stayed in power initially or rose far higher—most prominently John Kelly, the former head of the United States Southern Command, who became Secretary of Homeland Security and then, in July 2017, Trump's Chief of Staff in the White House. Nealon, who had been Kelly's right-hand man at Southcom in Miami before he became ambassador, followed Kelly to Homeland Security, where he became Assistant Secretary for International Affairs and then acting Under Secretary for Strategy, Policy, and Plans.[91] Thomas A. Shannon, who had been masterminding Honduras strategy at State since the coup, stayed high up top as Under Secretary for Political Affairs. When the Honduran foreign minister came to Washington in October to plead for the continuation of Temporary Protected Status for Honduran immigrants who had fled after Hurricane Mitch hit in 1998, it was Nealon and Shannon who she met with.[92] William Brownfield, though, the other key player at State, head of International Narcotics and Law Enforcement, quit in August. Whether he was pushed out or chose to walk remains unclear.[93] By March 2018, Nealon, Shannon, and Tillerson would all be gone, too.

Even before Kelly ascended to the White House, he was the one driving the train at a June 2017 major policy summit in Miami, entitled "Conference on Prosperity and Security in Central America." The presidents of Honduras, Guatemala, and El Salvador all attended, along with Tillerson, Vice President Mike Pence, Kelly, and Nealon. While the overall emphasis was on beefed-up security funding, Kelly made sure there was a day dedicated to "prosperity."[94] Six weeks before that conference, on May 4, he referred to President Hernández as a "great guy" and a "good friend."[95]

In July 2016, *BuzzFeed* revealed that Trump himself had sourced shirts with his company's label from a factory in Choloma, Honduras. Cited by the Workers' Rights Consortium for multiple labor rights violations, the factory was a hellhole, workers told the reporters. "We suffer from the moment we come in until the moment we leave," said one interviewee.[96]

But there was one key difference between the Trump Administration's approach and Obama's. In his budget request for 2018, presented to Congress in May 2017, Trump wanted to increase security aid—so-called hard power aid—while dramatically cutting back, by seventy-five percent, humanitarian and development aid—so-called soft power—including USAID. Development aid to Honduras would be cut entirely. Congress, though, including powerful Republican senators, balked, and supported the continuation of soft power funding.[97]

By the time of the 2009 military coup, the days of United Fruit—known popularly as *El Pulpo* (The Octopus)—and its blatant control of Honduran politics and economic affairs were long past (and Hondurans remain offended at the use of "banana republic" to describe their country). But in the long arc of its post-coup policy in Honduras, the United States was more ominously tentacular than ever. From the immediate legitimation of de facto president Roberto Micheletti within days of the coup, through the invention of Porfirio Lobo's illegitimate regime as a "government of national reconciliation," to the perpetual reign of Juan Orlando Hernández, the United States continued to dance with dictators, just as it had for decades in Central America and throughout the hemisphere, twisting, sidestepping, even tripping up its partner deliberately at times, but always locked in a loving embrace, eyes wide open, leading.

Why has the United States so shamefully and shamelessly backed the post-coup Honduran regime? First, for geopolitical reasons: to re-establish and expand US political power in Latin America and push back against the left and center-left governments that were elected beginning in the 1990s, especially in Venezuela. The United States also had its eye on China, Russia, even Iran, and any power that might conceivably assert itself in the region. It still adhered to the Monroe Doctrine, and still considered Latin America its "backyard," as Secretary Kerry put in 2013, infuriating the region by repeating the long-offensive phrase.[98] Second, the United States's long-term geopolitical agenda served an underlying commitment to the brutal economic project of transnational corporate capitalism. Finally, the United States Southern Command, enforcing that project at the point of gun, was also an engine that ran of itself, with its own lust for ever-increasing funding and political power, as Kelly's cynical use of the imaginary Ebola threat from Central America made clear. Drugs, "terrorists" of any sort, however fictitious, poor migrating women and children—all were useful in identifying a "threat" in the region that had to be addressed with military power, in turn deployed against the Honduran opposition and its defenders.

We have no clearly documented smoking gun showing that the United States green-lighted the coup in advance. We do know the Obama Administration did everything in its power to enable the coup to stabilize. But it's not just a question of what happened in 2009. The United States had multiple moments when it could have changed course, separated itself from the ongoing coup regime, and allowed other actors to lead Honduras. It could have declared that the 2009 elections were utterly illegitimate and called for Zelaya's return and new, free, and fair elections under international observation, with civil liberties restored. During the 2013 election season, as it became clear that opposition activists and candidates were being mowed down, and that the National Party would steal the election by every means necessary, it could have intervened on multiple fronts; it didn't have to declare the elections clean. It could even have chosen to swing its weight behind Xiomara Castro for president. She would have been no great friend of the United States; but neither, presumably, would she have overseen the military takeover of Honduran society or the further decimation of the economy and the Honduran state and of civil liberties. Again, in the 2013-14 election season, the United States could have adhered to its much-vaunted promotion of the rule of law and "good governance" and publicly condemned Juan Orlando Hernández for the criminal act of running for reelection. The United States could have taken a different course at so many points, not just after the coup. Instead, the Obama and then Trump Administrations flashed green light after green light after green light.

But there were always powerful constraints against US power and the greed of the Honduran elites and their transnational corporate friends. Journalists throughout the world did heroic work, shedding the light of day on what was happening inside Honduras. The solidarity movement in the United States put formidable pressure on Congress, producing real constraints on the administration's behavior, if with limited effectiveness. Congressional demands to enforce the Leahy Law did mean that US funding was withheld from multiple units and individuals who had committed human rights abuses—although the money could still flow in from other sources to compensate, and the embassy refused to publicly disclose the cases in which it was, in fact, enforcing the law. Beginning in 2012, conditions placed on funding for Honduras in the State and Foreign Operations Appropriations Acts did mean that certain senators and members in the congressional leadership had new powers to withhold funds—albeit not indefinitely—until certain requirements were met, empowering them to try to influence the Honduran government around specific issues such as the Aguán, attacks against journalists, and Berta Cáceres's case. Public letters from members and senators continuously objected to broader US policy in Honduras, placing the administration on the defensive and helping keep Honduran human rights activists and journalists alive. Finally, as the list of its cosponsors continued to grow, the Berta Cáceres Act held out the possibility of a day in the future when Congress might, indeed, suspend the aid by law.

But in the long Honduran night, the ultimate constraint on US imperial power was the Honduran people, who rose up again and again to protest the criminals who ran their government with a US blessing and pocketbook. The National Front of Popular Resistance; campesinos who launched land recuperations; LIBRE and the PAC; the Indignados; years and years of grassoots activism by the women's, labor, and LGBTI movements; Indigenous and Afro-Indigenous people struggling for land and legal rights; journalists who reported on all this and died for it; lawyers who defended them and died for it; prosecutors and judges who went after the criminals and died for it—all continued in the face of pervasive terror to hope for a new Honduran future, and worked to build it from below. They kept dancing, too.

We Hondurans have a choice, wrote the Honduran Jesuit Padre Melo (Ismael Moreno, SJ) in July 2017. Washington "treats Honduras and its people based on its own interests and sees us eternally as its backyard. . . . Honduras for the Americans and never Honduras for the Hondurans." There are "only two paths," he wrote, "either we continue as we have up until now, resigned to being a backyard, or we gamble on the construction of a country with sovereignty and identity, and from within that house build fair and complementary relationships with the United States or any other nation. One can't travel both paths. One can't please both God and the devil. We have to choose between God and money."[99]

Anniversary Gifts

On the eighth anniversary of the coup, in 2017, I had dinner with three Honduran activist friends at a pizza restaurant in downtown San José, California. We each gave a *"discursito"*—a little speech—on the occasion. Zenaida Velásquez, a public health educator and one of the founders of COFADEH in Honduras, whose brother had been disappeared in the early 1980s, said that the coup had had an enormous impact on all Latin America, beginning a US pushback against other governments as well. She said if there hadn't been the coup, her sister Ilse, who had been killed when a tear gas canister knocked her down and then a TV truck ran her over during the 2011 teachers' demonstration, would still be alive. Porfirio Quintano, a hospital orderly and a Vice President of the National Union of Healthcare Workers, drew parallels between the Honduran General Strike of 1954 and the Resistance to the coup in 2009, as the two great moments in Honduran history. He, too, talked about the coup's impact on all Latin America, but said the Resistance had politicized a whole new generation of Honduran youth—following the "lost generation" before—who were continuing to rise up in student protests during that summer of 2017. Marleni Quintano, a preschool teacher, talked about the transformation of young people, too. I said that the coup, while it had been and still was so, so, terrible, had also changed my life, and given it great meaning because I was able to be part of something larger than myself and be useful, for which I was deeply grateful.

On the seventh anniversary of the coup, I woke up at 2:45 a.m. from a nightmare in which Hondurans were somehow attacking the United States militarily, and I was afraid I would be charged with treason. I spent the day making forty-three phone calls to members of Congress, asking them to please co-sponsor the Berta Cáceres Human Rights in Honduras Act. Then I went for a long walk on the beach alone and thought about what the coup had meant and tried to honor all the people who had died because of it.

On the sixth anniversary of the coup, I went to a very sparse but nonetheless spirited demonstration organized by the National Front of Popular Resistance in downtown San Pedro Sula. I got bored by the speeches, hugged a couple of friends I ran into, and tried not to feel too depressed by how pathetically small it was and how the black and red paint was all gone from the *Plaza Central.*

On the fifth anniversary of the coup, I joined friends at the big highway flowing into San Pedro Sula and marched with them proudly, helping push the little kids' strollers, in an FNRP demonstration of maybe ten thousand people. I saw a man dressed in red and black, alone, with bulging muscles and a thick neck, watching me closely as he darted in and out and tried to listen to my conversations. After I made eye contact with him, he slipped away. The march ended in the Plaza Central, where I met up with friends, watched a clump of cops watch our clump of demonstrators watch the cops, then went off to lunch in an air-conditioned chain restaurant with two members of the Association of Honduran Judges for Democracy.

On the fourth anniversary, I drove from Santa Cruz to San Francisco and had lunch with five colleagues who I'd worked closely with on Honduras solidarity projects for years. Then we trotted off to the office of Global Exchange for a modest anniversary event at which Zenaida Velásquez and Porfirio Quintano spoke, and so did I.

On the third anniversary, I realized I didn't remember who I was before the coup.

I don't remember the second anniversary; my emails tell me that I was interviewed by NPR and Al Jazeera. Whatever I did got buried in the media coverage of the return of deposed former President Manuel Zelaya a month before, when I'd written two op-eds saying "Zelaya Returns, but Justice Doesn't."

On the first anniversary, I rode with a small pickup truck full of friends to Choloma, outside San Pedro Sula, where the Resistance blockaded the big highway to the port. When the tear gas tanks and riot cops arrived, I called the US Embassy to convey my alarm about potential human rights violations. I rode in a car in ninety-six-degree heat into San Pedro Sula. When we got into the city, we met up with thousands and thousands of marchers, including a high school marching band. Three months later, a few blocks away, in a Honduran Independence Day march, those same happy, proud high school students in their uniforms would be tear-gassed by the police.

On June 28, 2009, I watched the coup unfold on Spanish language television all day long and tried desperately to figure out what was going on, and had not a clue what a coup would or wouldn't mean to the lives of hundreds of friends, to the Honduran people, or to my own daily life for years to come.

Protesters wearing diapers with "Fuera JOH" (Juan Orlando Hernández Out) while taunting security forces at a women's demonstration protesting the November 2017 elections, on Honduran Women's Day, January 25, 2018, in Tegucigalpa. Photo Credit: Criterio.hn.

Acknowledgments

This book and the story it tells are possible because of the vast networks of Hondurans and their allies who have struggled for social justice in Honduras since June 28, 2009, and long before. Let me begin by thanking those in the Honduras solidarity movement within the United States, Canada, Mexico, Europe, and beyond, who have been such a joy to work with: Michael Bass, Beverly Bell, Diana Bohn, Laura Carlsen, Vicki Cervantes, Jesse Freeston, Babette Grunow, Matt Ginsberg-Jaeckle, Brigitte Gynther, Jack Herbert, Kate Hubbard, Sharon Hunter-Smith, Chuck Kaufman, Celeste Larkin, Susan Letendre, Tom Loudon, Michael Ring, Dale Sorenson, and Karen Spring. My special thanks to Gary Cozette, Lucy Edwards, and Elise Roberts. I want to especially thank Vicki Cervantes, who held it all together, and Daniel Langmeier for the invaluable updates. I am most deeply grateful for the opportunity to work with Hondurans and Honduran Americans in the United States: Silvio Carrillo, Tanya Cole, Alexy Lanza, Tito Meza, Lucy Pagoada, Roberto Quesada, Porfirio Quintana, and above all Zenaida Velásquez, who gave me the great gift of her comradeship and *cariño*.

My first home in this work was always the US Labor in the Americas Project (USLEAP)—Stephen Coats, Rebecca Van Horn, Gloria Kanu, and especially the wonderful Lupita Águila Arteaga, who taught me so much and sustained me in our dark times.

In Washington, D.C., a host of colleagues and friends provided help, perspective, and tireless labors on many fronts, including Jeremy Bigwood, Beth Gaglia, Judy Gearhart, Eric Gottwald,

Walker Grooms, Lisa Haugaard, Kathryn Johnson, Lora Lumpe, Caitrin McKee, Laura Raymond, Gabby Rosazza, Alexis Stombelis, Lisa VeneKlasen, Arturo Viscarra, and José Miguel Vivanco. The AFL-CIO has been firm and essential in its commitment to justice in Honduras from the very day of the coup; my thanks go to Alexis deSimone, Celeste Drake, Héctor Sánchez, Brian Finnegan, and especially Cathy Feingold; thanks also to Tim Beaty at the Teamsters. I want to express my particular gratitude to the Center for Economic and Policy Research for teaching me so much and welcoming me in so generously; thanks to Mark Weisbrot, Alexander Main, Jake Johnston, Eileen O'Grady, and Rebecca Watts. Special thanks to Dan Beeton for teaching me so much about the media and for sharing so much information. Closer to home, John Lindsay-Poland taught me about the military, about US policy, and about how to keep myself grounded at the grassoots below.

I am deeply grateful to dozens of congressional aides who took up the cause of Honduras and worked tirelessly on its behalf. None of them is responsible for the ideas presented in this book. Among them, my special thanks to Fulton Armstrong, Nina Besser, Cindy Buhl, Joel Colony, Andrew Goczkowski, Eric Jacobstein, Daniel Mauer, Brieana Marticorena, Erin Neill, Angel Nigaglioni, Erik Sperling, Cathy Hurwit, Ben Weiner, Caitie Whelan, and Cassandra Varanka. My special thanks to Jenny Perrino for being so dedicated and so much fun, to Wyndee Parker for bestowing on me the amazing honor of taking me seriously, and to the magnificent Algene Sajery for the great gift of her caring, dedication, and smarts. Sascha Foertsch (formerly Thompson) came through for years and years and was a great joy to work with for every one of them; I am grateful, especially, for the enormous gift of the bill and the joy of working on it together. Peter Quilter always astonished me with his commitment, his respect, his analysis, and his wit. Thank you. Finally, I am grateful above all to Tim Rieser, for his trust, his patience, and over six years of painstaking, dedicated, and beautiful work on behalf of the Honduran people. My additional thanks to Algene, Angel, Peter, Sascha, and Tim for giving me permission to discuss them in this book.

I want to thank all the members of Congress and senators who spoke up on behalf of human rights and justice in Honduras, year after year. In the face of so much Honduran terror, I remain thrilled when a single member speaks up and chooses to use their power for the side of good. My special thanks to Representatives Raúl Grijalva, Mike Honda, Betty McCollum, José Serrano, Jared Polis, and especially Sam Farr for letters about Honduras; to Representative James McGovern for his commitment to Honduras on so many fronts, as well as to all Latin America. Thanks to both Representatives McGovern and Frank Wolf for their attention to Honduras while co-chairing the Tom Lantos Human Rights Commission. Thanks to Representative Nancy Pelosi for paying close attention and caring. My thanks especially to the glorious Representative Marcy Kaptur for her warmth, dedication, and example; to Representative Keith Ellison for the gifts of his respect and his ongoing commitment to Honduras; and to Representative Hank Johnson for years of concern for Honduras, including sponsorship of the Berta Cáceres Human Rights in Honduras Act. Representative Janice Schakowsky remains an inspiring miracle who has not only led on Honduran issues for years and years, but always astonished me with her clarity, humor, and politics. Among senators, I am especially grateful to Senators Tim Kaine, Jeff Merkley, Barbara Mikulski, Jack Reed, and especially Benjamin Cardin. My thanks above all, to Senator Patrick Leahy, for his years of support for the people of Honduras.

My thanks to my academic friends and colleagues who sustained me in this work and inspired and informed me with their own research and analyses: Mark Anderson, Lauren Carasik, Darío Euraque, Greg Grandin, Suyapa Portillo Villeda, Miguel Tinker Salas, and David Vine. Special thanks to Jonathan Fox and Helen Shapiro for hospitality as well as intellectual companionship. I am especially indebted to Adrienne Pine, for her blog *Quotha,* and Russell Sheptak and Rosemary Joyce, for *Honduras Culture and Politics.*

I also want to thank the dedicated journalists who covered Honduras during these years and did the work of drawing back the curtains: Luis Alonso, Alberto Arce, Parker Asmann, Jonathan Blitzer, Chris Brooks, Carrie Kahn, Jeremy Kryt, Matt Lee, Danielle

Mackey, Elisabeth Malkin, Martha Mendoza, Adam Raney, Tracy Wilkinson, and Karla Zabludovsky; thanks also to Ginger Thompson for her earlier work on B-316. Thanks to Marc Charney for that astonishing editing experience. I want to especially thank Betsy Reed for publishing me in *The Nation* in a crucial period, and Amy Goodman, Juan Gonzáles, Laura Gottesdeiner, and Nermeen Shaikh at *Democracy Now!* for inviting me on the show, and more importantly, for their tireless and incisive commitment to covering Honduras. I am grateful, also, to Daniel Alarcón for his support for the book and for his reporting on Honduras.

At UC Santa Cruz I am grateful to Carlos Calierno, Anne Callahan, Alison Galloway, Robin Jacobs, William Ladusaw, Judit Moschkovich, Catherine Ramírez, Scott Rappaport, Juan Poblete, Irena Polic, David Symonik, the Academic Senate, the Vice Chancellor for Research, the Chicano/Latino Research Center, and especially Matt O'Hara, Stephanie Hinkle, Stephanie Sawyer, Kayla Ayers, and Cindy Morris in the History Department. I remain utterly in debt to Jay Olson, who came through year after year after year, so efficiently, so fast, and with such joyful commitment to the cause. My thanks to the UC in D.C. staff as well.

Thanks to the many people who answered research queries at the last minute, including Jerold Block, Vicki Cervantes, Lucy Edwards, Darío Euraque, Tirza Flores Lanza, Chuck Kaufman, Babette Grunow, Bertha Oliva, Mandel Pandey, and Karen Spring.

I am so grateful to Haymarket Books for wanting this book, for doing such a great job on previous projects, and for their commitment to progressive publishing. They have been an enormous pleasure to work with. My thanks to Anthony Arnove, Dana Blanchard, Nisha Bolsey, Rachel Cohen, Julie Fain, and especially to Amy Rosenberg for the terrific editing.

On the home front and beyond, my greatest thanks to my beloved friends who sustained me, as always, with their love, while graciously accepting and cheering on my sudden and obsessive transformation into a Honduran Freedom Fighter. Thanks to Craig Alderson, Frank Bardacke, Eva Bertram, Joe Chrastil, Adriana Craciun, Miriam Frank (no relation!), Frank Galuszka, Toni Gilpin,

Lorchen Heft, Jean Ingebritson, Lisbeth Haas, Desma Holcomb, Nelson Lichtenstein, John Logan, Priscilla Murolo, Ron Pomerantz, Mary Beth Pudup, Judy Shizuru, Bill Spencer, Vanessa Tait, Jane Weed-Pomerantz, and Alice Yang. Thank you to Cheri Brooks and Andrea Weiss for being my writing club. Thanks to Julie Greene for the hospitality and friendship in D.C., and especially to Gwendolyn Mink for the friendship, advice, and safe haven. Thanks to my beloveds, Becky McCabe, Ramona McCabe, Gerri Dayharsh, Josh MacCallister, and Stephen McCabe; to the wisdom and caring of Karin Stallard (including for the Montana writing retreat); and to my mother, Carolyn Frank, and my sister Laura. Thank you, Hamsa Heinrich, for sustaining me next door through the joys and pains of daily life, and for all that listening.

This book is the result of seventeen years working in Honduras and sharing close friendships there. Even as caring for Honduras has torn my heart apart, its people have filled it up with joy, solidarity, wisdom, and the example of their dedication, as they have given me the great privilege of their friendship and comradeship. My great thanks to José María Martínez, Nelson Nuñez, Belkis Castro, Gloria García, Tomás Membreño Pérez, and Gloria Guzmán of the FESTAGRO team. Deepest love and gratitude to my beloved Honduran family, Jessika Isela Álvarez Munguía, Roberto Enrique Vásquez Mejía, Adolfo Antonio Álvarez Munguía, Ivan Álarez Munguía, Dafhne Darian Zelaya Vargas, and all the nieta/os and primas/os. During the years of this book and its research, dozens of Hondurans shared with me their time and their insights in interviews. None of them is responsible for the ideas expressed in this book. It's not safe, alas, for me to thank them all by name. Those I can thank include Efraín Aguilar, María Luisa Borjas, Mario Díaz, Ruy Díaz, Rodolfo Pastor Fasquelle, Rodolfo Fasquelle de María y Campos, Matías Funes, Tirza Flores Lanza, Zoila Lagos, Orfilia de Mejía, Miriam Miranda, Leticia Salomón, Guillermo López Lone, Victor Meza, Enrique Reina, Carlos H. Reyes, Guadalupe Ruelas, President José Manuel Zelaya Rosales, and the late Berta Cáceres. I am especially deeply indebted to Ismael Moreno, SJ (Padre Melo) and Bertha Oliva for their lifetimes of courage, dedication, and insight, and for the honor of their friendships and respect. Iris Munguía remains at the center of my Honduran life. After seventeen years, I am still so grateful for her warmth, her humor, and her limitless hospitality, and still amazed by what she has to teach me, and so many others, about how to be an empowered woman.

Finally, I want to deeply thank four close colleagues and friends in the United States, without whom none of this would have been possible and who have been a great joy to work with on Honduran solidarity for many years. I am grateful to them, as well, for taking time out of their own pressing work in order to read parts of the manuscript and answer my pestering research queries. Jenny Atlee sustained me through ups and downs and offered a model of committed, lifelong activism, as well as a bridge to earlier struggles. Alexander Main was a caring partner on the Hill, inspiring in his writing, his acceptance of quirks, and his knowledge of the big picture. Annie Bird's exhaustive knowledge, amazing commitment, and labors both invisible and visible were always an inspiration, and it was a joy to share our love for research and for Honduras. Finally, the spectacular Jean Stokan provided me with a moral center and was an inspiring role model for how to work a room, and, most importantly, how to move through the world from the heart.

This book is dedicated to two men who anchored me in this work and kept me politically and personally grounded from my first trip to Central America in 2000 onward, sustaining me with their wisdom, clarity, and lifelong commitment to social justice. In Honduras, German Zepeda, from that first meeting in Guatemala through the next seventeen years of labor solidarity work, the coup, and its long, wrenching aftermath, offered me the great gift of his political analysis and above all his respect and comradeship. In the US, Stephen Coats first invited me to work with the banana unions in 2000, changing my life with one phone call. He was the one who taught me to do this work and to respect our partners, even when they drove us crazy. "We work for them," he taught me. He was the one I called the morning of the coup, and to whom I turned when I was cracking up from the horrors. He was my guide, my rock. All through the first four years after the coup, as I braced myself for messages that might tell me of the deaths of Honduran friends, I never imagined it would be him I'd lose. In April 2013, he left us at age sixty-one, without warning, in his sleep. As I have stumbled forward since then with a hole in my heart, I only hope that my work has lived up to what he would have wanted of me.

Notes

A Note on the Sources

While I have endeavored to provide notes for as much material as possible, the sources for some of what is presented here remain confidential, in many cases because of the danger involved for those who provided information or whose experiences I witnessed. Unless otherwise indicated, Spanish-language newspapers cited below are from Honduras. Until late 2015, *El Tiempo* (San Pedro Sula) was issued as a print newspaper; thereafter it has been web-only. Here I am providing URLs to *El Tiempo* articles only for the period since it became web-only. Much of the digital archive of the paper, from both periods, is apparently unavailable, however. Citations to several articles in *El Heraldo* (Tegucigalpa) have in a few cases been changed online by the paper to a uniform date of April 7, 2014 (including at the top of the article itself) although they originally appeared months or years earlier. In the notes here, I have used the correct date in cases in which I kept an original copy of the article or know the original date. In other cases, I have left the April 7, 2014, date in place and tried to indicate an approximate date. For newspapers, I have provided the country of origin for those published outside Honduras; those from within Honduras include *El Heraldo, La Prensa, Proceso Digital* (online only), *El Tiempo*, and *La Tribuna*.

Introduction

1. The best overview of modern Honduran history is Marvin Barahona, *Honduras en el siglo XX: una síntesis histórica* (Tegucigalpa, Honduras: Editorial Guaymuras, 2005). For the Honduran elites and the coup: Darío A. Euraque, "La configuración histórica de las élites de Honduras ante del Golpe de Estado del 2009," unpublished paper, 2012, presented at Workshop on Central American Elites, American University Center for Latin American and Latin Studies and the Instituto de Investigaciones y Gerencia Política of the Universidad Rafael Landívar, Antigua, Gua-

temala, February 16–19, 2012, in possession of the author. For further background on the Palestinians: Alberto Amaya Banegas, *Los árabes y palestinos en Honduras, 1900–1950* (Tegucigalpa: Editorial Guaymuras, 1997); Rodolfo Pastor Fasquelle, *Biografía de San Pedro Sula, 1536–1954* (San Pedro Sula: Centro Editorial, 1990); Darío A. Euraque, *Reinterpreting the Banana Republic: Region and State in Honduras, 1870–1972* (Chapel Hill: University of North Carolina Press, 1996). For accessible summaries in English of modern Honduran history up through the 1980s, see Richard Lapper and James Painter/Latin American Bureau, *Honduras: State for Sale* (London: Latin American Bureau, 1985); and Alison Acker, *Honduras: The Making of a Banana Republic* (Cambridge, MA: South End Press, 1988). See also James Dunkerley, *Power in the Isthmus: A Political History of Modern Central America* (London and New York: Verso Books, 1988); and William Robinson, *Transnational Conflicts: Central America, Social Change, and Globalization* (London and New York: Verso Books, 2003), 118–32.

2.   Nancy Peckenham and Annie Street, *Honduras: Portrait of a Captive Nation* (New York: Praeger Publishers, 1985).

3.   Marvin Barahona, *Honduras en el siglo XX*; Victor Meza, *Historia del Movimiento Obrero Hondureño* (Tegucigalpa: Editorial Guaymuras, 1980); Mario Pozas, *Lucha Ideológica y Organización Sindical en Honduras (1954–65)* (Tegucigalpa: Editorial Guaymuras, 1980); Robert MacCameron, *Bananas, Labor, and Politics in Honduras, 1954–1963* (Syracuse, NY: Maxwell School of Citizenship and Public Affairs, 1983). For the general strike, the best sources are Marvin Barahona, *El Silencio Quedó Atrás: Testimonios de la Huelga Bananera de 1954* (Tegucigalpa: Editorial Guaymuras, 1994); Mario R. Argueta, *La Gran Huelga Bananera: Los 69 Días que Estremecioron a Honduras* (Tegucigalpa: Editorial Universitaria,1995); and Suyapa Portillo Villeda, "Campeñas, Campeños, y Compañeros: Life and Work in the Banana Fincas of the North Coast of Honduras, 1944–1957," PhD diss., Cornell University, 2011.

4.   For example, William Robinson, *Transnational Conflicts*, 119–20.

5.   For *mano duro*, Lirio Gutiérrez Rivera, *Territories of Violence: State, Marginal Youth, and Public Security in Honduras* (New York: Palgrave Macmillan, 2013). For neoliberalism, Mario Posas, "Ajusta: dos caras de la moneda," *Envío*, no. 134 (January 1993); William I. Robinson, "Transnational Processes, Development Studies and Changing Social Hierarchies in the World System: A Central American Case Study," *Third World Quarterly* 22, no. 4 (August 2001): 529–63; Arne Ruckert, "The Poverty Reduction Strategy Policy of Honduras and the Transformations of Neoliberalism," *Canadian Journal of Latin American and Caribbean Studies/Revue canadienne des études latino-américaines et caraibes* 35, no. 70 (2010): 113–39.

6.   Stephen Schlesinger and Stephen Kinzer, *Bitter Fruit: The Story of the American Coup in Guatemala* (New York: Doubleday, 1982); Richard H. Immerman, *The CIA in Guatemala: The Foreign Policy of Intervention* (Austin: University of Texas Press, 1982).

7. William M. LeoGrande, *Our Own Backyard: The United States in Central America, 1977–1992* (Chapel Hill: University of North Carolina Press, 2000); Richard Lapper and James Painter, *Honduras: State for Sale*; Alison Acker, *Honduras: The Making of a Banana Republic*. For Battalion 3–16 and the US role in support of it, see the 1995 four-part series in the *Baltimore Sun* by Ginger Thompson and Gary Cohn, "A Carefully Crafted Deception," June 18, 1995; "A Survivor Tells Her Story," June 15, 1995; "Torturers' Confessions," June 13, 1995; "Unearthed: Fatal Secrets," June 11, 1995.

8. United States Southern Command, "Joint Task Force-Bravo," www.jtfb .southcom.mil/Units/.

9. Suyapa G. Portillo Villeda, "The Coup That Awoke a People's Resistance," *NACLA: Report on the Americas*, 43, no. 2 (March/April 2010): 26–27; Dana Frank, "Out of the Past, a New Honduran Culture of Resistance," *NACLA: Report on the Americas*, 43, no. 3 (May/June, 2010): 6–10.

10. Dana Frank, *Bananeras: Women Transforming the Banana Unions of Latin America* (Cambridge, MA: South End Press, 2005), in Spanish as *El Poder de las Mujeres es Poder Sindical* (Tegucigalpa: Editorial Guaymuras, 2006).

Chapter One

1. For contemporary English-language reporting about the Honduran coup through the fall of 2009, see Greg Grandin's articles for *The Nation*, "Democracy Derailed in Honduras," June 30, 2009; "Waiting for Zelaya," August 3, 2009; "Battle for Honduras—and the Region," August 12, 2009; "Honduran Coup Regime in Crisis," October 26, 2009; "Honduras: Solution or Stall?," October 31, 2009; see also Grandin, "Manuel Zelaya's Nighttime Return to Honduras," *Huffington Post*, n.d. (September 2009), www.huffingtonpost.com /greg-grandin/manuel-zelayas-nightime-r_b_294194.html. For a brief summary, see also Tyler A. Shipley, *Ottawa and Empire: Canada and the Military Coup in Honduras* (Toronto: Between the Lines, 2017), 35–47. For detailed documentation, Comisión de la Verdad y Reconciliación (CRV), *Para que los hechos no se repitan: Informe de la Comisión de la Verdad y la Reconciliación, Tomo I y Tomo II* (San José, Costa Rica: Editorama, 2011). For an excellent summary of the run-up to the coup, Zelaya, and US policy before and right after the coup, see Rene de la Pedraja, "Honduras: The Coup of June 2009," in de la Pedraja, *The United States and the Armed Forces of Mexico, Central America, and the Caribbean, 2000–2014* (Jefferson, NC: McFarland, 2014), 144–65.

2. Ibid.

3. Elisabeth Malkin, "Honduran President Ousted in Coup," *New York Times*, June 28, 2009.

4. Inter-American Commission on Human Rights (IACHR), *Honduras: Human Rights and the Coup D'Etat* (Washington: Organization of American States, December 30, 2009), 114, www.cidh.org/countryrep/honduras09eng /toc.htm. This IACHR report provides a comprehensive, detailed analysis of

human rights violations in the first six months after the coup. Another source for widespread abuses is Human Rights Watch, *After the Coup: Ongoing Violence, Intimidation, and Impunity in Honduras, December 10, 2009,* www.hrw.org/sites /default/files/reports/honduras1210webwcover_0.pdf. For comprehensive documentation, Comisión de Verdad, Final Report, *The Voice of Greatest Authority Is That of the Victims,* April 2013, ccrjustice.org/sites/default /files/attach/2015/01/TrueCommission_Report_English_04_13.pdf.

5.   Coordinadora de Sindicatos Bananeros y Agroindustriales de Honduras (COSIBAH), "Informamos a nuestros Compañeros de Lucha, a la comuni-dad en general y a las Organizaciones Cooperantes," June 30, 2009, received in email, COSIBAH to the author, June 30, 2009; Rights Action, "Honduran Military Regime Disappearing Youth in Olancho," June 30, 2009, hablahonduras.com/articles/3569-hondurean-military-regime-disappearing -youth-in-olancho.

6.   Ginger Thompson and Marc Lacey, "O.A.S. Votes to Suspend Honduras Over Coup," *New York Times,* July 4, 2009.

7.   "Statement from the President on the Situation in Hondruas," June 28, 2009, Office of the Press Secretary, The White House, obamawhitehouse .archives.gov/the-press-office/statement-president-situation-honduras.

8.   For a detailed summary and analysis of US policy in the six months following the coup, see Alexander Main, "'A New Chapter of Engagement': Obama and the Honduran Coup," *NACLA: Report on the Americas* 43, no. 1 (January/February 2010): 15–37, and Rosemary A. Joyce, "Legtimating the Illegitimate: The Honduran Show Elections and the Challenge Ahead," *NACLA: Report on the Americas* 43, no. 2 (March/April 2010), nacla.org /article/legitimizing-illegitimate-honduran-show-elections-and-challenge -ahead. See also articles at the time by MarkWeisbrot; for example, "Does the US Back the Honduran Coup?" The *Guardian,* July 1, 2009; "US leaves Honduras to its fate," The *Guardian,* July 8, 2009. For another, briefer ver-sion, close to that of the State Department, see United States Government Accountability Office, "Review of U.S. Response to the Honduran Political Crisis of 2009," October 20, 2011, www.gao.gov/products/GAO-12-9R and www.gao.gov/assets/590/585824.pdf. Note the title's reference to the "political crisis" of 2009, rather than the coup. Coup supporters at the time, and since, refer to the "constitutional crisis" or "political crisis" but refuse to call it a coup.

9.   "Honduran Leaders Shut Main Airport," *The Guardian,* July 6, 2000; "Zelaya's Plane Not Allowed to Land in Honduras," *Washington Post World Service,* July 6, 2009.

10. Comité de Familias de Detenidos y Desaparecidos de Honduras (COFADEH), *Informe Preliminar, Violaciones a Derechos Humanos en el Marco del Golpe de Estado en Honduras,* (Tegucigalpa, Honduras: July 15, 2009), 13–14, dataspace.princeton.edu/jspui/handle/88435/dsp01z029p477v; "Un hondu-reño muerto durante el frustrado regreso de Zelaya," *El País,* July 6, 2009.

11. Suyapa G. Portillo Villeda, "The Coup that Awoke a People's Resistance";

Dana Frank, "Out of the Past, a New Honduran Culture of Resistance"; Eugenio Sosa, *La protesta social en Honduras: Del ajuste al golpe de Estado* (Tegucigalpa: Federación Luterana Mundial/Editorial Guaymuras, 2010). For the deep roots and evolution of cultures of resistance in Honduras, including in Indigenous communities, before and after the coup, see James J. Phillips, *Honduras in Dangerous Times: Resistance and Resilience* (Lanham, MD: Lexington Books, 2015). For an ongoing, incisive and reflective analysis of the coup and the resistance, see the monthly articles by Ismael Moreno, SJ, in *Envío* (Managua, Nicaragua), available online in Spanish and English, e.g. "More from the Honduras Diary: From Jubiliation to Repression," no. 339 (October 2009).

12.   Ismael Moreno, SJ, "What I Saw, Felt and Discovered in a Three-Week Hunger Strike," *Envío* 27, no. 324 (July 2008): 33–48.

13.   Steven R. Weisman, "President Calls Nicaraguan Rebels Freedom Fighters," *New York Times*, May 5, 1983.

14.   Decreto Ejecutivo Numero PCM-M-016-2009, *La Gaceta*, República de Honduras, September 26, 2009; Inter-American Commission on Human Rights, *Preliminary Observations on the IACHR Visit to Honduras*, August 21, 2009, www.cidh.org/Comunicados/English/2009/60-09eng.Preliminary .Observations.htm.

15.   "Translation of Irma Villanueva's Testimony by María Soledad Cervantes," *Quotha* (blog), August 25, 2009, quotha.net/node/244; Comisión de Verdad, *The Voice of Greatest Authority Is That of the Victims*, 139–43. "Auto de prision dictan a vocero de la secretaría de seguridad," *El Heraldo*, April 7, 2014; "Justicia piden en caso de represion en Choloma tras golpe de estado," *Radio Progreso y ERIC* (blog), November 13, 2014, radioprogresohn.net/index.php /comunicaciones/noticias/item/1476-justicia-piden-en-caso-de-represi %C3%B3n-en-choloma-tras-golpe-de-estado; "Piden destituir a oficiales por agresión a manifestantes," *La Prensa*, August 21, 2013; Israel Cruz, "Dictan so-breseimiento definitivio a oficiales acusados de salvaje represion en Choloma, Cortés," *Conexion*, August 26, 2013, honduprensa.wordpress.com/2013/08/26 /dictan-sobreseimiento-definitivo-a-oficiales-acusados-de-salvaje-represion -en-choloma-cortes/; "Impunity for Police Abuse of Anti-Coup Demonstrators," *SOA Watch* (blog), n.d. (August 2013), www.soaw.org/about -us/equipo-sur/263-stories-from-honduras/4136-august14impunity; "Sobreseimiento definitivo a favor de dos comisionados de la Policía Nacional," *Proceso Digital*, August 26, 2013, www.proceso.hn/index.php /component/k2/item/15982.html.

16.   IACHR, *Human Rights and the Coup D'Etat*, 60–61; Mision Internacional de Observaciones Sobre la Situación de DDHH, *Informe Preliminar*, July 23, 2009, www.alainet.org/es/autores/misi%C3%B3n-internacional-de -observaci%C3%B3n-sobre-la-situaci%C3%B3n-de-los-ddhh.

17.   William Finnegan, "An Old-Fashioned Coup," *The New Yorker*, November 30, 2009; Main, "'A New Chapter of Engagement'"; Ginger Thompson, "Honduras Conflict Talks Yield Little Movement," *New York Times*, July 10,

2009; de la Pedraja, "Honduras: The Coup of June 2009."

18. David Luhnow and José de Cordoba, "US Decides Not to Impose Sanctions on Honduras," *Wall Street Journal*, August 7, 2009.

19. Main, "'A New Chapter of Engagement.'"

20. Omnibus Appropriation Act of 2009, Section 7008, Department of State, Foreign Operations, and Related Programs Act, 2009, Div. H, Pub. L. No. 111-8. S, March 11, 2009: "None of the funds appropriated or otherwise made available pursuant to titles III through VI of this Act shall be obligated or expended to finance directly any assistance to the government of any country whose duly elected head of government is deposed by military coup or decree."

21. For an incisive analysis of the failure of the Obama Administration to name it a military coup and act accordingly, see Rep. Howard Berman (at the time Chair of the Committee on Foreign Affairs of the United States House of Representatives), "Honduras: Make It Official—Call It a Coup," *Los Angeles Times*, September 3, 2009. Former Secretary of State Hillary Clinton would later claim in an April 9, 2016, interview with the editorial board of the *New York Daily News* that she never called it a coup and, that indeed, it was not. "Transcript, Hillary Clinton Meets with *New York Daily News* Editorial Board," April 11, 2016, www.nydailynews.com/opinion/transcript-hillary-clinton-meets-news-editorial-board-article-1.2596292. For an extended discussion of her claims, "'She's Baldly Lying': Dana Frank Responds to Hillary Clinton's Defense of Her Role in Honduras," *Democracy Now!* April 13, 2016, www.democracynow.org/2016/4/13/shes_baldly_lying_dana_frank_responds.

22. Cable, Hugo Llorens to Department of State, "Open and Shut: the Case of the Honduran Coup," July 24, 2009, wikileaks.org/plusd/cables/09TEGUCIGALPA645_a.html.

23. Main, "'A New Chapter of Engagement.'"

24. "Four of Six Generals Tied to 2009 Coup Were Trained at the School of the Americas," *SOA Watch* (blog) September 6, 2012, www.soaw.org/category-table/3807-honduran-coup-generals; "Generals Who Led Honduras Military Coup Trained at the School of the Americas," *Democracy Now!* July 1, 2009, www.democracynow.org/2009/7/1/generals_who_led_honduras_military_coup.

25. Jake Johnston, "How Pentagon Officials May Have Encouraged a 2009 Coup in Honduras," *The Intercept*, August 29, 2017, theintercept.com/2017/08/29/honduras-coup-us-defense-departmetnt-center-hemispheric-defense-studies-chds/.

26. Phil Stewart, "Ecuador Wants Military Base in Miami," Reuters, October 22, 2007, uk.reuters.com/article/ecuador-base/ecuador-wants-military-base-in-miami-idUKADD25267520071022.

27. For Canadian interests, especially mining corporations, see Shipley, *Ottawa and Empire*.

28. "Over 150 Scholars and Latin America Experts Call for UN Pressure on Honduran de facto Regime," Press Release, September 25, 2009, reprinted

on *Quotha*, quotha.net/node/395.

29. "Horrifying Image from Honduras," *Havana Times*, September 27, 2009,
www.havanatimes.org/?p=14459; Inter-American Commission on Human
Rights, *Honduras: Human Rights and the Coup D'Etat*, chapter 3, no. 103;
Ian Roxborough, Philip O'Brien, and Jackie Roddick, *Chile: The State and
Revolution* (London: Macmillan, 1977), 239.

30. "Foto manipulada por el diario hondureño '*La Prensa*,'" February 8, 2009,
TerceraInformación (blog), www.tercerainformacion.es/antigua/spip.php
?article9279.

31. Inter-American Commission on Human Rights, *Human Rights and the
Honduran Coup D'Etat*, 25–26.

32. Esteban Felix, "Life Inside Embassy with Ousted Honduran Leader: Bad Food,
No Baths, Shared Toothbrushes," Canadian Press, September 24, 2009, www
.ctvnews.ca/supporters-hole-up-with-ousted-honduran-president-1.437346.

33. Jorge Castañeda, "Obama's Policy on Honduras," *Newsweek*, December 4, 2009.

34. For analyses of media reporting on the coup and its aftermath, see Robert
Naiman, "U.S. Media Fail in Honduras Coup Reporting," *NACLA: Report on the
Americas*, 42, no. 6 (2009): 54–56, nacla.org/article/us-media-fail-honduras
-coup-reporting; Michael Corcoran, "A Tale of Two Elections: Iran and
Honduras," *NACLA: Report on the Americas*, 43, no. 1 (January/February 2010):
46–48. For Amnesty International, see, for example, "Honduras: Human Rights
Crisis Threatens as Repression Increases," August 18, 2009. For a very brief
exception, see "Honduras: Military is Accused of Abuses," *New York Times*,
August 18, 2009. The article, however, which covered the Amnesty International
report about repression, gave one of its total of three sentences to the coup perpetrators: "The government of Roberto Micheletti, the country's de facto leader,
accuses demonstrators of engaging in violent acts and provoking the authorities." For Human Rights Watch, see for example "Honduras: Evidence Suggests
Soldiers Shot into Unarmed Crowd," *Human Rights Watch* (blog), July 8, 2009,
www.hrw.org/news/2009/07/08/honduras-evidence-suggests-soldiers-shot
-unarmed-crowd. For other bodies, see e.g. Inter-American Commission on
Human Rights, *Honduras: Human Rights and the Coup D'Etat*.

35. For example, Olga R. Rodriguez, "Ousted Honduran leader asks Clinton
stand on coup," Associated Press, November 5, 2009.

36. Dana Frank, "President Obama's Honduran Test," *San Francisco Chronicle*,
July 1, 2009; "Honduras: Are We Going to Make Concessions to Those
Who Perpetuate Coups?" *New America Media*, July 17, 2009; "Honduras
Coup Has Been Far from Bloodless," *San José Mercury-News*, September
4, 2009; "Obama Shouldn't Cave in to the Far Right on Honduras," *The
Progressive*, October 24, 2009; "No Fair Election in Honduras Under Military
Occupation," *Huffington Post*, November 26, 2009, www.huffingtonpost.com
/dana-frank/no-fair-election-in-hondu_b_371669.html.

37. For example, "Military Using 'Brutal' Force Against Anti-Coup Protests in
Honduras," *Democracy Now!*, July 1, 2009, www.democracynow.org/2009/7/1
/military_using_brutal_force_against_anti.

38. Elisabeth Malkin, "Ousted Leader Returns to Honduras," *New York Times*, September 21, 2009; Rory Carroll, "Honduran Forces Blast Sound Effects Outside Brazilian Embassy, *The Guardian*, October 22, 2009; Fabiano Maisonnave, "Manuel Zelaya Endures Strange Seige Inside Brazilian Embassy," *The Guardian*, October 25, 2009; Inter-American Commission on Human Rights, *Honduras: Human Rights and the Coup D'Etat*, 23–24.
39. Main, "'A New Chapter of Engagement'"; Joyce, "Legitimating the Illegitimate."
40. "US Stance Confuses Ousted Honduran Leader," CBS News, November 5, 2009; Finnegan, "An Old-Fashioned Coup."
41. Mary Beth Sheridan, "U.S. and Some Allies at Odds over Honduras Presidential Election," *Washington Post*, December 1, 2009.
42. "Carlos H. Reyes Anuncia Su Retiro de Los Comicios," *El Tiempo*, November 8, 2009; Frank, "No Fair Election in Honduras Under Military Occupation."
43. Joyce, "Legitimating the Illegitimate"; Elisabeth Malkin, "Conservatives Poised to Win in Honduras," *New York Times*, November 29, 2009.
44. United States Department of State, Press Statement, "Honduran Election," November 29, 2009, 2009-2017.state.gov/r/pa/prs/ps/2009/nov/132504. htm. At a special briefing on the Honduran elections held on November 30, 2009, Arturo Valenzuela, Assistant Secretary of State, Bureau of Western Hemisphere Affairs, stated: "I would like to commend the Honduran people for an election that met international standards of fairness and transparency despite some incidents that were reported here and there." United States Department of State, Special Briefing on the Honduran Elections, November 30, 2009, 2009-2017.state.gov/p/wha/rls/rm/2009/132777.htm.
45. Alexander Main, "Hillary Clinton's Emails and the Honduras Coup," *The Americas Blog*, Center for Economic and Policy Research, September 23, 2015, cepr.net/blogs/the-americas-blog/the-hillary-clinton-emails-and-honduras.
46. "Honduras: Full and Prompt Investigation Needed into Death of Human Rights Campaigner," Amnesty International, Press Release, December 14, 2009, www.amnesty.org/en/press-releases/2009/12/honduras-full-and -prompt-investigation-needed-death-human-rights-campaig/. For post-coup repression of members of the LGBTI community and movement, see Suyapa Portillo Villeda, "'Outing' Honduras: A Human Rights Catastrophe in the Making," *NACLA: Report on the Americas* 45, no. 3 (October 2012), nacla .org/news/2012/11/29/outing-honduras-human-rights-catastrophe-making.
47. "New Honduran President Takes Office," CNN, January 27, 2010, www.cnn .com/2010/WORLD/americas/01/27/honduras.president/index.html.
48. Alexandro Olson and Juan Carlos Llorca, "New Honduran Leader to Take Office, Ending Turmoil," *Newsday*, January 27, 2010, www.newsday.com/news /world/new-honduran-leader-to-take-office-ending-turmoil-1.1726373; Dana Frank, "Hondurans' Great Awakening," *The Nation*, March 18, 2010; "Romeo Vásquez nuevo gerente de Hondutel," *La Prensa*, March 10, 2010. For other top coup figures appointed to positions in the government, "And the Coup Goes On," *Honduras Culture and Politics* (blog) March 10, 2010, hondurasculture-politics.blogspot.com/2010/03/and-coup-goes-on.html; National Congress

of Honduras, Decree 2/2010, January 27, 2010; Inter-American Commission on Human Rights, "IACHR Expresses Concern about Amnesty Decree in Honduras," press release no. 14/10, February 3, 2010, www.cidh.org /Comunicados/English/2010/14-10eng.htm.

49. "Porfirio Lobo: Haremos un gobierno de unidad nacional," *El País* (Spain), November 30, 2009; for the president of the Organization of American States, José Miguel Insulza, on this theme, "Insulza valora esfuerza de Lobo por lograr reconciliación en Honduras," *La Prensa* (Nicaragua), January 22, 2010. For an analysis summarizing and supportive of the Obama Administration's positions regarding "national reconciliation," a truth commission, and Lobo, see Kevin Casas-Zamora, "Next Steps for Honduras," statement before the House Committee on Foreign Affairs Subcommittee on the Western Hemisphere," March 18, 2010, www.brookings.edu/testimonies /next-steps-for-honduras/.

50. See, e.g., Blake Schmidt, "Lobo Attempts Reconciliation in Honduras," *Tico Times,* February 5, 2010, www.ticotimes.net/2010/02/05/lobo-attempts -reconciliation-in-honduras.

51. "IACHR Condemns Murders, Kidnappings, and Attacks in Honduras," Inter-American Commission on Human Rights, press release no. 26/10, March 8, 2010, www.cidh.org/Comunicados/English/2010/26-10eng.htm.

52. "En Triunfo de la Cruz, deconocidos asaltan e incindian Radio Coco Dulce," *Radio Progreso* (blog), January 9, 2010, radioprogresohn.over-blog.com /article-en-triunfo-de-la-cruz-desconocidos-asaltan-e-incendian-radio -coco-dulce-42585467.html; "Arson Attack on Community Radio Station Previously Targeted by Coup Supporters," *Reporters Without Borders* (blog), January 7, 2010, rsf.org/en/news/arson-attack-community-radio -previously-targeted-coup-supporters.

53. Inter-American Commission on Human Rights, "IACHR Condemns Murders, Kidnappings, and Attacks in Honduras."

54. This subsection is based in large part on Dana Frank, "Hondurans' Great Awakening," *The Nation*, April 5, 2010.

55. Comité para la Defensa de los Derechos Humanos en Honduras (CODEH), "Asesinan a Claudia Larissa Brizuela Gonzalese Miembro del Frente Nacional de Resistencia," *CODEH* (blog), February 24, 2010, www.codeh.hn /inicio/index.php?option=com_k2&view=item&id=82:asesinan-a-claudia -larissa-gonzales-miembro-del-frente-nacional-de-resistencia&Itemid =36&lang=es.

56. "Another Journalist Gunned Down Eighth Since Start of 2010," *Reporters Without Borders,* June 16, 2010, rsf.org/en/news/another-journalist -gunned-down-eighth-start-2010.

57. Susan Fitzpatrick-Behrens, "Honduras: Repression Intensifies, Resistance Deepens, and Washington Promotes Recognition of the Post-Coup Regime," *NACLA: Report on the Americas,* March 19, 2010, nacla.org/node/6480.

58. August 14, 2009 rape: "Transcript of Irma Villanueva's testimony by Maria Soledad Cervantes," *Quotha*, August 25, 2009, quotha.net/node/244;

February 9, 2010 rapes: Inter-American Commission on Human Rights, "IACHR Condemns Murders, Kidnappings, and Attacks in Honduras."

59. Human Rights Watch, *After the Coup*, Dana Frank, "The Long Judicial Arm of the Honduran Coup," *Huffington Post*, February 4, 2015, www.huffingtonpost .com/dana-frank/the-long-judicial-arm-of-_b_6606416.html.

60. Mary Duran, "Honduran Partners Mobilize Against New Mining Law," January 26, 2012, *Development and Peace* (blog), www.devp.org/en/blog /honduran-partners-mobilize-against-new-mining-law; "Honduran New Laws Put Communities at a Disadvantage," *Development and Peace*, April 19, 2013, www.devp.org/en/blog/honduras-new-laws-put-communities -disadvantage; Phillips, *Honduras in Dangerous Times*, 46–47.

61. Office of Trade and Labor Affairs, Bureau of International Labor Affairs, US Department of Labor, *Public Report of Review of US Submission 2012-01 (Honduras)*, February 27, 2015, Annex 2, "National Plan for Employment by Hours," 95; Dana Frank, "Repression's Reward in Honduras? Dinner with Obama," *Huffington Post*, September 24, 2010; "Open Season on Teachers in Honduras," *TheNation.com*, May 5, 2011, www.thenation.com/article/open -season-teachers-honduras/.

62. Bertha Oliva, "A Real Truth Commission for Honduras," *Huffington Post*, June, 2010, www.huffingtonpost.com/bertha-oliva/a-real-truth-commission-f_b _563215.html; Jeremy Bigwood, "Truth in Honduras," June 11, 2010, *In These Times*, inthesetimes.com/article/6069/truth_in_honduras; Kevin Casas-Zamora, "Demanding the Truth in Honduras," *Brookings* (blog), April 19, 2010, www.brookings.edu/opinions/demanding-the-truth-in-honduras/.

63. Chrissie Long, "United States to Restore Aid to Honduras in Step Toward Normalized Ties," *Christian Science Monitor*, March 5, 2010; "Honduras: World Bank to Restore Aid," *New York Times*, February 22, 2010; "World Bank, IMF, and IDB Resume Links (and Loans) With Honduras," *MercoPress* (blog), March 18, 2010; en.mercopress.com/2010/03/18/world-bank-imf-and -idb-resume-links-and-loans-with-honduras; Fitzpatrick-Behrens, "Honduras: Repression Intensifies, Resistance Deepens . . ."; "IDB Lends Honduras $500 Million, *CentralAmericaData* (blog), May 24, 2010, en.centralamericadata.com /en/article/home/IDB_Lends_Honduras_500_Million.

64. Matthew Lee, "Clinton urges recognition of Honduras government," Associated Press, March 4, 2010. Clinton reiterated her points on June 7 in a meeting of the Organization of American States in Lima, Peru. Mark Landler, "Clinton Asks the O.A.S. to Readmit Honduras," *New York Times*, June 8, 2010.

65. Portions of this account originally appeared in Dana Frank, "Crisis of Legitimacy in Honduras?" *The Nation*, June 30, 2010.

66. *Quién Dijo Miedo: Honduras de un Golpe . . .*, dir. Katia Lara (Honduras-Argentina, Terco Productions, 2010).

Chapter Two

1. Karen Spring, "Honduras: Teachers and Students Resist Repression, *MonthlyReviewOnline* (blog), August 31, 2010, mronline.org/2010/08/31

/honduras-teachers-and-students-resist-repression/; Committee of Families of the Detained and Disappeared of Honduras (COFADEH), "August 2010—Deadly Month for Human Rights in Honduras," August, 2010, reprinted at *Quotha,* September 9, 2010, quotha.net/node/1167; Honduras Solidarity Network, "Take Action! End the Brutal Repression of the Honduran Social Movement," *UpsideDownWorld,* August 30, 2012.

2. Ibid.

3. Marc Lacey, "Latin America Still Divided Over Coup in Honduras," *New York Times,* June 5, 2010; Mark Weisbrot, "One Year On, Honduras Rift Persists," *The Guardian,* June 30, 2010.

4. Chuck Kaufman, "Resistance March in Tegucigalpa, Honduras," September 15, 2010, reprinted at *Rights Action* (blog); "Honduras—September 15: Resistance & Repression," *Honduras Resists* (blog), September 17, 2010, hondurasresists.org /pipermail/announce_hondurasresists.org/2010-September/001222.html.

5. Convergencia por los Derechos Humanos Zona Noroccidental, *Protesta Social y Libertad de Expresion en Honduras: El Caso de 15-S,* May 2012, www.academia .edu/11758259/Protesta_social_y_libertad_de_expresi%C3%B3n_en _Honduras_El_caso_del_15-S; documented report of the incidents, Comisión de Verdad, *The Voice of Greatest Authority Is That of the Victims.* 151–53; "Auto de prision dictan a vocero de la secretaria de seguridad," *El Heraldo,* April 7, 2014 [modified date]; "Justicia piden en caso de represion en Choloma tras golpe de estado," *Radio Progreso y ERIC* (blog), November 13, 2014, radioprogresohn.net/index.php/comunicaciones/noticias /item/1476-justicia-piden-en-caso-de-represi%C3%B3n-en-choloma-tras -golpe-de-estado; "Piden destituir a oficiales por agresión a manifestantes," *La Prensa,* August 21, 2013, www.laprensa.hn/vivir/recetasdecocina/380562 -96/piden-destituir-a-oficiales-por-agresi%C3%B3n-a-manifestantes; Israel Cruz, "Dictan sobreseimiento definitivio a oficiales acusados de salvaje represion en Choloma, Cortés," *Conexion,* August 26, 2013, honduprensa .wordpress.com/2013/08/26/dictan-sobreseimiento-definitivo-a-oficiales -acusados-de-salvaje-represion-en-choloma-cortes/; "Impunity for Police Abuse of Anti-Coup Demonstrators," *SOA Watch* (blog), n.d. (August 2013), www.soaw.org/about-us/equipo-sur/263-stories-from-honduras/4136 -august14impunity; "Sobreseimiento definitivo a favor de dos comisionados de la Policía Nacional," *Proceso Digital,* August 26, 2013; www.proceso .hn/index.php/component/k2/item/15982.html; COFADEH, "Audiencia inicial contra Héctor Iván Mejía y Abraham Figueroa tercero altos oficiales de la policía," *Defensores en Linea,* defensoresenlinea.com/cms/index .php?option=com_content&view=article&id=2735:audiencia-inicial-contra -hector-ivan-mejia-y-abraham-figueroa-tercero-altos-oficiales-de-la-policia &catid=42:seg-y-jus&Itemid=159.

6. "Translation of Irma Villanueva's Testimony by María Soledad Cervantes," *Quotha,* August 25, 2009; Comisión de Verdad, *The Voice of Greatest Authority Is That of the Victims,* 139–43; "Auto de prision dictan a vocero de la secretaría de seguridad"; "Justicia piden en caso de represion en Choloma tras golpe

de estado"; Cruz, "Dictan sobreseimiento definitivio a oficiales acusados de salvaje represion en Choloma, Cortés,"; "Sobreseimiento definitivo a favor de dos comisionados de la Policía Nacional."

7. Hillary Rodham Clinton, Press Statement, "Honduras's Independence Day," Secretary of State, Washington, D.C., September 13, 2010, 2009-2017.state .gov/secretary/20092013clinton/rm/2010/09/11147052.htm.

8. Press Release, "IMF Mission Reaches Agreement in Principle on a Stand-by Agreement for $196 million with Honduras," International Monetary Fund, press release no. 10/338, September 13, 2010, www.imf.org/en/News /Articles/2015/09/14/01/49/pr10338.

9. Annie Bird, "World Bank-Funded Biofuel Corporation Massacres Six Honduran Campesinos,"*Rights Action*, November 22, 2009, reprinted at www .scoop.co.nz/stories/HL1011/S00175/world-bank-funded-biofuel-corp -massacres-six-hondurans.htm; Annie Bird, "Predictable, Endless Repression Continues in Honduras," December 16, 2010, reprinted at *Quotha,* quotha .net/node/1442; Sorcha Pollak, "Death Valley: The Land War Gripping Honduras," *Irish Times*, May 9, 2015; "Policías y Militares Reprimen Huelga de Campesinos en Honduras," TeleSUR, December 17, 2010, telesurtv.net /secciones/noticias/85964-NN/policias-y-militares-reprimen-huelga-de -campesinos-en-honduras/; Movimiento Unficado Campesino de Aguán (MUCA), "Communicado," Tocoa, Colon, Honduras, *Movimiento MUCA* (blog), November 16, 2010, movimientomuca.blogspot.com/2010 /11/comunicado.html.

10. The most authoritative source on the Aguán Valley is Annie Bird, *Human Rights Violations Attributed to Military Forces in the Bajo Aguan Valley in Honduras, Rights Action*, February 20, 2013; and Annie Bird, *Petición ante la Comisión Interamericana de Derechos Humanos Presentada por Rights Action y MUCA en representación del Movimiento Unificado Campesino del Aguan (MUCA), Movimiento Campesino Recuperación Aguan (MOCRA), y el Movimiento Campesino Refundación Gregorio Chávez (MCRGC) contra La Republica de Honduras* Rights Action (2013). See also Tanya M. Kerrsen, *Grabbing Power: The New Struggles for Land, Food and Democracy in Northern Honduras* (Oakland, CA: Food First Books, 2013). For Facussé, see also Dana Frank, "Wikileaks Honduras: US Linked to Brutal Businessman," *TheNation.com*, October 21, 2011, www.thenation .com/article/wikileaks-honduras-us-linked-brutal-businessman/; [Hugo] Llorens, Cable, "TFH01: Ambassador Urges Regime Supporters to Persuade Micheletti to Sign San Jose Accord," September 8, 2009, wikileaks.org/plusd /cables/09TEGUCIGALPA900_a.html. Multiple news accounts report two hundred security guards at El Tumbador at the time of the massacre, but the exact number of Dinant's security force remains unclear. For land struggles, Phillips, *Honduras in Dangerous Times.*

11. Bird, *Human Rights Violations Attributed to Military Forces in the Bajo Aguán;* Telephone interview by the author with Annie Bird, October 6, 2017; "Nueva atentado contra dirigente popular en Colón," *HondurasLaboral* (blog), June 23, 2009, honduraslaboral.org/article/nuevo-atentado-contra-dirigente-popular

-en-colon/; Kerssen, *Grabbing Power.*

12. Interview by the author with Annie Bird, October 6, 2017; Bird, *Human Rights Violations Attributed to Military Forces in the Bajo Aguán*, 25–26; Human Rights Watch, *There Are No Investigations Here: Impunity for Killing and Other Abuses in Bajo Aguán, Honduras*, (Human Rights Watch, 2014), 21–25 www.hrw.org/report/2014/02/12/there-are-no-investigations-here /impunity-killings-and-other-abuses-bajo-aguan; Bird, *Petición ante la Comisión Interamericana de Derechos Humanos . . .*

13. Interviews conducted by the author, December 15, 2010, town of Guadalupe Carney; "Report on Evictions in Aguan," *Food First-FIAN*, November 15, 2010, reprinted at archive.maryknollogc.org/regional/latinamerica /Honduras_Aguan_Valley_attack.html.

14. Bird, *Human Rights Abuses Attributed to Military Forces in the Bajo Aguán*, 14–15.

15. Peter J. Meyer, Congressional Research Service, *Honduras-US Relations*, February 5, 2013 (Washington D.C.: Congressional Research Service, 2013), pp, 21–23; United States Government Accountability Office, *Review of US Response to the Honduran Political Crisis of 2009*, October 20, 2011 (Washington, D.C.: United States Government Accountability Office, 2011), 7.

16. John T. Stamm, United States Southern Command, "Joint Task Force-Bravo Troops Conduct Counter-Drug Training," December 16, 2010, www.jtfb .southcom.mil/News/Article-Display/Article/434755/joint-task-force -bravo-enhances-counter-drug-capabilities/.

17. "Dreams of an Insurgency," *Honduras Culture and Politics*, November 25, 2010, hondurasculturepolitics.blogspot.com/2010/11/dreams-of-insurgency.html.

18. "A Correction," *Quotha*, April 21, 2011, quotha.net/node/1732.

19. See Philip Agee, *CIA Diary: Inside the Company* (New York: Farrar, Straus, and Giroux, 1975).

20. Email communication, Babette Grunow to the author, April 16, 2014; Email communication, Babette Grunow to the author, December 26, 2010.

21. Cable, Paul Trivelli, "Embassy Managua Request for TDY for Greg Maggio," March 15, 2013, wikileaks.wikimee.org/cable/2006/03/06MANAGUA599.html.

22. Grandin, "Democracy Derailed in Honduras."

23. "Mas de un millon y cuarto de firmas soberanas exigen constituyente ye el re-torno de Manuel Zelaya," *TerceraInformación* (blog), November 22, 2010, www .tercerainformacion.es/antigua/spip.php?article18563; Ismael Moreno, SJ, "¿Huelga General? ¿Asamblea Constituyente?" *Envío*, no. 342, September 2010.

24. "Carlos H. Reyes anuncia su retiro de los comicios," *El Tiempo*, November 8, 2009; Frank, "No Fair Election in Honduras Under Military Occupation"; Multiple phone interviews by the author with German Zepeda, one of the UD candidates, November 2010.

25. For COFADEH, begin with their website and their news, report, and analysis website, defensoresenlinea.com/. For ERIC and Radio Progreso, begin with: radioprogresohn.net/.

26. Ismael Moreno, SJ, "¿Huelga General? ¿Asamblea Constituyente?"; "Reactions to the National Assembly of the FNRP: From Mel on Down,"

Honduras Culture and Politics, July 12, 2010, hondurasculturepolitics.blogspot. com/2010/07/reactions-to-national-assembly-of-fnrp.html; for background on Zelaya as cult figure and leader, Ismael Moreno, SJ, "Diálogo: Cambiar algo para que cambie nadie," *Envío,* no. 344 (November 2010). I witnessed the crowds thronging around the statue of Zelaya during a 2010 demonstration in San Pedro Sula.

27. "Honduran resistance movement decides not to participate in elections," (translation from Radio del Sur), *Quotha,* February 28, 2011, quotha.net/node/1582; Frank, "Open Season on Teachers in Honduras." For positions, see, e.g., "Posición de STIBYS ante la asamblea de FNRP del 26 Febrero 2011," February 8, 2011, February 22, 2011, copinh.org/article/posicion-del-stibys-ante-la -asamblea-del-fnrp-del-/; "Honduras: Propuesta del D-19-USA ante la asamblea de FNRP el 26 de Febrero," February 22, 2011, www.elsoca.org/index.php /america-central/hondu/1640-honduras-propuesta-del-d-19usa-ante-la -asamblea-del-fnrp-el-26-de-febrero. For Department 19, a good start is "Department 19: A New Political Player in Honduras?" *Honduras Culture and Politics,* March 22, 2011, hondurasculturepolitics.blogspot.com/2011/03 /department-19-new-political-player-in.html.

28. Giorgio Trucchi, "II Encuentro Nacional por la Refundacíon de Honduras: Refundar y construir el poder popular y constituyente en Honduras," UITA-Secretaría Regional Latinoamerica, March 16, 2010, www6.rel-uita.org /internacional/honduras/democradura/hacia_la_refundacion_de_honduras -2.htm.

29. Portions of the discussion that follows were originally published in Frank, "Open Season on Teachers in Honduras," *TheNation.com,* May 5, 2011, www.thenation.com/article/open-season-teachers-honduras/.

30. Annie Bird and Karen Spring, "Honduras: Protesters Challenge IDB-Funded Privatization of Education, despite Massive Violent Retaliation," *Monthly Review Online,* April 12, 2011, mronline.org/2011/04/12/honduras-protesters -challenge-idb-funded-privatization-of-education-despite-massive-violent -repression/; Lois Weiner and Mary Compton, eds., *The Global Assault on Teaching, Teachers, and Their Unions: Stories for Resistance* (New York: Palgrave Macmillan, 2008).

31. Bird and Spring, "Honduras: Protesters Challenge IDB-Funded Privatization of Education, despite Massive Violent Retaliation"; Frank, "Open Season on Teachers in Honduras."

32. Freddy Cuevas, "Trabajadores de la salud en paro por apoyo maestros de Honduras," *La Prensa,* March 28, 2011; www.laprensa.com.ni/2011/03/28 /internacionales/56186-trabajadores-de-la-salud-en-paro-por-apoyo -a-maestros-en-honduras. COFADEH, "Honduras: Continúan en emergencia los DDHH"/"Honduras: The Human Rights Emergency Continues," March 31, 2011, transl. Vicki Cervantes, reprinted at *Quotha,* April 3, 2011, quotha.net/node/1691.

33. Frank, "Open Season on Teachers in Honduras"; Zenaida Velásquez, "Slain Honduran Teacher Writes to Nancy Pelosi: Stop Supporting Porfirio Lobo's

Regime in Honduras," *Monthly Review Online* April 17, 2011, mronline.
org/2011/04/17/slain-honduran-teachers-sister-writes-to-nancy
-pelosi-stop-supporting-porfirio-lobos-regime-in-honduras/.

34. Ibid.
35. COFADEH, "Honduras: Continúan en emergencia los DDHH." See this
report as well for a fuller delineation of widespread repression at the time.
36. Miriam Miranda, "Honduras: The Coup d'Etat, Its Inheritors and the
Criminalization of Social Protest," March 29, 2011, transl. Matt Ginsberg-
Jaeckle, reprinted at *Quotha*, March 30, 2011, quotha.net/node/1669; "Joint
Appeal—Assault and Judicial Harassment of Human Rights Defender Ms
Miriam Miranda Chamarro," *Front Lines Defenders*, March 30, 2011,
www.frontlinedefenders.org/es/case/case-history-miriam-miranda-chamorro.
37. COFADEH, "Honduras: Continúan en emergencia los DDHH."
38. C-Libre Alert, "Periodistas víctimas de represión policial," *C-Libre* (blog),
March 25, 2011, www.clibrehonduras.com/alerta/periodistas-victimas-de
-represi%C3%B3n-policial; Frank, "Open Season on Teachers in Honduras."
39. Frank, "Open Season on Teachers in Honduras."
40. Email, Jeremy Spector to Jerold Block, March 30, 2011, in possession of the
author.
41. "Hong Kong in Honduras," *The Economist*, December 10, 2011; Danielle
Marie Mackey, "'I've Seen All Kinds of Horrific Things in My Time. But
None as Detrimental to the Country as This,'" *The New Republic*, December
14, 2014.
42. For an analysis of the continuities in this history, see Ismael Moreno, SJ, "A
Model City for a Society in Tatters," *Envío*, no. 357 (April 2011).
43. For the maquiladora sector, Benedicte Bull, F. Castellaci, and Yuri
Kasarahara, *Business Groups and Transnational Capitalism in Central America*,
(New York: Palgrave Macmillan, 2014); Ralph Armbruster-Sandoval,
*Globalization and Cross-Border Solidarity in the Americas: The Anti-Sweatshop
Movement and the Struggle for Social Justice*, (New York: Routledge, 2004).
44. Republic of Honduras, Decreto No. 230-2010, *La Gaceta*, November 4, 2010;
AFL-CIO, *Trade, Violence, and Migration: The Broken Promises to Honduran Workers*,
January 9, 2015, aflcio.org/sites/default/files/2017-03/Honduras.PDF, 12–13.
45. Secretaría de Relaciones Exteriores, Republic of Honduras, *Honduras is Open
for Business*, pamphlet (San Pedro Sula, Honduras, May 5 and 6, 2011); John
Perry, "Honduras, Open for Business," *LRB Blog* (London Review of Books),
www.lrb.co.uk/blog/2011/05/18/john-perry/honduras-open-for-business/;
Press Release, "Obama Trade Official Highlights International Investment
Opportunities in Honduras," International Trade Association, May 5, 2011,
www.trade.gov/press/press-releases/2011/obama-trade-official-highlights
-international-investment-opportunities-in-honduras-050511.asp.
46. Elisabeth Malkin, "Ex-Leader of Honduras Signs Accord Clearing Path for
Reform," *New York Times*, May 22, 2011; "Ousted Leader Manuel Zelaya to
Return to Honduras," *The Guardian*, May 23, 2011. For an extensive analysis
of debates regarding the accord, see "The Cartagena Accord," *Honduras*

Culture and Politics, May 22, 2011; "Reactions to the Cartagena Accord, Part One: The FNRP," May 24, 2011; "Reactions to the Cartagena Accord, Part Three: Artists in Resistance"; "There's a Hidden Agenda," May 25, 2011; "'The ancestral force of Lempira,' COPINH Responds," May 27, 2011; "Reactions to the Cartagena Accord, Part Four: The UCD Responds," May 29, 2011.

47. Ibid.

48. "Ousted Ex-President Zelaya Returns to Honduras," *CNN.com*, May 30, 2011, www.cnn.com/2011/WORLD/americas/05/28/honduras.zelaya/index .html; Gustavo Palencia, "Ex-President Zelaya Returns from Exile," Reuters, May 28, 2011. For more critical reporting, Tracy Wilkinson and Alex Renderos, "Ousted President Zelaya Returns from Exile," *Los Angeles Times*, May 29 2011; Dana Frank, "Zelaya Returns to Honduras, But Justice Is Still Not Done," *The Nation*, June 2, 2011, www.thenation.com/article/zelaya -returns-honduras-justice-still-not-done/; Frank, "Ousted President's Return Doesn't Mean Repression Is Over in Honduras," *TheProgressive.org*, May 27, 2011, available at www.commondreams.org/views/2011/05/27 /ousted-presidents-return-honduras-doesnt-mean-repression-over. For video coverage and a thorough analysis, "Out of Exile: Exclusive Report on Ousted President Zelaya's Return Home 23 Months after US-backed Coup," *Democracy Now!* May 31, 2011, www.democracynow.org/2011/5/31/out _of_exile_exclusive_report_on.

49. "OAS Lifts Honduras Suspension After Zelaya Agreement," BBC News, June 1, 2011, www.bbc.com/news/world-latin-america-13622939. The lone holdout was Ecuador.

50. "Honduras' Lobo Renews Commitment to Human Rights," *Latin America News Dispatch*, September 22, 2011, latindispatch.com/2011/09/22 /honduras-lobo-renews-commitment-to-human-rights/.

51. For an analysis of the drug war in Latin America, see Dawn Paley, *Drug War Capitalism* (Chico, CA: AK Press, 2014).

52. Portions of this section were originally published in Dana Frank, "Repression's Reward in Honduras? Dinner with Obama," *Huffington Post*, September 24, 2010.

53. Office of the Press Secretary, The White House, "Remarks by President Obama and President Lobo of Honduras Before Bilateral Meeting," October 5, 2011, obamawhitehouse.archives.gov/the-press-office/2011/10/05 /remarks-president-obama-and-president-lobo-honduras-bilateral-meeting.

54. Interviews by the author with residents in the town of Rigores, August 6, 2011; Amnesty International, "Violent Forced Eviction Leaves Families at Risk," UA 215/11, July 13, 2011, www.amnesty.se/engagera-dig/agera /aktuella-blixtaktioner/ua-21511-honduras-violent-forced-eviction-leaves -families-at-risk/.

55. For the footage, see Jesse Freeston, "Honduran Police Burn Community to the Ground," The Real News Network, July 30, 2011, available at www.youtube.com/watch?v=TRB8Pao3NzQ; and *Resistencia: The Fight for the*

Aguan Valley, dir. Jesse Freeston (2014).

56. Bird, *Human Rights Violations Attributed to Military Forces in the Bajo Aguán*, 28–29 and passim; Bird, *Petición ante la Comisión Interamericana de Derechos Humanos . . .* , 32, 34; Interviews by the author with Annie Bird, December 29, 2015, October 6, 2017. For the eviction see also Human Rights Watch, "There Are No Investigations Here"; Amnesty Interntaional, "Violent Forced Eviction Leaves Families at Risk."

57. Bird, *Human Rights Violations Attributed to Military Forces in the Bajo Aguán*, 49; Human Rights Watch, "There Are No Investigations Here."

58. Interview with Annie Bird, October 6, 2017. Interviews by the author with Rigores residents, August 6, 2017.

59. Bird, *Human Rights Violations Attributed to Military Forces in the Bajo Aguán*, 28.

60. Human Rights Watch, "There Are No Investigations Here."

61. For example, "Out of Control," *The Economist*, March 9, 2013.

62. Bird, *Human Rights Violations Attributed to Military Forces in the Bajo Aguán*, Bird, *Petición ante la Comisión Interamericana de Derechos Humanos . . .* , Appendix 1; Interview with Annie Bird, October 6, 2017; COFADEH, "Campesinos denuncian falta de voluntad política para resolver conflicto agrario e impunidad en Bajo Aguán," Defensores En Linea, November 17, 2017, defensoresenlinea.com/campesinos-denuncian-falta-de-voluntad-politica -para-resolver-conflicto-agrario-e-impunidad-en-el-bajo-agu/. For detailed reports on the Aguán, see, in addition, FIDH (International Federation for Human Rights), "Honduras: Human Rights Violations in Bajo Aguán," September 2011, www.fidh.org/IMG/pdf/honduras573ang.pdf; Human Rights Watch, "There Are No Investigations Here"; Kersson, *Grabbing Power.*

63. Bird, *Human Rights Violations Attributed to Military Forces in the Bajo Aguán*, 4; Bird, *Petición ante la Comisión Interamericana de Derechos Humanos . . .* ; Kersson, *Grabbing Power*, Elisabeth Malkin, "In Honduras, Land Struggles Highlight Post-Coup Polarization," *New York Times*, September 15, 2011.

64. Bird, *Human Rights Violations Attributed to Military Forces in the Bajo Aguán*, 40, 48, 51.

65. FIDH, "Honduras: Human Rights Violations in Bajo Aguán."

66. Bird, *Human Rights Violations Attributed to Military Forces in the Bajo Aguán*, 39, 49; Bird, *Petición ante la Comisión Interamericana de Derechos Humanos . . .* , 39.

67. Annie Bird (with Karen Spring), "Campesinos in Honduras Killed," *Rights Action*, August 2011, reprinted August 17, 2011, Alliance for Global Justice, afgj.org/campesinos-in-Honduras-killed; Bird, *Human Rights Violations Attributed to Military Forces in the Bajo Aguán*, 40; COFADEH quoted in Dana Frank, "Wikileaks Honduras: US Linked to Brutal Businessman," *TheNation. com*, October 21, 2011, www.thenation.com/article/wikileaks-honduras -us-linked-brutal-businessman/.

68. Bird, *Human Rights Violations Attributed to Military Forces in the Bajo Aguán*, 49–50.

69. Quoted in Frank, "Wikileaks Honduras."

70. Bird, *Human Rights Violations Attributed to Military Forces in the Bajo Aguan*, 12–13 and passim.

71. FIAN Honduras, "Campesino sometido al tortura en el Bajo Aguan," October 7, 2011, www6.rel-uita.org/agricultura/palma_africana /FIAN-campesino_sometido_a_torturas.htm.

72. John Lindsay-Poland, "Honduras and the US Military," *Fellowship of Reconciliation* (blog), September 21, 2011, archives.forusa.org/blogs/john -lindsay-poland/honduras-us-military/9943; The White House, Press Release, "Fact Sheet: United States Support for Central American Security," May 4, 2013, obamawhitehouse.archives.gov/the-press-office/2013 /05/04/fact-sheet-united-states-support-central-american-citizen-security. For an analysis of additional US bases in Honduras, and the "Lily Pad" strategy, see David S. Vine, "When a Country Becomes a Military Base: Blowback and Insecurity in Honduras, the World's Most Dangerous Place," in *Biosecurity and Vulnerability*, eds. Lesley A. Sharp and Nancy N. Chen, (Albuquerque, NM, School for Advanced Research Press, 2014) 25–44. See also Thom Shanker, "Lessons of Iraq Help US Fight a Drug War in Honduras," *New York Times*, May 5, 2012; "New US Bases in Honduras, *Honduras Culture and Politics,* November 28, 2011, hondurasculturepolitics.blogspot.com/2011/11 /new-us-bases-in-honduras.html.

73. Bird, *Human Rights Violations Attributed to Military Forces in the Bajo Aguan*, 14–15; Wednesday, October 5, 2011, report from delegation visit to the Aguán Valley, *Honduras Resists* (blog), hondurasresists.blogspot.com/2011/.

74. Portions of what follows were originally published in Frank, "Wikileaks Honduras."

75. For a summary of the Wikileaks regarding Facussé, see Frank, "Wikileaks Honduras." For the Wikileaks themselves, see, e.g., wikileaks.org. For the planes landing, cable, "Drug Plane Burned on Prominent Hondurans' Property," March 19, 2004. wikileaks.org/plusd/cables/04TEGUCIGALPA672_a.htm.

76. Ibid.

77. Malkin, "In Honduras, Land Struggles Highlight Post-Coup Polarization."

78. Ibid.

79. For example, MUCA comunicado, "Denuciamos a la ola de persecución y los asesinatos hacia los campesinos de Bajo Aguán," July 7, 2012, translated and reprinted at *Honduras Resists*, July 8, 2012, hondurasresists.blogspot.com/2012 /07/below-is-english-translation-of.html.

80. "Honduras arrests 176 in corruption purge," BBC News, November 4, 2011, www.bbc.com/news/world-latin-america-15586060.

81. "Honduras arrests 176 in corruption purge,"; "Police Suspected of Murdering Students," *Honduras Culture and Politics*, October 26, 2011, hondurasculturepolitics.blogspot.com/2011/10/police-suspected -of-murdering.html; "Police Shakeup," *Honduras Culture and Politcs*, October 31, 2011, hondurasculturepolitics.blogspot.com/2011/10/police-shakeup. html; "Policías los subieron a la patrulla y tomaron decision de asesinarlos," *La Tribuna*, October 31, 2011; "Policías separadados de la granja serán enviados a otras jefaturas," *La Tribuna*, November 12, 2011.

82. E.g., Sandra Rodríguez, "COFADEH demands complete overhaul of the

Ministry of the Attorney General and the Ministry of Security," translated by the Friendship Office of the Americas, reprinted at *Quotha*, November 1, 2011, quotha.net/node/2022.

83. "María Borjas dice que en Honduras policías atemorizan más que pandilleros," *El Tiempo*, November 4, 2011.

84. "COFADEH: Mas de 10,000 denuncias contra policías desde el 2009," *La Tribuna*, November 4, 2011.

85. Ronan Graham, "Honduras Politician: 40% Police Tied to Organized Crime" *Insight Crime* (blog), July 20, 2011, www.insightcrime.org/news-briefs /honduras-politician-40-police-tied-to-organized-crime.

86. "Mi hijo murió primero a Carlos, lo mataron con disparo en la cara," *La Tribuna*, November 1, 2011.

87. Dana Frank, "Honduras: Which Side Is the US On?" *The Nation*, May 22, 2012.

88. "Al ex 'zar antidrogas' lo asesinaron agentes de seguridad del Estado: Landaverde," *La Tribuna*, November 22, 2011; "Asesinan a Alfredo Landaverde," *La Tribuna*, December 7, 2011. For a later, full analysis, see Elisabeth Malkin and Alberto Arce, "Files Suggest Honduran Police Leaders Ordered Killing of Antidrug Officials," *New York Times*, April 15, 2016; for a longer, more detailed version in Spanish, Alberto Arce, "Tres generales y un cartel: violencia policial e impunidad en Honduras" *New York Times*, Spanish edition, April 15, 2016.

89. Malkin and Arce, "Files Suggest Honduran Police Leaders Ordered Killing of Antidrug Officials"; Arce, "Tres generales y un cartel: violencia policial e impunidad en Honduras."

90. Portions of what follows were originally published in Dana Frank, "Honduras in Flames," *TheNation.com*, February 16, 2012, www.thenation.com /article/honduras-flames/.

91. Christine Armario and Martha Mendoza, "Honduras fire inmates not convicted," Associated Press, February 16, 2012; Mark Stevenson and Martha Mendoza, "Prison Fire Exposes Chaos in Honduras," Associated Press, February 16, 2012; Mariano Castillo and Elvin Sandoval, "More than 300 Killed in Honduras Prison Fire," CNN.com, February 16, 2012, www.cnn .com/2012/02/15/world/americas/honduras-fire-deaths/index.html; Javier C. Hernández and Randall Archibold, "Blaze at Prison Underscores Broad Security Problems in Hodnuras," *New York Times*, February 15, 2012. Quote: Armario and Mendoza, "Honduras fire inmates not convicted."

92. Armario and Mendoza, "Honduras fire inmates not convicted"; Melissa Sanchez and Tim Johnson, "Inmates Trapped in Blazing Honduran Prison Say Guards Shot at Them," McClatchy News Service, February 15, 2012, www.mcclatchydc.com/news/nation-world/world/article24724234.html.

93. "Policía dice que incendio fue provocado y que ya tienen nombre de responsable," *Proceso Digital*, February 12, 2012, www.proceso.hn/component /k2/item/41481.html. For Mejía's earlier history, see chapters 1 and 2.

94. "Policía dice que incendio fue provocado y que ya tienen nombre de responsable"; Armario and Mendoza, "Honduras fire inmates not convicted";

"Honduras fire victims 'Burned up against the bars, stuck to them,'" *The Guardian*, February 16, 2012; Freddy Cuevas, "As many as 356 killed in Honduras prison fire" Associated Press, February 15, 2012.

95. Interviews on Radio Progreso, Honduras, February 15, 2012, cited in Dana Frank, "Honduras in Flames."

96. Javier C. Hernández and Randall Archibold, "Blaze at Prison Underscores Broad Security Problems in Honduras."

97. Frank, "Honduras in Flames."

98. "Deadly Fire at Overcrowded Prison Adds to Worsening Toll in Post-Coup Honduras," *Democracy Now!* February 16, 2012, www.democracynow.org/2012 /2/16/deadly_fire_at_overcrowded_prison_adds.

99. *El Porvenir*, dir. Oscar Estrada (Marabunta Films, 2008).

100. At the time it was Pinnacles National Monument. It became Pinnacles National Park in 2013.

Chapter Three

1. Malkin, "In Honduras, Land Struggles Highlight Post-Coup Polarization."

2. Elisabeth Malkin, "Honduras: Killings Prompt a Ban on Motorcycles Carrying Passengers," *New York Times*, December 8, 2011.

3. Rep. Howard L. Berman to Secretary of State Hillary Clinton, November 28, 2011, reprinted at *Just Foreign Policy* (blog), www.justforeignpolicy.org/sites /default/files/11-28-11.%20Letter%20to%20Secretary%20Clinton%20re. %20Human%20Rights%20in%20Honduras.pdf.

4. Alexander Main, "Congress Places Conditions on Military and Police Aid to Honduras," *CEPR Americas Blog*, December 28, 2011, cepr.net/blogs/cepr -blog/congress-places-conditions-on-military-and-police-aid-to-honduras.

5. "Honduras no califica a Cuenta del Milenio pero recibe voto de confianza de Estados Unidos," *El Heraldo*, December 15, 2011; "No estamos fuera de la Cuenta del Milenio," *La Tribuna*, December 21, 2011.

6. Randal Archibold, "Peace Corps to Scale Back in Central America," *New York Times*, December 21, 2011.

7. United Nations, *Global Study on Homicide*, www.unodc.org/gsh/en/data.html; Nick Miroff, "San Pedro Sula, Honduras, Is the World's Most Violent Place," *Washington Post*, January 13, 2012; "Central America's Bloody Drug Problem," *CNN.com*, January 19, 2012, www.cnn.com/2012/01/19/world/americas /narco-wars-guatemala-honduras/index.html.

8. Editorial, "Holding Honduras Accountable: President Porfirio Lobo Must Demonstrate That He's Taking Measurable Steps to Prevent Human Rights Abuses," *Los Angeles Times*, January 2, 2012.

9. Miroff, "San Pedro Sula, Honduras, Is the World's Most Dangerous Place"; Tim Johnson, "Crime Booms as Central Americans Fear Police Switched Sides," McClatchy News Service, January 23, 2012, www .mcclatchydc.com/news/nation-world/world/article24722638.html; Frances Robles, "Honduras Becomes Murder Capital of the World," *Miami Herald*, January 23, 2012; Editorial, "Central America's Free-Fire Zone. Dramatic

Crisis in Honduras Demands Action," *Miami Herald,* January 24, 2012.

10. Dana Frank, "A Mess in Honduras, Made in the U.S.," *New York Times,* January 27, 2012.

11. "US Policy in Honduras: Views of Two Diplomats," *New York Times,* February 5, 2012.

12. "En Honduras, un caos hecho en los EEUU," *El Tiempo,* January 28, 2012; "Ofensiva diplomática Hondureño en el *New York Times,*" *El Heraldo,* February 6, 2012.

13. For a full discussion of the prison fire, see chapter 2. Alberto Arce later wrote a book about his experiences covering Honduras, *Honduras a ras de suelo: Crónicas desde el país más violento del mundo* (Mexico City; Ediciones Culturales Paidós, 2016).

14. Press Release, "94 House Members Send Letter to Clinton to Suspend Security Assistance to Honduras," Representative Jan Schakowsky, March 12, 2012, schakowsky.house.gov/press-releases/94-house-members-send-letter -to-clinton-to-suspend-security-assistance-to-honduras/.

15. James McGovern and eighty-six additional members of Congress to Hillary Clinton, May 31, 2011, mcgovern.house.gov/news/documentsingle .aspx?DocumentID=397143.

16. "Congresista Estadounidosense denuncia ataques contra periodistas y gays," *El Tiempo,* May 22, 2012; for the original statement in English, "Human Rights in Honduras—Hon. Sam Farr," *Congressional Record,* 112th Congress May 17, 2012, E835, .

17. Bird, *Human Rights Violations Attributed to Military Forces in the Bajo Aguán,* 51–52.

18. COFADEH, "Campesinos detenidos en San Manuel Cortes por ordenes de terratenientes," *Defensores En Linea,* April 24, 2012, www.defensoresenlinea .com/cms/index.php?option=com_content&view=article&id=1974:136 -campesinos-detenidos-en-san-manuel-cortes-por-ordenes-de-terratenientes &catid=54:den&Itemid=171; Bird, *Petición ante la Comisión Interamericana de Derechos Humanos . . .* , 50–51.

19. "Missing Honduran journalist found dead," *BBC News.com,* March 12, 2012, www.bbc.com/news/world-latin-america-17990638. On repression of members of the LGBTI community, Portillo Villeda, "'Outing' Honduras."

20. "Abducted Honduras reporter Alfredo Villatoro found dead," *BBC News.com,* May 16, 2012, www.bbc.com/news/world-latin-america-18083550.

21. "Practicar periodismo responsable aconseja el portavoz de Seguridad," *El Tiempo,* May 12, 2012.

22. Thom Shanker, "Lessons of Iraq Help US Fight a Drug War in Honduras," *New York Times,* May 5, 2012.

23. "Should US Troops Fight the War on Drugs?," *New York Times,* May 8, 2012, www.nytimes.com/roomfordebate/2012/05/08/should-us-troops -fight-the-war-on-drugs.

24. Adam Davidson, "Who Wants to Buy Honduras?" *New York Times Magazine,* May 8, 2012.

25. For an extensive analysis of the incident, of two other related incidents, and

responses by the State Department, DEA, and Honduran government, Office of the Inspectors General, US Department of Justice, US Department of State, *A Special Joint Review of Post-Incident Responses by the Department of State and Drug Enforcement Administration to Three Deadly Force Incidents in Honduras, May 2017*, Office of the Inspectors General, Oversight and Review 17-02, Office and Evaluations and Special Projects ESP 17-01, available at oig.state.gov/system /files/esp-17-01_-_joint_report_-honduras.pdf. For a thorough investigation of the incident itself, including the perspectives of the victims, Annie Bird and Alex Main, with research contributions from Karen Spring, *Collateral Damage of a Drug War: The May 11, 2012 Killings in Ahuas and the Impact of US War on Drugs in La Moskitia, Honduras, August 12, 2012*, Center for Economic and Policy Research and Rights Action, available at: cepr.net/documents/publications /honduras-2012-08.pdf. For the aftermath, especially an assessment of the Honduran government's response, Alexander Main and Annie Bird, *Still Waiting for Justice: An Assessment of the Honduran Public Ministry's Investigation of the May 11, 2012, Killings in Ahuas, Honduras*, Center for Economic and Policy Research and Rights Action, April 2013, cepr.net/documents/publications /honduras-ahuas-2013-04.pdf. For a later analysis, see Mattathias Schwartz, "A Mission Gone Wrong," *The New Yorker*, January 6, 2014.

26. Adam Williams, "Honduras to Probe DEA for Death of Pregnant Woman in Drug Raid," Bloomberg News, May 16, 2012; Martha Mendoza and Freddy Cuevas, "US agents on deadly Honduran military operation," Associated Press, May 16, 2012; Damien Cave, "Anger Rises after Killings in US-Honduras Drug Sweep," *New York Times*, May 17, 2012; Damien Cave, "From a Honduras Hospital, Conflicting Tales of a Riverside Shootout" *New York Times*, May 18, 2012; Charlie Savage and Thom Shanker, "D.E.A.'s Agents Join Counternarcotics Efforts in Honduras," *New York Times*, May 16, 2012.

27. Alberto Arce and Katherine Corcoran, "Hunt for trafficker terrorizes Honduran villagers," Associated Press, May 23, 2012.

28. United States Department of State, Daily Press Briefing, May 17, 2012, available in transcript and video at 2009-2017.state.gov/r/pa/prs /dpb/2012/05/190242.htm; see also May 18, May 22, State Department Daily Press Briefings.

29. Main and Bird, *Still Waiting for Justice*, 5, 9.

30. Bird and Main, *Collateral Damage of a Drug War*; Office of the Inspectors General, US Department of Justice, US Department of State, *A Special Joint Review of Post-Incident Responses . . .*, chapter 12, "Information Provided to Congress."

31. The administration did allow *New York Times* reporters to see the video in June 2012. Charlie Savage and Thom Shanker, "Video Adds to Honduran Drug War Mystery," *New York Times*, June 22, 2012. Five years later, Mattathias Schwartz of *ProPublica* and the *New York Times* obtained the video and published it online and summarized it in print. Schwartz, "D.E.A. Says Hondurans Opened Fire During a Drug Raid. A Video Suggests Otherwise," *New York Times*, October 23, 2013; www.propublica.org/article/the-dea-says -it-came-under-fire-during-a-deadly-drug-raid-its-own-video-suggests

-otherwise; www.nytimes.com/2017/10/23/world/americas/drug
-enforcement-agency-dea-honduras.html?_r=0.

32. Frank, "Honduras: Which Side is the US On?"; Frank, "US has blinders on
in Honduras," *Los Angeles Times*, August 24, 2012; Frank, "Honduras Gone
Wrong," *Foreign Affairs.com*, October 16, 2012, www.foreignaffairs.com/articles
/americas/2012-10-16/honduras-gone-wrong.

33. Email, Roger Pineda to the author, March 16, 2012; email, Roger Pineda to
the author, April 12, 2012; email, Roger Pineda to the author, May 28, 2012,
and attached letter, Roger Pineda to the author, May 25, with suggestion that
I could be "held legally liable for the damage caused to the image of Miguel
Facussé and his companies."

34. Media Note, Office of the Spokesperson, US Department of State, "Meeting
with Honduran President Lobo," January 18, 2012, 2009-2017.state.gov/r
/pa/prs/ps/2012/01/181487.htm.

35. "Presidente Lobo se reunió con asesor estadunidense Oliver Garza," *Proceso
Digital*, February 9, 2012, www.proceso.hn/component/k2/item/41682.html;
Annie Bird, "The US's Drug War Should Not Hit Central America," *Rights
Action*, February 18, 2012, reprinted at *Quotha*, quota.net/node/2134.

36. "Biden Visits Honduras Amid Drug Legalization Debate," *CNN.com*, March
6, 2012, www.cnn.com/2012/03/06/world/americas/honduras-biden/index
.html; Press Release, The White House, "Vice President Biden to Travel
to Mexico and Honduras," White House Archives, February 22, 2010,
obamawhitehouse.archives.gov/the-press-office/2012/02/22/vice-president
-biden-travel-mexico-and-honduras.

37. Media Note, Office of the Spokesperson, US Department of State, "Travel of
Assistant Secretary Willim R. Brownfield Bureau for International Narcotics
and Law Enforcement Affairs," March 22, 2012, 2009-2017.state.gov/r/pa
/prs/ps/2012/03/186701.htm.

38. "'La Situación es algo crítica,'" *El País* (Tegucigalpa), March 26, 2012; "Reynoso:
a Honduras aún le falta mucho por hacer," *La Prensa*, March 26, 2012.

39. "DIECP recomienda sanciones a miembros de la carrera policial investigados
por delitos," *HRN* (blog), August 7, 2012, www.radiohrn.hn/l/node/12139;
"DIECP pide separar al menos 18 miembros de la policía que sometieron a
pruebas de confianza," *Proceso Digital*, September 1, 2012, www.proceso.hn
/component/k2/item/33059-DIECP-pide-separar-al-menos-18-miembros
-de-la-Polic%C3%ADa-que-se-sometieron-a-pruebas-de-confianza.html.

40. "Nombran a comisionados para depuración policial en Honduras," *La Prensa*,
April 17, 2012; "Comisión para la reforma avanza en pro de suguridad del
país," *La Tribuna*, April 24, 2012. For accusations against Blu, "Corrales:
Corruption Accusations are OK," *Honduras Culture and Politics*, April 27, 2012,
hondurasculturepolitics.blogspot.com/2012/04/arturo-corrales-corrruption
-accusations.html. For the embassy and Meza, Wikileaks cable, US Embassy,
Tegucialpa, "Possible Candidates to Serve as First Honduran Ambassador to
Cuba," April 8, 2003, wikileaks.org/plusd/cables/03TEGUCIGALPA856_a
.html. For a fuller discussion of the history of the CRSP, see chapter 4.

41. Austin Robles, "The Honduran Military Shouldn't Police," *Foreign Policy in Focus* (blog), July 10, 2012, fpif.org/the_honduran_military_shouldnt_police/; Geoffrey Ramsey, *InSight Crime*, November 30, 2011, www.insightcrime.org /news-analysis/new-powers-for-honduran-military-will-not-clean-up -law-enforcement.

42. Katherine Corcoran, "Honduras names new national police chief," Associated Press, May 22, 2012. "Embajadora de EEUU desea suerte a Bonilla," *El Tiempo*, May 23, 2012.

43. Katherine Corcoran and Martha Mendoza, "New Honduras top cop once investigated in killings," Associated Press, June 1, 2012.

44. Ibid.

45. For an analysis of the Leahy Law and its history, see Nina M. Serafino, June S. Beittel, Lauren Plonch Blanchard, and Liana Rosen, *"Leahy Law" Human Rights Provisions and Security Assistance: Issue Overview*, Congressional Research Service, January 29, 2014 2014) available at fas.org/sgp/crs/row/R43361.pdf.

46. State Department Daily Press Briefing, May 22, 2012.

47. United States Department of State, Report on the Government of Honduras's protection of human rights and the investigation and prosecution of security services personnel credibly alleged to have violated human rights, August 8, 2012, in possession of the author, reprinted at securityassistance.org /sites/default/files/120808hn.pdf.

48. Alberto Arce and Martha Mendoza, "US withholds funds to Honduran police,"Associated Press, August 11, 2012; Channel 3, Tegucigalpa, August 12, 2012; "El 'Tigre' Bonilla es caso juzgado señalamientos a violaciones de DDHH," *La Tribuna*, August 13, 2012; "Campaña contra el Tigre favorece la delincuencia," *La Prensa*, August 12, 2012. "'Denuncia y campaña contra el Tigre favorecen delincuencia,'" *La Prensa*, August 15, 2012; Martha Mendoza and Alberto Arce, "Honduras cooperating with US human rights probe," Associated Press, August 14, 2012; "Kubiske: No solo al 'Tigre' Bonilla se investiga por violación a derechos humanos," *Proceso Digital*, August 13, 2012; "Honduras reafirma apoyo al 'Tigre' Bonilla, tras investigaciones y recorte de ayuda de EEUU," *Proceso Digital*, August 12, 2012.

49. Office of the Inspectors General, US Department of Justice, US Department of State, *A Special Joint Review of Post-Incident Responses by the Department of State and Drug Enforcement Administration to Three Deadly Force Incidents in Honduras*; Alberto Arce, "DEA agents killed pilot of drug flight in Honduras," Associated Press, July 8, 2012; Alberto Arce and Martha Mendoza, "US suspends anti-drug radar support in Honduras," Associated Press, September 7, 2012; Damien Cave, "US Suspends its Antidrug Radar Sharing with Honduras," *New York Times*, September 7, 2012. See also, "F.F.A.A. respaldan la posición de presidente del Congreso," *La Tribuna*, March 30, 2012; "Fuerzas Armadas de Honduras no puede derribar aviones," *El Heraldo*, March 30, 2012.

50. Damien Cave and Ginger Thompson, "US Rethinks a Drug War After Deaths in Honduras," *New York Times*, October 12, 2012; Arce and Mendoza,

"US suspends anti-drug radar support in Honduras," Damien Cave, "US Suspends its Antidrug Radar Sharing with Honduras."

51. Cave and Thompson, "U.S. Rethinks a Drug War After Deaths in Honduras."

52. Schoolhouse Rock, *I'm Just a Bill*, www.schoolhouserock.tv/Bill.html.

53. Press Release, "South Florida Congress Members on Mission to Honduras," Representative Ileana Ros-Lehtinen, October 5, 2009, ros-lehtinen.house.gov /press-release/south-florida-congress-members-mission-honduras.

54. "Worldwide Threats to Media Freedom," Hearing Before the Tom Lantos Human Rights Commission, House of Representatives, 112th Congress, Second Session, June 25, 2012, humanrightscommission.house.gov/events /hearings/worldwide-threats-media-freedom.

55. Sam Farr and twenty-nine additional members of Congress to Hillary Clinton, October 19, 2010, in possession of the author.

56. For the Honduras Solidarity Network, see *Honduras Resists*, hondurasresists.blogspot.com/#.

57. Sisters of Mercy, "Advocating for Human Rights in Honduras," www.sistersofmercy.org/get-involved/advocate-for-social-justice/advocating -for-human-rights-in-honduras/; see, for example, the report from their December 11–15 delegation to Honduras, *A Furnace of Violence: Honduras, US Policy and the Root Causes of Violence,* Sisters of Mercy/Nicaragua-United States Friendship Office on the Americas, www.sistersofmercy.org/files /images/Justice/Initiative/2015-Honduras-delegation-report—-Eng.pdf.

58. James Parks, "AFL-CIO: Honduras Coup is 'Unconscionable,'" *AFL-CIO blog,* June 30, 2009, reprinted at www.laborstandard.org/New_Postings/Honduras _Update_July_28_2009.htm; "Resolution 40: Resolution on Military Coup in Honduras," September 13, 2009, aflcio.org/resolution/resolution-military -coup-honduras; Emile Schlepers, "AFL-CIO head denounces Honduras elections," *Peoples' World,* November 18, 2018, www.peoplesworld.org/article /afl-cio-head-denounces-honduras-elections/; AFL-CIO, *Trade, Violence, and Migration: The Broken Promises to Honduran Workers,* January 9, 2015, aflcio.org/ sites/default/files/2017-03/Honduras.PDF. For the impressive work of the AFL-CIO's Solidarity Center in Honduras, begin with its website, www.solidaritycenter.org/where-we-work/americas/629-2/; for an example of their work, Tula Connell, "2 More Honduran Union Leaders Threatened, Harassed," www.solidaritycenter.org/2-more-honduran-union-leaders -threatened-harassed/.

59. For LAWG's work on Honduras, see, for example, Lisa Haugaard and Sarah Kinosian, *Honduras: A Government Failing to Protect its People,* Report, Latin American Working Group, February 9, 2015, www.lawg.org/action-center /lawg-blog/69-general/1415-honduras-a-government-failing-to-protect-its -people; Omar Martínez, "LAWG and Other Groups Condemn Repression of Peasant Activists From Bajo Aguán, Honduras," August 31, 2012, lawg.org /action-center/lawg-blog/81-being-better-neighbors-towards-latin-america /1112-lawg-and-other-international-ngos-condemn-repression-of-peasant -activists-from-bajo-aguan-honduras.

60. Testimony of Vicki Gass, and remarks by Gass during the question and answer period (when she argues for the restoration of aid), "Next Steps for Honduras," Hearing, March 18, 2010, House Committee on Foreign Afffairs, Subcommittee on the Western Hemisphere, 111th Congress, Second Session, Serial No. 111-94, (Washington, D.C.: US Government Printing Office, 2010). For a critique of WOLA's role during and after the coup, Adrienne Pine, "WOLA vs. Honduran Democracy," *CounterPunch*, April 12, 2010, www.counterpunch.org/2010/04/12/wola-vs-honduran-democracy. For WOLA and police reform, "Police Reform in Honduras: Stalled Efforts and the Need to Weed Out Corruption," August 26 2013, *WOLA* (blog), www.wola.org/analysis/police-reform-in-honduras-stalled-efforts-and-the -need-to-weed-out-corruption/. For further information on WOLA's work on Honduras, begin at www.wola.org/?s=honduras.

61. Jared Polis and eighty-three additional members of Congress to Hillary Clinton, June 26, 2012, in possession of the author, and press release and letter available at quotha.net/docs/honduras/6.26.12.Honduras_LGBT _letter_press_release.pdf.

62. "Rep. Johnson, 57 Colleagues Call for Investigation into DEA-related killings in Honduras," January 30, 2013, hankjohnson.house.gov/media -center/press-releases/rep-johnson-57-colleagues-call-investigation-dea -related-killings. (Sascha Thompson has subsequently changed to her name to Sascha Foertsch.)

63. Howard L. Berman to Hillary Clinton, November 28, 2011, in possession of the author.

64. Howard L. Berman to Hillary Clinton, October 2, 2013, in possession of the author.

65. Barbara Mikulski and six additional senators to Hillary Clinton, March 5, 2012, available through a link in Alexander Main, "Twenty-one Senators Ask Kerry to Conduct at 'Thorough Review' of Security Assistance to Honduras," *CEPR Americas Blog*, June 19, 2013, cepr.net/blogs/the-americas -blog/twenty-one-us-senators-ask-kerry-to-conduct-thorough-review -of-security-assistance-to-honduras; Press Release, "Cardin Leads Senate Call for Accountability in Honduras for Human Rights Violations," Press Release, June 18, 2013, www.cardin.senate.gov/newsroom/press/release /cardin-leads-senate-call-for-accountability-in-honduras-for-human -rights-violations.

66. Email, Tim Rieser to the author, December 3, 2011.

67. United States Congress, Consolidated Appropriations Act, 2012, PL 112-74, Section 7041(d) and Conference Report, to Accompany HR 2055, Sections 7045(d), available at www.congress.gov/congressional-report/112th-congress /house-report/331/1?q=%7B%22search%22%3A%5B%22pl+112-74%22 %5D%7D.

68. Cave and Thompson, "US Rethinks a Drug War After Deaths in Honduras."

69. "Intervención de AJD en la audiencia de la CIDH del 31 de Octobre de 2012 sobre fortalecimiento del SIDH," Association of Honduran Judges

for Democracy, October 31, 2012, in possession of the author; "Audiencia
a la sociedad civil sobre el proceso de fortalecimiento del SIDH," October
31, 2012, Inter-American Commission on Human Rights/Organization of
American States, www.oas.org/es/cidh/fortalecimiento/audienciaSC.asp.

Chapter Four

1. Portions of this account appeared in Dana Frank, "How Low Can Honduras
   Go?" *TheNation.com,* October 15, 2012.
2. Alberto Arce, "Slain Honduran lawyer complained of death threats,"
   Associated Press, September 25, 2012.
3. "Extienden por seis meses el decreto de emergencia de seguridad," *El Tiempo,*
   September 26, 2012; "Honduras crime: Soldiers deployed on public buses," *BBC
   News,* September 28, 2012, www.bbc.com/news/world-latin-america-19768043;
   Hannah Stone, "Honduras Uses Security Tax to Send Army to City Streets,"
   InSight Crime, February 12, 2013, www.insightcrime.org/news-briefs/honduras
   -security-tax-army-capital. Security tax: República de Honduras, *La Gaceta,*
   January 25, 2012, www.tasadeseguridad.hn/_assets/docs/Reglamento-de-la
   -Ley-de-Seguridad-Poblacional.pdf; "Honduras: Tasón de seguridad tendrá
   vigencia por 10 años más," *La Prensa,* December 17, 2013. For an historical
   analysis by eminent Honduran sociologist Leticia Salomón, including the
   military's long desire to have the police under military control, see "Están
   retomando esquema militarista de la seguridad," *El Tiempo,* May 7, 2013. For a
   summary of the constitutional issues, "Military Policing," *Honduras Culture and
   Politics,* November 17, 2011, hondurasculturepolitics.blogspot.com/2011/11
   /military-policing.html.
4. "Militarization Ramped up in Honduras," *Honduras Accompaniment Project,*
   April 1, 2013, hondurasaccompanimentproject.wordpress.com/2013/04/01
   /militarization-ramped-up-in-honduras/; Email, Jennifer Atlee to the
   author, July 7, 2017.
5. "'Tigres' Are Honduras' New Battalion 3-16," July 12, 2012, *Upside Down
   World,* August 1, 2012, upsidedownworld.org/news-briefs/news-briefs
   -news-briefs/qtigresq-are-honduras-new-battalion-3-16/. The Tigres
   proposal would ultimately be approved by the Honduran Congress on June
   5, 2013; "En tercer y últimos debate CN aprueba unidad Tigres," *Proceso
   Digital,* June 5, 2013, www.proceso.hn/component/k2/item/20202.html.
6. Charles Parkinson, "Honduras Congress Votes for Military Police Force,"
   InSight Crime, August 17, 2013, www.insightcrime.org/news-briefs/honduras
   -congress-votes-for-military-police-force; Marguerite Cawley, "Honduras
   Gives Green Light to Military Police, *InSight Crime,* August 23, 2013,
   www.insightcrime.org/news-briefs/honduras-gives-green-light-to-military
   -police.
7. 18 U.S. Code § 1385 (1878).
8. Alberto Arce, "Dad seeks justice for son slain in broken Honduras,"
   Associated Press, November 12, 2012.
9. Amnesty International, Urgent Action, "Army Fires on Protesters in

Honduras," *Amnesty International*, July 23, 2013, www.amnestyusa.org/files
/uaa18813.pdf.

10. "Sisma entre Defensa y Seguridad," *El Heraldo*, May 6, 2013; "Marlon Pascua
dice que no acatará ordenes de Corrales," *El Tiempo*, May 6, 2013.

11. "Tres militares asume altos cargos en seguridad," *La Tribuna*, May 3, 2012.

12. "Comunicado, Movimiento Unificado Campesino del Aguán," November
11, 2012, in possession of the author; Bird, *Human Rights Violations Attributed to
Military Forces in the Bajo Aguán*, 32; Bird, *Petición ante la Comission Internacional
de Derechos Humanos*, 85.

13. COFADEH, "Secuestran por varias horas a Karla Zelaya, periodista de
MUCA," *Defensores en Linea*, October 2012, defensoresenlinea.com
/cms/?option=com_content&view=article&id=2293:secuestran-por-varias
-horas-a-karla-zelaya-periodista-de-muca&catid=71:def&Itemid=166;
translated as "MUCA Journalist Karla Zelaya Kidnapped for Hours," *Quotha*,
October 24, 2012, quotha.net/node/2396.

14. Tracy Wilkinson, "In Honduras a Controversial Tycoon Responds to
Critics," *Los Angeles Times*, December 21, 2012.

15. Press Release, "Honduras Must Investigate Killing of Murdered Activist's
Brother," *Amnesty International*, February 21, 2013, www.amnesty.org
/en/press-releases/2013/02/honduras-must-investigate-killing-murdered
-activist-s-brother/.

16. "Comunicado," COFADEH, November 23, 2012, in possession of the author;
Dina Meza, *Kidnapped: Censorship in Honduras*, transl. Jill Powis (Amsterdam:
Evatas Foundation, 2015).

17. For Battalion 3-16 and the US role in support of it, see the 1995 four-part
series in the *Baltimore Sun* by Ginger Thompson and Gary Cohn, "A Carefully
Crafted Deception," June 18, 1995; "A Survivor Tells Her Story," June 15,
1995; "Torturers' Confessions," June 13, 1005; "Unearthed: Fatal Secrets,"
June 11 1995.

18. This story is recounted with permission from Fr. Ismael Moreno, SJ (Padre
Melo).

19. For summaries, see Yanina Parada, "Marlon Escoto y su desempeño como
ministro de Secretaría de Educación," *Criterio*, January 10, 2017,
criterio.hn/2017/01/10/marlon-escoto-desempeno-ministro-la-secretaria
-educacion/; "Las facturas no pagadas de Marlon Escoto," *El Pulso*, January 8,
2017, elpulso.hn/las-facturas-no-pagadas-de-marlon-escoto/.

20. Meza, *Kidnapped*, 59.

21. "Alcaldía inicia recuperación del parque de San Pedro Sula," *La Prensa*,
December 18, 2012.

22. "LIBRE: Libertad y Refundación: Declaration of Principles," reprinted at
Honduras Culture and Politics, hondurasculturepolitics.blogspot.com/p
/libre-libertad-y-refundacion.html; Tyler A. Shipley, *Ottawa and Empire*,
87–88; Ismael Moreno, SJ, "The country that gave birth to the new LIBRE
party," *Envío*, no. 373, August 2012, www.envio.org.ni/articulo/4575; Dawn
Paley, "In Honduras Election, the People's Will is Hushed but Not Silenced,

The Nation, December 10, 2013; Phillips, *Honduras in Dangerous Times*, 241.

23. "Asesinan a alcalde de MRP," *El Tiempo*, November 3, 2012; Karen Spring, "Context of the Honduran Electoral Process 2012-2013: Incomplete List of Killings and Armed Attacks Related to Political Campaigning in Honduras," May 2012 to October 19, 2013, *Rights Action*, October 21, 2013, rightsaction .org/sites/default/files/Honduras-Violence-Political-Campaign.pdf.

24. "Honduras: Smears Put Activists at Risk," *Human Rights Watch*, November 8, 2013, www.hrw.org/news/2013/11/08/honduras-smears-put-activists-risk; "Diputado lamenta que Libre desprestigie Policía Militar," *La Prensa*, November 13, 2013; "Lobo critica a malos hondureños que quieren despre-tigiar el proceso electoral en el exterior," *Proceso Digital*, November 14, 2013, www.proceso.hn/component/k2/item/11974.html.

25. For a positive summary of the Stein commission's history and related documents and reports, see "Truth Commission: Honduras, 2010," *United States Institute of Peace*, February 9, 2012, www.usip.org/publications /2012/02/truth-commission-honduras-2010.

26. Comisión de Verdad, *The Voice of Greatest Authority Is That of the Victims.* While the commission's report did not have the powerful impact its authors had hoped for, it remains a rich, painstakingly documented source for the historical record.

27. "TSE declara a ganadores de elecciones internas," *El Heraldo*, December 9, 2012.

28. Portions of this account originally appeared in Dana Frank, "Hernández's Election Was Built on Corruption," *Houston Chronicle*, January 26, 2014.

29. Comisión de la Verdad y Reconciliación (CRV), *Para que los hechos no se repitan: Informe de la Comisión de la Verdad y la Reconciliación* I, 145n48; volume II, 639, 640, 641, 642, 643 and 649–653. My thanks to Darío Euraque for research support on this issue.

30. Cable, US Embassy, Tegucigalpa, "Subject: National Congress Chooses Provisional Executive Board," January 22, 2010, wikileaks.org/plusd/cables /10TEGUCIGALPA58_a.html. For his official biography, see Government of Honduras, "Juan Orlando Hernández," www.presidencia.gob.hn /index.php/gob/el-presidente/biografia2.

31. "Inconstitucional decreto de 'ciudades modelo,'" *El Heraldo*, October 18, 2012; Alberto Arce, "Honduran supreme court rejects 'model cities' idea," Associated Press, October 18, 2012, newsarchive.ohchr.org/SP/NewsEvents /Pages/DisplayNews.aspx?NewsID=12958&LangID=S.

32. "Police Clean Up Law Appears Unconstitutional," *Honduras Culture and Politics*, November 28, 2012, hondurasculturepolitics.blogspot.com /2012/11/police-clean-up-law-appears.html?m=0.

33. For a summary, "Ducktatorship in Honduras," *Honduras Culture and Politics*, December 15, 2012, hondurasculturepolitics.blogspot.com/search?q =primary+alvarez.

34. "Congeso de Honduras asesta golpe técnico a la CSJ," *El Heraldo*, December 12, 2012; "Oposición hondureña tilda de golpe ténico destución de cuatro magistrados," *La Tribuna*, December 12, 2012; Annie Bird, "The December

12, 2012 'Coup' in Honduras: The Constitutional Court Dismissed as Primary Elections are Challenge," *Rights Action,* January 8, 2013, www.rightsaction.org /action-content/december-12-2012-coup-honduras-constitutional-court -dismissed-primary-elections-are. For disturbing US press coverage casting Lobo in a heroic role, see Christina Costantini, "Honduran President Fears Coup, Four Supreme Court Judges Fired," ABC News.com, December 12, 2012, abcnews.go.com/ABC_Univision/News/honduran-congress-fires -supreme-court-judges/story?id=1794442. For a response from the United Nations, Office of the High Commissioner on Human Rights, Comunicado de Prensa, "Grave atentado a la democracia en Honduras la destitución de magistrados de la Sala Constitucional," January 29, 2013, newsarchive.ohchr .org/SP/NewsEvents/Pages/DisplayNews.aspx?NewsID=12958&LangID=S.

35. "El congreso juramenta al cuarto magistrado de sala constitucional," *El Tiempo,* December 20 2012.

36. Inter-American Court of Human Rights, "Case of López Lone et al. v. Honduras, Judgement of October 5, 2015," www.corteidh.or.cr/docs/casos /articulos/seriec_302_ing.pdf; Press release, "IACHR Takes Case Involving Honduras to the Inter-American Court," Inter-American Commission on Human Rights, April 2, 2012, www.oas.org/en/iachr/media_center/preleases /2014/032.asp. For background, Dana Frank, "The Long Judicial Arm of the Honduran Coup," *Huffington Post,* February 4, 2015, www.huffingtonpost.com /dana-frank/the-long-judicial-arm-of-_b_6606416.html.

37. Marguerite Cawley, "Honduras Attorney General Resigns After Pressure From Congress," *InSight Crime,* June 28, 2013, www.insightcrime.org/news -briefs/honduras-attorney-general-resigns.

38. For the illegality of the five-year term, Tirza Flores Lanza, "Testimony of Ms. Tirza Flores Lanza, Tom Lantos Human Rights Commission," Hearing, Tom Lantos Human Rights Commission, "Human Rights in Honduras," July 25, 2013, humanrightscommission.house.gov/sites/humanrightscommission.house.gov /files/documents/Tirza%20Flores%20Lanza%20testimony_ESP.pdf. For the the selection procedures, "Honduras Wants a New Public Prosecutor in the Worst Way Possible," *Honduras Culture and Politics,* September 2, 2013, hondurasculturepolitics.blogspot.com/2013/09/honduras-has-new-public -prosecutorthe.html.

39. "JOH se despide de Congreso para dedicarse a su campaña," *Proceso Digital,* June 13, 2013, www.proceso.hn/component/k2/item/19771.

40. C-Libre Alerta 00067-2013, "Acéfala la Fiscalía de Derechos Humanos en Honduras," *C-Libre,* September 28, 2013, www.clibrehonduras.com/alerta /ac%C3%A9fala-la-fiscal%C3%ADa-de-derechos-humanos-en-honduras.

41. United States Department of State, Maria Otero, "Remarks at the Opening of the Bilateral Human Rights Working Group," September 13, 2012, 2009- 2017.state.gov/j/197775.htm.

42. "Acuerdo de seguridad ciudadana Honduras EUA," *El Heraldo,* September 13, 2012; "Honduras y EEUU firman convenio de seguridad ciudadana y fortalecimiento de DDHH," *El Tiempo,* September 13, 2012.

43. "Las elecciones son el momento para exigir a candidatos planes de trabajo," *El Tiempo*, November 12, 2012.

44. "US Embassy Weighs in on Firing of Justices—Sort of," *Honduras Culture and Politics*, December 26, 2012, hondurasculturepolitics.blogspot.com /2012/12/us-embassy-weighs-in-on-firing-of.html. The statement is also quoted in part in Alberto Arce, "Honduran congress dismisses Supreme Court justices," Associated Press, December 12, 2012, establishing that the statement was not, as reported, issued a week later.

45. Press Statement, US Embassy, Tegucigalpa, "Subject: National Congress Chooses Provisional Executive Board," January 22, 2010.

46. For funding levels that are publicly available, see *Security Assistance Monitor* (blog), securityassistance.org/data/program/military/Honduras/.

47. Martha Mendoza, "US military expands its drug war in Latin America," Associated Press, February 3, 2013.

48. Damien Cave, "As U.S. Shares Intelligence with Honduras, Other Antidrug Aid Stays Frozen," *New York Times*, November 27, 2012.

49. "Difícil lograr compacto de la MCC," *El Heraldo*, November 9, 2012.

50. News Release, "IDB lends $60 million to Honduras for violence prevention and criminal investigation program," Inter-American Development Bank, June 21, 2012, www.iadb.org/en/news/news-releases/2012-06-21/crime -reduction-and-public-safety-in-honduras,10038.html.

51. Alberto Arce, "Honduras police accused of death squad killings," Associated Press, March 17, 2013.

52. United States Department of State, "Report on the Government of Honduras' Protection of Human Rights and the Investigation and Prosecution of Security Services Personnel Credibly Alleged to Have Violated Human Rights," August 8, 2012, in possession of the author, reprinted at securityassistance.org/sites/default/files/120808hn.pdf.

53. Alberto Arce and Katherine Cocoran, "US aids Honduran police despite death squad fears," Associated Press, March 23, 2013.

54. United States Department of State, Daily Press Briefing, March 25, 2013, 2009-2017.state.gov/r/pa/prs/dpb/2013/03/206637.htm; and March 27, 2013, 2009-2017.state.gov/r/pa/prs/dpb/2013/03/206713.htm.

55. US Embassy, Tegucigalpa, cable from Ambassador Larry Palmer, "Anti-Corruption in Honduras—Is Ricardo Maduro Willing to Follow Through with More Than Just Rhetoric?" Wikileaks, September 26, 2003, cables.mrkva.eu/ cable.php?id=5967.

56. Katherine Corcoran and Martha Mendoza, "New Honduras top cop once investigated in killings," Associated Press, June 1, 2012.

57. For a sympathetic summary of Brownfield's career at the time of his retirement from the State Department in September 2017, Nick Miroff, "For veteran drug warrior and diplomat, retirement comes with tinge of regret," *Washington Post*, September 17, 2017. On Venezuela, Al Kamen and Colby Itkowitz, "William Brownfield doesn't enjoy discussing those tough years in Venezuela," *Washington Post*, May 21, 2014.

58. "Estados Unidos apoyará a policía Hondureña pero ignorará a su director," *El Universal*, March 28, 2013; Arce and Corcoran, "US aids Honduran police despite death squad fears"; "Zar antidrogas de Estados Unidos reitera que seguirá apoyando proceso de depuración de la Policía hondureña," *Proceso Digital*, March 28, 2013, www.proceso.hn/nacionales/9-nacionales/Zar -antidrogas-de-Estados-Unidos-reitera-que-seguir%C3%A1-apoyando -proceso-de-depuraci%C3%B3n-de-la-Polic%C3%ADa-hondure%C3 %B1a.html; transcript, LiveAtState press conference, US Department of State, March 28, 2013, in posession of the author.

59. "Hay mucho que hacer en depuración policial," *El Heraldo*, April 4, 2013.

60. "EEUU alaba el trabajo del 'Tigre' Bonilla."

61. "Escalofriante: Fiscal admite que el 80 por ciento de los delitos queda im- pune," *Proceso Digital*, April 10, 2013, www.proceso.hn/component/k2/item /23025.html.

62. "Altos oficiales de las FFAA acusados en los tribunales por muerte de un menor," *Proceso Digital*, April 11, 2013, www.proceso.hn/component/k2 /item/22983.html.

63. "Funcionarios y empresarios participan en narcoactividad," *El Tiempo*, April 11, 2013; Press Release, "Treasury Designates Honduran Drug Traffickers," United States Department of the Treasury, April 9, 2013, www.treasury.gov /press-center/press-releases/Pages/jl1888.aspx.

64. Russell Sheptak, "US suspends aid to Honduras police cleanup," *Christian Science Monitor*, June 6, 2013, www.csmonitor.com/World/Americas/Latin-America -Monitor/2013/0606/US-suspends-aid-to-Honduras-police-cleanup; "Fiscal acusa a doce policías," *La Prensa*, April 10, 2013.

65. "EEUU alaba el trabajo del 'Tigre' Bonilla."

66. "A FFAA les preocupa rezago en armanento," *La Tribuna*, May 14, 2013.

67. "Suspenden a todo el personal de la DNIC por sospechas: Secretaria de Seguridad," *El Tiempo*, June 6, 2013.

68. "Policia cero muertes realidad 12 muertos," *El Tiempo*, May 14, 2013.

69. Benjamin Cardin and twenty additional senators to John Kerry, June 18, 2013, Press release, senator Bejamin Cardin, "Cardin Leads Senate Call for Accountability in Honduras for Human Rights Violations," June 18, 2013, www.cardin.senate.gov/newsroom/press/release/cardin-leads-senate -call-for-accountability-in-honduras-for-human-rights-violations.

70. Amnesty International, "Declaración pública," "Honduras: Amnistía Internacional condena los recientes asesinatos de personas que defienden la justicia, la igualdad y los derechos humanos," July 29, 2013, AMR No. 37/007/2013; International Commission of Jurists, "La CIJ condena asesinato de la jueza Mireya Mendoza Peña en Honduras," July 27, 2012, www.icj.org /la-cij-condena-asesinato-de-la-jueza-mireya-mendoza-pena-en-honduras/.

71. Embassy official to the author, July 24, 2013.

72. "Public Clarification of the Circumstances Surrounding the Abduction of Two Observers from PROAH in La Nueva Esperanza," *Honduras Accompaniment Project*, November 15, 2013, hondurasaccompanimentproject.wordpress.com/2013/11

/15/public-clarification-of-the-circumstances-surrounding-the-abduction-of
-two-observers-from-proah-in-la-nueva-esperanza-2/; Amnesty International,
"Honduras: human rights activists abducted in Honduras," July 30, 2013, AMR
No. 37/008/2013, www.amnesty.org/en/documents/AMR37/008/2013/en/.

73. Stephen Posivak to the author, email, August 29, 2013.

74. Alberto Arce, "Top cop is US go-to man in Honduras for war on drugs,
denies death squad charge," Associated Press, November 1, 2013.

75. Suyapa Portillo Villeda, "Honduras on the Brink of Change," *CounterPunch*,
September 13, 2013, www.counterpunch.org/2013/09/13/honduras-on-the
-brink-of-change/; Nina Lakhani, "Honduras elections: Leftist party
challenges right's grip on power," *The Guardian*, November 22, 2013; Paley,
"In Honduras Election, the People's Will is Hushed but Not Silenced"; Dana
Frank, "A High-Stakes Election in Honduras," *The Nation*, November 6, 2013.

76. For a thorough summary and analysis of the polling data over time, see,
"Polling, polling, polling," *Honduras Culture and Politics*, August 29, 2013,
hondurasculturepolitics.blogspot.com/2013/08/polling-polling-polling.
html; "Last Polls in Honduran Presidential Election: Dead Heat," October
24, 2013, hondurasculturepolitics.blogspot.com/search?q=last+polls; see
additional articles throughout 2013.

77. Frank, "A High-Stakes Election in Honduras."

78. "Presidenciable nacionalista aboga por un militar en cada esquina hasta
recuperar la paz," *Proceso Digital,* July 15, 2013, www.proceso.hn/component
/k2/item/18086.html. For an overall analysis of the militarization, Dana
Frank, "In Honduras, Military Takes Over with U.S. Blessing," *Miami Herald,*
September 11, 2013.

79. "Juan Orlando manda a diputados ratificar policía militar con cinco mil
soldados," *El Tiempo,* July 31, 2013; "Congreso Nacional aprueba decreto que
crea la Policía Militar," *Proceso Digital,* August 22, 2013,www.proceso.hn
/component/k2/item/16204.html; "Policía Militar a las calles mañana," *El
Heraldo,* November 3, 2013.

80. "Alegres los diputados aprueban compra de mil millones de cemento," *Proceso
Digital,* March 19, 2013, www.proceso.hn/component/k2/item/24029.html.

81. "Entrega de bono Diez mil se convierte en propaganda política," *Radio Progreso,*
November 18, 2013, reprinted at honduprensa.wordpress.com/2013
/11/18/entrega-de-bono-diez-mil-se-convierte-en-propaganda-politica/. For
a longer-term analysis of the Bono de Diez Mil, see "Un gran proyecto
con millones de incautos," *Radio Progreso y ERIC,* September 7, 2016,
radioprogresohn.net/index.php/comunicaciones/nuestra-palabra/item
/3157-un-gran-proyecto-con-millones-de-incautos-07-septiembre-2016.

82. Karen Spring, *Context of the Honduran Electoral Process 2012-2013: Incomplete List
of Killings and Armed Attacks Related to Political Campaigning in Honduras,* May
2012 to October 19, 2013, *Rights Action,* October 21, 2013 (Washington D.C.:
Rights Action, 2013).

83. Raúl M. Grijalva, Hank Johnson, and Michael Honda to John Kerry, October
15, 2013, available at grijalva.house.gov/press-releases/reps-grijalva

-honda-hank-johnson-urge-secretary-kerry-to-speak-against-militarization
-of-civil-society-ahead-of-honduran-election/.

84. Tim Kaine and 12 additional senators to John Kerry, November 13, 2013,
Press Release, "In letter to Secretary Kerry, Kaine calls for free and fair
elections in Honduras," November 13, 2013, democrats-foreignaffairs
.house.gov/news/press-releases/engel-speech-council-americas-upcoming
-elections-central-america.

85. Press Release, "Engel Speech at Council of Americas on Upcoming Elections
in Central America," United States House of Representatives Committee on
Foreign Affairs, November 13, 2013, democrats-foreignaffairs.house.gov
/news/press-releases/engel-speech-council-americas-upcoming
-elections-central-america.

86. "Kubiske: Ojalá que las elecciones sean tan limpias como a todos les gustaría,"
Proceso Digital, November 3, 2013, ww.proceso.hn/component/k2/item
/12529.html.

87. "Kubiske dice que 'es probable' que resultados electorales no se obtengan la
misma noche," *Proceso Digital*, November 8, 2013, www.proceso.hn/component
/k2/item/12529.html; Lisa Kubiske, "El poder de voto es de ustedes," *El
Heraldo*, November 8, 2013.

88. Sandra Cuffe, "Policía Militar intenta centrar a la sede de LIBRE de la
Colonia Kennedy," *HonduPrensa* (blog) November 23, 2013, honduprens
a.wordpress.com/2013/11/23/policia-militar-intenta-entrar-a-la-sede-de
-libre-de-la-colonia-kennedy/.

89. COFADEH, "Alerta: Asunto, Mesa de Análisis sobre grave situación de
derechos humanos este domingo en las eleccciones," Proyecto Monitoreo
de Derechos Humanos en el Proceso Electoral 2014, November 24, 2013, in
possession of the author.

90. "Simpatizantes de Libre mueren en emboscada," *La Prensa*, November 24, 2013.

91. "Alerta: Radio Globo, TV Globo y Cholusat Sur denuncian censura con
firma de protocol moral previo a las eleccciones," Movimiento Amplio por la
Dignidad y Justicia, November 23 2013, in possession of the author.

92. COFADEH, "Alerta: Agentes del Estado Hondureño hostigan e intimidan a
observadores internacionales de DDHH," Proyecto Monitoreo de Derechos
Humanos en el Proceso Electoral, 2013, November 22, 2013, in possession of
the author.

93. "Escalation in Intimidation Towards Election Observers and Accompaniers
in Honduras," *Rights Action*, November 23, 2013, reposted at:
www.hondurassolidarity.org/2013/11/23/alarming-escalation-in-the
-intimidation-towards-international-election-observers-and-accompaniers
-in-honduras/.

94. For a summary, see Lisa Haugaard, "Honduras Elections: No Cause for
Celebrations," *Latin America Working Group* (blog), December 6, 2013, reprinted at: www.huffingtonpost.com/lisa-haugaard/honduran-elections-no-cause
-for-celebration_b_4384713.htmlr; FIDH (Federación Internacional de
Derechos Humanos), "International Mission of FIDH with the Support of

CIPRODEH on the Honduran Elections," December 20, 2013, www.fidh .org/en/region/americas/honduras/14429-international-mission-of-fidh -with-the-support-of-ciprodeh-on-the-honduran.

95. European Union Election Observation, Honduras, General Elections—24 November 2013, "Preliminary Statement: Transparent voting and counting after an unequal and opaque campaign," Tegucigalpa, November 26, 2013. For the final report in February 2014, European Union Election Observation Mission, Honduras 2014, Honduras, *Final Report on the General Elections*, 2013, February 13, 2014, www.eods.eu/library/EUEOM%20FR%20 HONDURAS13.02.2014_en.pdf.

96. Giorgio Trucchi, "The Results of the Elections in Honduras Were Changed, Says European Union Observer," transl. Adrienne Pine, *Upside Down World*, November 29, 2013, upsidedownworld.org/archives/honduras/the-results-of -the-elections-in-honduras-were-changed-says-european-union-observer; also quoted in Mark Weisbrot, "Why the world should care about Honduras' recent election," *The Guardian*, December 3, 2013.

97. Nicholas Phillips and Elisabeth Malkin, "Honduras Election Results Challenged," *New York Times*, November 20, 2013.

98. Ibid.

99. Ibid.

100. Jeremy Relph and Dominic Bracco II, "Postcard from Honduras: On the Eve of the Election," *The New Yorker*, November 23, 2013.

101. Dana Frank, "Honduras Gone Wrong," *Foreign Affairs*, October 16, 2012, www .foreignaffairs.com/articles/americas/2012-10-16/honduras-gone-wrong.

102. Nick Miroff, "Honduras election brings risks of more instability," *Washington Post*, November 23, 2013.

103. "Embajadora Kubske visita a sala de cómputo de TSE y asegura que todo 'es normal y transparente,'" *Proceso Digital*, December 5, 2013, www.proceso .hn/politica/item/10924-Embajadora-Kubiske-visita-sala-de-c%C3 %B3mputo-del-TSE-y-asegura-que-todo-%E2%80%9Ces-normal-y -transparente%E2%80%9D.html; "Kubiske califica como normal y tranpar-ente revisión de actas," *El Heraldo*, December 5, 2013.

104. "Embajadora Kubiske visita a sala de cómputo de TSE."

105. Government of Honduras, Tribunal Supremo Electoral, *La Gaceta*, Acuerdo no. 12-2013, December 12, 2013, www.tse.hn/WEB/documentos/Acu-2013 /Acuerdo%20No.%20012-2013_LG-Decla-01.PDF.

106. Government of Honduras, Tribunal Supremo Electoral, "Declaratoria de ciudadanos(as) electados(as) al cargo de diputados al Parlamento Centroamericano, Diputados al Congreso Nacional, y corporaciones municipales, eleccciones generales 2013," *La Gaceta*, Acuerdo No. 13-1013, December 13, www.tse.hn/WEB/documentos/Acu-2013/Acuerdo%20 No.%20013-2013_LG-Decla-02.PDF.

107. United States Department of State, Press Statement, Secretary John Kerry, "Honduras Elections," December 12, 2013, 2009-2017.state.gov/secretary /remarks/2013/12/218646.htm.

108. For the concept and history of "demonstration elections," see Edward S. Herman and Frank Broadhead, *Demonstration Elections: U.S.-Stage Elections in the Dominican Republic, Vietnam, and El Salvador* (Cambridge, MA: South End Press, 1984).

109. "Honduras fires top cop dogged by death squad claim," Associated Press, December 20, 2013; "Ruedan las cabezas de jefes militar y policías," *Proceso Digital*, December 19, 2013, www.proceso.hn/component/k2/item/10226.html.

110. "Masiva approbación de contratos y decretos," *El Heraldo,* January 20, 2014; "Honduras: Congreso hondureño cierra legislativa con aprobación de leyes lesiva para el pueblo," *El Libertador,* January 22, 2014, honduprensa.wordpress .com/2014/01/20/congreso-hondureno-cierra-legislatura-con-aprobacion -de-leyes-lesivas-para-el-pueblo/; Sandra Cuffe, "Congress' Last Stand: Privatizations among New Laws in Honduras," *Upside Down World,* January 28, 2014, upsidedownworld.org/archives/honduras/congress-last-stand -privatizations-among-new-laws-in-honduras/; Paola Nalvarte, "Honduran Secrecy Law endangers access to public information: RSF," *Journalism in the Americas* (blog), Knight Center for Journalism in the Americas, January 21, 2014; "Honduran Congress ends mining projects moratorium," Reuters, January 24, 2014, www.reuters.com/article/honduras-mining/honduran-congress -ends-mining-projects-moratorium-idUSL1N0AT9EF20130124.

111. For the history and dynamics of the US breeding loyalty from Latin American police and military, see two superb analyses: Martha K. Huggins, *Political Policing: The United States and Latin America* (Chapel Hill: University of North Carolina Press, 1998) and Lesley Gill, *The School of the Americas: Military Training and Political Violence in the Americas* (Chapel Hill, NC: Duke University Press, 2004).

112. For the CRSP, "Comisión de Reforma a la Seguridad Pública nació destinada a fracasar," *Radio Progreso y ERIC,* January 31, 2014, radioprogresohn.net /index.php/comunicaciones/noticias/item/665-comisi%C3%B3n-de -seguridad-p%C3%BAblica-naci%C3%B3-destinada-a-fracasar; "L. 30 millones tirados a la basura en reformas a la seguridad pública que JOH ni leyó," *Criterio,* April 19, 2016, 0.0.7.224/04/19/l-30-millones-tirados -la-basura-reformas-la-seguridad-publica-joh-leyo/; "'Planchón del Congreso en disolución de la CRSP," *El Heraldo,* January 22, 2014; "Depuración policial un fracaso más de Pepe Lobo," *Revistazo,* January 22, 2014, 0.0.7.224/04 /19/l-30-millones-tirados-la-basura-reformas-la-seguridad-publica-joh-leyo/; Interview by the author with Matías Funes, January 30, 2014.

113. For photographs of empty seats in the stadium, see Adrienne Pine's analysis and clips, "Juan Orlando's inauguration: Stadium empty, streets full. A photo-essay," *Quotha,* January 28, 2014, quotha.net/node/2626.

114. "Medirán impacto de reformas al 'paquetazo,'" *El Heraldo,* January 28, 2014. "Partido Liberal logra revisar el 'paquetazo' sin recurrir a la anarquía y al caos," *El Heraldo,* January 2, 2014.

115. For an early analysis of machinations, Ismael Moreno, SJ, "Will the bipartite system get the opposition back under control?" *Envío,* no. 393 (April 2014),

www.envio.org.ni/articulo/4838. For an overview, Giorgio Trucchi, "Los 100 días de Juan Orlando Hernández y la creciento militarización de Honduras," *Resumen Latinamericano,* May 5, 2014, www.resumenlatinoamericano.org/2014 /05/07/los-100-dias-de-juan-orlando-hernandez-y-la-creciente-militarizacion -de-honduras/. For media coverage, e.g. "Diputados de Libre protagonizan nueva protesta en Congreso de Honduras," *El Heraldo,* May 7, 2014.

116. "TVC Tomas de posesión—Juan Orlando Hernández discurso presidencial," January 27, *Televicentro HN,* posted at www.youtube.com/watch?v =tkYwoFp6_pM; "JOH anuncia que tigres entrance en funcion hoy," *La Tribuna,* January 27, 2014.

117. "Inauguran programa 'Guardianes de la Patria,'" *La Tribuna,* March 29, 2014. For the image of the children crawling under barbed wire, see "Movimiento mundial por la infancia pide revisar programa 'Guardianes de la Patria,'" *Presencia Universitaria* (blog), May 16, 2014, presencia.unah.edu.hn/seguridad /articulo/movimiento-mundial-por-la-infancia-pide-revisar-programa -guardianes-de-la-patria. For tree planting, Government of Honduras, Secretaría de Defensa, "Guardianes del la Patria al cuidado del medio ambiente," May 26, 2016, sedena.gob.hn/2016/05/26/guardianes-del-la -patria-al-cuidado-del-medio-ambiente/.

118. AFL-CIO, *Trade, Violence, and Migration,* 13; "Ya trabajan 300 jóvenes 'Con Chamba vivís mejor,'" *La Prensa,* February 4, 2014.

119. Press Release, "Honduras: Special Investigative Unit for Bajo Aguán Crimes," *Human Rights Watch,* March 6, 2014, www.hrw.org/news/2014/03/06/honduras -special-investigative-unit-bajo-aguan-crimes.

120. See "NGO Purge," *Honduras Culture and Politics,* March 9, 2014, for a summary as well as links to the laws themselves, hondurasculturepolitics .blogspot.com/2014/03/ngo-purge.html.

121. Amnesty International USA, Urgent Action, "Children's Rights Defender Beaten, Detained," UA 122/4, May 12 2014, www.amnesty.org.uk/blogs /childrens-human-rights-network/childrens-rights-defender-hondu- ras-beaten-detained; "Case History: Guadalupe Ruelas García," *Front Line Defenders,* 2014, www.frontlinedefenders.org/en/case/case-history-jose -guadalupe-ruelas-garcia; "Beating and arbitrary detention of children's rights defender Mr José Guadalupe Ruelas," *Honduras Accompaniment Project,* March 2014, hondurasaccompanimentproject.wordpress.com/2014 /05/15/beating-and-arbitrary-detention-of-childrens-rights-defender -mr-jose-guadalupe-ruelas/; "Director de Casa Alianza en Honduras denuncia supuesta golpiza por policias," *La Prensa,* May 9, 2012; "Se agranda escándolo del director de Casa Alianza," *La Prensa,* May 12, 2014.

122. Marvin Palacios, "La orden desde el Congreso Nacional fue reprimir toda acción de la oposición," *Defensores en Linea,* May 13, 2014, reposted at hondu- prensa.wordpress.com/2014/05/13/la-orden-desde-el-congreso-nacional-fue -reprimir-toda-accion-de-la-oposicion/. For video images, see www.youtube .com/watch?v=1C2cQQOeqxo&feature=youtu.be&app=desktop; *Univision,* May 13, 2014. For media coverage, e.g.: "Diputados de Libre encabezan acto

bochornoso en el Congreso Nacional," *El Heraldo*, May 14, 2014.

123. "'Lucha de Honduras contra el narcotráfico es impresionante,'" *La Prensa*, June 2, 2014.

124. "Realizan Foro de DDHH en Honduras," *El Heraldo*, April 29, 2014.

125. Elisabeth Malkin, "Lawmakers Ask State Department to Review Support for Honduras," *New York Times*, May 29, 2014, www.nytimes.com/2014 /05/29/world/americas/lawmakers-ask-state-dept-to-review-support-for -honduras.html?_r=0. For the letter itself, Press Release, "More than 100 Members of Congress Urge Action on Human Rights in Honduras," May 28, 2014, schakowsky.house.gov/press-releases/more-than-100-members -of-congress-urge-action-on-human-rights-in-honduras/.

126. United States Senate Committee on Foreign Relations, Hearing, "Nominations: Ambassadors to Qatar, Iraq, and Honduras," June 22, 2014, www.foreign.senate.gov/hearings/nominations-ambassadors-to-qatar -iraq-and-honduras-06-11-14a.

127. For FESTAGRO, begin with its website, festagro.org.

128. For background on the banana unions in Honduras, Marvin Barahona, *El Silencio Quedó Atrás: Testimonios de la Huelga Bananera de 1954* (Tegucigalpa: Editorial Guaymuras, 1994); Victor Meza, *Historia del Movimiento Obrero Hondureño* (Tegucigalpa: Editorial Guaymuras, 1980); Robert MacCameron, *Bananas, Labor, and Politics in Honduras: 1954–1963* (Syracuse, NY: Foreign and Comparative Studies/Latin American Series, no. 5, Maxwell School of Citizenship and Public Affairs, Syracuse University, 1983); Dana Frank, *Bananeras: Women Transforming the Banana Unions of Latin America* (Cambridge, MA: South End Press, 2005); Suyupa Portillo Villeda, "Campeñas, Campeños, y Compañeros: Life and Work in the Banana Fincas of the North Coast of Honduras, 1944–1957," PhD diss., Cornell University, 2011. Number of Dole workers in 2014, and their gender composition: Email, Iris Munguía to the author, August 1, 2017.

129. Ramón Amaya Amador, *Prisión Verde* (Mexico City: Editorial Latina, 1950); Juan Ramón Martínez B, *Ramón Amaya-Amador: biografía de un escritor* (Tegucigalpa: Editorial Universitaria, 1999).

130. For the history of women's projects in the banana unions of Honduras and Latin America, and biographical information on Iris Munguía, see Frank, *Bananeras*.

Chapter Five

1. Rebecca Bratek, "57,000 migrant children picked up at US border since Oct. 1," *Los Angeles Times*, July 9, 2014.

2. United Nations High Commissioner for Refugees, *Children on the Run: Unaccompanied Children Leaving Central America and Mexico and the Need for International Protection* (Washington, D.C.: United Nations, 2014), available at www.unhcr.org/en-us/about-us/background/56fc266f4/children-on-the -run-full-report.html/.

3. Brandon Darby, "Leaked Images Reveal Children Warehoused in Crowded

US Cells, Border Patrol Overwhelmed," *Breitbart* (blog), June 5, 2014,
www.breitbart.com/texas/2014/06/05/leaked-images-reveal-children
-warehoused-in-crowded-us-cells-border-patrol-overwhelmed/; Ben
Shapiro, "8 Reasons to Close the Border Now," *Breitbart*, July 8, 2014,
www.breitbart.com/big-government/2014/07/08/8-reasons-to-close-the
-border-now/; Caroline May, "Report: More Than Half of Central American
Immigrants on Welfare," *Breitbart*, July 8, 2014, www.breitbart.com/big
-government/2014/07/08/report-central-american-immigrants-use-welfare
-at-high-rate/.

4. Lindsey Boerma, "Is the surge of illegal child immigrants a national security
    threat?" *CBS News*, July 7, 2014, www.cbsnews.com/news/is-the-surge-of
    -illegal-child-immigrants-a-national-security-threat/.
5. Cindy Carcamo, "Children crossing border alone create 'urgent humanitari-
    an situation,'" *Los Angeles Times*, June 2, 2014.
6. See, e.g. Rick Jervis, "Immigrant children continue to surge into South
    Texas," *USA Today*, June 17, 2014. For analyses of the media coverage of
    the issues, see Laura Carlsen, "Child Migrants and Media Half-Truths,"
    TruthOut, July 2, 2014, www.truth-out.org/news/item/24739-child
    -migrants-and-media-half-truths; Steve Rendall, "All They Will Call You
    Will Be Detainees," *FAIR* (Fairness and Accuracy in Reporting), July 14,
    2014, fair.org/home/all-they-will-call-you-will-be-detainee/.
7. William Wilberforce Trafficking Victims Protection Reauthorization Act of
    2008, Public Law 110-457, available at www.gpo.gov/fdsys/pkg/PLAW
    -110publ457/content-detail.html.
8. For example, Molly Hennessy-Fiske and Cindy Carcamo, "Overcrowded,
    unsanitary conditions seen at immigrant detention centers," *Los Angeles Times*,
    June 18, 2014. For multiple stories, American Civil Liberties Union, "Media
    Coverage of Family Detention," September 19, 2014, www.aclu.org/sites
    /default/files/assets/14_9_19_media_coverage_of_family_detention.pdf.
    For a later, extensive story, Wil S. Hylton, "The Shame of America's Family
    Detention Centers," *New York Times Magazine*, February 4, 2015. For the
    dangers of the journey, UNICEF Child Alert, *Broken Dreams: Central American
    children's dangerous journey to the United States*, August 2016, www.unicef.org
    /infobycountry/files/UNICEF_Child_Alert_Central_America_2016_report
    _final(1).pdf.
9. Swati Sharma, "Harrowing images of police battling gang violence in
    crime-stricken Honduras," *Washington Post.com*, August 1, 2014,
    www.washingtonpost.com/news/worldviews/wp/2014/08/01/harrowing
    -images-of-police-battling-gang-violence-in-crime-stricken-honduras
    /?utm_term=.8e530cfa3795.
10. "Honduras Special Forces Work to Keep Kids From Fleeing Country," NBC
    News, July 15, 2014, www.nbcnews.com/news/latino/honduran-special
    -forces-work-keep-kids-fleeing-country-n164791. See also Cindy Carcamo,
    "Elite Honduran unit works to stop flow of child emigrants to U.S.," *Los
    Angeles Times*, July 9, 2014.

11. The literature on gangs in Honduras is extensive; good starting points are Lirio Gutiérrez Rivera, *Territories of Violence: State, Marginal Youth, and Public Security in Honduras* (New York: Palgrave Macmillan, 2013); Adrienne Pine, *Working Hard, Drinking Hard: Violence and Survival in Honduras* (Berkeley: University of California Press, 2008). For gangs and migrants, see, for example, Jo Tuckman, "'Flee or die': violence drives Central America's child migrants to US border," *The Guardian,* July 9, 2014.

12. The impact of extortion is immense, especially on small businesses. See, e.g. "Por extorsión cerraron 1,500 pulperías en la capital de Honduras," *El Heraldo,* September 7, 2017. By 2016, according to the Honduran government's Fuerza Nacional Antiextorsion, Hondurans paid 26,418,400 Lempiras to extortionists (approximately $1,064,447 in US dollars), "Guadalupe Ruelas: Hondureños pagaron más por Tasa de Seguridad que por extortiones," *El Tiempo,* November 3, 2017.

13. "Ciudadanos pagaron más por la Tasa de Seguridad que por las extorsiones: Guadalupe Ruelas," *Criterio,* November 3, 2017, criterio.hn/2017/11/03/ciudadanos-pagaron-mas-la-tasa-seguridad-las-extorsiones-guadalupe-ruelas/.

14. *Honduras 2013 Human Rights Report,* United States Department of State, www.state.gov/documents/organization/220663.pdf.

15. "World Report 2014: Honduras," *Human Rights Watch,* www.hrw.org/world-report/2014/country-chapters/honduras.

16. See, for example, Belkis J. Argueta, "'En Honduras las mujeres no valen nada'; femicidios aumentan," *El Tiempo,* May 4, 2017, tiempo.hn/femicidios-en-honduras-no-valen-nada/; "El 90% de los femicidios en Honduras están engavetados en el Ministerio Público," *Criterio,* July 3, 2017, criterio.hn/2017/07/03/90-los-feminicidios-honduras-estan-engavetados-ministerio-publico/; "Femicidios: Van más de 4,500 hondureñas asesinadas," *La Prensa,* August 18, 2016; JuJu Chang, Jackie Jesko, Ignacio Torres, and Jenna Millman, "'Men can do anything they want to women in Honduras': Inside one of the most dangerous places on Earth to be a woman," *ABC News,* May 3, 2017, abcnews.go.com/International/men-women-honduras-inside-dangerous-places-earth-woman/story?id=47135328.

17. Sarah Chayes, *When Corruption Is the Operating System: The Case of Honduras,* Carnegie Endowment for International Peace, May 30, 2016, available at carnegieendowment.org/2017/05/30/when-corruption-is-operating-system-case-of-honduras-pub-69999.

18. By September 2017, the Honduran government's public debt was reportedly over ten billion US dollars; "La deuda pública alcanza 10,626.8 millones de dólares," *El Heraldo,* November 8, 2017.

19. Camila Pérez, "IMF Survey: IMF Approves $202 Million Loan for Honduras," International Monetary Fund, October 1, 2010, www.imf.org/en/News/Articles/2015/09/28/04/53/socar100110a.

20. News Release, "Honduras to boost human capital of families in extreme poverty with support from IDB," Inter-American Development Bank, December

4, 2014, www.iadb.org/en/topics/social-protection/honduras-to-boost -human-capital%2C11005.html.

21. Press Release, "IMF Executive Board Approves US$113.2 Million Stand-By Arrangement and US$75.4 Million Stand-By Credit Facility for Honduras," International Monetary Fund, press release no. 14/545, December 4, 2014, www.imf.org/en/News/Articles/2015/09/14/01/49/pr14545.

22. Nina Lakhani, "World Bank lending arm forced into U-turn after Honduras loan row," *The Guardian,* January 27, 2014; John Vidal, "World Bank facing renewed pressure over loan to Honduran palm oil firm," *The Guardian,* March 12, 2014.

23. Ibid.

24. For a thorough analysis, Stephan Lefebvre, *Honduras: IMF Austerity, Macroeconomic Policy, and Foreign Investment,* Center for Economic and Policy Research, September 2015, cepr.net/publications/reports/honduras-imf -austerity-macroeconomic-policy-and-foreign-investment.

25. For Maduro, Mario Posas, "Ajusta: dos caras de la moneda," *Envío,* no. 134 (January 1993), www.envio.org.ni/articulo/767; William I. Robinson, "Transnational Processes, Development Studies and Changing Social Hierarchies in the World Ssytem: A Central American Case Study," *Third World Quarterly* 22, no. 4 (August, 2001), 529–563; Arne Ruckert, "The Poverty Reduction Strategy Paper of Honduras and the Transformations of Neoliberalism," *Canadian Journal of Latin American and Caribbean Studies/Revue canadienne des études latino-américaines et caraibes,* 35, no. 70 (2010), 113–39.

26. "Gobierno de Honduras anuncia 7,000 despidos para 2015," *La Prensa,* December 2, 2014; Press Release, "IMF Executive Board Concludes 2014 Article IV Consultation with Honduras," International Monetary Fund, June 13, 2014, press release no. 14/282, www.imf.org/en/News/Articles /2015/09/14/01/49/pr14282; "Empresas estatáles reducidas a su mínima expresión, según analistias," *Radio Progreso y ERIC,* January 16, 2015, radioprogresohn.net/index.php/comunicaciones/noticias/item/1550 -empresas-estatales-reducidas-a-su-m%C3%ADnima-expresi%C3 %B3n-suman-10-mil-trabajadores-separados.

27. Lefebvre, *Honduras: IMF Austerity, Macroeconomic Policy, and Foreign Investment.* For poverty rates in later years, UNICEF, "Honduras. Statistics," www. unicef.org/infobycountry/honduras_statistics.html.

28. For a summary, Javier Suazo, "A evitar el frijolazo," *América Latina en movi- miiento* (blog), August 14, 2014, www.alainet.org/es/active/76215.

29. AFL-CIO, *Trade, Violence, and Migration,* 7.

30. Jacob Wilson and Jake Johnston, *Honduras: Social and Economic Indicators Since the 2009 Coup, Center for Economic and Policy Research,* November 22, 2017, cepr. net/blogs/the-americas-blog/honduras-social-and-economic-indicators -since-the-2009-coup.

31. "House Resolution No. 51 — Relative to immigration," California Assembly, August 4, 2014, Amended in Assembly August 14, 2014, August 22, 2014, leginfo.legislature.ca.gov/faces/billTextClient.xhtml?bill_id=201320140HR51.

32. Matt Hansen and Mark Boster, "Protesters in Murrieta block detainees' buses in tense standoff," *Los Angeles Times,* July 1, 2014; "Both Sides of the Murrieta CA Debate," *Fox News,* July 3, 2014, video.foxnews.com /v/3658126583001/?#sp=show-clips.

33. Hearing, Judiciary Committee, California Assembly, August 14, 2014, Video available at the California Channel, calchannel.granicus.com/MediaPlayer /php?view_id=7&clip_id=2362.

34. "Perez state resolution on Central American immigrants approved by California Assembly," *The Desert Review,* August 27, 2014, www.thedesertreview .com/perez-state-resolution-on-central-american-immigrants-approved-by -california-assembly/.

35. Office of the Press Secretary, The White House, "Fact Sheet: Unaccompanied Children from Central America," June 20, 2014, obamawhitehouse .archives.gov/the-press-office/2014/06/20/fact-sheet-unaccompanied -children-central-america.

36. Press Release, The White House, "Statement by the Press Secretary on the Visit of the Presidents of Guatemala, Honduras, and El Salvador," *The American Presidency Project,* July 18, 2014, www.presidency.ucsb.edu/ws/?pid=105358.

37. "Children Migrating From Central America: Solving a Humanitarian Crisis," Hearing before the Subcommittee on the Western Hemisphere of the Committee on Foreign Affairs, House of Representatives, 113th Cong., Second Session, June 25, 2014, Serial No. 113-18, available at www.gop.gov/fdsys/.

38. Jim Garamone, United States Department of Defense, "Kelly: Southcom Keeps Watch on Ebola Situation," *DoD News* (blog), Defense Media Activity, October 8, 2014, www.defense.gov/News/Article/Article/603408/.

39. Peter J. Meyer and Clare Ribando Seelke, *Central America Regional Security Initiative: Background and Policy Issues for Congress* (Congressional Research Service, December 17, 2015), fas.org/sgp/crs/row/R41731.pdf; quote: 22. For an analysis of CARSI funding's effectiveness, see David Rosnick, Alexander Main, and Laura Jung, *Have US-Funded CARSI Programs Reduced Crime and Violence in Central America?, Center for Economic and Policy Research,* September 2016, cepr.net/publications/reports/have-us-funded-carsi-programs-reduced- crime-and-violence.

40. Ninoska Marcano, "Honduran President Says U.S. Weak Laws to Blame for Child Migration Crisis," *Fox News.com,* June 13, 2014, www.foxnews.com /politics/2014/06/13/honduran-president-says-us-to-blame-for-child -migration-crisis.html.

41. "Primera dama de Honduras llega a la frontera con EUA," *La Prensa,* July 3, 2014; Cindy Carcamo, "U.S. sends first planeload of moms, children back to Honduras," *Los Angeles Times,* July 14, 2014.

42. "Cierran el Inhfa por ser incapaz de velar por la niñez," *La Prensa,* June 4, 2104; "Trabajadores de desaparecido Inhfa denuncian al Estado de Honduras," *La Tribuna,* June 26, 2014.

43. "Policia de Fronteras recupera en occidente de Honduras a ocho menores que viajaban sin autorización," *Proceso Digital,* July 6, 2015, www.proceso

.hn/migrantes/1-migrantes/Polic%C3%ADa-de-Fronteras-recupera-en
-occidente-de-Honduras-a-ocho-menores-que-viajaban-sin-autorizaci
%C3%B3n.html. For another example, "Honduras retiene a cinco niños que
iban para Estados Unidos," *La Prensa,* July 3, 2014.

44. "Ayudados de caninos EEUU y Honduras buscan prevenir migración
    infantil," *Proceso Digital,* February 23, 2014, www.proceso.hn/migrantes/1
    -migrantes/ayudados-de-caninos-eeuu-y-honduras-buscan-prevenir
    -migracion-infantil.html.

45. Ioan Grillo, "President of Honduras Expects Mass Deportations of Minors
    From U.S.," *Time.com,* July 22, 2014, time.com/3020874/honduras
    -immigration-border-crises-children/.

46. Susan B. Glasser, "'Our Neighbor Isn't Doing Its Part,'" *Politico Magazine,* July
    25, 2014, www.politico.com/magazine/story/2014/07/honduras
    -president-hernandez-interview-109400.

47. "Congresistas de EEUU vienen a Honduras por crisis migratoria que afecta
    a niños," *El Heraldo,* July 4, 2014; "Congresistas de EEUU verifican inversion
    de recursos," *El Tiempo,* July 19, 2014.

48. Quoted in Molly Hennessy-Fiske and Richard Simon, "Republicans blame
    Obama policies for immigration crisis on the border," *Los Angeles Times,* June
    19, 2014.

49. For subsequent arguments by Republicans in the House of Representatives,
    see House Subcommittee on State, Foreign Operations and Related
    Programs, of the Committee on Appropriations, "Budget Hearing—
    Assistance to Central America," March 24, 2015, appropriations.house.gov
    /calendararchive/eventsingle.aspx?EventID=394076.

50. Press Release, "Sens. Menendez, Durbin, Hirono, and Reps. Gutierrez and
    Roybal-Allard Discuss Humanitarian and Refugee Children Crisis at the
    Border," June 19, 2014, www.menendez.senate.gov/news-and-events/press
    /sens-menendez-durbin-hirono-and-reps-gutierrez-and-roybal-allard
    -discuss-humanitarian-and-refugee-children-crisis-at-the-border.

51. Press Release, "Engel and 61 House Members Send Letter to President
    Urging Greater Resources for Central America," United States House of
    Representatives Committee on Foreign Affairs, June 20, 2014, democrats
    -foreignaffairs.house.gov/news/press-releases/engel-and-61-house-members
    -send-letter-president-urging-greater-resources. For the previous letters, James
    McGovern and 86 additional members of Congress to Hillary Clinton, May 31,
    2011, mcgovern.house.gov/news/documentsingle.aspx?DocumentID=397143;
    Sam Farr and 29 additional Members of Congress to Hillary Clinton, October
    19, 2010, in possession of the author; Press Release, "94 House Members Send
    Letter to Clinton to Suspend Security Assistance to Honduras," March 12, 2012,
    schakowsky.house.gov/press-releases/94-house-members-send-letter
    -to-clinton-to-suspend-security-assistance-to-honduras.

52. Press Release, "Progressive Caucus Urges President Obama to Adopt a Kids
    First Approach to the Humanitarian Crisis on the Border," Congressional
    Progressive Caucus, July 10, 2014, cpc-grijalva.house.gov/press

-releases/progressive-caucus-urges-president-obama-to-adopt-a-kids-first
-approach-to-the-humanitarian-crisis-on-the-border1/.

53.   Plan of the Alliance for Prosperity in the Northern Triangle, *A Road Map:
       Regional Plan Prepared by El Salvador, Guatemala and Honduras*, September, 2014;
       available at www.iadb.org/en/news/news-releases/2014-11-14
       /northern-triangle-presidents-present-development-plan,10987.html
       ?valcookie=&actionuserstats=close&isajaxrequest=.

54.   Editorial Board, "The immigration crisis solution: A Plan Honduras,"
       Washington Post, July 26, 2014. For Plan Colombia, John Lindsay-Poland,
       Plan Colombia: US Ally Atrocities and Community Activism, (Durham, NC: Duke
       University Press, 2018); Winifred L. Tate, *Drugs, Thugs, and Diplomats: U.S.
       Policymaking in Colombia* (Stanford, CA: Stanford University Press, 2015); For
       another example of Plan Colombia as the model, see Daniel Runde, "To
       Stop the Surge of Migrants, Central America Needs a 'Plan Colombia,'"
       Foreign Policy.com, August 18, 2014, foreignpolicy.com/2014/08/18/to-stop
       -the-surge-of-migrants-central-america-needs-a-plan-colombia/.

55.   "A surprisingly safe haven," *The Economist,* January 28, 2012.

56.   *Plan of the Alliance for Prosperity in the Northern Triangle.*

57.   Joseph R. Biden, Jr., "Joe Biden: A Plan for Central America," *New York
       Times,* January 29, 2015.

58.   H.R. 2029, Consolidated Appropriations Act, 2016, 114th Cong.,
       www.congress.gov/bill/114th-congress/house-bill/2029/text, including
       Joint Explanatory Statement with funding and restrictions for specific
       regions and countries, www.congress.gov/congressional-record/2015/12/18
       /senate-section/article/S8844-1. For supportive summaries of the funding
       and conditions, Adriana Beltrán, "U.S. Increases Central America Aid, But
       It's No Blank Check," *WOLA*, December 22, 2015; www.wola.org/analysis
       /us-increases-central-america-aid-but-its-no-blank-check/; and Steven
       Dudley and Mimi Yagoub, "5 Takeaways from US Congress Northern
       Triangle Aid Package," *InSight Crime*, December 18, 2015, www.insightcrime
       .org/news-analysis/5-takeaways-from-us-congress-proposed-northern
       -triangle-aid-package.

59.   Sanjay Badri-Maharaj, "The Israeli Factor in Honduras Efforts to Modernise
       its Air Force," *IDSA Comment* (blog), Institute for Defence Studies and Analysis,
       February 9, 2017, idsa.in/idsacomments/israel-factor-in-honduras-efforts-to
       -modernise-air-force_sbmaharaj_090217#footnote17_ehe3ht2; Herb Keinon,
       "Exclusive: US objections could kill $209 million Honduras deal," *Jerusalem
       Post*, December 14, 2016, www.jpost.com/Israel-News/Politics-And-Diplomacy
       /Exclusive-US-objections-could-kill-209-million-Honduras-deal-475426.
       The United States held up approval of part of that funding beginning in 2016.
       Evidently it was the work of the Defense Department, which has to approve
       any third-party funds for refurbishing of equipment—in this case jets and
       helicopters—which were originally US-funded.

60.   "Honduras page $13.5 millones por buque a Colombia," *El Heraldo*,
       November 27, 2016; "Oficiales de FFAA viajaron a Colombia para super-

visón de construcción del modern Buque BAL-CC," *Proceso Digital*, March 3, 2017, www.proceso.hn/actualidad/7-actualidad/oficiales-de-ffaa-viajaron -a-colombia-para-supervision-de-avances-de-construccion-del-moderno -buque-bal-c.html.

61. A few weeks after the Honduran-Israel deal was agreed upon, the US granted $38 billion in security aid to Honduras. Peter Baker and Julie Hirschfeld Davis, "U.S. Finalizes Deal to Give Israel $38 Billion in Military Aid," *New York Times*, September 13, 2016.

62. For examples of the "bad parenting" charge, and criticism of that, see "Children Migrating from Central America," Hearing before the Subcommittee on the Western Hemisphere of the House Committee on Foreign Affairs, 5, 32; for the propaganda, 9-10, 26; for an analysis of the "bad parenting" question, Laura Carlsen, "Child Migrants and Media Half-Truths."

63. Email, Roger Pineda to the author, March 16, 2012; Email, Roger Pineda to the author, April 12, 2012; Email, Roger Pineda to the author, May 28, 2012, and attached letter, Roger Pineda to the author, May 25, with suggestion that I could be "held legally liable for the damage caused to the image of Miguel Facussé and his companies."

64. Alison Galloway, "Living on the Sidelines of Death: Anthropologists and Violence," in *Bioarcheological and Forensic Perspectives on Violence: How Violent Death Is Interpreted from Skeletal Remains*, ed. Debra L. Martin and Cheryl P. Anderson (New York: Cambridge University Press, 2014), 311–20.

65. *So I Married an Axe Murderer*, dir. Thomas Schlamme (1993).

66. My thanks to Vilashini Coopan for this insight.

67. "Cynthia Nixon Shocked to Learn Her Ancestor Was an Axe Murderer," *ABC News.com*, July 24, 2014, abcnews.go.com/blogs/entertainment/2014/07 /cynthia-nixon-shocked-to-learn-her-ancestor-was-an-axe-murderer/. As of this writing, Nixon is a candidate for governor of the State of New York.

68. Galloway, "Living on the Sidelines of Death."

69. "Axe Murder," *Wikipedia* (blog), accessed November 9, 2017, en.wikipedia.org /wiki/Axe_murder.

70. Roy Greenslade, "Honduras radio journalist murdered," *The Guardian*, March 13, 2012.

71. "Denuncia urgente: intentan asesinar a la compañera María Santos Domínguez, a su esposo e hijo, familia destacada en la lucha en Río Blanco y miembra del COPINH," *COPINH* (blog), March 7, 2014, copinh.org /article/denuncia-urgente-intentan-asesinar-a-la-companera/.

72. "Honduras: Luto y dolor por vil asesinato de cuatro niños en Colón," *El Heraldo*, May 4, 2014.

73. Press Release, The White House, "Statement by the Press Secretary on the Visit of the Presidents of Guatemala, Honduras, and El Salvador," *The American Presidency Project*, July 18, 2014, available at www.presidency.ucsb .edu/ws/?pid=105358.

74. 60,000 estimate: "Honduran protesters stage biggest march yet to demand

president resign," *The Guardian,* July 3, 2015.

75. Portions of this section were originally published in Dana Frank, "Protests light up long Honduran night," *Miami Herald,* July 16, 2015.

76. "Documentos ligan directamente al Partido Nacional con el fraude practicado al IHSS," *Criterio,* May 8, 2015, criterio.hn/2015/05/08/documentos -ligan-directamente-al-partido-nacional-con-el-fraude-practicado-al-ihss/; "Presentan mas pruebas de multimillonaria estafa al IHSS," *Criterio,* May 29, 2015, criterio.hn/2015/05/29/presentan-mas-pruebas-de-multimillonaria -estafa-al-ihss/. For Romero revealing the checks on TV Globo, "Periodista no se retracta ante accusasiones y amenazas contra su vida," *You Tube,* (2015) www.youtube.com/watch?v=Z3Vk6hN72Dw2015; "David Romero—Hay mas Cheques del IHSS (29-May-15)," You Tube, (2015), www.youtube.com /watch?v=OowGOS44__s. For Hernández admitting the checks were real, "Presidente Honduras admite que su campána recibió fondos vinculados a corrupción," Reuters, June 3, 2015, lta.reuters.com/article/domesticNews /idLTAKBN0OJ21520150604; "JOH: Partido Nacional debe devolver fondos al IHSS," *El Heraldo,* June 3, 2015. For the attorney general, "'El fiscal general confirmó cheques al nombre del Partido Nacional," *El Libertador,* May 26, 2015, www.web.ellibertador.hn/index.php/noticias/nacionales/88-el-fiscal-general -confirmo-cheques-a-nombre-del-partido-nacional.

77. "Fiscalía: L4.6 millones recibió Bertetty por ambulancias sobrevaloradas del IHSS, *La Prensa,* July 21, 2015; "Cerca de tres mil personas han muerto por decalabro en el IHSS," *La Tribuna,* May 28, 2015; "El Escándolo que llevó al ejercito a controlar los medicamentos en Honduras," *BBC Mundo,* July 19, 2015, www.bbc.com/mundo/noticias/2015/06/150619_america_latina _salud_honduras_corrupcion_militares_amv; "Las muertes inducidas en el IHSS por la corrupción del Partido Nacional de Honduras," *Honduras Laboral,* June 15, 2015, honduraslaboral.org/article/las-muertes -inducidas-en-el-ihss-por-la-corrupcion./.

78. For Varela, see his website, www. arielvarela.com. The pro-coup group is 300 Con Dignidad; its statements refer to the 2009 coup as a "constitutional crisis," using the language of those who supported the coup at the time, and since. For Méndez, see CIPRODEH's website, ciprodeh.org.hn/.

79. "Hondureños 'indignados' inician huelga de hambre," *La Prensa,* June 22, 2015; "Etnia Tolupán se suman a huelga de hambre de Honduras," *Criterio,* June 30, 2015, criterio.hn/2015/06/30/etnia-tolupan-se-suman-a-huelga-de -hambre-en-honduras; "Siete tolupanes se unen a huelga de hambre a inmediaciones de Casa Presidencial," *Proceso Digital,* June 30, 2015, proceso. hn/nacionales/item/105224-siete-tolupanes-se-unen-a-huelga-de-hambre-a -inmediaciones-de-casa-presidencial.html; "Wilfredo Méndez se une a hulega de hambre a partir del lunes," *Criterio,* June 10, 2015, criterio.hn/2015/07/10 /wilfredo-mendez-se-une-a-huelga-de-hambre-a-partir-del-lunes/.

80. "Embajador Nealon recibe a 'indignados' tras marcha," *El Heraldo,* July 17, 2015. For an analysis of the Embassy's relationship to the Indignados, Ismael Moreno, SJ, "What will we be? Their backyard or our own home?," *Envío,* no.

432 (July 2017), www.envio.org.ni/articulo/5372.

81. Frank, "Protests light up long Honduran night." For visual imagery, "Para sacar a JOH," *FESTAGRO* (blog), June 26, 2015, festagro.org/?p=3149.

82. For the CICIG's history and achievements, start with its website, www.cicig .org/index.php?page=home.

83. Azam Ahmed and Elisabeth Malkin, "Otto Pérez Molina of Guatemala Is Jailed Hours After Resigning Presidency," *New York Times*, September 3, 2015. For the importance of the CICIG, Nina Lakhani, "Guatemala president's downfall marks success for coruption investigators," *The Guardian*, September 9, 2015.

84. E.g. Louisa Reynolds, "Are We Witnessing a Central American Spring?," *ForeignPolicy.com*, June 26, 2015, foreignpolicy.com/2015/06/26 /guatemala-honduras-baldetti-la-linea/; "A Central American spring?" *The Economist*, August 15, 2015.

85. "Presidente Hernández inicia hoy diálogo nacional con grupos de Sociedad Civil," *Proceso Digital*, June 24, 2015, proceso.hn/nacionales/item/104824 -presidente-hern%C3%A1ndez-inicia-hoy-di%C3%A1logo-nacional -con-grupos-de-sociedad-civil.html.

86. US Ambassador's Twitter feed, @USAMBHonduras, twitter.com/search ?q=U.S.%20finds%20proposal%20of%20%23JOH%20very%20interesting %2C%20worthy%20of%20serious%20study.&src=typd&lang=en.

87. "ONU y OEA confirman acompañamiento en diálogo nacional," *La Prensa*, June 29, 2015.

88. Press Release, "OAS Secretary General Announces Initiative to Combat Corruption and Impunity in Honduras," Organization of American States, September 28, 2015, www.oas.org/en/media_center/press_release .asp?sCodigo=E-303/15.

89. Coalition Against Impunity, "We Reject the OAS and Urge the Installation of a CICIH," September 16, 2015, in possession of the author; reported in *Criterio*, criterio.hn/2015/09/17/coalicion-contra-la-impunidad -decepcionada-con-propuesta-de-la-oea/. For another critique by prominent intellectuals, see "Otra decepción pero también otra resistencia," September 24, 2015, reprinted in *El Libertador*, (n.d.) www.web.ellibertador .hn/index.php/avance/551-honduras-analisis-otra-decepcion-pero-tambien -otra-resistencia. For critiques in the US, Alexander Main, "An Anti-Corruption Charade in Honduras," *New York Times*, February 15, 2016; and regularly at *Honduras Culture and Politics*, e.g. "Why the OAS MACCIH Will Likely Fail," October 28, 2015, hondurasculturepolitics.blogspot.com /2015/10/why-oas-maccih-will-likely-fail.html.

90. Eric L. Olson, "Nine questions and observations about Honduras's new anti-corruption mechanism," *Woodrow Wilson Center* (blog), October 5, 2015, www.wilsoncenter.org/article/nine-questions-and-observations-about -hondurass-new-anti-corruption-mechanism.

91. Hannah Stone, "With Extradition Law, Honduras Outsources Justice to US," *InSight Crime*, January 30, 2012, www.insightcrime.org/news-analysis

/with-extradition-law-honduras-outsources-justice-to-us.

92. David Gagne, "Completing Chapter, Honduras Extradites Valle Brothers," *InSight Crime*, December 19, 2014, www.insightcrime.org/news-briefs /honduras-extradites-valle-drug-clan-brothers-to-us.

93. Joseph Goldstein and Benjamin Weiser, "Murderous Drug Lord Helps US in Secret Deal," *New York Times*, October 7, 2017.

94. Azam Ahmed, "US Indicts Members of Powerful Honduran Family," *New York Times*, October 7, 2015; Press Release, United States Department of Justice, US Attorney's Office, Southern District of New York, "Former Honduran Cabinet Officials Pleads Guilty in Manhattan Federal Court to Money Laundering Charge," August 29, 2017, www.justice.gov/usao-sdny/pr/former-honduran -cabinet-official-pleads-guilty-manhattan-federal-court-money-laundering; Press Release, United States Department of Justice, US Attorney's Office, Southern District of New York, "Former Honduran Congressman and Businessman Pleads Guilty in Manhattan Federal Court to Money Laundering Charge," July 26, 2017, www.justice.gov/usao-sdny/pr/former-honduran -congressman-and-businessman-pleads-guilty-manhattan-federal-court-money; "CSJ: Extradición de Jaime Rosenthal no procede," *El Heraldo*, January 28, 2016; "Deconstructing the Grupo Continental?" *Honduras Culture and Politics*, October 12, 2015, hondurasculturepolitics.blogspot.com/2015/10/deconstructing -grupo-continental.html; "Diario El Tiempo Deja de Circular en Honduras," *El Heraldo*, October 26, 2015.

95. Benjamin Weiser, "Honduras: Ex-President's Son Arrested," *New York Times*, May 22, 2015; Press Release, United States Department of Justice, US Attorney's Office, Southern District of New York, "Son Of The Former President Of Honduras Sentenced To 24 Years In Prison For Conspiring To Import Cocaine Into The United States," September 5, 2017, www.justice.gov /usao-sdny/pr/son-former-president-honduras-sentenced-24-years-prison -conspiring-import-cocaine.

96. Rebecca R. Ruiz, "Former Head of Honduran Federation Pleads Guilty in FIFA Case," *New York Times*, March 28, 2016.

97. Nealon's tweets are available at twitter.com/usambhonduras?lang=en.

98. The Fourth of July party took place on July 1, 2015. For the torches, "Embajada de Estado Unidos celebra con antorchas su independencia," *Criterio*, July 1, 2015. criterio.hn/2015/07/01/embajada-de-estados-unidos-celebra -con-antorchas-su-independencia/.

99. "James Nealon: Relaciones entre EEUU y Honduras pasan por 'el mejor momento de la historia,'" *La Tribuna*, July 1, 2015. In an interview on July 2, I confirmed with Ambassador Nealon that the quote was correct. Dana Frank, Interview with James Nealon, Tegucigalpa, July 2, 2015.

Chapter Six

1. Katie Pisa, "Berta Cáceres' family seeks justice in anniversary of fearless activist's death," *CNN.com*, March 3, 2017.

2. United Nations, "United Nations Declaration on the Rights of Indigenous

People," www.un.org/development/desa/indigenouspeoples/declaration
-on-the-rights-of-indigenous-peoples.html; International Labor
Organization (ILO), "C169—Indigenous and Tribal Peoples Convention,
1989" (No. 169), www.ilo.org/dyn/normlex/en/f?p=NORMLEXPUB:12100
:0::NO::P12100_ILO_CODE:C169.

3. Annie Bird, *The Agua Zarca Dam and Lenca Communities in Honduras:
    Transnational Investment Leads to Violence against and Criminalization of Indigenous
    Communities, Rights Action,* October 3, 2013, rightsaction.org/sites/default
    /files/Rpt_131001_RioBlanco_Final.pdf; interview by the author with Annie
    Bird, October 6, 2017.

4. Bird, *The Agua Zarca Dam and Lenca Communities in Honduras;* Interview
    with Annie Bird, October 6, 2017. For Indigenous Land struggles, Phillips,
    Honduras in Dangerous Times.

5. For details, see "Case History: Berta Cáceres," *Front Line Defenders,* (n.d.,
    2013–2017), www.frontlinedefenders.org/en/case/case-history-berta
    -c%C3%A1ceres.

6. Urgent Action, "Army Fires on Protesters in Honduras,'" *Amnesty International,*
    July 23, 2013, www.amnesty.org/en/documentsamr37/006/2013/en/.

7. "'Defending human rights in Honduras is a crime," *Amnesty International,*
    November 22, 2013, www.amnesty.org/en/latest/news/2013/11/honduras
    -human-rights-defenders-under-threat/.

8. "Carlos H. Reyes anuncia su retiro de los comicios," *El Tiempo,* November 8,
    2009; Frank, "No Fair Election in Honduras Under Military Rule."

9. Nina Lakhani, "'Time was running out': Honduran activist's last days marked
    by threats," *The Guardian,* May 25, 2016.

10. For the prize, and the video of her speech, Goldman Environmental Prize,
    "Berta Cáceres," *Goldman Environmental Prize* (blog), www.goldmanprize.org
    /recipient/berta-caceres/.

11. "Photos and Highlights from the 2015 Prize Tour," Goldman Environmental
    Prize, April 29, 2015, www.goldmanprize.org/blog/photos-and-highlights
    -from-the-2015-prize-tour/.

12. Barbara J. Fraser, "Honduran activists hope pope's climate encyclical gives
    them boost," *CatholicPhilly.com* (blog), April 22, 2015, catholicphilly.com
    /2015/04/news/world-news/honduran-activists-hope-popes-climate
    -encyclical-gives-them-boost/.

13. Danielle Marie Mackey, "An Interview with Gustavo Castro, Sole Witness
    to Assassination of Berta Cáceres," *The Intercept,* April 18, 2016, theintercept.
    com/2016/04/18/an-interview-with-gustavo-castro-sole-witness-of-the-
    murder-of-berta-caceres. While some accounts report her death to be on
    March 3, the correct date—used by COPINH and her family—is March 2,
    just before midnight.

14. Mackey, "An Interview with Gustavo Castro"; Joshua Partlow and Gabriela
    Martinez, "Suspensions mount in slaying of noted Honduran environmentalist,"
    Washington Post, March 18, 2016; Jonathan Blitzer, "No Answers in the Murder
    of Berta Cáceres," *The New Yorker.com,* April 11, 2016, www.newyorker.com

/news/news-desk/no-answers-in-the-murder-of-berta-caceres.

15. Nina Lakhani, "Berta Cáceres's name was on Honduran military hitlist, says former soldier," *The Guardian,* June 21, 2016; Nina Lahkani, "US investigating allegations Honduran military had hitlist of activists to target," *The Guardian,* July 8, 2016.

16. For the most thorough and reliable evidence in the case, including regarding dam owners as the alleged intellectual authors of the assassination, see GAIPE (Grupo Assesor Internacional de Personas Expertas), *Dam Violence: The Plan That Killed Berta Cáceres,* November 2017, www.gaipe.net/english/. Another major source is Global Witness, *Honduras: The Deadliest Country in the World for Environmental Activism,* January 31, 2017, www.globalwitness.org/en /campaigns/environmental-activists/honduras-deadliest-country-world -environmental-activism/.

17. "Honduras: opposition radio journalist narrowly escapes murder attempt," Reporters Without Borders, May 3, 2016, updated May 4, 2016, rsf.org /en/news/honduras-opposition-radio-journalist-narrowly-escapes-murder -attempt; Jason McGahan, "Journalist Survives Two Murder Attempts in One Day," *Daily Beast,* May 5, 2016, www.thedailybeast.com/journalist -survives-two-murder-attempts-in-one-day.

18. Elisabeth Malkin and Alberto Arce, "Berta Cáceres, Indigenous Activist, Is Killed in Honduras," *New York Times,* March 3, 2016; Nina Lakhani, "'Time was running out,'" "Berta Cáceres's name was on Honduran military hitlist," "US investigating allegations Honduran military had hitlist of activists to target," and other stories for *The Guardian.*

19. For example, "High profile Honduran activist Berta Cáceres murdered," *Friends of the Earth International* (blog), March 3, 2016, www.foei.org/press /archive-by-subject/economic-justice-resisting-neoliberalism-press/high -profile-honduran-activist-berta-caceres-murdered; Press Release, "Sierra Club Statement on the Assassination of World-Renowned Activist Berta Cáceres," *Sierra Club* (blog), March 3, 2016, content.sierraclub.org/press -releases/2016/03/sierra-club-statement-assassination-world-renowned -activist-berta-c-ceres.

20. For hemispheric-wide solidarity with Berta see regular coverage in *Indian Country Today,* e.g. Grahame Russell, "The Day Berta Cáceres was Assassinated," *Indian Country Today,* March 4, 2016; Comisión Intercontinental Abya Yala, "Pronunciamiento del MAPCA al cumplirse un año del asesinato de nuestra compañera Berta Cáceres Flores," *Somos America* (blog), somosunaamerica.org/2017/03/03/pronunciamiento-del-mapca-al-cumplirse -un-ano-del-asesinato-de-nuestra-companera-berta-caceres-flores/.

21. Press Release, "Remarks of Senator Patrick Leahy On Remembering Berta Cáceres," March 3, 2016, www.leahy.senate.gov/press/remarks-of-senator -patrick-leahy-on-remembering-berta-caceres. From Leahy, see also Press Release, "Statement of Senator Patrick Leahy On the Life of Berta Cáceres," March 15, 2016, www.leahy.senate.gov/press/statement-of-senator-patrick -leahy-on-the-life-of-berta-caceres-.

22. Press Release, "Reps. Johnson, Ellison call for independent murder investigation of human rights activist Cáceres," March 17, 2016, hankjohnson.house .gov/media-center/press-releases/reps-johnson-ellison-call-independent -murder-investigation-human-rights.

23. Press Release, "Cardin Condemns Murder of Human Rights Activist Berta Cáceres," March 3, 2016, www.cardin.senate.gov/newsroom/press/release /cardin-condemns-murder-of-honduran-human-rights-activist-berta-caceres; Press Release, "Rep. Schakowsky Statement On the Murder of Berta Cáceres," March 3, 2016, schakowsky.house.gov/press-releases/rep-schakowsky -statement-on-the-murder-of-berta-caceres/; Press Release, "Rep. Ellison Statement on the Assassination of Berta Cáceres," March 3, 2016, ellison. house.gov/media-center/press-releases/rep-ellison-statement-on -the-assassination-of-berta-caceres; Tweet, Rep. Nancy Pelsoi, March 3, 2016, twitter.com/nancypelosi/status/705426227553824769?lang=en ; Press Release, "Rep. Ellison speaks on House Floor About the Assassination of Honduran Activists," March 18, 2016, ellison.house.gov/media-center /press-releases/rep-ellison-speaks-on-house-floor-about-the-assassination -of-honduran; Representative Betty McCollum to Secretary of State John Kerry, March 8, 2016, in possession of the author.

24. "Condolence Message to the Honduran People from Ambassador James D. Nealon on the Murder of Berta Cáceres," March 3, 2016, hn.usembassy .gov/condolence-message-ambassador-nealon-murder-berta-caceres/; Representative Sam Farr and 17 Additional Members to John Kerry, March 8, 2016, in possession of the author; "Demócratas piden a Kerry vigilar investi- gacíon Berta Cáceres," *El Nuevo Herald*, March 8, 2016, www.elnuevoherald.com /noticias/estados-unidos/article64826747.html.

25. For Torres's official biography, see her website, "Biography," torres.house.gov /about/full-biography.

26. Julian Hattem, "Lawmakers launch Central American Caucus in meeting with Guatemalan leader," *The Hill*, February 24, 2016, thehill.com/policy /national-security/270667-lawmakers-launch-central-america-caucus -in-meeting-with-guatemalan.

27. Torres's voting record was particularly conservative regarding criminal justice and environmental issues. For example, she voted against the ban on hydraulic fracking, against sentence reconsideration for juvenile offenders, and against the ban on single-use plastic bags in stores. Quite often she did not vote at all on progressive bills. See votesmart.org for her full voting record.

28. Press Release, "Congressman Serrano and 53 Members Call for Creation of UN-sponsored Commission on Corruption and Impunity in Honduras," December 4, 2015, serrano.house.gov/media-center/press-releases /congressman-serrano-and-53-members-call-creation-un-sponsored -commission. Bizarrely, a self-appointed 'Indignado leader' named Fernanda López claimed out of whole cloth that she herself had produced the letter. notibomba.com/toque-todas-las-puertas-en-ee-uu-hasta-que-los -congresistas-me-escucharon-fernanda-lopez/.

29. The Kaptur/Johnson letter was a follow-up letter from one that Representative
     Jan Schakowsky and Farr himself had co-led. Jan Schakowsky, Sam Farr, and
     28 additional members to John Kerry, January 15, 2016, schakowsky.house.gov/
     common/popup/popup.cfm?action=item.print&itemID=3189; Marcy Kaptur,
     Henry C. "Hank" Johnson and 23 additional members to John Kerry, March
     16, 2016, 201 ilrf.org/sites/default/files/publications/Kaptur%20and%20
     Johnson%20sign-on%20letter%20to%20Kerry%20on%20Honduran%20
     trade%20unionists%2C%20March%202016.pdf.

30. Sascha Thompson has since changed her name to Sascha Foertsch.

31. Berta Caceres Human Rights in Honduras Act, H.R. 5474, 114th Cong.
     (2015–16), www.congress.gov/bill/114th-congress/house-bill/5474.

32. John James Conyers, Jr, Keith Ellison, Hank Johnson, Marcy Kaptur, Jan
     Schakowsky and José E .Serrano, "America's funding of Honduran security
     forces puts blood on our hands," *The Guardian*, July 8, 2016.

33. "H.R. 5474, Cosponsors," www.congress.gov/bill/114th-congress/house-bill
     /5474/cosponsors.

34. Witness for Peace, "Organizational Endorsements for the Berta Cáceres
     Act," (n.d., November 2017), witnessforpeace.org/organizational
     -endorsements-for-the-berta-caceres-act/. For Torres and WOLA, see e.g.
     "The Central America Tracking Monitor: Tracking U.S. Assistance and
     Assessing Impact," *WOLA*, May 16, 2017, www.wola.org/events/central
     -america-monitor-tracking-u-s-assistance-assessing-impact/.

35. "Honduran Human Rights Organizations Call for Suspension of US Aid,"
     Americas Program, September 1, 2016, www.americas.org/archives/19058.

36. Berta Cáceres Human Rights in Honduras Act, H.R. 1299, 115th Cong.
     (2017–18), www.congress.gov/bill/115th-congress/house-bill/1299/cosponsors
     ?overview=closed.

37. "Washington: 'Ley Berta,' candatos a PPTN y el viaje de JOH," *El Tiempo*,
     July 12, 2016, tiempo.hn/washington-ley-berta-viaje-joh/.

38. Press Release, "Central America Caucus Meets with Honduran President,"
     website of Representative Norma Torres, July 12, 2016, torres.house.gov/media
     -center/press-releases/central-america-caucus-meets-honduran-president.

39. "Washington, D.C.: Honduran President Faces Protests over Cáceres's
     Murder," *Democracy Now!* March 22, 2017, www.democracynow.org/2017/3
     /22/headlines/washington_dc_honduran_president_faces_protests_over
     _caceress_murder; Laura Gambino, "Protesters in DC confront Honduran
     president over Berta Cáceres murder," *The Guardian*, March 21, 2017.

40. Norma Torres to the Family of Berta Cáceres, March 17, 2017, in possession
     of the author; Family of Berta Cáceres to Norma Torres, March 2, 2017,
     in possession of the author; Sarah Lazare, "How the US Created a Human
     Rights Disaster in Honduras—and How It Can Be Stopped," *AlterNet*, March
     6, 2017, www.alternet.org/world/how-us-created-human-rights-disaster
     -honduras-and-how-it-can-be-stopped.

41. Nina Lakhani, "Fellow Honduran activist Nelson García murdered days
     after Berta Cáceres," *The Guardian*, March 16, 2016; David Agren, "Honduras

confirms murder of another member of Berta Cáceres's activist group," *The Guardian,* July 7, 2016.

42. "Honduran and international march to commemorate Berta Cáceres attacked by counter-protesters," *Front Line Defenders* (blog), April 20, 2016, www.frontlinedefenders.org/en/statement-report/honduran-and -international-march-commemorate-berta-caceres-attacked-counter.

43. "Honduras: Protestan por el cierre de transmision de Globo TV," *El Libertador,* May 23, 2016, www.web.ellibertador.hn/index.php/noticias/nacionales /1387-honduras-protestan-por-el-cierre-de-transmision-de-globo-tv.

44. Nina Lakhani, "Two More Honduran land rights activists killed in ongoing violence," *The Guardian,* October 19, 2016.

45. Tula Connell, "Honduran union leader, family leave home after threats," *AFL-CIO Solidarity Center* (blog), November 17, 2015, www.solidaritycenter. org/honduran-union-leader-family-leave-home-after-threats-3/; Jan Schakowsky, Sam Farr, and 28 additional members to John Kerry, January 15, 2016, schakowsky.house.gov/common/popup/popup.cfm?action=item .print&itemID=3189; Marcy Kaptur, Henry C. "Hank" Johnson and 23 additional members to John Kerry, March 16, 2016, 201 ilrf.org/sites/default /files/publications/Kaptur%20and%20Johnson%20sign-on%20letter%20 to%20Kerry%20on%20Honduran%20trade%20unionists%2C%20 March%202016.pdf.

46. Paula Nalvarte, "Honduran Congress approves jail sentences for journalists who make justifications for terrorism," *Knight Center Journalism in the Americas* (blog), February 23, 2017, knightcenter.utexas.edu/blog/00-18055-honduran -congress-approves-jail-sentences-journalists-who-make-justifications-terroris.

47. Heather Gies, "Honduras, the Deadliest Country in the World for Environmental Defenders, Is About to Get Deadlier," *Upside Down World,* September 29, 2017, upsidedownworld.org/archives/honduras/honduras -deadliest-country-world-environmental-defenders-get-deadlier/.

48. "Honduras: Conoce las reformas al Código Penal y Procesal," *El Tiempo,* May 16, 2017, tiempo.hn/conoce-las-reformas-al-codigo-penal/.

49. "Observadora europea de DD.HH. sufre ataque de xenofobia y campaña de odio en Honduras," *C-Libre,* Alerta 79-16, Honduras, April 12, 2016, www.clibrehonduras.com/alerta/observadora-europea-de-dd-hh-sufre -ataque-de-xenofobia-y-campa%C3%B1a-de-odio-en-honduras.

50. Llamado urgente, "Honduras: Retención y deportación del observador internacional de Derechos Humanos Luis Díaz de Terán López," FIDH, November 3, 2016, www.fidh.org/es/temas/defensores-de-derechos-humanos /honduras-retencion-y-deportacion-del-observador-internacional-de.

51. Dana Frank, "End US Support for the Thugs of Honduras," *New York Times,* September 22, 2016, www.nytimes.com/2016/09/23/opinion/end-us -support-for-the-thugs-of-honduras.html?_r=0.

52. "La oposción y medios internacionales continúan campaña para dañar a Honduras," *Nos Queda Claro* (blog), September 22, 2016, nosquedaclaro.com /la-oposicion-medios-internacionales-continuan-campana-danar-honduras.

53.　See Chuy Ramos' Facebook entry, September 25, 2016, www.facebook.com
　　/SoyChuyRamos/posts/1795128800702374.

54.　"Denuncian campaña de odio contra periodistas," *CERIGUA* (blog), October 1,
　　2016, cerigua.org/article/honduras-denuncian-campana-de-odio-contra
　　-periodis/; www.youtube.com/watch?v=LRbxW3W5Wgc; Honduras,
　　izquierda arremete contra imagen del pais," *Quien Opina?* (blog), September
　　30, 2016, www.quienopina.com/2016/09/honduras-izquierda-arremete
　　-contra-imagen-de-pais/; "Extranjeros incitan a la violencia y el odio en
　　Honduras," *Nos Queda Claro*, May 10, 2016, nosquedaclaro.com/extranjeros
　　-incitan-a-la-violencia-y-el-odio-en-honduras/; "Activistas piden sus-
　　pension de ayuda Honduras por violaciones de DD.HH," *Nos Queda Claro*,
　　December 16, 2016; nosquedaclaro.com/activistas-piden-suspension-ayuda
　　-honduras-violaciones-dd-hh/. For an especially insidious and dangerous
　　attack against COFADEH's Bertha Oliva and Karen Spring of the Honduras
　　Solidarity Network, "Modus operandi de algunas ONG's que protegen a
　　narcotraficantes en el Bajo Aguán," *Nos Queda Claro*, November 21, 2016,
　　nosquedaclaro.com/modus-operandi-las-algunas-ongs-protegen
　　-narcotraficantes-aguan/. For the *You Tube* video attacking me, Annie Bird,
　　and Amy Goodman for our statements on *Democracy Now!*, Chuy Ramos, "La
　　izquierda ataca a Honduras de la mano de Mel Zelaya," *You Tube*, September
　　25, 2016, www.youtube.com/watch?v=LRbxW3W5Wgc.

55.　Global Witness, *Honduras: The Deadliest Country in the World for Environmental
　　Activism*; "ONU rescata a delegado de Global Witness," *El Libertador*, February
　　2, 2017, www.web.ellibertador.hn/index.php/noticias/nacionales/2061
　　-onu-rescata-a-delegado-de-global-witness; "Honduras: Increasing Smear
　　Campaign Against Defenders," *Amnesty International*, February 2, 2017, AMR
　　37/5613/2017, www.amnesty.org/en/documents/amr37/5613/2017/en/.

56.　"Public Clarification of the Circumstances Surrounding the Abduction of Two
　　Observers from PROAH in La Nueva Esperanza," *Honduras Accompaniment
　　Project*, November 15, 2013, hondurasaccompanimentproject.wordpress.com
　　/2013/11/15/public-clarification-of-the-circumstances-surrounding-the
　　-abduction-of-two-observers-from-proah-in-la-nueva-esperanza-2/; *Amnesty
　　International*, "Honduras: human rights activists abducted in Honduras," July
　　30, 2013, *Amnesty International*, AMR No. 37/008/2013, www.amnesty.org/en
　　/documents/AMR37/008/2013/en/.

57.　"Estamos investigando denuncia que una norteamericana desestabiliza en el
　　Aguan," *La Tribuna*, December 12, 2013, reposted at *HonduPrensa*,
　　honduprensa.wordpress.com/2013/12/12/estamos-investigando-denuncia
　　-que-una-norteamericana-desestabiliza-en-el-aguan/; Canal 11,
　　Tegucigalpa, Honduras, July 16, 2014.

58.　"Norteamericana promueve acciones violentas e invasiones en Bajo Aguán, acu-
　　sa titular del INA," *Proceso Digital*, July 17, 2014, www.proceso.hn/component
　　/k2/item/616.html; "DDHH Extranjera buscar discreditar exhumaciones," *La
　　Tribuna*, July 16, 2014, www.latribuna.hn/2014/07/16/dd-hh-extranjera-busca
　　-desacreditar-exhumaciones/; "Polemica presencia de defensora de DDHH en

zona del Bajo Aguán," *El Tiempo*, December 16, 2013, reprinted at honduprensa.wordpress.com/2013/12/16/polemica-presencia-de-defensora -de-ddhh-en-zona-del-bajo-aguan/; Canal 5, Tegucigalpa, December 12, 2013.

59. "Polemica presencia de defensora de DDHH en zona del Bajo Aguán." Comments included *y esta vieja puttttta de donde salio, hay que ir a quemarla.* [sic] ("and this old whore here did she come from, we have to burn her.") (translated by the author).

60. For example, "Presidente Hondureño ataca a defensores de DDHH que piden en EEUU 'Ley Berta,'" July 15, 2016, *El Confidencial*, confidencialhn.com /2016/07/15/presidente-hondureno-ataca-a-defensores-de-ddhh-que -piden-en-ee-uu-ley-berta/.

61. For an excellent analysis of the reelection question and Hernández's power grab, see Joaquín Mejía, "El despotismo amenaza a Honduras," *New York Times*, Spanish edition, October 17, 2016; www.nytimes.com/es/2016/10/17/el -despotismo-amenaza-a-honduras; see also "Re-Election a Done Deal," *Honduras Culture and Politics*, April 25, 2015, hondurasculturepolitics.blogspot.com /2015/04/re-election-done-deal.html; "Presidential Re-Election?!" April 23, 2015, *Honduras Culture and Politics*, hondurasculturepolitics.blogspot.com/search ?q=supreme+court&max-results=20&by-date=true.

62. "Completos resultados las elecciones primarias," *La Tribuna*, March 31, 2017.

63. "Salvador Nasralla es el candidato oficial de la alianza de oposición," *La Prensa*, May 21, 2017. For the alliance's program, "Alianza de oposición a Salvador Nasralla como presidenciable y presenta sus propuestas de gobierno," *El Heraldo*, September 15, 2017.

64. US Embassy in Honduras, "Statement Regarding Comments in Washington on Honduran Presidential Reelection," November 2016, hn.usembassy .gov/statement-regarding-comments-washington-honduran-presidential -reelection/.

65. For lobbying activities, "ASJ pide que se mantenga la cooperación bilateral de Defensa y Seguridad," *La Tribuna*, December 13, 2016, www.latribuna.hn /2016/12/13/asj-pide-se-mantenga-la-cooperacion-bilateral-defensa -seguridad/. For funding, www.usaspending.gov/Pages/AdvancedSearch. aspx?sub=y&ST=C,G&FY=2018,2017,2016,2015,2014,2013,2012,2011,2010 ,2009,2008&A=0&SS=USA&DUNS=850661463.

66. Sonia Nazario, "How the Most Dangerous Place on Earth Got Safer: Programs funded by the United States are Helping Transform Honduras," *New York Times*, August 11, 2016.

67. David Rosnick, Alexander Main, and Laura Jung, *Have US-Funded CARSI Programs Reduced Crime and Violence in Central America? An Examination of LAPOP's Impact Assessment of US Violence Prevention Programs in Central America*, Center for Economic and Policy Research, September 2016, cepr.net /publications/reports/have-us-funded-carsi-programs-reduced-crime -and-violence.

68. República de Honduras, Poder Legislative, "Decreto No. 2102016," *La Gaceta*, April 8, 2016, www.observatoriodescentralizacion.org/download

/decretos_vigentes/DECRETO-DE-EMERGENCIA-DEPURACION
-POLICIAL-08-DE-ABRIL-2016.pdf.

69. For a summary and analysis of the commission and its members, see Laura Jung, "Honduras' Special Commission on Police Reform: Genuine Cleanup Effort or Yet Another Scheme?" *CEPR Americas blog*, July 8, 2016, cepr.net /blogs/the-americas-blog/honduras-special-commission-on-police -reform-genuine-cleanup-effort-or-yet-another-pr-scheme.

70. "Ministerio de Seguridad, Julian Pacheco, señalado por los Cachiros," *La Prensa*, March 7, 2017; Jake Johnston, "Top U.S.-Backed Honduran Security Minister is Running Drugs, According to Court Testimony," *The Intercept*, November 26, 2017, theintercept.com/2017/11/26/honduras-election -pacheco-security-minister-is-running-drugs-according-to-court-testimony/.

71. For an example of his preeminence in the media soon after Pacheco Tinoco was named by the Cachiro, "Omar Rivera: 'Empresarios utilizaron dinero de procedencia ilícita para actividades comerciales e industriales,'" *El Heraldo*.

72. See Chapter Four.

73. "Comisión depuradora cancela 377 policías más en Honduras," *La Tribuna*, February 14, 2017. In May, 2017, Omar Rivera "confessed" that some of those had been separated because they were working in the wrong place, and that new places would be found for them. "Comisión busca empleo para buenos policías depurados," *La Prensa*, May 19, 2017.

74. "'Se ha sembrado la semilla' para la transformación de la policía nacional," *Association for a More Just Society* (blog), November 2, 2017, asjhonduras.com /webhn/comision-depuradora-en-washington-se-ha-sembrado-la-semilla -para-la-transformacion-de-la-policia-nacional/.

75. "Héctor Iván Mejía sería el nuevo Director de la Policía Nacional," *Once Noticias*, February 27, 2017, www.oncenoticias.hn/hector-velasquez-seria -director-la-policia/; "Secretaría de Seguridad realize cambios en la cúpula de la Policía," *El Heraldo*, January 21, 2017; "Comisionado Héctor Iván Mejía será nombrado como enlace en la OEA," *La Prensa*, April 29, 2017; "Héctor Iván Mejía de agregado en la OEA," *La Tribuna*, May 3, 2017.

76. For examples of the supposed drop in the murder rate being used to make Hernández look good, see "A would be-strongman? Juan Orlando Hernández headed for re-election in Honduras: His tough-on-crime policies are paying a political dividend," *The Economist*, November 25, 2017; and Gabriel Stargardter, "US ally seen clinching re-election in Honduras vote, eight years after coup," Reuters, November 23, 2017, www.reuters.com/article/us -honduras-election/u-s-ally-seen-clinching-re-election-in-honduras-vote -eight-years-after-coup-idUSKBN1DN1CS. When Arturo Corrales became Minister of Security in May 2014, the next day his spokesman sent a message to all police requiring them to limit information-sharing, and saying that information would only be available from press statements from the top. "Los asesinatos de mujeres aumentan un 65 por ciento en Honduras," *La Prensa*, March 7, 2014.

77. "Cerca de 4.000 mujeres fueron asesinadas en Honduras entre 2002 and

2013," *El Mundo* (Spain)/EFE, April 29, 2014, www.elmundo.es/internacional /2014/04/29/53600cb4268e3ec52a8b458b.html; "Honduras on 'red alert' over female murders, say activists," BBC, July 6, 2017, www.bbc.com/news /world-latin-america-40518212.

78. For the State Department's official explanation of Leahy vetting, see United States Department of State, "Leahy Fact Sheet," Bureau of Democracy, Human Rights, and Labor, July 18, 2017, www.state.gov/j/drl/rls/fs /2017/272663.htm; Interview by the author with John Lindsay-Poland, October 6, 2017.

79. Alberto Arce, "Dad seeks justice for son killed in broken Honduras," Associated Press, November 12, 2012, www.usatoday.com/story/news/world /2012/11/12/dad-seeks-justice-for-son-slain-in-broken-honduras/1699289/.

80. "Absuelven a policías TIGRES acusados de hurtar dinero decomisado a los Valle," *El Heraldo*, March13, 2016; "Dólares por los que acusaron a policías 'Tigres' fueron declarados en abandono," *El Heraldo*, September 25, 2016.

81. "Honduras: Policías 'Tigres' dejaron en libertad al capo Wilter Blanco Ruiz," *El Heraldo*, October 2, 2016; "Policías depurados donde están?" *Proceso Digital*, November 27, 2016, www.proceso.hn/component/k2/item/135916-policias -depurados-donde-estan.html.

82. Partrow and Martinez, "Suspicions mount in killing of noted Honduran environmentalist."

83. Elisabeth Malkin, "In Honduras Election, Ex-Sportscaster Takes Lead Over President," *New York Times*, November 27, 2017; "Nasralla practically assured of Honduras election win—official," Reuters, November 17, 2017; "Honduran candidate says Nasralla won, urges president to concede," Reuters, November 27, 2017; Kate Linthicum, "Hondruas still hasn't declared a winner in its presidential vote—and tensions are still rising," *Los Angeles Times*, November 28, 2017; Kaelyn Forde, "3 days after election, 2 men declare themselves president amid rising tensions," ABC News, November 29, 2017, abcnews.go.com/International/days-election-men -declare-honduran-president-amid-rising/story?id=51462579; Sarah Kinosian, "Calls for fresh Honduras election after President Juan Orlando Hernández wins," *The Guardian*, December 18, 2017.

84. Comité de Familiares de Detenidos y Desparecidos de Honduras, "Informe 2: Violaciones a los Derechos Humanos en el contexto de las protestas anti fraude en Honduras," Defensores en Linea, January 11, 2018, defensoresenlinea .com/segundo-informe-del-cofadeh-violaciones-a-los-derechos-humanos -en-el-contexto-de-las-protestas-anti-fraude-en-honduras/.

85. Press Release, "Statement by the OAS General Secretariat on the Elections in Honduras," Organization of American States, December 17, 2017, www. oas.org/en/media_center/press_release.asp?sCodigo=E-092/17.

86. "Leahy Statement on the Election in Honduras," *Congressional Record*, December 5, 2017, www.leahy.senate.gov/press/leahy-statement-on-the -election-in-honduras; Press Release, "Merkley Statement on Honduras," December 5, 2017, www.merkley.senate.gov/news/press-releases/merkley

-statement-on-honduras; Press Release, "Cardin Expresses Concern about the Political Crisis in Honduras," December 5, 2017; www.cardin.senate.gov /newsroom/press/release/cardin-expresses-concern-about-the-political -crisis-in-honduras_; Press Release, "Reed Statement on Democracy and Human Rights Concerns in Honduras," December 14, 2017, www.reed.senate .gov/news/releases/reed-statement-on-democracy-and-human-rights -concerns-in-honduras.

87. Jan Schakowsky, "The Honduran Candidate," *New York Times,* November 23, 2017, www.nytimes.com/2017/11/23/opinion/honduras-juan-orlando -hernandez-election.html; Press Release, "Merkley, Schakowsky Join Calls for New Election in Honduras," December 19, 2017; www.merkley.senate.gov /news/press-releases/merkley-schakowsky-join-calls-for-new-election-in -honduras.

88. Press Release, "Letter on Honduran Elections," December 21, 2017, ellison .house.gov/media-center/press-releases/letter-on-honduras-elections; Keith Ellison, "We Must Fight the Rising Oligarchy in the United States," *Huffington Post,* January 3, 2018, www.huffingtonpost.com/entry/we-must-thwart -the-rising-oligarchy-in-the-united-states_us_5a4d0086e4b025f99e1f3f30.

89. Press Release, "Rep. Torres Leads House Democrats in Objecting to Trump Administration Response to Honduras Crisis," December 21, 2017, torres .house.gov/media-center/press-releases/rep-torres-leads-house-democrats -object-trump-administration-response. Rep. James McGovern was the only member to sign both letters.

90. US Department of State, "Statement by Heather Nauert, Spokesperson, on the Presidential Elections in Honduras," December 22, 2017, hn.usembassy.gov /statement-heather-nauert-spokesperson-presidential-elections-honduras/.

91. United States Department of Homeland Security, Office of Strategy, Policy, and Plans, "Organizational Chart, (November 2017)," www.dhs.gov/office-policy.

92. "Shannon y Nealon reconocen avances de Hondruas," *La Prensa,* October 31, 2017. At the UN General Assembly in September in New York, Hernández's first meeting was with Shannon. "JOH inicia agenda en New York con Thomas Shannon," *La Prensa,* September 18, 2017.

93. Nick Miroff, "For veteran drug warrior, retirement comes with tinge of regret," *Washington Post,* September 17, 2017.

94. Eric Olson, "Miami summit an opportunity to rethink Central America," *Miami Herald,* June 13, 2017; for a critical perspective, Jake Johnston, "Miami Conference Signals Further Militarization of US Policy in Central America," *CEPR Americas Blog,* June 14, 2017, cepr.net/blogs/the-americas-blog /miami-conference-signals-increased-militarization-of-us-policy-in-central -america; Conversation by the author with State Department official. For official missives about the conference, Office of the Vice President, The White House, "Remarks by the Vice President at the Northern Triangle Conference," June 15, 2017, www.whitehouse.gov/the-press-office /2017/06/15/remarks-vice-president-northern-triangle-conference; United States Department of State, Rex W. Tillerson, "Remarks at the Conference

for Prosperity and Security in Central America Opening Plenary Session," June 15, 2017, www.state.gov/secretary/remarks/2017/06/271926.htm.

95. John Kelly, speech at the Atlantic Council, "A New Strategy for Engagement in Central America," May 4, 2017, Washington D.C., www.atlanticcouncil.org /events/webcasts/a-new-strategy-for-us-engagement-in-central-america.

96. Karla Zabladovsky and Daniel Wagner, "Meet the Workers Who Sewed Donald Trump Clothing For a Few Dollars A Day," *BuzzFeed*, July 22, 2016, www.buzzfeed.com/karlazabludovsky/meet-the-workers-who-sewed-donald -trump-clothing-for-a-few-d?utm_term=.ooBJz2rNk#.naVVNmQnl.

97. Nancy Hiemstra, "Trump's 'Skinny' Central America Budget," *NACLA: Report on the Americas*, July 25, 2017, nacla.org/blog/2017/08/04/trump%E2%80 %99s-%E2%80%9Cskinny%E2%80%9D-central-america-budget; "Development Assistance to Latin American and the Caribbean in Trump's 'Skinny Budget,'" *Global Americans* (blog), May 3, 2017, theglobalamericans.org /2017/05/just-facts-development-assistance-latin-american-caribbean-trumps -state-skinny-budget/.

98. "Bolivia expels US aid agency after Kerr 'backyard' comment," Reuters, May 1, 2013, www.reuters.com/article/us-bolivia-usaid/bolivia-expels-u-s-aid -agency-after-kerry-backyard-comment-idUSBRE94013V20130501.

99. Ismael Moreno, SJ, "What will we be? Their backyard or our own home?" *Envío*, no, 432, July 2017, www.envio.org.ni/articulo/5372.

Index

ABOUT THE AUTHOR

The author at a highway blockade in Choloma, Cortés, June 28, 2010. Photo credit: Dana Frank.

Dana Frank is professor of history emerita at the University of California, Santa Cruz. She is the author of *Bananeras: Women Transforming the Banana Unions of Latin America* (2005; reprinted Haymarket, 2016); *Buy American: The Untold Story of Economic Nationalism* (Beacon, 1999); *Purchasing Power: Consumer Organizing, Gender, and the Seattle Labor Movement, 1919–1929* (Cambridge, 1994); *Local Girl Makes History: Exploring Northern California's Kitsch Monuments* (City Lights, 2007); and, with Howard Zinn and Robin D. G. Kelley, *Three Strikes: Miners, Musicians, Salesgirls and the Fighting Spirit of Labor's Last Century* (Beacon, 2001). Her contribution to *Three Strikes* has been reprinted with a new introduction by Haymarket Books as *Women Strikers Occupy Chain Store, Win Big* (2012). Since the 2009 military coup her articles about human rights and US policy in Honduras have appeared in *The Nation, New York Times, Politico Magazine, Foreign Affairs.com, Foreign Policy.com, Miami Herald, Los Angeles Times, The Baffler,* and many other publications, and she has testified before both the US Congress and Canadian Parliament.

CPSIA information can be obtained
at www.ICGtesting.com
Printed in the USA
JSHW050157040422
24382JS00004B/4